Educational Leaders Encouraging the Intellectual and Professional Capacity of Others

A Social Justice Agenda

A Volume in:
Educational Leadership For Social Justice

Series Editors:
Jeffrey S. Brooks , Denise E. Armstrong
Ira Bogotch, Sandra Harris, Whitney H.
George Theoharis

Educational Leadership for Social Justice Book Series

Series Editors

Jeffrey S. Brooks
University of Missouri

Denise E. Armstrong
Brock University

Ira Bogotch
Florida Atlantic University

Sandra Harris
Lamar University

Whitney H. Sherman
Virginia Commonwealth University

George Theoharis
Syracuse University

Educational Leaders Encouraging the Intellectual and Professional Capacity of Others
A Social Justice Agenda

Elizabeth Murakami-Ramalho
University of Texas at San Antonio

Anita Pankake
The University of Texas–Pan American

INFORMATION AGE PUBLISHING, INC.
Charlotte, NC • www.infoagepub.com

Library of Congress Cataloging-in-Publication Data

Educational leaders encouraging the intellectual and professional capacity
of others : a social justice agenda / [edited by] Elizabeth
Murakami-Ramalho, Anita Pankake.
    p. cm. – (Educational leadership for social justice)
  Includes bibliographical references.
  ISBN 978-1-61735-623-0 (pbk.) – ISBN 978-1-61735-624-7 (hardcover) –
ISBN 978-1-61735-625-4 (ebook)
1. Educational leadership–Social aspects–United States. 2. School
principals–Professional relationships–United States. 3.
Teachers–In-service training–United States. 4. Educational
equalization–United States. 5. Social justice–United States. I.
Murakami-Ramalho, Elizabeth. II. Pankake, Anita M., 1947-
  LB2805.E347 2011
  371.200973–dc23
                                    2011035164

CONTENTS

PART 1
THE FOUNDATION OF SOCIAL JUSTICE:
DEVELOPING OTHERS

PART II

BUILDING SOCIAL JUSTICE: INTELLECTUAL AND PROFESSIONAL CAPITAL

PART III

MENTORING STRATEGIES FOR BUILDING INTELLECTUAL AND PROFESSIONAL CAPACITY

ACKNOWLEDGEMENTS

To my sons Julio and Fabio, who consistently support my professional journey.

—Elizabeth Murakami-Ramalho

To David Pankake, my husband, my mentor, and my best friend.
I am so blessed to have had you in my life these many years.

—Anita McCoskey Pankake

The authors are indebted to Ashley Oleszewski and Christine Weiland for assisting with editorial and peer-review processes.

EXTERNAL REVIEWERS

The editors would like to express their gratitude to the following reviewers. Their knowledge and expertise were vital assets to the development of this book.

Vangie Aguilera, San Antonio Independent School District
Rebecca Bustamante, Sam Houston State University
Gary Crow, Indiana University Bloomington
Michael Dantley, Miami University
Sonya Douglass Horsford, University of Nevada Las Vegas
Stacy Edmonson, Sam Houston State University
Rebecca Garza, The University of Texas at San Antonio
Miguel Guajardo, Texas State University
Patricia Guerra, Texas State University
Beverly Irby, Sam Houston State University
Gary Ivory, New Mexico State University
Estelle Kamler, Long Island University
Frances K. Kochan, Auburn University
Brad Kose, Madison Metropolitan School District
Melinda M. Mangin, Michigan State University
Martha McCarthy, Indiana University Bloomington
Norma Mertz, The University of Tennessee Knoxville
Matthew Millitello, North Carolina State University
Patrick Pauken, Bowling Green State University
Nan Restine, Texas Women's University
Charol Shakeshaft, Virginia Commonwealth University
Jennifer Stotts, The University of Texas at San Antonio
Linda Thurston, Kansas State University
Kathleen Wilcox, Spring Arbor University
Ralph M. Wirth, San Antonio School for Inquiry and Creativity
Ron Zimmer, Michigan State University

PREFACE

Educational Leadership and Social Justice: Paths to the Present, Possibilities for the Future and Future

Jeffrey S. Brooks

A few years ago, my co-author Mark Miles and I wrote a book chapter tracing pedagogical trends in educational leadership from scientific management to social justice (Brooks & Miles, 2008). As often happens, we ended the chapter with quite a few questions. Among these, we asked:

> Will social justice become another historical era, fondly recalled by a few and gladly forgotten by some, or a paradigm shift that actually produces the liberation pedagogy it promises? Will social justice be washed away by a second wave of scientific management? Surely, educational leaders stand at a crossroads, with critical decisions to be made about the direction of the present and the future (108).

Several of the authors in this edited volume by Elizabeth Murakami-Ramalho and Anita Pankake, *Educational Leaders Encouraging the Intellectual and Professional Capacity of Others: A Social Justice Agenda*, stand boldly at that

Educational Leaders Encouraging the Intellectual and Professional Capacity of Others: A Social Justice Agenda, pages xi–xiii.
Copyright © 2012 by Information Age Publishing

crossroads, pointing the way for a new generation of educators. They explore some of the questions Mark and I raised and pose new ones for those of us who choose social justice as an area of inquiry—but of course, social justice is much more than an area of inquiry.

Social justice is many things to many people. To some it is a way of looking at the world through a critical lens that highlights justice and injustice. To others it is a way of thinking about and practicing education and schooling that demands action that speaks truth to power, rallies for freedom, liberates minds and bodies, wrests freedom from tyranny of mind or body from tyrants, and emancipates thought and deed. Social justice can be as quiet and calm as a teacher's caring and compassionate look and as unrelenting as the storm of fury unleashed on a racist educator by someone bold enough to confront them. To be sure, it is a combination of these things to some, these things and more to others, and none of them to many more. So, why study something so ambiguous? How can such inquiry hope to help when we can't even agree on the most basic of definitions? I will hazard a brief answer. Because all social justice educators do believe that putting human rights at the core of our work is the most fundamental and necessary change that must take place in education. Indeed, it is human care and compassion for the body, mind and soul that distinguishes education for social justice from any other kind of education.

And leadership? The authors in this book are convinced that educational administration and leadership are essential to the practice of a socially just education. They share research about schools where they've led, taught and studied and help us see possibility where none seemingly exists—they show us the darkness, but also the light in the darkness that may lead us to improved practices in schools. I invite you to join me as a reader of this fine volume. Let's ask questions, seek answers, critically reflect on our own thoughts and behaviors, change, grow, and learn.

ABOUT THE EDUCATIONAL LEADERSHIP FOR SOCIAL JUSTICE BOOK SERIES

I am pleased to serve as series editor for this book series, *Educational Leadership for Social Justice*, with Information Age Publishing. The idea for this series grew out of the work of a committed group of leadership for scholars associated with the American Educational Research Association's (AERA) Leadership for Social Justice Special Interest Group (SIG). This group existed for many years before being officially affiliated with AERA, and has benefitted greatly from the ongoing leadership, support, and counsel of Dr. Catherine Marshall (University of North Carolina-Chapel Hill). It is also important to acknowledge the contributions of the SIG's first President, Dr. Ernestine Enomoto (University of Hawaii at Manoa), whose wisdom, stewardship, and guidance helped ease a transition into AERA's more formal organizational structures. This organizational change was at times difficult to reconcile with scholars who largely identified as non-traditional thinkers and push toward innovation rather than accept the status quo. As the second Chair of the SIG, I appreciate all of Ernestine's hard work and friendship. I am now privileged to work under the leadership of Dr. Gaetane Jean-Marie, University of Oklahoma, the third chair of the LSJ SIG.

I am particularly indebted to my colleagues on the SIG's first Publications Committee, which I chaired from 2005-2007: Dr. Denise Armstrong, Brock University; Dr. Ira Bogotch, Florida Atlantic University; Dr. Sandra Harris, Lamar University; Dr. Whitney Sherman, Virginia Commonwealth University, and; Dr. George Theoharis, Syracuse University. This committee was a joy to work with and I am pleased we have found many more ways to collaborate as we seek to provide publication opportunities for scholarship in the area of leadership for social justice.

This book by Dr. Elizabeth Murakami-Ramalho and Dr. Anita Pankake, the fifth in the series, presents many new and exciting voices. We are exited to help provide a forum for this important voice in the ongoing conversation about equity and excellence in education, and the role(s) that leadership can assume in educational organizations.

Again, welcome to this fifth book in this Information Age Publishing series, *Educational Leadership for Social Justice.* You can learn more about the series at our web site: http://www.infoagepub.com/series/Educational-Leadership-for-Social-Justice. I invite you to contribute your own work on equity and influence to the series. We look forward to you joining the conversation.

REFERENCE

Brooks, J. S., & Miles, M. T. (2008). From scientific management to social justice...and back again? Pedagogical shifts in educational leadership. in A. H. Normore, (Ed.), *Leadership for social justice: Promoting equity and excellence through inquiry and reflective practice* (pp. 99–114). Charlotte, NC: Information Age Publishing.

EDUCATIONAL LEADERS ENCOURAGING THE INTELLECTUAL AND PROFESSIONAL CAPACITY OF OTHERS

A Social Justice Agenda

Elizabeth Murakami-Ramalho and Anita Pankake

Sometime in his mid-career, Sergiovanni had a break-through experience when around 1992, principals and superintendents shared perspectives of their daily work in and around schools (Mullen, 2006). He realized that all "school leaders were morally-oriented, connected to a sense of purpose and feeling of responsibility" (line 854). Later in 1998, Sergiovanni presented us with the concept of pedagogical leadership as an effective alternative to constrained narratives and hierarchies of domination in school leadership, none of which seemed to improve student success, parent involvement, or teacher development.

Educational Leaders Encouraging the Intellectual and Professional Capacity of Others:
A Social Justice Agenda, pages xv–xxviii.
xv

Pedagogical leadership, affirmed Sergiovanni (1998), "invests in capacity building by developing social and academic capital for students and intellectual and professional capital for teachers" (p. 37). He explained that pedagogical leadership is focused on building various forms of human capital, with special attention to its development. Human capital development, he affirmed, is the key mediating variable that stands between pedagogical leadership and value added to students. We argue that even though efforts to promote the professional development of educators at all levels exist, these are planned and delivered by simply addressing immediate or pressing needs, or organized in order to communicate the adoption of new policies and regulations. Teachers and school administrators also attend professional development activities on their own, choosing subject-specific or thematic leadership workshops to fulfill district requirements. We contend that both those seeking workshops and professional development opportunities, and those who deliver them, may not be necessarily building capacity for pedagogical leadership. Building a pedagogical approach in the preparation of educators requires a more inclusive alignment and professional mentoring, from teachers, school administrators, district leaders, and higher education professors and researchers in the field of education.

This book is a contribution from the voices of scholars and practitioners in building pedagogical leadership. While understanding social justice is important, in this book, the chapters present a more proactive stance. What do those involved in the wide spectrum of education, from P–20 to those that continue in the mission to prepare professionals in education, need to do to be effective social justice advocates? What are the pitfalls—sometimes hidden, sometimes obvious—educators can avoid and thus disrupt cycles of social inequities? Adding to the Educational Leadership for Social Justice Series, scholars and practitioners in this new volume focus on building a social justice agenda. They offer ways to encourage intellectual and professional capital in others serving in different capacities in the P–20 continuum. Their goal is to create possibilities for building social and academic capital for students, and fulfill an intrinsic sense of purpose and responsibility in educators.

ENCOURAGING INTELLECTUAL AND PROFESSIONAL CAPACITY

Even though the United States may produce examples of excellence in its educational structures and human development, Kose (2007) reminds us that we are still on a long journey to eliminating social inequities in schools when he affirmed that "Ample evidence suggests that K–12 schools still have a long journey in becoming affirming, equitable, and high achieving. Rather, schools often perpetuate social inequities and discrimination" (p. 135).

In this volume, we focus not only on schools as systems, but also as people perpetuating social inequities and discrimination in such structures. A sustained effort to improve intellectual and professional capital therefore takes precedence, as an important social justice agenda, if creating or perpetuating systems that may unconsciously replicate social inequities is to be avoided.

We consider schools as fundamental social institutions and significant centers of community activity. Encouraging social and academic capital for students, and encouraging intellectual and professional capital for educators, creates a cycle that is only complete when sustained by a pedagogical leadership that includes a social justice agenda. A social justice agenda in building professional capacity involves not only being an advocate for students in the P–20 path, but also advocating for ways to provide access, retention, and continued growth of all professionals serving in education, such as educators, service providers, and administrators. These stakeholders compose the body of leadership that will better serve students from pre-school to college. When the cycle of building human capital is fragmented, educators, service providers, administrators, and professors are doomed to join in the perpetuation of the status quo—of what *is*—rather than what can or should be.

Without a concerted pedagogy to prepare these professionals, individuals then craft their own agendas, creating self-serving systems and disarray while serving in different capacities, resulting in a disservice to students. Countermeasures to such development of practitioners can be strengthened through research-based inquiry. However, inquiry and research are not sufficient. Application of knowledge is also necessary to level the playing field in order to create social justice, and as a consequence, effective educational institutions. As the field begins to level, individuals also need the tools to understand the field and to encourage other professionals in this environment.

EDUCATIONAL LEADERSHIP AND SOCIAL JUSTICE

It is essential that educational leaders are prepared to understand how their advocacy and social justice agenda is an important part of their intellectual and professional capital. As Theorharis (2007) rightly declared, "Social justice in schools has not happened by chance" (p. 253). He speaks of the need to go beyond what has been seen as good leadership and calls for the redefining of good leadership as leadership for social justice. Social justice becomes a more significant concept when we identify those serving in educational institutions who fail to deliver the promise of quality education to every student (Connell, 1993; Miller, 1979; Tyler, 1997). What is the significance of social justice and advocacy in encouraging the development of others?

In seminal discussions about justice and fairness, Rawls (1958), asserted that justice is dependent on a balance of a complex of three ideas: "liberty, equality, and reward, for services contributing to the common good" (p. 166). Rawls extensively explored the topics of liberty and equality, discussing where the pendulum of fairness and moral purpose may lie within each individual. Important to the pedagogy of leadership, however, are the contributions of educators toward a common good. In fact, Rawls expands on individualism as being a benefit and a burden when trying to determine the concept of justice. Similarly, Etzioni (1988), among early theorists, discussed the need of deontological ethics (moral dimensions of action based on rules and duties), especially in individualistic societies such as the one in which we live.

A collective and firm grasp of the concept of justice is necessary, affirmed Rawls (1958), arguing that "this notion involved mutual acceptance" (p. 193). Mutual understanding requires a continuous engagement of communications and negotiations is paramount. He affirmed that "persons engaged in a just, or fair practice can face one another openly and support their respective positions, should they appear questionable, by reference to principles which it is reasonable to expect each to accept" (Rawls, p. 178). Nonetheless, in building intellectual and professional capacity among educators, we are keenly aware that even when consistently negotiating moral and utilitarian values, individual interpretations of justice, and individual actions toward justice in education, these may be enveloped in emotional, and less rational attitudes.

Scholars like Spring (1998), then, remind us how complex such interrelationships are, especially when we try to transfer theory into practice. Interrelationships among multiple stakeholders in education, for example, are charged with emotional liberty, equality, and reward values in determining the students' future. Such emotions are present in "the political organization of schools, student achievement, and equality of educational opportunity" (p. 102). Such decisions involve parents, boards of education, courts, politicians, school administrators, and teachers, to include just a few. When these stakeholders are not mentoring each other for a common purpose, or common agenda, people may be exercising what Etzioni (1988) perceived as people rendering independent decisions as free-standing individuals, but who are disconnected from their social contexts. For example, people smoke even after exercising, or "brush their teeth but do not fasten their seat belts" (p. xi). This may be the reason why scholars like Bogotch (2000) argued about the importance of continuously engaging theory and practice together, and continuously confronting "the issue of social justice in all its guises and to deliberately make social justice a central part of educational leadership discourse and actions, while, at the same time, vigilantly critique such actions and motives such that when the material conditions change, we have to start all over again" (p. 2).

More recently, scholars writing about social justice focused on connecting an authentic application of advocacy into the field of educational leadership (Anderson, 2002; Bogotch, 2002; Capper, Theoharis, & Sebastian, 2006; Marshall & Oliva, 2006; Shoho, Merchant, & Lugg, 2004; Theoharis, 2007). These scholars examine the skills needed to build a new social order that includes mentoring and supportive networks for the active role of educational leaders as social justice agents (Capper et al., 2006; Merchant & Shoho, 2006; Sergiovanni, 1998). These tasks encompass developing professional capital through shared purposes, moral connections between roles and responsibilities, modeling, enabling, and in turn, motivating others.

INTELLECTUAL AND PROFESSIONAL
CAPACITY THROUGH MENTORING

Instead of merely pointing out social injustices, this book takes a proactive approach. As noted earlier, Sergiovanni (1998) affirmed human capital as the key mediating variable that stands between pedagogical leadership and value added to students. In the principalship, for example, Kose (2007) noted that "principals for social justice influence professional development toward socially just teaching and socially just student learning" (p. 280). Among his findings regarding the actions of principals for social justice is the recentering and enhancing of staff capacity, "Principals used this strategy to increase the capacity of staff with ongoing staff development focused on building equity, developing staff investment in social justice, hiring and supervising for justice, and empowering staff" (p. 235). In this regard, one of the most often included strategies on the agendas for addressing social justice issues in the writings of the authors in this volume is to nurture the development of others through mentoring. The chapters on new teacher induction, the shortage of women in the superintendency, induction of new faculty to the academy, and even the chapter on undergraduate students assisting P–12 students in high-need schools advocate some form of mentoring.

The very essence of mentoring is to provide guidance, assistance, and support to new members of the system. Mentoring is, by definition, encouraging the development of intellectual and professional capital in others. When initiated and implemented with forethought and moral purpose, mentoring taps the best thinking and behavior of those within the existing system, offering these as the guideposts and support mechanisms for those new to the system.

Quality mentoring creates entry points for new members that socialize them according to "the best" the current system has to offer. Beginning with "the best" as the baseline empowers, even demands, that as new members continue their work in the system, their development increases the quantity of performance that is modeled on the best. Their development then makes the best, better. It is this upward spiral that ultimately improves the organization as the critical mass of mentors and mentees begin to populate the system. While enriched funding is always welcomed, quality mentoring can be done with existing resources. Consequently, quality mentoring may be among the most cost-efficient and results-oriented means of changing the climate, the community, and, ultimately, the nature of schools as systems.

A PROACTIVE SOCIAL JUSTICE AGENDA

In proposing a social justice agenda and a proactive pedagogy of leadership we highlight the importance of an alignment of the purpose of schooling with the roles and contributions of individuals, using their purposeful intellectual and professional capital to create the social and academic capital for students. Within this book, the authors provide various voices and perspectives in order to encourage the development of others. In particular, processes of development that include mentoring, coaching, professional development, the reculturing of a work environment, and collaborative partnerships are offered as possibilities. The possibilities influence individuals and groups involved in the social justice agenda, such as new teachers, veteran teachers, teacher leaders, emergent campus leaders, veteran campus leaders, district leaders, and alternative school leaders.

Educators involved in building the social and academic capital of students will be able to identify key issues that, when adopted and operationalized, will help improve their own intellectual and professional capital and increase the academic capital of students. Most important, however, is the proactive exercise of learning from the several recommendations made by the professionals who collaborated with researchers in these chapters, who are leading examples in building a social justice agenda. By sustaining mentoring and collaborative cycles among professionals in education that approaches leadership as a planned and structured organizational characteristic (not as an individual or a position), educational leaders will build strong and sustainable leadership capacity.

ORGANIZATION OF CHAPTERS

The book is divided in three sections. The first section focuses on the foundations of social justice. The chapters highlight the importance of developing others by intentionally adopting measures to improve and change school cultures, and new approaches for social justice practices.

In the first chapter, "Building Capacity: The Foundation of Developing Others," Pankake and Abrego address the issue of building leadership capacity. They take the perspective that leadership needs to be an organizational characteristic, rather than a role assignment in schools. They advocate that leadership operate in every part of the organization and be a responsibility assumed by every member. Pankake and Abrego see building capacity as a necessary condition, to enable schools to become more socially just institutions in both their purpose and delivery. The voices they share come from individuals at all levels of leadership in the school; they felt this range of voices was important to depict the reciprocity principle of building leadership capacity (Elmore, as cited in Farrace, 2002) and used to frame the authors' thinking in this chapter.

Hirsh and Hord in Chapter 2, "A Context for Developing Social Justice for Staff and Students: Communities of Professional Learners," stress the importance of valuing the organization of communities of professional learners among teachers. Communities of professional learners can nurture social justice attitudes and actions in schools through a structured agenda. Hirsh and Hord explain that professional learners are intentional about providing learning options for K–12 schools, assess and monitor the progress from individual interests, to an appreciation, acceptance, and integration of goals in order to create a collective belief system geared toward effective programs and the preparation of students. The authors call attention to the importance of emotional and psychological aspects of preparing a community of learners toward change, providing, for example, more time for teachers to be connected to a larger network of teachers, be more connected with administrators and the school operations, and be provided time to reflect and learn from each other. Hirsh and Hord attest that professional learning communities are instrumental in creating a sustained social justice culture.

Huffman focuses on reculturing organizations in Chapter 3. While reculturing is the process, the purpose is to create more socially just school organizations. Reculturing requires school leaders to increase their own awareness of existing discrimination in their organizations. Once aware, the school leaders must seek the places and practices that perpetuate this discrimination. Huffman encourages the initiation of dialogue between and among the various stakeholders in the organizations. She offers descriptions of the voices to be engaged and heard through this recommended dialogue—administrators, teachers, students, and parents. She then moves beyond those in the immediate environs of the school to the larger contexts of communities, districts, and state agencies. She goes on to identify three necessary conditions to engender the changes that will aid in reculturing schools toward more socially just organizations.

In Chapter 4, Klinker and Thompson enlighten us on a deeper understanding of leadership for social justice in "Philosophical Reflections on Moral Transformative Leadership." Drawing from law and ethics, Klinker and Thompson theorize about underlying philosophies related to deep-seated principles, and the subsequent use of a code of ethics in order to understand ideas of individual wants, individual rights, and connections with the common good. Providing us with several examples to understand ethical and moral values, they remind us of the struggle of the mind to shape social agendas (Foster, 1989).

Most importantly, they contend that a moral, transformative leadership is needed, which among educational leaders, emerges from a combination of conflicts, including one's personal needs and wants, and problems that cannot be ignored. Such negotiations, they argue, form the values that propel decision making and actions among educational leaders. They remind us that even in a current data-driven society, the collection of data has no impact, unless educators and educational leaders negotiate and determine their approach using moral transformative leadership.

"Leadership for Social Justice: A Matter of Influencing Policy Development" is the last chapter of this section. Surface, Smith, Keiser, and Hayes address the creation of policies for social justice as a means of strengthening the relationships between schools and communities. They emphasize the importance of well-crafted policies to guide decision making. Policies encompass our intent, our ideals, that which we want to be. Though policies may not always describe the reality of today, they are essential in leading us toward the ideal by ensuring that the actions today align with the intent we have for the future. These authors delve deeply into the knowledge, skills, and dispositions school leaders need and leadership preparation programs must emphasize if schools are to truly serve the immediate needs of children and ultimately the needs of society. Surface and her colleagues call upon school leaders to be the stewards of the communities' schools; they advocate that leaders must have both the penchant and the skills to draft the policies that drive actions for social justice.

The second section of the book more purposefully provides elements of building social justice and the intellectual and professional capital in K–12 environments. Areas highlighted by the authors in building a social justice agenda include teacher induction processes; teacher, principal, and superintendent leadership; and the importance of leadership capacity building through professional development. Also in this section is the important consideration of preparing democratic leaders in different forms of public education, such as charter schools.

In Chapter 6, Roberts and Pankake examine the process of teacher induction. They discuss concerns about teacher turnover, especially in low-performing schools. Based on the voices of new and veteran teachers, they explore what makes a quality induction program and analyze different components educational leaders can consider in building strong programs for teacher retention and subsequent effectiveness that generates the academic success of students. "Teacher Induction: A Process for Advancing Social Justice" highlights how purposeful action to support individuals new to the organization can simultaneously support and improve the social justice agenda of the organization as a whole.

Mills and Schall follow, in Chapter 7, "Barriers and Marginalization in Female Teacher Leadership." They focus on teacher leaders, and more specifically, female leadership, discussing how females can challenge the barriers that marginalize their efforts. Issues that merit attention among female leaders include pay differentials and nonlegitimization of their roles. As a consequence, teachers are both informal as well as formal leaders in their schools and communities, invested in improving learning through leadership. Mills and Schall remind us of the value of teacher leaders in building intellectual and professional capital among their colleagues. Including the voices of six teachers, the authors evidence the impact female teacher leaders can have in replacing structures that work against their contributions as female leaders and the impacting force they provide in reforming schools with their agenda to influence student learning.

In Chapter 8, "Professional Development to Strengthen Department Chair Instructional Leadership Capacity: Advancing Social Justice in Urban High Schools," Klar and Bredeson indicate how strengthening department chairs' instructional leadership capacity advances social justice in urban high schools. Department chairs can address teachers' instructional and professional capacity, and focus on deeply rooted inequalities in student learning outcomes. Klar and Bredeson report on a professional development program they developed for department chairs using specific tasks related to developing a shared vision, identifying goals, and supporting both student and adult learning. As well as monitoring and promoting the teaching and learning at the school and departmental level (Bredeson, Kelley, & Klar, 2009), department chairpersons were able to recognize their roles as instructional leaders. The outcomes of professional development speak to the importance of establishing agendas to build professional capital, and becoming proactive in involving principals and teachers in urban areas to advance school improvement goals.

In Chapter 9, "Lessons from a Principal Preparation Program: Creating Support through Social Justice Practices," Murakami-Ramalho, Garza, and Merchant discuss the importance of sustaining preparation programs for emerging principals in urban areas geared specifically toward a social justice agenda. They report on successful outcomes in preparing leaders through a university–district partnership named Urban School Leaders Collaborative (USLC). Goals for the USLC include courses that focus on attitudes and skills needed to become social justice agents, mentoring structures for social and professional support, and the support of a team of professors, district officials, and experienced principals. By exposing emerging principals to research on social justice cases, these emerging leaders developed critical consciousness and culturally relevant preparation in order to exercise their leadership in socially just places and highly diverse urban communities.

In "Voices of Veteran Administrators," Grady, Williams, and Gaddie, share interviews with 32 administrators regarding their leadership experiences. The administrators demonstrated how social justice can be a part of a school administrator's daily work. The veteran administrators talked about the importance of being dedicated to the improvement of the lives of students and the required changes to be more prepared to support diverse students. The scholars concluded that veteran administrators used self-driven initiatives as well as professional development sessions to be informed about current research and practices.

In Chapter 11, "Critical Differences in Superintendency Seekers," Muñoz, Mills, Pankake, and Murakami-Ramalho offer some insights into a growing concern regarding the shortage of quality candidates for the superintendency in the nation's schools. They rely on the work of others and research of their own to argue that there is not a shortage of qualified candidates, but rather some subtle paradigm limitations regarding who is seen and who sees themselves as quality candidates for the top leadership positions in the nation's schools. The chapter offers a brief review of the history of women in the superintendency, data on the current status of women in the superintendency, and voices of both males and females regarding their aspirations for attaining this top-level position. The most advocated action to address the inequities is mentoring, through which a strong professional network for women can be developed. The responsibility for preparing, encouraging, and sponsoring women for the superintendency is seen as belonging to current superintendents, both males and females.

In Chapter 12, Valle and Mendez-Morse discuss the importance of advancing social justice through support personnel. These scholars contend that if principals practice inclusivity, they can create important venues to inspire and bring to life the commitment and passion of not only educators, but also support personnel, in order to create schools that work toward a social justice agenda. Principals can foster the development of support personnel to enhance a vision of inclusion, collaboration, and social empowerment. Creating socially just and equitable schools is a collective endeavor in which support personnel has much to contribute, especially when they are prepared and actively participating in school decisions.

In "Charter Schools: Meeting the Democratic Mission of Public Education," Allen and Gawlik examine the charter movement and social justice issues related to the rise of charter schools 15 years ago. They analyze the challenges charter school leaders experience, especially in delivering socially just education in such a nontraditional school system. The schools compete with schools in the public system, but differ in their organizational and structural differences when compared to schools connected through a district and also in their lack of central office support. Most importantly, Allen and Gawlik indicate that there are no specific professional leadership programs to prepare charter school principals, especially preparation toward creating charter school leaders committed to social justice goals, including access and equity in educational opportunities for students.

The third and final section of this volume focuses on mentoring strategies for building intellectual and professional capacity. The section looks at mentoring issues as an important element when considering the social injustices in diverse forms of underrepresentation in higher education environments. Social justice issues as related to mentoring reveal disconnects beyond the K–12 environment, and discloses further concerns as related to the absence of a seamless pedagogy among the adults serving students in education. Mentoring relations, especially in building the intellectual and professional capital of underrepresented groups, is examined, further exploring the possibilities of building a PK–higher education social justice agenda.

In Chapter 14, Schiller and Charles discuss how service learning provides university students with a vehicle to address inequities in urban education. They demonstrate how college students can help elementary and secondary students in two different programs, where college students serve K–12 students as academic coaches in underperforming urban schools. This chapter inspires us to reflect on the potential of such programs in actively addressing social justice issues, and infusing autonomy and stimulating enthusiasm both in mentors and mentees, college students and elementary and secondary children.

In "Mentoring Women and Minority Educational Leaders: The Need for Research," Crisp discusses the need for research specific to the underrepresentation of women and minorities in leadership. Crisp critically examines the literature related to race and ethnicity as directly affecting mentoring relationships/outcomes. The thorough literature review informs how mentoring is approached through different schools of thought (i.e., psychology, business, and education). Crisp proposes a research agenda to examine mentoring as enhancing the representation of women and minorities in K–12 educational leadership.

In Chapter 16, Oleszewski and Murakami-Ramalho examine yet another facet in educational leadership preparation. In "Building Bridges and Epistemologies among Practitioners and Researchers in Educational Leadership," they still perceive that educational leadership students who pursue careers as practitioners are not treated the same as those who are pursuing a career in higher education. Part-time doctoral students in educational leadership doctoral programs in universities especially endure limitations and disregard in relation to developing "real" research. Mentoring and advocacy are key elements in building bridges between practitioners and researchers in higher education and K–12 environments, who, when divided, do not engage in improving the overall landscape of education.

Sherman and Grogan continue the conversation about the importance of mentoring in higher education in Chapter 17, this time as it relates to females in the academy. In "Mentoring as a Social Justice Equalizer in Higher Education for Women," the authors warn us of the importance of distinguishing mentoring processes that are meant to promote ascension rather than those meant to preserve the status quo. In this chapter, they expand the knowledge related to social justice and female issues in educational leadership from K–12 to higher education settings, demonstrating challenges female academics face in a traditionally "chilly" higher education setting that includes fewer opportunities for advancement and unequal distribution of responsibilities. The authors highlight the importance of disrupting myths and biases that prevent women from being recognized and valued by proactively acting through mentor–protegé relations. Mentoring through women-to-women relations in order to promote social justice as an equalizer, then, takes a different role in the preparation of future generations of female professionals in higher education.

In the last chapter, Simonsson and Muñoz reaffirm the importance of mentoring in higher education by providing perceptions from both mentors and mentees. In "Mentoring Relationships in Higher Education: An Important Means for Encouraging the Development of Others," Simonsson and Muñoz describe the critical role that mentoring can play in postsecondary education institutions. They share perceptions of the mentoring process from both those being mentored and those serving as mentors. In addition to defining mentoring and reviewing literature regarding the importance of mentoring to the success of individuals new to academia, they present the voices of mentees and mentors to emphasize the influence this process can have. As higher education institutions seek to increase diversity in the makeup of the faculty, mentoring becomes a social justice concern. Recruiting, selecting, and retaining minority faculty is a challenge postsecondary institutions must meet. Simonsson and Muñoz provide evidence that quality mentoring can be a powerful assist in making this goal a reality. Readers will be convinced of this when learning about the voices included in this presentation.

We hope that the voices of scholars and practitioners in this volume not only confirm the steps still needed to be taken in building pedagogical leadership, but highlight the many paths each educator and educational administrator may take to improve the quality of other professionals. Beyond the pitfalls of social inequities lies the responsibility of building a social justice agenda. As the authors demonstrated, building a social justice agenda that encourages the intellectual and professional capital in others serving in different capacities in the P–20 continuum is vital. Such efforts do not lie in one-day professional development sessions or individual preparation, but in developing intellectual and professional capital for educators and leaders and fulfilling the intrinsic sense of purpose and responsibility of generating social and academic capital for students.

REFERENCES

Anderson, G. L. (2002). Reflecting on research for doctoral students in education. *Educational Researcher, 31*(7), 22–25.

Bogotch, I. E. (2000, November). *Educational leadership for social justice: Theory to practice.* Proceeding of the annual conferences of the University Council for Educational Administration, Albuquerque, NM. Available at http://eric.ed.gov/PDFS/ED452585.pdf.

Bogotch, I. E. (2002). Educational leadership and social justice: Practice into theory. *Journal of School Leadership, 12,* 138–156.

Bredeson, P. V., Kelley, C. J., & Klar, H. W. (2009). [Instructional leadership framework]. Unpublished raw data.

Capper, C. A., Theoharis, G., & Sebastian, J. (2006). Toward a framework for preparing leaders for social justice. *Journal of Educational Administration, 44*(3), 209–224.

Etzioni, A. (1988). *The moral dimension: Toward a new economics.* New York: Free Press.

Farrace, B. (2002). Building capacity to enhance learning: A conversation with Richard Elmore. *Principal Leadership (High School Edition), 2*(5), 39–43.

Foster, W. (1989). The administrator as a transformative intellectual. *Peabody Journal of Education, 66*(3), 5–18.

Kose, B. W. (2007). Principal leadership for social justice: Uncovering the content of teacher professional development. *Journal of School Leadership, 17*(3), 276-312.

Marshall, C., & Oliva, M. (Eds.). (2006). *Leadership for social justice: Making revolutions in education.* Boston: Pearson/Allyn & Bacon.

Merchant, B., & Shoho, A. (2006). Bridge people: Civic and educational leaders for social justice. In C. Marshall & M. Oliva (Eds), *Leadership for social justice: Making revolutions in education* (pp. 85–109). Boston: Pearson.

Miller, D. (1979). *Social justice.* New York: Oxford University Press.

Mullen, C. (2006). Exceptional scholarship and democratic agendas: Interviews with John Goodlad, John Hoyle, Joseph Murphy, and Thomas Sergiovanni. *Connexions.* Retrieved March 6, 2010, from cnx.org/content/m14103/latest.

Rawls, J. (1958). Justice as fairness. *Philosophical Review, 67*(2), 164–194.

Sergiovanni, T. J. (1998). Leadership as pedagogy, capital development, and school effectiveness. *International Journal of Leadership in Education, 1*(1), 37–46.

Shoho, A., Merchant, B., & Lugg, C. A. (2004). Social justice: seeking a common language. In F. W. English & G. L. Anderson (Eds.), *The Sage handbook of educational leadership: Advances in theory, research, and practice* (pp. 46–67). Thousand Oaks, CA: Sage.

Spring, J. H. (1998). *Conflict of interests: The politics of American education*. Blacklick, OH: McGraw-Hill.

Theoharis, G. (2007). Social justice educational leaders and resistance: Toward a theory of social justice leadership. *Educational Administration Quarterly, 43*(2), 221–258.

Tyler, T. R. (1997). *Social justice in a diverse society*. Boulder, CO: Westview Press.

PART 1

THE FOUNDATION OF SOCIAL JUSTICE:
DEVELOPING OTHERS

CHAPTER 1

BUILDING CAPACITY

The Foundation of Developing Others

Anita Pankake and Jesus (Chuey) Abrego, Jr.

In Good to Great, Collins (2001) talks about the importance of leadership that "builds enduring greatness" in the organization, rather than focusing on short-term results. In the same vein, Mintzberg (2004) claims "successful managing is not about one's own success but about fostering success in others" (p. 16). Similar declarations are found referring specifically to leadership in education. For example, Fullan, Bertani, and Quinn (2004) state "the main mark of successful leaders is not their impact on student learning at the end of their tenure, but rather the number of good leaders they leave behind who can go even further" (p. 44). Earlier, Fullan (2002) stated that the criterion for selecting an educational leader should be based on that individual's capacity to "...create the conditions under which other leaders will flourish, leaving a continuing effect beyond their term" (p. 7). All of these remarks refer to the importance of building leadership capacity within the organization.

Educational Leaders Encouraging the Intellectual and Professional Capacity of Others:
A Social Justice Agenda, pages 3–23.

In this chapter, we argue that in order to foster such a legacy it is essential to have the perspective that leadership is not a position, but rather a characteristic of the organization. Individuals with this perspective believe that leadership can and should be found in thought and active practice throughout the organization—in every classroom, office, bus, cafeteria, foyer, playground, and so on. The true power of capacity building lies in this simultaneous focus—on the organization and the individual. We believe that it is not enough for leaders to foster individuals if the organizational policies and practices do not also change to both accommodate and catalyze these new ways of thinking and behaving. Primary among these new ways of thinking and behaving are those that advance the agenda of social justice. For us, building the leadership capacity of the organization is key to meeting the social justice agenda.

Leithwood and Riehl (2003) offer affirmation of our perspective. They declare, "school leaders can promote equity and justice for all students by establishing school climates in which patterns of subtle or explicit discrimination are challenged and negated" (p. 7). Creating school climates in which various forms of discrimination are disputed and worked against is instrumental to advancing changes that address a significant moral purpose and a more socially just system.

In this regard, Ogawa and Bossert (1995) note that leadership does not focus on a few individuals in certain parts of the organization, but rather as "a quality of organizations—a systemic characteristic" (reprinted in the Jossey-Bass Reader, 2000, p. 39). They go on to point out that,

> leadership flows through the networks of roles that comprise organizations. The medium of leadership and the currency of leadership lie in the personal resources of people. And, leadership shapes the systems that produce patterns of interaction and the meanings that other participants attach to organizational events. (Ogawa & Bossert, 1995, reprinted in the Jossey-Bass Reader, 2000, p. 39)

Creating an organization with leadership as a systemic characteristic is a challenging but worthy effort. A major component for accomplishing this effort is to build the leadership capacity of individuals within the organization.

The purpose of this chapter is to examine the literature on building capacity. Specific focus is on what building leadership capacity means and how it can be done. Following this discussion are quotes from individuals who have been involved in capacity building; the voices of these practitioners provide support for many of the ideas found in the literature. The chapter closes with a section on strategies for building capacity based on both the literature and the voices.

WHAT DOES BUILDING CAPACITY
MEAN AND HOW CAN IT BE DONE?

What is capacity? Locating a succinct and obvious definition of capacity is difficult. The term is often used in tandem with other terms: leadership capacity, capacity for change, instructional capacity. Thus, a measure of inference is necessary if a sense of meaning for building capacity is to be gleaned from those who write about it. Additionally, it is almost impossible to define capacity building without also discussing actions that cause it to occur. The meaning and the means of building capacity are overlapping and interdependent concepts and difficult to arbitrarily separate for the sake of discussion. Thus, we acknowledge here that some actions are included when attempting to define capacity and the meaning of capacity is often clarified when presenting literature on how it is done.

Fullan (2002) refers to capacity building as a "collective phenomenon" and stresses that the entire school, district, and larger education system should work to build capacity, not just as individuals, but also as groups. Building capacity involves increasing "the collective effectiveness" of everyone at all levels and thus the effectiveness of the organization (Fullan, Hill, & Crevola, 2006; Leithwood & Riehl, 2003). The veracity of the collective nature of capacity building will be seen in the numerous admonitions to create and sustain professional learning communities that we describe in the section on how to build leadership capacity.

In her study of teachers and principals through open-ended questions from schools located in North Carolina, Ohio, Missouri, Kansas, Texas, California, Washington, and Alberta, Canada, Lambert (2005) defined leadership capacity as the broad-based, skillful participation in the work of leadership. Her research was based on data from "3 high schools, 1 junior high school, and 11 elementary schools" and "most of the schools, some high-performing and others low-performing with nowhere to go but up, were urban and high-poverty" (p. 63). Her findings revealed that:

> schools that have developed high leadership capacity take on a different character, however. Even if the principal is reassigned while the school is still in the transitional phase—which often happens—staff commitment can survive the change and even energize the new principal. Teachers find leadership in one another, assigning both credibility and authority to their peers. They tap into mutual authority by expecting others to identify problems and bring them to the group. (p. 65)

Building capacity is often seen as connected with the successful initiation and implementation of change in the organization. For example, Elmore claims that when the topic of discussion is "capacity" it really means that the conversation is about knowledge and skills. For Elmore, the basics of knowledge and skills for teachers and principals must be dramatically increased if there are to be changes in students' learning, especially as the current accountability requires. The uniqueness of Elmore's ideas come in realizing that the knowledge and skills he is referencing are not those with which we are already familiar. For him, capacity means:

> making available the skill and knowledge for people to do things that they have not yet been able to do or not yet learned how to do—and that involves connecting people to sources of knowledge and skill outside of their own workplace; connecting people within the workplace to develop knowledge and skill; and substantially increasing professional development that is instructionally focused and designed to enhance student learning. "Capacity" also means putting teachers and principals in a stream of professional knowledge that lies outside of their immediate workplace and encouraging them to bring it into the workplace. (cited in Farrace, 2002, p. 40)

The connection between capacity building and successful change is also found in the works of Newmann, King, and Youngs (2000) and Fullan (2005a). Newmann et al. (2000) identified five components of change capacity within the school: (1) developing teachers' knowledge, skills, and dispositions; (2) professional community; (3) program coherence; (4) technical resources; and (5) principal leadership. They suggest that schools and their communities must develop new cultures of learning in order to improve.

Building capacity is also one of several drivers of change identified by Fullan (2005a). He sees building capacity as involving policies, strategies, resources, and actions designed to increase people's collective power to move the system forward, as well as developing new knowledge, skills, and competencies; new resources (time, ideas, materials); and new shared identity and motivation to work together for greater change. As with the perspective that we take regarding the simultaneous individual and organizational building of capacity, Fullan points out that building capacity is important not only for and with individuals, but also the organization itself. He sees the building of capacity for the organization occurring through improvements in the infrastructure, that is, "agencies at the local, regional, and state levels that can deliver new capacity in the system, such as training, consulting, and other support" (Fullan, 2005a, p. 55).

The links between capacity and change can also be found in the work of Hargreaves and Fink (2004). They found inspiring examples of leaders who did more than just manage change. They argue that the actions of these leaders provide insights regarding what it means to build capacity, specifically because they pursued and modeled sustainable leadership in their schools. Hargreaves and Fink note that sustainable leadership is defined by: (1) committing to and protecting deep learning in their schools; (2) trying to ensure that improvements last over time, especially after the leader has moved on; (3) distributing leadership and responsibility to others; (4)

considering the impact of their leadership on the schools and communities around them; (5) sustaining themselves so that they can persist with their vision and avoid burning out; (6) promoting and perpetuating diverse approaches to reform rather than standardized prescriptions for teaching and learning; and (7) engaging actively with their environments (pp. 12–13). Their study demonstrated that leadership efforts must be focused on the system rather than the individuals. No matter how talented, charismatic, and dedicated an individual leader may be, "If we want change to matter, to spread, and to last, then the systems in which leaders do their work must make sustainability a priority" (Hargreaves & Fink, 2004, p. 13). This, according to Supovitz (2006), is the "engine of sustainability." He quotes Senge (1990), saying, "the organizations that will truly excel in the future will be the organizations that discover how to tap people's commitment and capacity to learn at all levels in an organization" (p. 161).

Regarding understanding the change process, the change process is about establishing the condition for continuous improvement in order to persist and overcome inevitable barriers to reform. It is about innovativeness, not just innovation (Fullan, 2005a).

How to build capacity? Building leadership capacity requires numerous opportunities for educators to engage in identifying their shared beliefs and values, to examine the ways in which personal and professional values and beliefs align with those of others and, most especially, with the principles social justice demands. This purposeful process of engagement and examination is best supported through "a learning climate, characterized by trust and openness" (Kouzes & Posner, 2002, p. 309). These are among the important elements and actions that form a foundation for building leadership capacity and ultimately result in successful organizational change (Kouzes & Posner, 2002).

Locating, learning, and sustaining new ways of working together are also key to building capacity. These new ways cannot be short-lived and they need to pervade the daily interactions and activities of the organization. Learning to work together in new ways (i.e., building capacity) requires more than increasing the forms and types of learning typically used. Beyond providing professional learning opportunities with follow-up to ensure implementation, building capacity requires organizational initiatives that aid in sustaining the new way of working together. Two of these organizational initiatives are succession planning and the development of professional learning communities.

Succession planning is a means for building capacity in an organization. Fullan (2002) stated that while succession planning is needed at all levels of an organization, the topic is generally neglected in research, policy, and practice. Succession planning can, however, help ensure that schools select "leaders in terms of their capacity to create the conditions under which other leaders will flourish, leaving a continuing effect beyond their term" (p. 7). When a new principal is selected to replace the outgoing occupant, there is most often a failure to take the faculty's concerns or opinions into account. This in turn causes friction between the new leader and the old staff. Much to the detriment of our educational organizations, succession planning is not highly practiced among educational institutions in the United States. Capacity building is needed to implement successful leadership succession; on the other hand, successful leadership succession planning is key to building and sustaining capacity. When the school is run by a team and not by an individual, it is more likely than not to continue to run smoothly after its formal, positional leader is replaced.

The development of professional learning communities requires individual and organizational efforts that promote collaboration, job-embedded professional development, and a supportive culture. Research from Louis and Kruse (1995), Newmann and Wehlage (1995), and Fullan (1999) offer encouraging evidence that developing professional learning communities make a positive difference in supporting reform initiatives. In addition, this same research suggests that professional communities may have significant effects on student achievement and enhanced organizational capacity. Based on a 4-year multischool study, Giles and Hargreaves (2006) concluded, "that the learning organization and professional learning community model may provide a more robust resistance to conventional processes of the attrition of change and of surrounding change forces" (p. 124). Evidence from the study ties together the existence of professional learning communities and the sustainability of improvement initiatives, that is, "schools as learning organizations and professional learning communities seem to have the capacity to offset change forces that threaten the sustainability of innovative efforts" (Giles & Hargreaves, 2006, p. 152).

Mason (2003) explored the role of professional learning communities in promoting effective use of data by school administrators and teachers in 11 schools from the Milwaukee Public Schools over 6 years. Mason's research "was designed to identify capacity issues, organizational problems, and the needs of district and school staff in using data" (p. 9). She found:

> that in addition to building school-level culture, processes, and skills, schools also need to create organizational and structural mechanisms for using data to improve teaching and learning. We learned that decision making and reform capacity needed to be distributed beyond the scope of administrators to include classroom practitioners. We have learned that many schools are simply not organized to use data to improve teaching and learning. In our most recent study, school teams worked collaboratively to learn about continuous improvement, decision-making and data inquiry processes, and the analysis, application, and use of data. Ongoing field research has revealed that these school teams and the processes they employed exemplify the key characteristics of learning communities. (p. 24)

In terms of building capacity of both the organization and individual, Andrews and Lewis (2004) studied educators involved in a process of whole-school renewal in Australia. Efforts were focused on "sharing purpose, developing identity and new systems of meaning which enhance the professional capacity of teachers to improve school outcomes such as student learning, relationships with the community, and the coherence of school operation" (p. 130). As a result of these activities, teachers reported that their previous behavior was competitive, that is, "they operated independently—each doing their own thing and competing for resources," but now they "have a shared purpose—a common language, which reflects their work" (p. 146).

Providing support for teacher learning and collaborations appears to be an important means for building capacity and is endemic to the existence of professional learning communities. For example, Printy's (2004) works, "support the popular conception that communities of practice can play a substantial role in how teachers gain knowledge, acquire their attitudes and beliefs, and refine their instructional practices" (p. 20). The findings from this research also seem to support the idea that teachers involved in communities of practice offer an opportunity for "improving the quality of instruction in our schools" (p. 23).

In what has now become a classic study, Susan Rosenholtz (1989) found that teachers could be effective in meeting the needs of students, when they felt supported through teacher networks, were in a cooperative atmosphere among colleagues, and expanded professional roles were encouraged among faculty. She identified *five outcome measures*: goal consensus, teacher collaboration, teachers' learning opportunities, teachers' instructional certainty, and teacher commitment. Rosenholtz concluded that successful schools possessed a capacity to cherish individuality while at the same time inspiring community.

In schools, fostering success in others includes adults as well as students. In this regard, Fullan et al. (2004) emphasized that tending to both student learning and the leadership development of the adults in the school is not only possible, but desirable. The learning they advise is described as lifelong and found not only in workshops but in the numerous interactions that occur daily in the organization (i.e., formal and job-embedded).

The concepts of leadership, change, and succession are largely informed through a growing body of research in each of these areas. Leadership is described and defined in numerous ways. Some see leadership as a function whereas others have asserted that leadership is about relationships. Leithwood and Riehl (2003) are among those that perceive leadership as a function. They state, "at the core of most definitions of leadership are two functions: providing direction and exercising influence. Leaders mobilise and work with others to achieve shared goals" (p. 3). Kouzes and Posner (2002), on the other hand, claim that "leadership is a relationship. Leadership is a relationship between those who aspire to lead and those who choose to follow" (p. 20). Similarly, Fullan (2001) cited that "new relationships (as found in a professional learning community) are crucial, but only if they work at the hard task of establishing greater program coherence and the addition of resources. The role of leadership is to 'cause' greater capacity in the organization in order to get better results (learning)" (p. 65).

According to Astin and Astin (2000), "a leader can be anyone—regardless of formal position who serves as an effective social change agent. Every faculty and staff member and student is a potential leader" (p. 12). The mission of leaders, in whatever position they may be, is to "create communities of reciprocal care and shared responsibility where every person matters and each person's welfare and dignity is respected and supported" (p. 11). Such a mission is the essence of social justice and therefore aligns with the moral purpose for building leadership capacity.

Fullan (2002) identified five action-and-mindsets that effective leaders possess. They include the following: "a strong sense of moral purpose, an understanding of the dynamics of change, an emotional intelligence as they build relationships, a commitment to developing and sharing new knowledge, and a capacity for coherence making" (p. 15). He claimed the aforementioned action-and-mindsets are characteristics of leaders in effective organizations that might help in improving working conditions and development of future leaders—"thus great leadership is ensured for the future" (p. 17).

Newman and Wehlage (1995), researchers with the Center on Organization and Restructuring of Schools (CORS), studied over 1,500 United States schools from a variety of campus grade levels from 1990 through 1995. The study consisted of a mixed methods approach and included in-depth case studies and survey data. It focused on "schools at different stages of restructuring that participated in a variety of district and state reform strategies, including public school choice, radical decentralization, and state level systemic reform" (p. 6). They concluded from their findings "that the level of professional community in a school had significant effects on student achievement whether achievement was measured as authentic performance or tested in more conventional ways" (p. 32).

The principal's role, according to Barth (1990), is that of *head learner* in a community of learners. According to Wood and Killian (1998), job-embedded staff development is learning that takes place as teachers and administrators engage in their daily work activities—such as discussion with others, peer coaching, mentoring, study groups, and action research. In addition, Sparks and Hirsh (1997) elaborated that "successful job-embedded staff development calls for principals to see themselves as leaders of learning and as designers of organizational structures that support high levels of learning by being facilitators of adult learning" (p. 2).

Lambert (2002) claims that by understanding that learning and leading are firmly linked in community, the first essential step in building shared instructional leadership capacity is taken. The importance of "teacher culture resides in and reinforces the fact that principals are not the only leaders in their schools. They do not have a monopoly on vision and wisdom. Locating, respecting, and collaborating effectively with such teacher leaders are strategies that will significantly enhance a principal's impact when he or she takes up a new position in another school" (Macmillan, 2000, p. 69). "Educators and policymakers alike seek a framework for instructional leadership that will produce sustainable school improvement" (Lambert, 2002, p. 38). According to Lambert, our mistake has been in looking to the principal alone for instructional leadership, when instructional leadership is everyone's work. Not only must the learning journey be shared, so must the leading journey (Frankel & Hayot, 2001).

Fullan (2005b) defined capacity building as a development that increases the collective power in the school in terms of new knowledge and competencies, increased motivation to engage in improvement actions, and additional resources. To assure this occurs, Fenwick and Pierce (2001) stated that our challenge as an educational society is to encourage those who are qualified to assume leadership roles. The challenge to school leaders today is to encourage the participation of every professional in shaping a vibrant and dynamic environment for students.

Furthermore, Wood and Killian (1996; cited in Wood & Killian, 1998) identified several factors associated with successful school-based improvement and the role of staff development. The research findings cited that the impact on the success of schools in improving instruction and student learning was staff development "linked to the school's and the faculties' improvement goals and to job-embedded learning"...and described "11 major shifts in staff development" (p. 1).

Thus the change from a traditional professional development approach that emphasized the development of individual teachers to a current focus on job-embedded learning where learning is much more "on-the-job" than it was before and seen as an essential ingredient for creating learner-centered schools is in line with the characteristics of a professional learning community—building a collective learning community that focuses on the school, the value of professional networks, and site-based professional development activities (National Association of State Boards of Education, 1997) and on building organizational cultures that support teacher development over time (Loucks-Horsley, 1995).

A study on educational accountability in Texas by McGhee and Nelson (2005) found that the current culture of educational accountability created by well-intended policymakers aiming to improve schools has instead become a culture of fear, driven by the unanticipated consequences of the

Texas accountability system. What matters for instructional improvement and student achievement is not that leadership is distributed, but how it is distributed so that stakeholders can contribute effectively to the development of the organization.

Elmore suggests several strategies that can be implemented by principals seeking to be instructional leaders. First, he recommends that the principal should take an interest in instructional practice and budget time within the school schedule to focus specifically on issues of instruction with department heads and teachers to create opportunities for teachers to learn. Additionally, like Kouzes and Posner (2002), he advocates that a powerful leadership strategy for principals to use in creating a high level of internal coherence in an organization is to " model what they say" (pp. 13–14). For example, principals can demonstrate their own competence in working with teachers on problems of instructional practice. According to Farrace (2002, p. 41), their primary contribution is to enhance their own knowledge and skill and the knowledge and skill of others.

Elmore also observes that most successful schools work on the internal accountability problem. This results in their creating greater coherence within the organization and working on the development of their own measures of whether they think they are succeeding with kids. Elmore goes on to claim that "successful schools have internal intelligence about whether the quality of teaching is what it should be and the quality of student learning is what it should be and, frankly, are not particularly surprised by the test results they get back because they already know basically how well they're doing" (Farrace, 2002, p. 43). Unfortunately, most districts and schools believe that accountability systems are external and focused on one or more high-stakes tests, and therefore helping educational leaders to begin to understand the power of internal intelligence and quality monitoring is difficult (Elmore, cited in Farrace, 2002).

PRACTITIONERS' VOICES:
BUILDING LEADERSHIP CAPACITY

The voices heard here come from individual educators from a variety of formal positions in educational organizations (i.e., teachers, principals, central office administrators, and state agency representatives). Their words were obtained through personal interviews focused on leadership, professional learning communities, and professional development. The majority of voices come from educators in Texas, with a few taken from interviews with educators in Louisiana, Oklahoma, and Arkansas.

The educators interviewed mentioned opportunities when they had to engage with others regarding their beliefs and practices about teaching, learning, and leadership. In their comments you hear their desires to align their individual work into a coherent whole. For example, the following comments are from a principal and central office administrator, respectively; each elaborates on the development of vision and mission through the strategic planning committee process. The principal discussed development of the mission and vision within the context of the district's standards.

> We have vision and mission statements and they're done as a team...we just have finished our 5-year district plan for the future and we have our standards and everybody in the district knows our standards. Everyone receives the statements, the mission statement, and the vision statements and our statements of beliefs. They are included in our campus plans to coincide, go hand in hand. The district standards are placed at our campus plans so that we align everything campus-wise to district-wise. Our goals must be aligned with district goals...action...our action statements must be aligned with district actions so we're very consistent...yes.

The central office administrator from that same district shared how the vision and mission were developed from his perspective.

> Okay, the vision and mission statements are done through that strategic planning process. We have a district commitment statement...is what we have...we have a set of district goals and then campuses set their goals and have mission statements as well but it's all linked back to the district set of goals.

Several principals from one district spoke of the importance of coming together to increase the alignment of their thinking and practice with those of other schools and with the district as a whole. Also mentioned as equally important is the increased alignment of teachers' thinking and practice.

> When we got together on Thursday afternoons it was about learning, vertical alignment pieces, horizontal, looking at our plan, looking at our data. It could be a committee, a small committee action team working on something specifically.

> ...they'll [teachers] meet early in the year...talk about what they want to discuss...collect data over months...come back and look at the data that everybody's collected...review it, then make another plan...so often it works like that...

Whereas another principal reported:

> ...to me if I'm going to be supportive...cheerleading doesn't do any good. Let's go try it, let's see if it works and let's try to provide the people who are doing the training with some accurate data.

From another interview, one of the superintendents from a different district emphasized the need to share responsibility and accountability if people are going to grow. He also stated the importance of teamwork in making changes in organizations as complex as schools and school districts:

> If you are teaming and have a collection of individuals, that means you stand together, have mutual respect, and, of course, support each other. But, it also means that responsibility is parceled out and accountability goes with it. I think all of the organizations, the really lasting and significant things, they are complex. I am not minimizing the importance of individuals. There may be key points when individuals absolutely make the difference, probably on their own. But I really think that the most important things were done in strong teams and I think it's true.

Similarly, another superintendent addressed the collective nature of developing leadership that closely aligns with the literature on building leadership capacity:

> . . . we have high expectations for each other, we communicate that, our campus improvement plans that I think look so much different today than they did four or five years ago. Where you saw so much maintenance kind of things on campus improvement plans you really have principals and teachers talking about student improvement and academic success and what needs to be done to improve the achievement levels of kids.

He went on to say:

> We try to stress that teachers are just as important leaders in this district as anyone else is and they are indeed really good teachers. We all have jobs just to support teachers and prove the environment for the kids to learn and I guess the things we do to tell people that things like normal things that a lot of people, I guess, do but advisory committees and decision-making committees, you know. I meet with teachers on a regularly scheduled basis, the students the same way, but the organizational interaction that goes on each of the campuses are very important, essential.

Kouzes and Posner's (2002) admonition of the importance of creating a climate "characterized by trust and openness" (p. 309) was evidenced in several of the voices we heard. The following comment comes from a superintendent discussing how the organization can either encourage or stifle the leadership of its employees. Though the words trust and openness are not specifically used, it can be easily inferred that in order to accomplish what the superintendent is describing, openness and trust must be characteristics of the organization.

> Any organization that doesn't value its employees is in trouble. And so, to create a culture, environment and values of learning that means people's potential is being enhanced . . . I think you have to look to people you think have potential and you got to actually encourage them and you got to have

organizational support systems to enable them to do whatever else they need to do to develop.

A similar message is heard in the following list of actions for encouraging leaders shared by other district leaders:

> Oh, that's easy for me . . . encourage, appreciate your employees through pay, benefits, being positive to employees in a constructive way when possible. Give them latitude and be individual . . . I have learned not to be nearly as controlling as I used to be . . . really delegating. I think once you allow people to get involved in real good projects . . . and allow new ideas, look at new areas, don't be still with everything. If you can change, it would be very good.

Openness and trust can be demonstrated by leaders being accessible.

> For leaders to be accessible to others is an important thing. To share and just to talk with people to be available for maybe an unimportant conversation may be to them a tremendous learning experience. That is the kind of thing that helps them to decide if they want to move on up the ladder or not move up the ladder.

Openness and trust can also be evidenced through the sharing of information. One superintendent commented on the importance of openly sharing information with others in the organization by stating:

> The major thing they can do to encourage is to share information and share opportunities. That is what was done for me. Share participation and allow you to participate and to be informed . . . information is power and an organization that doesn't keep people informed or doesn't even want them to be informed, that is cruelty in the first order. It shows that you don't trust them, that you don't respect them. If you really want to keep someone from growing or getting promoted, don't let them know what is going on, keep the information away from them.

Among the strategies for building leadership capacity described earlier in the chapter was the development of professional learning communities. Included in the development of community among education professionals are shared leadership, collective learning, shared learning, and human and nonhuman supportive conditions. The following words shared by a teacher reflect the collective learning and supportive conditions essential to the development of a professional learning community and, thus, an increase in leadership capacity.

> And she's [principal] also been very, very good at finding inservice and learning—really, really good things for us to go and learn. I had been involved a long time ago in lots of workshops that you just meet and they go on and on and on. But she's found us some really good material and sent us all. There's

been lots of times when either all or lots of us have gone to the same place, so we're all getting the same input and it makes it a lot easier to work together when we've all come from the same place.

The voice from a central office administrator credits the superintendent of that district with bringing a vision for community with her when she accepted the position. Of particular interest here is that the superintendent not only is an advocate of learning and development of others, but also of herself.

I think she had a vision of coming to a district and have the potential to really grow and it's academic excellence without losing sight that children come with different needs and that a lot of training is required at all levels—the board, administrators, teachers, and the staff. I think that was the way she looked at it really. She's a strong believer in training. And leads by example, so she's always learning. She's always participating in training.

Elmore's comments that the knowledge and skills necessary to build capacity should be different than doing more of what we already know are heard in the following voices. Each of these educators reports on new ways of doing things that have enhanced their personal growth and increased the capacity of their schools and teams.

… every year basically is a new year … is a little different. Our curriculum changes as the times change. You know we went from TAAS to TAKS and so you see change in that…and expectations and I do see we have a lot of teamwork. A lot more teamwork…where we're really developed into some vertical teams and some alignments … and getting our curriculum really put together well.

Well, we disaggregate everything we have … our TAKS scores are disaggregated … we take each individual student …We go through … by [social] economics, we do it every way…and we see which ones are doing well, which ones are not. How many … we have you know … What their learning levels are. And we discuss all of those you know through meetings. In our team meetings uh we talk about the individual kids and who needs extra help and who doesn't … all kinds of things.

As Fullan and Elmore both noted, capacity needs support from all levels of the organization. An example of this is found when one particular principal shared her experience regarding the freedom to implement at her campus. She reported that teachers' freedom to implement new programs and ideas was supported by her.

At this campus that [freedom to implement] has always been a strength and in fact when we did the first organization health inventory, innovation was very high on our scale … and supportive innovation … [comments about teachers' freedom to implement] so they can ... now as long as they are following the essential knowledge and skills and they follow the scope and sequence.

A teacher from another school and district had similar reactions to share. These comments are particularly relevant to the collective learning and shared personal practices dimensions of professional learning communities. Additionally, the support offered by the CLT is an excellent example of providing supportive conditions for developing capacity.

> . . . any time anyone goes to a workshop or institute or whatever, usually unless they just pay out of their pocket, they'll bring it before the CLT and pay for it. I don't think we've ever turned anyone down. Well, if we pay for it, then you definitely have to share once you come back. And it's always nice if we don't pay for it, if you do, if you come back and share. So that'll happen. And with the grade-level group, that person will come over the loudspeaker and say, I went to this memory conference yesterday and I got some good ideas; if you want to know more about it, come in my room and see me. That's real important.

She goes on to mention the supportive conditions and collective learning that she offers to a colleague in her own teaching sphere. Interestingly, a physical constraint in the building itself has provided a means for fostering collaboration and shared personal practice.

> For instance, my grade level, my team partner, she shares a back door with me and she's a first-year teacher. So we leave our door open all the time. So all during the day, if she has a question about something, she just runs through and says oh, you know, what do I do, that sort of thing. So that is something that, and I started out here in a portable building, which is completely different, the way this building is laid and put together, it's shorter to go through classrooms than it is to go around the outside perimeter. And so people are constantly running through even during the day, which you would think would be real destructive but the kids are used to it and we're all used to it. . . . Who would have thought of it?

Elmore proffered that successful schools not only created increased coherence within their organizations, but also developed internal intelligence regarding how to measure their success with students. Some evidence of this internal monitoring and the use of school- and district-specific tools for measuring progress toward goals are found in the comments below.

> Every department has a scorecard but we've got strategic outcomes or indicators ... strategic data that we're measuring ... that you know if we boil everything down ... of our work, these are the things that are most vital ... and keep people ... measuring and setting goals off of that but for improvement.

Another central office administrator shared some background regarding the scorecard and how it came about.

> ... we have looked at other districts who've done very [well] ... successful at using the continuous improvement model. And one of the districts that we looked at is Aldine, and a couple of years ago they had a scorecard and we saw it and we looked at it and ... I mean it worked for [another district] ... so Executive Director of Student Services and myself, we kinda developed the scorecard and it is gone probably through nine versions now ... it's not the fact that it's a form but what works so that you can keep the data in front of you ... to judge ... are we being successful or not...

Some principals saw the scorecard as a way to self-monitor, while for others, it was a way of impacting district accountability.

> I have a scorecard and that's how the directors and the central office staff... that has the mission statements...the strategic goals...and it's their report card, [in terms of] how are we doing.

> It's a personal way. It's [the scorecard] a way of monitoring personal progress toward those goals. If you are a leader of that particular area then there are things that you have agreed to do that you feel that would move toward [that] goal and so those are... become the checkpoints...there are things that can't be measured.

From a central office perspective, the scorecard was seen as a way to "keep up with how we are doing on our department plan." It was also identified as a way of aligning efforts to the district strategic plan.

> ...what is different here than what was there [another district] is there are measures [the use of the scorecard] ... indicators of success that you look at and we monitor those indicators of success ... through measures either on a quarterly basis or on an annual basis ... but I think that before ... we had our strategic plan ... it was something that was there and I think we are making a huge effort to make the strategic plan be what guides our work.

In this same district, principals talked about how data was used at all levels to monitor performance internally and based on that information adjust practice appropriately. The following words operationalize the internal intelligence element of building capacity offered by Elmore.

> Oh we monitor. We monitor and evaluate and readjust and everything is based on data. What's the focus of the district goals, our campus goals ... we look at our data to try to figure out how far away are we from those goals and so we're all a part of that process and then we give the draft to the general staff and then they approve it or wordsmith it or whatever they want to do ... I have to say that we look at our kids and that is the focus is our kids and how far can we take them ... pretty much the same process that she uses at the district level.

… so our campus we went over all our data, TAKS data, parent survey, teacher survey; all the data that we had and identified some specific areas. Five … we made five teams of that worked on some strategic areas and then throughout the year they had action plans connected to that and then we looked [at] our growth at the end of the year.

We do a lot of data … and by looking at data it reveals if we're meeting our goals … well like our benchmark scores, our 6-week assessments … we always look at the TAKS scores…other data depends on what … depends on what data. I have a reading data wall, I'll have like a math data wall … so if I'm doing reading, I might look at their … reading fluency … the kids can … they can see where … if they're improving or if they're not … it really opens their eyes.

We do a lot of gathering of information … we do whether it's your own grade-level team, whether it's the school team, whether it's vertical teams we constantly come back and look at is that goal successful, we do a lot of disaggregating in TAKS data, we do a lot of disaggregating in just data in our classrooms with our benchmarks. We have the computer program that we can you know that's done by the district that allows us to look at those scores.

Look at their attendance rates, their home life, what we know about that. We look at their test scores, we look at the grades in their classes, we look at everything that we can look at so that we can determine if we're going to be able to, what we can do to intervene to make sure this student is going to … graduate and be successful.

Superintendents reported that getting others involved was an important means for increasing the capacity of others. Strategies such as shared decision making and effective delegation were among those most frequently mentioned.

This is simple and old, but the failure to delegate stifles participatory management and encourages giving opportunity to be seen and present and to be recognized for their contributions as opposed to letting them do the work of it and then you get up and do it yourself. I know people that do that. I have had that experience a few times in my life . . .

Getting people involved in genuine ways seemed to be a theme with many of the superintendents when they talked about what could be done to encourage leadership. See these comments below:

I think that the most critical thing that an organization can do is to have people that are involved, be able to relate to people who are actually involved in the work these people do. In other words, to be given some practical experiences.

I think, if the leader does share the responsibility and accountability, and they [others] know that, well that's not development, they are not going to grow. If I am going to run things by orders or to make the decisions, what are they gonna do? They are gonna know that he's gonna make the decision anyway. So I think that if you have that kind of philosophy, you are gonna stifle development or people I believe strongly in sense of teaming and work as a team.

The voices shared in this section provide affirmation for much of the literature presented earlier. In the work environments for all of the voices here, one or more of the means for building leadership capacity are heard to greater or lesser degrees. Some voices are stronger, some have more strategies in place, but all are moving to improve the micro and macro environments that allow leadership capacity to increase as a means to improve education for all children.

CONCLUSION

In an interview with Faracce (2002), Richard Elmore referenced the "principle of the reciprocity of accountability for capacity." He explained this by stating, ." . . when others in the organization are asked to add to their performance, those doing the asking have " . . . an equal and opposite responsibility to provide the capacity to acquire the knowledge and skill to do that performance" (pp. 41–42). Elmore's principle of reciprocity of accountability for capacity reminds us that while it is easy to say we should build capacity, the reality is that capacity building is neither easy nor quick and it involves changes in every part of and everyone's part in the organization. However, it is also important to note that while building capacity is neither easy nor quick, capacity building is most definitely possible and desirable. Most importantly, building capacity does not just happen; it must be led and nurtured; it must be achieved through "intentional leadership" on the part of the administrative team (Moller & Pankake, 2006).

Within the literature reviewed and the voices presented, some strategies emerged that can become a part of the intentional leadership needed. Bringing individuals together for conversation and collaboration regarding their work is basic to building capacity. Conversations can focus on such topics as vision, mission, classroom practice, allocation of resources, and changes in structures. Using the conversations to gain a greater coherence of beliefs and values between and among staff can be important in creating an organization in which leadership pervades every activity and role.

Looking both beyond the basic skills and knowledge of educators for tools and solutions that have rarely if ever been used in our profession can be strategies for building leadership capacity and advancing a social justice agenda in schools. Going beyond the usual and familiar is a form of capacity building that can enhance performance of both the adults and children within the system.

Succession planning is a practice that has evidence to support its importance in sustaining improvement initiatives and yet is rarely done. Leadership capacity that pervades the organization will accomplish at least two major objectives: a smooth transition when personnel in formal leadership positions turn over and a critical mass of individuals available for placement in various formal leadership roles.

Working with building-level and district personnel to create a professional learning community (PLC) is probably the most advocated strategy for building leadership capacity. A PLC includes other recommended strategies as a part of its makeup. The dimensions of a PLC include shared and supportive leadership, shared values and vision, collective learning and application, shared personal practice, and supportive conditions (Hord, 2004). Initiating the development of a professional learning community encompasses many of the other strategies offered in isolation—collaboration, professional development, shared leadership, and supportive structures.

Whether educators choose strategies to building leadership capacity that are targeted as specific practices or a more comprehensive approach such as creating a PLC, the intended outcomes are the same: Creating the capacity of the organization and the individuals within it to deliver quality teaching and learning to all students.

REFERENCES

Andrews, D., & Lewis, M. (2004). Building sustainable futures: Emerging understandings of the significant contribution of the professional learning community. *Improving Schools*, 7(2), 129–150.

Astin, A. W., & Astin, H. S. (2000). *Leadership reconsidered: Engaging higher education in social change*. Battle Creek: MI: W. K. Kellogg Foundation.

Barth, R. S. (1990). *Improving schools from within: Teachers, parents, and principals can make the difference*. San Francisco: Jossey-Bass.

Collins, J. (2001). *Good to great: Why some companies make the leap and others don't*. New York: HarperCollins.

Farrace, B. (2002). Building capacity to enhance learning: A conversation with Richard Elmore. *Principal Leadership (High School Edition)*, 2(5), 39–43.

Fenwick, L., & Pierce, M. L. (2001). The principal shortage: Crisis or opportunity. *Principal*, 80(4), 24–32.

Frankel, M. T., & Hayot, P. T. (2001). School leadership at a crossroads: An agenda for developing a new generation of leaders. *Independent School*, 60(2), 68–78.

Fullan, M. (1999). *Change forces: The sequel*. Philadelphia: The Falmer Press.

Fullan, M. (2001). *Leading in a culture of change*. San Francisco: Jossey-Bass.

Fullan, M. (2002). Leadership and sustainability. *Principal Leadership*, 3(4), 14–17.

Fullan, M. (2005a). 8 forces for leaders of change. *Journal of Staff Development*, 26(4), 54–64.

Fullan, M. (2005b). *Leadership and sustainability: System thinkers in action.* Thousand Oaks, CA: Corwin Press.

Fullan, M., Bertani, A., & Quinn, J. (2004). New lessons for districtwide reform. *Educational Leadership, 61*(7), 42–46.

Fullan, M., Hill, P., & Crevola, C. (2006). *Breakthrough.* Thousand Oaks, CA: Corwin Press.

Giles, C., & Hargreaves, A. (2006). The sustainability of innovative schools as learning organizations and professional learning communities during standardized reform. *Educational Administration Quarterly, 42*(1), 124–156.

Hargreaves, A., & Fink, D. (2004). The seven principles of sustainable leadership. *Educational Leadership, 61*(7), 9–13.

Hord, S. M. (Ed.). (2004). *Learning together, leading together.* New York: Teachers College Press.

Kouzes, J. M., & Posner, B. Z. (2002). *The leadership challenge* (3rd ed.). San Francisco: Jossey-Bass.

Lambert, L. (2002). A framework for shared leadership. *Educational Leadership, 59*(8), 37–40.

Lambert, L. (2005). Leadership for lasting reform. *Educational Leadership, 62*(5), 62–65.

Leithwood, K., & Riehl, C. (2003). What we know about successful school leadership. Retrieved February 5, 2006, from http://www.cepa.gse.rutgers.edu/whatweknow.pdf

Loucks-Horsley, S. (1995). Professional development and the learner centered school. *Theory into Practice, 34*(4), 265–271.

Louis, K., & Kruse, S. (1995). *Professionalism and community: Perspectives on reforming urban schools.* Thousand Oaks, CA, Corwin Press.

Macmillan, R. B. (2000). Leadership succession, cultures of teaching and educational change. In N. Bascia & A. Hargreaves (Eds.), *The sharp edge of educational change: Teaching, learning and the realities of reform* (pp. 52–71). New York: Routledge-Falmer.

Mason, S. (2003, April). *Learning from data: The role of professional learning communities.* Paper presented at the annual conference of the American Education Research Association, Chicago. Retrieved February 1, 2006, from http://www.wcer.wisc.edu/mps/AERA%202003/Learning%20from%20Data%204%2016%2002%20FINAL.doc

McGhee, M. W., & Nelson, S. W. (2005). Sacrificing leaders, villainizing leadership: How educational accountability policies impair school leadership. *Phi Delta Kappan, 86*(5), 367–372.

Mintzberg, H. (2004). *Managers not MBAs.* San Francisco: Berrett-Koehler.

Moller, G., & Pankake, A. (2006). *Lead with me: A principal's guide to teacher leadership.* Larchmont, NY: Eye on Education.

National Association of State Boards of Education. (1997). *Financing student success: Beyond equity and adequacy.* Report of the NASBE Study Group on Funding Education in the 21st Century. Retrieved January 26, 2006, from http://www.nasbe.org/Educational_Issues/Reports/Financing%20Student%20Success.pdf

Newmann, F., & Wehlage, G. (1995). *Successful school restructuring.* Madison, WI: Center on Organization and Restructuring of Schools.

Newmann, F. M., King, M. B., & Youngs, P. (2000). Professional development that addresses school capacity: Lessons from urban elementary schools. *American Journal of Education, 108*(4), 259–299.

Ogawa, R., & Bossert, S. (1995). Leadership as an organizational quality. *Educational Administration Quarterly, 31,* 224–243. Reprinted in the *Jossey-Bass Reader on Educational Leadership* (pp. 38–58). San Francisco: Jossey-Bass, 2000.

Printy, S. M. (2004, Winter). The professional impact of communities of practice. *UCEA Review,* 21–23.

Rosenholtz, S. (1989). *Teacher's workplace: The social organization of schools.* New York: Longman.

Senge, P. M. (1990). *The fifth discipline: The art and practice of the learning organization.* New York: Currency Doubleday.

Sparks, D., & Hirsh, S. (1997). *A new vision for staff development.* Alexandria, VA: ASCD and Oxford, CA: National Staff Development Council

Supovitz, J. A. (2006). *The case for district-based reform: Leading, building, and sustaining school improvement.* Cambridge, MA: Harvard Education Press.

Wood, F., & Killian, J. E. (1998). Job-embedded learning makes a difference in school. *Journal of Staff Development, 19,* 52–54.

CHAPTER 2

A CONTEXT FOR DEVELOPING SOCIAL JUSTICE FOR STAFF AND STUDENTS

Communities of Professional Learners

Stephanie A. Hirsh and Shirley M. Hord

The purpose of schools is student learning, and social justice in education is about ensuring that all students regardless of race, creed, color, socioeconomic status, gender, or disability have access to and receive the highest quality education (Cochran-Smith et al., 2009; Curren, 2009). The most significant factor in whether students learn well is quality teaching (Haycock & Crawford, 2008; Peske & Haycock, 2006). Such teaching is increased, enhanced, and expanded through continuous professional development (Hord, 2009, 2010). Teachers cannot promote social justice if they do not possess the knowledge and skills, beliefs and attitudes necessary to ensure success for all students. Principals likewise cannot lead a school committed to social justice if they do not believe in social justice and possess a vision for advancing it in a high-performing school, knowing how to prioritize resources, and support the needs of faculty to achieve this vision. Both are

Educational Leaders Encouraging the Intellectual and Professional Capacity of Others:
A Social Justice Agenda, pages 25–43.
Copyright © 2012 by Information Age Publishing
25

possible and substantive research demonstrates so (American Institute for Research, 2007).

A fundamental purpose for professional development has always been to advance learning for educators and students. Placing this purpose in the context of a discussion of social justice demands that all students achieve at high levels. Social justice advocates posit that successful academic achievement alone does not address inequities that occur as a result of the "isms" of racism, oppression, and others (Sensoy & Diangelo, 2009). And that the goals of a successful education are not defined solely as academic achievement, but include proficiencies related to participatory membership in a democratic society. As Trueba (1998) so elegantly stated, "perhaps the main dream of our democracy, is that education is for all and that education can empower all peoples to participate in our democratic structures and make an important contribution to our society" (p. 166). Additional goals are the capacities and confidence to conduct oneself responsibly in support of one's own well-being; the ability to contribute to the well-being of others whose circumstances bar them from completing successful attainment of well-being for themselves; and facilitating the translation of the society's beliefs and values to upcoming generations, ensuring community service and social justice are maintained and remain an integral part of society's fabric (Arneson, 2007). To contribute to this robust and broader vision for schooling and its multiple outcomes, there must be a consideration of the value systems that educators bring, and to their understanding "the light in the eyes of their students as evidence that they are capable and worthy human beings, then schools can become places of hope and affirmation for students of all backgrounds and all situations" (Nieto, 1999, p. 176). Professional development must include appropriate *content*, use effective *designs*, and strengthen the *context* necessary to sustain these efforts.

IDENTIFYING CONTENT FOR CONTINUOUS LEARNING CYCLES

Schools that are successful at achieving the vision (articulated above) are places where all staff are members of a community committed to professional learning. In the work of this learning community (Darling-Hammond, Wei, Andree, Richardson, & Orphanus, 2009; Hord & Hirsh, 2008), the faculty is focused on what the data regarding student academic performance, as well as other measures, tells them. They examine all data from multiple perspectives. They determine whether gaps exist between gender groups, between races, between students who have disabilities and those who do not, between English language learners and the rest of the students, between students who are eligible for free and/or reduced-price lunches and those who are not (Guerra & Nelson, 2007). As members of a learning community, they know that their own learning is essential to closing gaps as well as positioning all students, and especially their minority group students, to develop the knowledge and skills to achieve all aspects of the comprehensive vision set forth by the school. Therefore, they establish a purposeful learning agenda that they feel confident will support their own acquisition of the new knowledge and skills they need in order to assist all students in achieving the school's vision and goals.

Determining the Content for School Wide Learning

Ensuring that every student experiences great teaching every day is not as simple as it sounds. Well-intentioned teachers can be committed to great teaching, and still the beliefs, habits, and strategies they have adopted over the years may work against them. As an example, there are skillful teachers who view slowing the pace of instruction as an appropriate strategy for serving struggling students. And yet, research reports that acceleration, not remediation, has a greater impact (Coalition for Student Success, 2009). There are teachers who lower expectations because of students' home living circumstances. Exposing and discussing these issues as a faculty can expose misinterpretations of research and ultimately strengthen the community's commitment to the school vision for social justice (DeMulder, Ndura-Ouédraogo, & Stribling, 2009).

Schoolwide learning is essential to achieving a school vision committed to social justice (Bustamante, Nelson, & Onwuegbuzie, 2009). Identifying the appropriate content for schoolwide learning initiates the process. In addition to examining data regarding students, schools must examine data regarding teacher knowledge, skills, and attitudes. These data provide insights into the learning topics that would most effectively and efficiently respond to the needs of the staff.

When a school staff limits its learning goals to academic performance and its technical focus only, the data analyses and subsequent decisions for learning may be a bit easier. But, when social justice as an outcome is added to the mix, the content needs expand and in many cases become much more complicated. In addition to understanding literacy, math, or differentiation strategies, for example, principals and teachers must understand the foundation and requirements for social justice. It is not solely about "appreciating" racial or class differences; it is about helping all staff identify and understand the impact of organizational and individual practices on each person—staff and students, those in the majority and those in the minority (Berman, Chambliss, & Geiser, 1999). It is each staff member creating a lens of deep-seated beliefs, a philosophy, or social justice worldview from which all decisions are made. A school cannot say we did cultural literacy last year, or we had our hard conversations about race and class last year, and expect a different and meaningful learning agenda to appear for their next attention. Serving in a community of professional learners that is concerned solely about its structural dimensions is not the answer; the answer is in what the members believe in and are doing while in their community. A school must determine how social justice becomes a component of every conversation and how the goals for social justice are used to influence the decisions at each level of the content discussion.

As we know, not all content is created equal and embracing the wrong learning agenda can result in wasted resources (Kennedy, 1998). This is why the learning community must be thoughtful in its research and discussion regarding the content in which it will invest. It must not only examine the research that appears to support a particular program or strategy it is considering, it must also seek information about the demographics of the "testing grounds" for the program or strategy (National Staff Development Council, 2001). In other words, was the research on the program or strategy conducted in a location similar to our school? Were their goals similar to our school? What did they gain from the experience?

Three critical questions guide the selection of content for professional development (National Staff Development Council, 2001):

- To what degree are educators able to use the content to capitalize on the unique qualities of each student; able to create safe, orderly, and supportive learning environments; and demonstrate high expectations for all students?
- To what degree do educators possess deep content knowledge, rich instructional strategies expertise, and ability to develop and use appropriate classroom-based assessments?
- To what degree are educators prepared to engage families in support of students' outcomes?

Through a social justice lens, additional questions are necessary: Are multiple goals influenced by the selection of a particular content-learning agenda? What are they? Does the content take into consideration the many student differences and challenges teachers face in classrooms and provide accommodations for them? Are the needs that teachers have for working with children of different backgrounds met?

Does the content facilitate teacher reflection in terms of what the teacher learns about the students and him- or herself through the course of the learning process, as opposed to a strict script that ignores the needs of individual students or fails to promote continuous growth on the part of the teacher? Does the content prepare students to become empowered citizens? Do the system's policies support or deny equitable access of appropriate content that advances learning for all?

Content that promotes social justice will be rich and will require the faculty to determine the appropriate learning foci that once again advances the goals they have set for students. Thus, staff select new practices that accommodate both academic performance and social justice goals. From here the faculty determines learning outcomes, the policies they want to reexamine, the teaching strategies they want to be able to implement in classrooms, and how they want to learn the strategies, as well as how they will monitor and assess the impact of their efforts.

Under the best circumstances, schoolwide staff learning promotes collaboration, joint responsibility, and schoolwide implementation of a compelling vision for teacher and student performance. Team learning at the grade level or subject area increases consistency across classrooms and helps teachers address the more specific academic challenges associated with grade level or content-specific learning objectives. Learning that occurs at the schoolwide community level builds commitment, promotes common understandings and a common purpose, and supports the challenges associated with substantive change. Teacher learning is further supported in learning team settings where teachers are able to apply schoolwide learning to their specific grade level and subject area challenges (Darling-Hammond et al., 2009; Hirsh & Hord, 2008).

Extending Learning at the Team Level

Learning team members work together to apply schoolwide learning to their classrooms and their students. Some begin by determining where students are struggling, and planning how to apply new schoolwide learning to those challenges. Some wait to see how schoolwide learning supports their own cycle of improvement. A cycle might begin with the identification of a new unit of study or set of standards, wherein a first step is an assessment that identifies what students know and where they have learning needs. When the learning teams identify student learning needs, they can isolate their own learning questions and create their own learning agenda. How they address their learning agenda can differ. They can look for clues as to whether certain teachers among them have been more successful with certain objectives. They can then ask them to lead the learning on a particular objective (Jackson & Bruegmann, 2009). If they are not comfortable with the expertise within the team or school, they can look for assistance beyond the school. They might invite a subject-matter expert to work with them, attend a workshop, take a course, or visit another school experiencing greater success. These are just a few examples of how they might gain new knowledge and skills.

As they increase their knowledge and skills, team members begin to design new lessons and learning opportunities for students based on a stronger understanding of the content and the skills their students need to achieve academic and social justice outcomes. Together they test the lessons and critique them afterward, looking for ways to improve them. They create classroom assessments to determine if their strategies produced desired results. And when they do not, they identify additional strategies for re-teaching and reinforcing. As lessons are designed, implemented, assessed, and revised, the staff is able to "bank" lessons to which they can return next year. When they feel confident their students have mastered the desired objectives or content, they repeat the cycle with another set of objectives or unit of study, each time identifying new learning priorities that lead to improved instruction and student growth (Lewis, Perry, & Hurd, 2004; Perry & Lewis, 2009).

SELECTING THE LEARNING PROCESSES

How educators approach their own learning is key to successful implementation of any new program and/or strategy (Hall & Hord, 2010). If the learning community makes poor design decisions then it jeopardizes the potential outcome of its plans. Schoolwide and grade-level teams can increase the likelihood of successful social justice implementation by addressing questions and issues related to social justice and adult learning. Questions may include: How will educators acquire the necessary knowledge and skills to implement the strategies successfully? How will the effort be monitored and ultimately evaluated? How will accommodations be made to support educators throughout the change process? How will the relationships within the school be leveraged to advance the implementation? And, importantly, who is going to ask these hard questions and monitor the tough conversations? Also, what are the dispositions required around these questions so that they may be asked? Within each question are other questions that must promote learning and reflection at a deeper level for an educator to be truly effective at promoting social justice. Self-examination and reflection are critical at each stage with a synthesizing experience at the conclusion so that new learning becomes an institutional practice and expectation (York-Barr, Sommers, Ghere, & Montie, 2006).

Providing Learning Options

How will educators acquire the necessary knowledge and skills to achieve the agreed-upon goals and specific program expectations or strategies? If the learning community is committed to substantive change in knowledge, skills, and dispositions, then research suggests that it will need to set aside time for traditional workshop learning supported by follow-up coaching sessions (Joyce & Showers, 2002). Workshop learning is used as a broad term to include sessions with experts, colleagues, or external assistance providers that may occur on staff development days, early-release day sessions, courses, online courses, and some conferences. While some teachers may be able to acquire and demonstrate new knowledge and skills absent of some form of organized learning, most teachers will require such learning and support in order to develop a foundation for making instructional and philosophical (social justice) changes. If schoolwide changes regarding attitudes and expectations are a desired outcome, then settings that convene the entire staff for hard conversations and facilitated dialogue are more apt to be the necessary first steps. This is not a technical challenge but the need to support and guide staff to look deeply into their beliefs and values, their predispositions and worldviews (Guerra & Nelson, 2009).

Initially we can change behaviors, but if we do not move deeper beyond behaviors to modify beliefs about our children's needs and what is truly required to provide them social justice, we will make changes at the superficial level and will not initiate nor sustain true and lasting change (Guerra & Nelson, 2009). That is, we can realize technical changes through behaviors, but not significant change that results in social justice. Once new knowledge and skills are being authentically and deeply implemented, there are many options for reinforcing their application through different modes of continuous professional development: learning team meetings, classroom observations, support groups, peer coaching, classroom walkthroughs, and more. While educators in the school and even on different teams may, at times, take different paths to developing knowledge, skills, and beliefs, there is no uncertainty about what the goals are and each person's individual accountability for achieving them.

Assessing Progress

How will the progress of the effort be monitored and ultimately evaluated? Establishing goals for professional learning is key to ensuring results. Schoolwide and learning team members can move from goals to setting benchmarks that will demonstrate appropriate progress is being made. They can determine what documentation will serve as evidence of progress. If changes in teacher beliefs and their attendant practices are expected, they may develop innovation configurations (Hall & Hord, 2010), a road map that will allow each staff member to understand what the innovation looks like in practice, and what it will potentially mean for the entire school. The road map ensures everyone has a common understanding and vision for an implementation plan that carries with it fidelity. If changes in student achievement are expected, they will create formative and summative assessments to provide the feedback necessary to know if they are on track. Grade-level and subject-matter teams can use student work as another indicator of the impact of staff and students' sense of efficacy, the belief that they can impact or influence (their own and others') circumstances in order to make a difference. For example, to assess the adoption and implementation of a social justice agenda, a complex method will be needed in order to track its development. Initially, however, conducting conversations and listening intently to staff and students' expressions about social justice and inequities of the system (such as the overrepresentation of special education students), and about taking responsibility for one's own support and livelihood (from the vision), can be used to gain understandings about where individuals "are" in their appreciation, acceptance, and integration of social justice into their own belief systems. A larger question looms, How do you change the system's priorities, in order to make social justice possible at the individual level?

Supporting Change

How will educators be supported through the emotional and psychological aspects of making change? Will there be accommodations for new teachers, experienced teachers, teacher leaders, and administrators? The school learning community has many strategies to draw from to support teachers from all backgrounds and at all stages as they attempt to make substantive changes in their practice. These strategies might include organizing support groups to discuss challenges, and to receive help and suggestions for addressing them, or sending a coach to the classroom to assist with implementation or provide feedback on the effectiveness of implementation efforts. Providing a substitute so that a teacher may observe another teacher experiencing more success is another strategy, as is inviting an expert teacher to present a model lesson with a teacher who is challenged by students. The bottom line is that while there may be predictable patterns of beliefs and behaviors that educators transcend through the change process, the community will be able to access multiple strategies to assist themselves in dealing with the technical and personal challenges associated with change (Hall & Hord, 2010). But to get to deep social justice change, there must be individuals ready to step up to the plate to ask, What is it that we are trying to do? What does it mean? There will be a need for a social justice lens through which all activities are viewed and contemplated.

Building Relationships

Finally, how will the relationships within the school be leveraged to advance the implementation? The potential impact of any change initiative is only as powerful as the number of staff members committed, as well as the depth of expertise (Hord, Roussin, & Sommers, 2010). Implementation must be supported at the school's leadership level as well as the grade and/or subject level (Hall & Hord, 2010; Leithwood, Louis, Anderson, & Wahlstrom, 2004). Without the expectations and support of colleagues at all levels with whom one shares responsibility for the success of a larger group of students, there is very little incentive, pressure, or support to work through what is necessary to achieve success with the innovation (Hord et al., 2010). Schoolwide as well as team-level improvement efforts benefit from the establishment of ground rules for working together, for special training for group facilitators, and opportunities for everyone's voice to be heard on the most critical decisions (National Staff Development Council, 2001). Trust and transparency should permeate the community and allow for each voice (Bryk & Schneider, 2004). Each person must feel empowered to speak; the outliers must have a voice and be listened to, with the opportunity for others to exert persuasion. No issue is more critical than ensuring all students achieve success, and gaining this success from all possible sources. Staff learning and its attendant work are impacted by and evolve in a setting—whatever it may be. In the next section, a powerful environment for adult learning is the focus.

CREATING A CONTEXT CONDUCIVE TO LEARNING

What has been the focus of attention in this chapter is essentially the work of the professional learning community, described in intimate alignment with its purpose: the continuous learning of all professionals, and subsequently, all students. As the most powerful means for improving the performance of the school's educators and the learning outcomes of its students, we have identified the community of professional learners as providing the context most conducive to the learning of both the educators and their students, thus promoting social justice for all citizens of the school.

The "professional learning community," as an innovation du jour, has become ubiquitous globally, with the emphasis on community. This emphasis that provides for grade-level teams and subject-matter departments to meet (it appears that for some schools, meeting is all there is to it) allows for various teams and groups to conduct conversations about instruction, to share repertoire, and to do collaborative work, easily misses the most important point—the deep learning needed by educators to effectively enable all students to learn well. Because we understand the significant element to be the *learning* of the community, we have tweaked the term a bit and may use at times the phrase, "communities for professional learners..." with the hope that this places the emphasis on the learning. Certainly, learning in a social context, in community, is richer but it is the learning, not the community that begs the attention.

For this learning, the leadership team and the grade-level and content-area teams—the entire faculty—require a supportive culture in order to assist all in their efforts to achieve all goals (including social justice goals) rather than merely academic goals. When examining whether the culture exists to support the attainment of the goals, key questions emerge: How does the school organize itself for the purpose of professional learning? How do leaders responsible for guiding professional learning go about this work? Do leaders themselves have a social justice lens through which they anchor their work (Berman & Chambliss, 2000)? How are resources allocated to support the learning agenda that advances the social justice agenda? The responses to these questions are embedded in the research-based components of professional learning communities identified by Hord (2004).

Social justice questions begin with educators' self-examination and result in their true investment, in not only acknowledging content needs/gaps in their own learning, but also lack of understanding regarding society, their students, their students' circumstances, and what students truly need from schools and teachers to be successful. When process decisions are made, social justice demands the addition of a few more questions: What system policies and power structures are prohibiting our students from being truly successful in these areas? At what level do we believe our students can achieve the vision and goals we have set forth for them? What do we need from everyone—administrators, parents, community—to achieve this vision (National Staff Development Council, 2001)?

Organizing for Professional Learning

Two structures for the conduct of the professional learners' work have been fully elaborated and must be part of the context. That is, the necessity for grade-level teams and subject-matter departments, and the entire professional faculty, to work in parallel ways, side by side, has been described. Without this interaction with each other, the school's common purpose is not defined and the subparts of the school move in disparate and possibly conflicting directions. As noted, it is important for the various grade levels and academic departments to create the specific objectives, agenda, and activities necessary for their particular area of responsibility. In the large group, as well as in the subgroups, it is vital that each staff member develops the necessary beliefs and values, capacities and expertise, to effectively teach their students. But, expertise must be equitably addressed for each of the staff members, and their needs met, so that social justice resides in the entire population of the school.

As noted, two *formats* advance the professionals' learning/social justice context. These are large group learning sessions and one-to-one or small-group follow-up or coaching incidents. The large group sessions, typically labeled "workshops," introduce new curriculum, programs, processes, or projects that the professionals have decided to adopt to close the gap (see the section "Selecting the Learning Processes") in students' learning. Staff development research (Joyce & Showers, 2002), as well as change process research (Hall & Hord, 2010), reveals these typical sessions, as a stand-alone, or one-shot session, will not be sufficient for the adult learners to become proficient. Thus, organizing for the continuous attention, follow-up, or coaching will be required. Even champions continue their process of continuous learning, changing their grip for golf, footwork for tennis, and so on, and their use of coaches to support them in this learning. Do the coaches also have social justice beliefs, and do they ask the hard questions of their clients when they see discrepancies?

These two organizational arrangements are found in the research-based components of the communities of professional learners (Hord, 2004). In the first, the community determines the area of intentional collegial learning they will undertake (note descriptions of these activities earlier in this chapter in the section "Identifying Content for Continuous Learning Cycles"), and how they will arrange for their learning (note the "Selecting the Learning Processes" section). Second, the coaching or peers-helping-peers component will supply the observation and coaching essential for the adults' deep learning (Jackson & Bruegmann, 2009; Joyce & Showers, 2002). Only when these two formats have been considered and organizing for them has been accomplished can the learning be successful for each teacher and administrator (Joyce & Showers, 2002). The coaching element makes it possible to address each educator's particular needs and respond with support so that social justice has been served within and across the faculty (Killion & Harrison, 2006).

Advising Leaders in Guiding Professional Learning

The community of professional learners is a self-organizing entity, characterized by democratic participation of all members, teachers, and administrators (Hord & Hirsh, 2009). This participation promotes the sharing of power, authority, and decision making, one of the research-based components of the professional learning community. This sharing is not the typical positional leader's behavior, but it is foundational to the professional learning community and to a community committed to social justice (McKenzie et al., 2008). Sharing power, authority, and decision making allows for all voices to be expressed—and counted—a place to initiate equity (Cambron-McCabe & McCarthy, 2005).

The professional learning community setting is also characterized by members' shared values and vision, which derive from the participants' beliefs. The concept of a school staff's shared vision is especially compelling, for a social justice agenda to move forward or not is dependent on the beliefs/values held by its members related to social justice (Theoharis, 2007). In multiple additional ways, the professional learning community setting is ideal and consistent with the essentials of a social justice agenda.

In both cases (professional learning community and social justice), staff learning is determined by the needs of students so that the staff becomes more effective in areas where students are not performing well; this adult learning translates into successful learning for students.

In these and other ways the community of professional learners/professional learning community context fosters the ideals of social justice. Leaders will need to elaborate especially on the imperative of uncovering and changing inequities through the articulation of a challenging yet attainable vision and its related goals (Skrla, Scheurich, Garcia, & Nolly, 2004). They do this while engaging the entire community with all its perspectives. The result is a more complete and rich vision for students that demands a richer and more complex learning agenda for staff.

As authors, we acknowledge our own "whiteness" and our inability, perhaps, to identify all the intricacies relating to high-quality professional development and social justice. We can immerse ourselves in the literature, and yet we will not fully understand all aspects. We can take the next step and introduce ourselves into schools committed to social justice and learn, ourselves, by keen and critical observations and reflections, and by taking action. Our experiences have contributed to our understandings, but we acknowledge the limitations of these experiences. We can turn to colleagues with other perspectives, from other groups, and with different experiences, and ask them to read and comment on our propositions and help us to broaden our perspectives and improve our message. We have done this, and we are hopeful the results in this chapter demonstrate that step.

An additional word here about trust, a most important factor for achieving social justice and an imperative for the conduct of schoolwide and team learning (Bryk & Schneider, 2004). Teachers, who for the most part have not had the experience of participating democratically in making decisions about important school matters, will initially be reluctant to express themselves. Developing their skills in conversation modes—dialogue and discussion and when to use each (Garmston & Wellman, 1997)—and helping them to learn various models for decision making, and supporting them before conflict erupts, will prepare teachers for their new roles. They should also learn about how to provide feedback to each other. These skills make for an atmosphere and a culture that encourages interaction based on trust. Patience and persistence is required of the Head Learner, the principal, as he or she goes about developing skills, encouraging participation, sharing the leadership roles, and building trust so that leadership becomes widely dispersed, distributed, and practiced by an ever-widening array of teachers who are becoming leaders.

Who is in the professional learning community and what is their worldview? Leaders must observe, understand, and act so as to allow disagreement to happen, but resolve the disagreements in various ways (both public and private), such as a private conversation, a note by email. These activities can also ensure that social justice becomes the characterizing factor of the school culture, where students and staff are treated with consideration, compassion, and equity (Spence, 2009).

The wise leader uses data to engage staff members in exploring their success, or lack thereof, related to efforts at improvement and consequently student learning. We are reminded of one of our favorite stories here. In our early years working in the field for school change and improvement, we were assigned to "turn the school around" in a 450-member small rural community. While intensely studying the student state achievement data with the entire 18-member faculty, the young secondary science teacher leaped to his feet and loudly exclaimed, "They didn't get it!" After a pause, he then continued, "I'm gonna have to learn to teach that differently next year!" He got it.

But what about data that is less specific to academics and more about the choices students feel they have if they do succeed in school? By collecting such data from all students and analyzing it, a faculty learns that their high-achieving Title I students carry the same aspirations and expectations as their high-achieving, high-socioeconomic-status students. Is a faculty provided this information; does it know to collect it; and what resources exist to assist it in analyzing and responding to this kind of information?

Of significant importance then is the leader ensuring that the staff has developed the abilities to read, understand, and interpret the multiple sources of student data to be examined through a social justice lens. Over time in this learning school context, school leaders learn and work to exemplify a collaborative style (Hord & Sommers, 2008), participating as an equal in studying data, decision making with the staff, and sharing power and authority. Clearly, the staff must be skillful in reviewing student data in order to use it to make sound decisions directed to student academic performance and to social justice. This responsibility resides initially in the positional leader. It is uncomfortable for many leaders to continuously guide conversations about social justice. Even though it is hard, it will be necessary to continue this talk.

The literature about professional learning communities reports that not only is leadership shared, but leadership development is encouraged and supported for all the staff. This is done by cultivating the leadership skills of teachers and providing opportunities for their practice of the skills (Copland & Knapp, 2007; Leithwood et al., 2004). In these communities, leadership is widely distributed so that novice leaders, especially teacher leaders, can be supported in their development. Sharing the power, authority, and decision making with all staff increases staff commitment to the decisions in which they are involved. However, individuals vary in their comfort level about making decisions. Leaders will need to understand these differences and identify where individuals are and help them to grow into these capacities. In addition, it contributes measurably to the development of professionalism among the staff (Boutte, 2008; Landreman, Edwards, Balón, & Anderson, 2008), modeling once again the dual desirable outcomes of high-achieving schools and social justice.

A culture of shared leadership is foundational for effective professional learning in many school systems internationally. In fact, it is one of the characteristics that distinguishes teacher learning in the United States and other countries whose students perform higher on international benchmark exams (Darling Hammond et al., 2009). Thus, the positional leader (the principal) may initiate the professional learning as the "sage on stage" but over time this administrative leader becomes the "guide on the side" as others take on multiple responsibilities formerly the domain of the principal. The principal's role in developing and supporting learning communities may be concisely summarized (Hord & Hirsh, 2009):

- Emphasize to teachers that you know they can succeed—together
- Expect teachers to keep their knowledge fresh
- Guide communities toward self-governance
- Make data accessible
- Teach discussion and decision-making skills
- Share research with teachers
- Take time and effort to build trust.

This list clearly requires amending to include:

- Maintain a continuous orientation for student needs
- Continue the conversations focused on social justice

Allocating Resources

The demands on the context for developing staff's commitment to social justice include the provision of supportive conditions for the work and study/learning of the staff. These conditions are of two types, structural and relational, and they constitute another component of the Professional Learning Community (PLC), as identified in the research base. The structural conditions include time for meeting, a place for meeting, and sharing expectations for what will happen in the meetings (National Staff Development Council, 2001). These conditions also include policies that impact the staff's schedules and thus their opportunities for convening for professional learning. It also includes attention to budgets and financing and consistency in maintaining funding for supporting these endeavors.

Time, the first item noted, can be a challenge. It is critical that staff have regularly scheduled time to convene in communities for the purposes of improving instruction and focusing attention on the outcomes of a social justice agenda. Without adequate time, the staff cannot prepare itself to deliver an effective instructional program so that social justice is served for students. While many schools use the challenge of finding time as an excuse, rarely has either author met a school faculty committed to a social justice agenda and to their own learning, unable to agree upon the most effective way to organize time for consistent and sustained professional learning.

There are countless examples of how schools have structured their time to make learning for adults as much a priority as learning for students. (See *Journal of Staff Development*, volumes *20*(2) and *28*(2); von Frank, 2008).

In some schools, the scarcity of space challenges the community for a location in which to meet. One school leader solved this problem by rotating the meetings around all the classrooms. Not only did this solve the space issue, but it also provided the opportunity for each teacher to showcase his or her classroom, offering others a brief glimpse into classrooms that they might never visit. A not-so-isolated incident occurred after being in a classroom to meet—a teacher requested she be able to return to the host teacher's room and learn more about how she uses "word walls," which was displayed in this room. While there are obvious benefits to this model, there are other benefits that occur when teachers have a regular and professional place to meet, where materials are stored, and refreshments are accessible.

An additional structural factor is that of expectations about what will happen in the community meetings. Because issues related to the social justice goals are sensitive and complicated, early investments in skillful facilitation will pay off for introducing this new dimension to the professional community (Marshall & Oliva, 2010). This is, again, initially the principal's responsibility. The supply of protocols and/or agendas with summaries of the meetings to be submitted to the principal's mailbox can encourage thoughtful planning for the meetings (Jolly, 2008). Systematic preparation of instructional coaches and teacher leaders to serve as facilitators contributes to focused learning and accelerated success. As the community's practice becomes mature, teachers assume leadership responsibilities and the group's democratic participation is the norm, another opportunity for teacher leadership and for social justice to develop.

The second type of supportive conditions, relational conditions, focus on the respect and regard that the staff feels and expresses for each other and is perhaps the most critical factor in whether or not the community of professional learners succeeds or not. A school that has procedures for establishing staff agreements or ground rules lays the foundation for relational trust that is essential in a school committed to social justice. Campus educators' attitudes about their roles in the school, their students, and their parents is another aspect of the relations developed across the entire school community (Ames, 1995). The NSDC Standards for Staff Development (2001, p. 30) address the issue of equity, "Staff development that improves the learning of all students prepares educators to *understand* and *appreciate* (emphasis added) all students...." Furthermore, the Standards address family involvement (p. 34), "Staff development that improves the learning of all students provides educators with knowledge and skills to involve families...." Securing parent/family cooperation and support of social justice goals can be a sticky issue, especially when parents have competing goals (e.g., wanting social justice and learning for all students, but wanting their child to excel sometimes at the expense of other students). At the root of all relational conditions is trust and the imperative for trust has been noted above.

Members' reflection, transparency, and porosity (Hord & Sommers, 2008) are embedded in trust that is consistently nurtured and developed. There can be no social justice in the presence of distrust, thus, the professional learning community's cornerstone of trust is a compelling variable.

CONCLUSION

The sensitive reader will have noted that this chapter's text has now folded over itself. That is, it began with rich description about how the school staff works to learn and to accelerate improved academic performance and social justice for its students. In these descriptions, the reader was provided information about the attitudes, actions, and agenda of the staff as they work together to deliver a powerful instructional program to students, making certain that each unique student is promoted toward the vision of the school.

In the latter part of the chapter, we learn that the staff's activities have been in authentic alignment with the research-based components of professional learning communities. Thus, may we conclude that the culture provided by the community of professional learners can nurture social justice and directly contribute to social justice for students and staff of the school? We believe so; a school organized to support schoolwide as well as team-based professional learning offers a very powerful setting for social justice to grow, develop, and impact the school's citizens.

ACKNOWLEDGMENTS

Abundant and grateful thanks to Dr. Stella Bell, Dr. Patricia Guerra, Dr. Cheryl Harris, and Dr. Maria Lourdes De Hoyos, scholars who reviewed this paper during its development and contributed valuable feedback and suggestions; and to Nancy Reynolds, information specialist and librarian extraordinaire who tracked citations and references.

REFERENCES

American Institute for Research. (2007). *Successful California schools in the context of educational adequacy.* Washington, DC: Author.

Ames, C. (1995). *Teachers' school-to-home communications and parent involvement: The role of parent perceptions and beliefs* (Report No. 28). East Lansing: Center on Families, Communities, Schools, and Children's Learning, Michigan State University.

Arneson, R. J. (2007). Does social justice matter?: Brian Barry's applied political philosophy. *Ethics, 117*(3), 391–412.

Berman, P., & Chambliss, D. (2000). *Readiness of low-performing schools for comprehensive reform.* Emeryville, CA: RPP International.

Berman, P., Chambliss, D., & Geiser, K. D. (1999). *Making the case for a focus on equity in school reform.* Emeryville, CA: RPP International.

Boutte, G. S. (2008). Beyond the illusion of diversity: How early childhood teachers can promote social justice. *The Social Studies Teacher, 9*(4),165–173.

Bryk, A. S., & Schneider, B. (2004). *Trust in schools: A core resource for school improvement.* New York: Russell Sage Foundation.

Bustamante, R., Nelson, J., & Onwuegbuzie, A. (2009). Assessing schoolwide cultural competence: Implications for school leadership preparation. *Educational Administration Quarterly, 45*(5), 793–827.

Cambron-McCabe, N., & McCarthy, M. (2005). Educating school leaders for social justice. *Educational Policy, 19*(1), 201–222.

Coalition for Student Success. (2009). *Smart option: Investing recovery funds for success.* Washington, DC: Author.

Cochran-Smith, M., Shakman, K., Jong, C., Terrell, D. G., Barnatt, J., & McQuillan, P. (2009, May). Good and just teaching: The case for social justice in teacher education. *American Journal of Education, 115*(3), 347–377.

Copland, M., & Knapp, M. (2007). *Connecting leadership with learning: A framework for reflection, planning, and action.* Alexandria, VA: Association for Supervision and Curriculum Development.

Curren, R. (2009). Education as a social right in a diverse society. *Journal of Philosophy of Education, 43*(1), 45–56.

Darling-Hammond, D., Wei, R.C., Andree, A., Richardson, N., & Orphanus, S. (2009). *Professional learning in the learning profession: A status report on teacher development in the United States and abroad.* Oxford, OH: National Staff Development Council and the School Redesign Network, Stanford University.

DeMulder, E., Ndura-Ouédraogo, E., & Stribling, S. (2009). From vision to action: Fostering peaceful coexistence and the common good in a pluralistic society through teacher education. *Peace and Change, 34*(1), 27–48.

Garmston, R., & Wellman, B. (1997). *The adaptive school: Developing and facilitating collaborative groups.* El Dorado Hills, CA: Four Hats Press.

Guerra, P. L., & Nelson, S. W. (2007). Assessment is the first step to creating a school that educates everybody. *Journal of Staff Development, 28*(3), 59–60.

Guerra, P. L., & Nelson, S.W. (2009). Changing professional practice requires changing beliefs. *Phi Delta Kappan, 90*(5), 354–359.

Hall, G. E., & Hord, S. M. (2010). *Implementing change: Patterns, principles, and potholes* (3rd ed.). Boston: Pearson/Allyn & Bacon.

Haycock, K., & Crawford, C. (2008). Closing the teacher quality gap. *Educational Leadership, 65*(7), 14–19.

Hirsh, S. A., & Hord, S. M. (2008). The role of professional learning in advancing quality teaching and student learning. In T. L. Good (Ed.), *21st century education: A reference handbook.* Thousand Oaks, CA: Sage.

Hord, S. M. (Ed.). (2004). *Learning together, leading together: Changing schools through professional learning communities.* New York: Teachers College Press.

Hord, S. M. (2009). Foreword. In D. B. Lindsey, L. D. Jungwirth, J. V. N. C. Pahl, & R. B. Lindsey (Eds.). *Culturally proficient learning communities: Confronting inequities through collaborative curiosity.* Thousand Oaks, CA: Corwin Press.

Hord, S. M. (2010). Foreword. In K. K. Hipp & J. B. Huffman, *Demystifying professional learning communities: School leadership at its best.* Lanham, MD: Rowman & Littlefield.

Hord, S. M., & Hirsh, S. A. (2008). Making the promise a reality. In A. M. Blankstein, P. C. Houston, & R. W. Cole (Eds.), *Sustaining professional learning communities* (pp. 23–40). Thousand Oaks, CA: Corwin Press.

Hord, S. M., & Hirsh, S. A. (2009). The principal's role in supporting learning communities. *Educational Leadership, 66*(5), 22–23.

Hord, S. M., Roussin, J. L., & Sommers, W. A. (2010). *Guiding professional learning communities: Inspiration, challenge, surprise, and meaning.* Thousand Oaks CA: Corwin Press.

Hord, S. M., & Sommers, W. A. (2008). *Leading professional learning communities: Voices from research and practice.* Thousand Oaks, CA: Corwin Press.

Jackson, C. K., & Bruegmann, E. (2009). Teaching students and teaching each other: The importance of peer learning for teachers. *American Economic Journal: Applied Economics, 1*(4), 85–108.

Jolly, A. (2008). *Team to teach: A facilitator's guide to professional learning teams.* Oxford, OH: National Staff Development Council.

Joyce, B., & Showers, B. (2002). *Student achievement through staff development* (3rd ed.). Alexandria, VA: Association for Supervision and Curriculum Development.

Kennedy, M. (1998). Education reform and subject matter knowledge. *Journal of Research in Science Teaching, 35,* 249–263.

Killion, J., & Harrison, C. (2006). *Taking the lead: New roles for teachers and school-based coaches.* Oxford, OH: National Staff Development Council.

Landreman, L., Edwards, K., Balón, D., & Anderson, G. (2008). Wait! It takes time to develop rich and relevant social justice curriculum. *About Campus, 13*(4), 2–10.

Leithwood, K., Louis, K. S., Anderson, S., & Wahlstrom, K. (2004). *How leadership influences student learning.* New York: Wallace Foundation. Retrieved from http://www.wallacefoundation.org/SiteCollectionDocuments/WF/Knowledge%20Center/Attachments/PDF/ReviewofResearch-LearningFromLeadership.pdf

Lewis, C., Perry, R., & Hurd, J. (2004). A deeper look at lesson study. *Educational Leadership, 61*(5), 18–22.

Marshall, C., & Oliva, M. (2010). *Leadership for social justice: Making revolutions in education* (2nd ed.). Boston: Allyn & Bacon.

McKenzie, K. B., Christman, D. E., Hernandez, F., Fierro, E., Capper, C. A., Dantley, M., et al. (2008). From the field: A proposal for educating leaders for social justice. *Educational Administration Quarterly, 44*(1), 111–138.

National Staff Development Council. (2001). *NSDC's standards for staff development* (2nd ed.). Oxford, OH: Author.

Nieto, S. (1999). *The light in their eyes: Creating multicultural learning communities.* New York: Teachers College Press.

Perry, R. R., & Lewis, C. C. (2009). What is successful adaptation of lesson study in the US? *Journal of Educational Change, 10*(4), 365–391.

Peske, H. G., & Haycock, K. (2006). *Teaching inequality: How poor and minority students are shortchanged on teacher quality.* Washington, DC: The Education Trust. Retrieved from http://www.wallacefoundation.org/SiteCollectionDocuments/ WF/Knowledge%20Center/Attachments/PDF/ReviewofResearch-Learning-FromLeadership.pdf

Sensoy, O., & Diangelo, R. (2009). Developing social justice literacy. *Phi Delta Kappan, 90*(5), 345–352.

Skrla, L., Scheurich, J. J., Garcia, J., & Nolly, G. (2004). Equity audits: A practical leadership tool for developing equitable and excellent schools. *Educational Administration Quarterly, 40*(1), 133–161.

Spence, C. M. (2009). *Leading with passion and purpose: Creating schools that help teachers teach and students learn.* Markham, ON, Canada: Pembroke.

Theoharis, G. (2007). Social justice educational leaders and resistance: Toward a theory of social justice leadership. *Educational Administration Quarterly, 43*(2), 221–258.

Trueba, E. (1998). *Latinos unidos: From cultural diversity to the politics of solidarity.* Lanham, MD: Rowman & Littlefield.

von Frank, V. (2008). *Finding time for professional learning.* Oxford, OH: National Staff Development Council.

York-Barr, J., Sommers, W., Ghere, G., & Montie, J. (2006). *Reflective practice to improve schools* (2nd ed.). Thousand Oaks, CA: Corwin Press.

CHAPTER 3

RECULTURING ORGANIZATIONS

Jane B. Huffman

Creating effective schools that are sustainable organizations and incorporate social justice theory in their policies and operations is a goal to which
most leaders would subscribe. To do this, school leaders might consider
incorporating the tenants of social justice in a series of democratic and
empowering relationships among stakeholders who share common beliefs
and purposes (Jones, Webb, & Neumann, 2008). In our democratic society,
educators use the term social justice to describe a set of interactions that
reflect ethical and caring decisions applied equitably to all learners within
a larger connected community. These interactions relate to characteristics
of students such as race, class, gender, sexual identification, abilities, and
disabilities. As educators work collaboratively for the purpose of reculturing their schools using a social justice perspective, not only will students
and teachers be treated more fairly, but members of the larger school community will also be involved in a more humane and equitable manner and
student learning will be advanced.

DEFINITION OF SOCIAL JUSTICE

For this chapter, the perspective of social justice that guides the discussion
is taken from Theoharis's (2007) definition and the definition proposed

Educational Leaders Encouraging the Intellectual and Professional Capacity of Others:
A Social Justice Agenda, pages 45–60.

by McKenzie et al. (2008). Theoharis defines social justice leadership in the following statement: "[social justice is when] principals make issues of race, class, gender, disability, sexual orientation, and other historically and currently marginalizing conditions in the United States central to their advocacy, leadership, practice, and vision" (p. 223). McKenzie et al. suggest that any social justice effort must have three goals. These goals, as identified by Grant and Sleeter in 2007, are academic achievement, critical consciousness, and inclusive practices. Thus, school leaders should be able to address all three tasks as they facilitate school programs and practices. Specifically, they should increase student achievement as evidenced, in part, by high test scores; raise the critical consciousness among their students and staff; and accomplish these tasks by creating intentional, heterogeneous learning communities for students and staff (McKenzie et al., 2008).

McKenzie et al. (2008) explain their view of social justice is nonessentialized. This means that there is no one meaning that can be universally applied to every inequitable situation for each marginalized individual. However, they reiterate that first, student academic achievement is important, and should include not only standardized testing, but also other measures of student learning. Second, they believe that students should use their intellectual abilities to be critical and activist members of society and to challenge inequities. And, third, all students should have access to a rigorous and challenging curriculum and be able to interact with all members of the student population. In doing so, students are encouraged to learn and work together in heterogeneous and untracked classrooms. This paves the way for students to learn how to live and work in community with people who may initially appear different or unusual as compared to themselves. To create a school, such as one that would include all three of these goals, much careful planning, implementation, and constant communication is required. While the challenge to reculture schools is significant, it remains imperative to create more equitable learning opportunities for all our learners.

Ravitch (2000) described many "progressive" educational movements that occurred during the early part of the 20th century that were designed to differentiate schooling for students. This led to vocational education programs that provided alternative and more practical education for those students deemed not as academically advanced as others. In the mid-1900s school leaders introduced the open schooling concept that emphasized social and emotional learning rather than a more academic-oriented focus. These movements and others such as outcomes- based education illustrate the piecemeal reform that too often drives school reform. Tyack and Cuban (1995) suggested that instead of reacting to ideas, educators and the larger community should engage in public dialogue based on the United States' cultural and historical progress. While it is difficult and time consuming, this approach would provide substantive evidence to not only challenge the long-held practices such as grading systems and the Carnegie units, but to also produce effective reforms that meet the needs of the students.

More recently, programs such as the Whole School Reform Models in the 1990s and the 2001 legislation known as the No Child Left Behind (NCLB) Act are examples of national programs and policies that may have been positively proposed, but resulted instead in short-term solutions that failed to serve students well. Critics admit the NCLB requirements include equity issues, especially as they relate to underserved populations; however, most agree the implementation methods have served to emphasize strict accountability measures and high-stakes testing. These actions have resulted in repetitive remediation steps and memorization activities that have replaced enriched curriculum, hands-on activities, higher-order thinking, and holistic learning (Grogan, 2004).

Siskin (2003) examined the high school environment as related to the high expectations for all students. These findings emphasize the time it takes for schools that have low internal alignment to create structures and processes for essential and systemic school reform. Especially in under-funded urban schools who cannot meet the standards, these high-stakes expectations are out of touch with the practical realities of struggling schools. For administrators, students, and teachers, these reform efforts have produced fear, marginalization of student groups, competition, and false expectations of improvement.

In addition, the leaders of social equity concerns such as the civil rights movement (1950s) and the special education rights movement (1970s) provide additional concerns and evidence to question the effectiveness of past reforms. They call for new reforms that provide all children with adequate and equitable education. Thus to provide appropriate education for all students, including those of color, those who have learning differences, and those who are poor, reformers must create schools that address the needs of all students and that are held accountable. While some advocates for NCLB have deemed this legislation as supportive of civil rights and educating minority children, others question that claim. Skrla and Scheurich (2004) maintain that, for the most part, social forces in the United States have produced the institutional racism evident in our society and schools. They believe that the accountability measures outlined by NCLB would be a first step in requiring schools to be accountable for students learning and progressing through the system.

This is a contentious argument and Valenzuela (2004) has a different opinion. She believes that critical race and critical social theory drive the school equity debate and that the accountability requirements in NCLB are not enough to address the serious problems of minority and English language learners. She suggests that there be multiple assessments, including state tests, teacher observations, reading inventories, student presentations, portfolios, and other classroom products to determine decisions about a child's fitness for promotion. Thus the challenge for educators is to redesign schools into learning organizations based on social justice theory where all students are valued, and stakeholders are empowered to not only share leadership and authority in decision making, but also to support learning that encourages social and ethical responsibility.

For this chapter several areas related to social justice are explored. Specifically the author examines the challenges of social justice, suggests who would be involved and what roles they would play in the reculturing effort, and finally reviews processes needed for this social justice development.

THE CURRENT CHALLENGE

While educators in each district in America struggle to develop a school system that provides equitable opportunities, a lack of discrimination in any form, and adequate resource allocations for all participants, there are complex issues to confront. The social and political relationships within the school and with the families and community members often pose ethical challenges for educational leaders. The challenges, in many cases, deal with discriminatory situations that may be overt and obvious, or covert and silent.

To confront these challenges, school administrators must be intellectually and emotionally aware of the existing discrimination. These situations may be related to the ableness (or not) of a student, or the student's race, social class, socioeconomic status, gender identification, or sexual orientation. There are many ways discrimination practices may exist in schools. Some ways might be individual to individual, which would include bullying or other kinds of verbal, emotional, or physical harassment or abuse. Other instances might include the choice of courses to various groups of students, advance placement or enrollment in higher-level courses, or identification and placement in special programs. Additionally, manifestations of discrimination might be in the services students are offered such as counseling, special education, job placements, or alternative classes or schools. And finally, punitive consequences related to discipline issues might be handled in an inequitable manner.

To address these existing discriminatory situations, administrators may want to consider providing more education related to social justice for staff, students, parents, and community members. Areas for dialogue, such as safe spaces or safe classrooms, may also need to be identified and promoted. These important reculturing efforts, built around social justice beliefs, will not only reinforce student emotional and physical safety issues, but will also provide opportunities for all stakeholders to fully participate in creating and maintaining a culture conducive to student academic growth and achievement (Fullan, 2006; Fullan, Hill, & Crevola, 2006). In fact, school leaders must take this as their challenge by garnering whatever resources, such as time, money, or political clout, to lead the effort in developing strong and inclusive cultures.

THE VOICES TO BE HEARD IN THE RECULTURING EFFORT

In transforming schools, there are multiple stakeholders whose interactions and relationships contribute to the success or failure of this effort. These stakeholders include internal constituencies such as administrators, teachers, and students. External stakeholders are identified as parent and family member voices; community members, district administrators, and state policymakers; and university faculty members in Educational Administration/Leadership departments. From the professional learning community research (Huffman & Hipp, 2003) we note that empowering all members of the school community results in a more democratic and informed system of problem solving and decision making. Thus, by proactively including and honoring all stakeholders, decisions more closely address the collective need, can be implemented more quickly, and have a greater chance of being maintained and sustained. In the following sections the voices of each stakeholder group are discussed.

Administrators

In Theoharis's (2007) definition of social justice, he identified four actions needed for a strong social justice environment: advocacy, leadership, practice, and vision. His research highlighted principals who were committed to empowering their staffs and who included the teachers in the decision-making processes. These principals served as advocates and supporters rather than bureaucratic managers. Regarding leadership implementation, Theoharis's research revealed that the administrators were purposeful and authentic in facilitating change. They prioritized professional learning for all and sharing of information through supportive networks. In their practice, Theoharis noted the principals were proactive in anticipating and providing necessary time, space, and resources for teachers. And finally, the research uncovered the importance of vision. The principals stayed focused on developing the social justice awareness and amidst resistance and discouragement, continued to keep moving toward the goal.

Another viewpoint by Shields (2004) suggests that educational leaders should be transformative leaders. She contrasts transformative leaders with transformational leaders. Transformational leaders focus on collective action within the organization, and transformative leaders emphasize accountability in schools based on strong moral and ethical beliefs, and applied at all levels in a social context. Thus, the transformative approach builds democratic experiences incorporating dialogue, supportive relationships, and more involvement with parents and the community. This interaction provides opportunities for students to interact and to share their similarities as well as their differences; thus these varied realities and shared experiences broaden and deepen understanding among students, teachers, administrators, and parents. To provide these realities, one needs a starting place.

Thus, an important piece for the administrator is how to begin. As administrators work to create their recultured organization and as they develop strategies for change, administrators who start by reviewing the data generally find that this is a neutral yet productive point to begin the conversation. In looking longitudinally at demographic trends, resource allocations, test results, and other information, patterns and omissions can emerge that serve as a basis for the initial questions to be considered. Often these data themes are discovered by teachers, which results in an even more convincing discovery. What generally follows these data discoveries are conversations and dialogue that instead of blaming and criticizing, serve to motivate teachers and administrators to work together to learn from the data and find ways to use the data so students' achievement can improve.

Teachers

The teachers' role in social justice development is multifold. The initial expectation is that teachers will incorporate social justice issues into their courses. However, teachers need to do more than present these issues; they need to be able to teach about these issues and provide students a more interactive and authentic experience. As a result of these experiences, students leave the classroom with a better understanding of the larger global discourse and the responsibility they have in that social and political environment.

Prior to the classroom involvement is the development of the pre-service teacher in the certification programs. In these programs students are generally taught about lesson plans, classroom management, and teaching strategies and often participate in internships or practica in which they shadow and are mentored by a teacher. Little thought or time is given to the considerations of social justice theory in pre-service education. And all too often the veteran teacher conveys strategies that may be expedient and efficient, but may not be comprehensive enough to provide the individualized information needed for equitable student treatment.

Once in the school, the first-year teacher may or may not experience interactions and professional development that support and implement strategies and information consistent with social justice theory. The question often arises as to who is responsible to see that policies and examples of social justice are incorporated into the students' lives.

More specifically, Jones et al. (2008) maintain that literacy teachers "are responsible for helping students understand how they have the power to be transformational in their own lives" (p. 9). They suggest that by teaching language and how to critically evaluate words and the meaning of those words, literacy teachers influence students in their perception of their world and other people. However, literacy teachers (and other teachers as well) also have the option to oppress or otherwise unduly influence students in their perceptions. Jones et al. explain that the best result would be for teachers to "provide students with the opportunities to critically reflect on the text from different viewpoints" (p. 10). Examples of classroom practices that would illustrate this reflection include reading circles, journal writing, writing to learn strategies, role playing, Socratic seminars, and reader's theatre.

Developing socially responsible students requires more than literacy teachers working with the students. A schoolwide awareness of social justice issues and a thoughtful approach by all faculty will result in teachers providing content and reflection opportunities for all students to "find meaningful ways to contribute to the world" (Berman, 2006, p. 194). Shields (2004) argues that we should "open our curriculum (formal, informal, and hidden) and create spaces in which all children's lived experiences may be both reflected and critiqued in the context of learning" (p. 123). She continues to explain that our classrooms should not be based solely on middle-class experiences. By opening the classroom doors, more meaningful and authentic experiences will enter and then emerge into the broader society. Ayers (in Ayers, Quinn, & Stovall, 2009) concludes "a social justice classroom examines and undermines the achievement gap and celebrates powerful engagement and success for all students" (p. 658).

Students

Social justice education must have meaning for all students—whether they are marginalized or privileged—and this education must be actualized through practices and interactions in the classroom, in the school, and in the wider community. What is most important is for students to learn to be critically aware of their world, understand and be compassionate as related to the people in it, and be able and willing to take action when needed for the purposes of equity and social justice (Ayers et al., 2009). Our schools must be places where students have access to resources, time to use and learn from these resources, and the opportunities to benefit from those experiences in order to achieve a productive job post high school, or to enter an institution of higher education.

So how does a student learn to incorporate social justice into their knowledge base? One way students learn is through constructivism and transfer of learning. This model is based on students' active involvement in problem solving and critical thinking regarding a learning activity that they find relevant and interesting. They construct their new knowledge by testing ideas based on their earlier knowledge, and then apply or transfer these to a new situation.

Another very important consideration is that of a student feeling like he or she belongs and fits in with the school culture. For students to feel connected, each student must be able to identify with someone and establish a solid and healthy relationship with another person, preferably an adult. If students can find conversation and authentic experiences reflected in the classroom, they will be more likely to engage in learning activities, construct their own learning, and have greater success in school.

On a different note, Shields (2004) cautions that it is important that students never be blamed for the circumstances that may or may not have contributed to their perceived lack of success in school. It is important students feel supported and are viewed as capable by their teachers and administrators. This being the case, they have more opportunity to achieve at their highest levels and learn related information based on their interests and capabilities.

Parents

From a parent's perspective it is expected that the school will provide an equitable and fair environment for their student(s) to learn and to become a productive member of society. Parents' involvement in the school is based on myriad reasons, experiences, and perceptions, generally related to how they experienced school as a student. Moreover, for many parents, visiting and participating in school events is not a preferred or easy task. Adams, Forsyth and Mitchell (2009) stated "cooperative relationships between parents and schools are too important to leave their existence to chance or to place the responsibility for their development on parents" (p. 5). The challenge for administrators and teachers is to establish a school climate that is purposeful and welcoming, open to all, and considers parents' needs and schedules in planning and conducting parent involvement events.

Recognizing parents as partners in the educational system requires a major shift in long-held expectations by parents, teachers, and administrators. To do this and to bring parents into the mainstream of teaching and learning means that relationship formation must be intentional and ongoing. The interdependent interactions of parents, teachers, administrators, and students is often, however, a goal that schools struggle to achieve. In 2002, Bryk and Schneider identified teacher trust as a significant mediator in the reform of several Chicago schools. Providing opportunities for parents to have frequent interactions with school personnel is another way to establish the connections needed for reculturing. Adams et al. (2009) also confirm that "contextual conditions, such as socioeconomic status, school size, diversity, and so forth, influence parent trust to the degree that they shape social exchanges within the relational network" (p. 29).

Community Members, District Leaders, and State Officials

Too often voices and concerns from community members, district leaders, and state officials have either been absent, unsupportive, or directive. However, by encouraging these groups and individuals to fully participate and to engage in comprehensive and long-range strategic planning, much progress regarding the social justice agenda can be made. Murphy (1991) commented: "Change is more likely to occur when all the significant players—the state, the district, the school, the community—align their efforts around a common agenda, with each doing what it can at its level to make improvement a real possibility" (p. 32).

Gaining the involvement and support of multiple constituencies is a difficult task requiring skill and patience on the part of school leadership. Barber and Fullan (2005) identify this involvement by multiple constituencies as *tri-level development.* They believe that for institutions to engage in sustained efforts for change or innovation, these efforts must be intentional and related.

The role of the community member is similar to that of the parent. It is a supportive and reinforcing role in which supplemental and additional information, resources, or time is given as needed and requested by the school administrator or teacher. Often community groups will provide grants or other types of financial or structural support for teachers and the school.

District leaders provide a more comprehensive view of the school environment. They would offer a commitment to provide time and resources for staff and students so they could all have opportunities to interact and study the social justice agenda. When district leaders understand that they serve to facilitate and to provide support for school leaders, the changes and improvements will emerge.

State or province leaders provide the policy development, implementation strategies, and monitoring processes required at the state level. They also maintain the connection and gate keeping to the federal policy and procedures. Even though the short-term solutions seem to be more urgent at the state level, the conversation and interaction regarding the long-term plans and solutions that involve all levels provide the best hope for emergent and sustained collaboration. It is through the strategic mindset of wise leaders, and carefully planned inclusion of all people involved, that critical issues such as social justice can be studied and a plan can be formulated. Using this model, the district and site leaders can work collaboratively with the state leadership to initiate, implement, and sustain important initiatives.

Faculty in Educational Administration/Leadership Departments

Reframing the traditional courses and content in Educational Administration (EDAD) programs continues to be a challenge. Moreover, this group, the faculty in EDAD, holds much of the power to provide change and clear direction for the social justice agenda. Not only should new content be added, changed, or deleted, but faculty should spend formative time with each other and with practitioners to identify salient issues and possible remedies related to social justice issues in the field. This collaboration would also result in conversations and continuing dialogue addressing other emerging issues.

Specifically, faculty members should address the process for student admission and selection as related to the social justice agenda. In their courses they should also consider if any ideology, practice, or other discourse that would possibly marginalize the private or public school student is being taught. Another issue to examine is to determine if field-based activities are designed to include projects for internship and practicum assignments that would directly address these equity issues.

In summarizing this section, it is clear that educators and others concerned about students and social justice have much to do. Epstein (2001) reports that when many groups join to influence students' lives, they share in the responsibility for learning. This type of integration brings the groups closer together and they learn to appreciate each other. Shields (2004) suggests that we do not need to work harder, but we do need to work smarter:

> We need to critique the way in which our present practices marginalize some students and their lived experiences and privileges others—both overtly and through our silences. We need to act agentically, to lead deliberately, to facilitate transformative dialogue, and to achieve socially just learning environments for all children. (p. 127)

PROCESSES THAT DEVELOP
AND SUPPORT THE VOICES
IN THEIR WORK

So how do these stakeholders modify and create their interactions to allow a more open, equitable, and democratic conversation to emerge? Three processes are considered as necessary for the development, implementation, and sustainability of this reculturing effort: trust, relationships, and dialogue. The following sections suggest ways in which stakeholders can effect change within the organizations and for the students as related to these processes (see Figure 3.1).

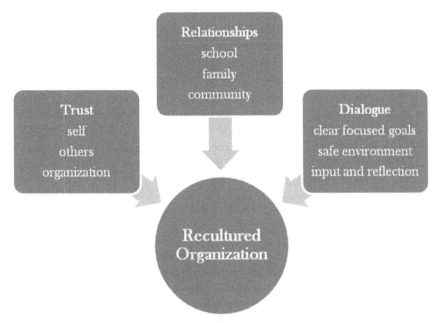

FIGURE 3.1. Recultured organization components.

Trust

How schools are organized and the management style of the principal contribute to the overall climate of the school and the resulting levels of participation and dedication of teachers. One important factor in creating and maintaining a more professional and positive attitude is the establishment of trust among administrators and teachers. Hacker and Willard (2002) suggest there are three components of trust—consistency, commitment, and capability—and each are necessary for the development of a trusting relationship. They also explain there are several levels at which trust can be established. Initially one would work on the ability to trust oneself and thus be trustworthy in interactions with other people. The next level is interpersonal trust. This includes a trusting relationship with other individuals and also a reliable trustworthy foundation with members of a team. The final level is the organization or institutional trusting interaction. In all of these interactions, and especially in the institutional level, issues such as priorities, resources, and communication patterns often appear as troublesome issues.

Huffman and Hipp (2003) examine critical attributes of the professional learning community (PLC) process and find that trust is included in the *supportive conditions* dimension. Trust is one of the attributes that help to establish the personal interactions essential for teachers and administrators in their work together. Thus administrators may want to cultivate and support efforts to foster great trust among staff. Tschannon-Moran (2009) reports that in high-trust environments, people are more honest, communicate more openly, share more accurate information, and have, in general, greater satisfaction with the leader and the organization. Also, principals who are successful in creating trustful environments refrain from micromanaging and concentrate instead on sharing power and decision making. Working toward a trusting climate in school requires planning, constant communication and reinforcement, and an intentional mindset to develop healthy, open relationships.

Relationships

For two decades, Noddings (1986) has maintained that relationships between and among people in schools and their ideas should be at the center of educational practice. She calls this a pedagogy of care and believes it is the foundation for all learning. She is supported in this belief by Grumet (1995), who believes that the way people construct meaning from curriculum and knowledge is the way they interact and talk with each other. Thus the way learning is constructed is based on our interactions and relationships with other learners. Thus in social justice terms, students who have opportunities to interact with students and teachers of many cultures and who are presented with beliefs that are both similar and different will have more success in constructing democratic and equitable learning outcomes.

How people interact with each other can affect the academic achievement of students, as reported by Shields, Mazawi, and Bishop (2002), while studying indigenous populations in the United States. They found that attitudes and relationships of people within schools were more significantly related to student achievement than buildings or other resources. Yet, school relationships are only part of the collaboration that is needed. Fox (2005) reports that multiple forms of collaboration are needed to create the partnerships. These would include family-centered, interorganizational, and community collaboration efforts to create the meaningful and productive relationships needed.

Dialogue

As educators strive for understanding as related to social justice, the idea of dialogue assists in developing norms of inclusion, trust, and respect. Using dialogue as a strategy in schools, educators open the door for differing realities to be exposed and reviewed within a safe environment. Dialogue has been defined by many researchers (Argyris, 1990; Bohm, 1996; Wellman & Lipton, 2004; Wheatley, 2002) and the process can be summed up by reviewing important considerations:

- the participants should be in mixed groups across grade and subject levels;
- the goals should be stated clearly, the conversation would be focused yet open and accepting of ideas;
- participants should feel safe and in a trusting environment;
- the process should have several opportunities for input and reflection; and
- there should be plans for implementation and monitoring built into the outcomes.

Preskill and Brookfield (2009) encourage leaders to be part of the dialogue and participate—not dominate—the conversation. In doing so, the group can developmentally and formatively arrive at the new idea or program by crafting a meaningful (not prescribed) outcome. The leader might offer some guidelines or issues that would be included for the group to consider. In social justice terms these issues may be the related theories, programs, or conditions that are present in the school and that might hinder or support the social justice ideology. From the teacher's perspective, Olivier and Hipp (as cited in Hipp & Huffman, 2010) suggest that staffs need to involve themselves in the beliefs and values of the organization, and listen to the voices and experiences of all staff. This would provide the information to reflect on all options, develop priorities, and to begin action in areas of greatest need.

CONCLUSION

Voices of the stakeholders in schools are important and meaningful in the journey to create schools incorporating the social justice agenda. Preskill and Brookfield (2009) state "...learning to lead collectively and democratically depends in part on the leader's ability to absorb the stories of co-workers" (p. 215). Leaders, thus, play a critical part in this reculturing. They serve as the gatekeepers for action. It is not enough for the voices to be present in the school. Efforts must be made to nurture and bring forth the voices so they can be heard. As supportive conditions develop people will begin to believe they can fully participate, communicate honestly, and trust those around them. Dialogue and reflection about prior learning and new experiences are central to the cultivation of new ideas and new perspectives. It is from these conversations that people begin to relate to others and open their minds and hearts to multiple and different viewpoints. Moreover, norms of respect and inclusion develop, and when combined with inquiry, collaboration, and healthy skepticism, they serve to create social change that forms the basis for continuous improvement in the schools.

Considering another viewpoint, Kincheloe and Steinberg (1995) suggest that personnel in socially just educational organizations consider developing their policies and procedures with these four terms in mind: just, democratic, empathic, and optimistic. In doing so, teachers and leaders will make educational decisions and take actions that are grounded in respectful, equitable, and open beliefs.

Regarding institutions of higher education, and specifically the principal and superintendent preparation programs, Grogan (2004) suggests that faculty pay attention to the "courageous practice" by leaders in the field, and "recenter our principal and superintendent preparation programs around ways to resist the dominant discourse" (p. 234). She contends that in some districts an organizational consciousness develops that ensures the inculcation of social justice principles. It is in these districts that data can be gathered qualitatively and quantitatively to provide research for university faculty and practitioners to analyze and replicate. This type of collaboration allows academics and practitioners to learn and work together so each can benefit from the other's expertise. Then, also combining these actions with leaders at the state educational level, policies and decisions can be made that broaden and deepen the goals we have for our students. Thus, preparing leaders to have the data, information, and dispositions they need to engage their schools and districts in socially just learning allows them to have a greater degree of agency as they deal with externally imposed accountability reforms.

Finally, it should be mentioned that while it may seem there is one way to provide equity and a more inclusive education for our students, we must be cognizant that there is really no one voice. Thus it remains important for those concerned with the social justice issues to be open to additional narratives and opinions. Providing a culture for discourse that is based on trust, relationships, and dialogue may prove to be a process that can give everyone involved respect for their opinions, and voice in the decisions.

REFERENCES

Adams, C., Forsyth, P., & Mitchell, R. (2009). The formation of parent–school trust: A multilevel analysis. *Educational Administration Quarterly, 45*(4), 4–33.

Argyris, C. (1990). *Overcoming organizational defenses.* Needham, MA: Allyn & Bacon.

Ayers, W., Quinn, T., & Stovall, D. (2009). *Handbook of social justice in education.* New York: Routledge.

Barber, M., & Fullan, M. (2005). Tri-level development: It's the system. *Education Week, 24*(25), 32–35.

Berman, E. (2006). Teaching about language, power, and text: A review of classroom practices that support critical literacy. *Journal of Adolescent and Adult Literacy, 49*(6), 490–498.

Bohm, D. (1996). *On dialogue.* London: Routledge.

Bryk, A., & Schneider, B. (2002). *Trust in schools: A core resource for improvement.* New York: Russell Sage Foundation.

Epstein, J. (2001). *School, family, and community partnerships: Preparing educators and improving schools.* Boulder, CO: Westview Press.

Fox, E. (2005). Tracking U.S. trends. *Education Week, 24*(35), 40–42.

Fullan, M. (2006). *Turnaround leadership.* San Francisco: Wiley.

Fullan, M., Hill, P., & Crevola, C. (2006). *Breakthrough.* Thousand Oaks, CA: Corwin Press.

Grant, C., & Sleeter, C. (2007). *Doing multicultural education for achievement and equity.* New York: Routledge.

Grogan, M. (2004). Keeping a critical, postmodern eye on educational leadership in the United States: In appreciation of Bill Foster. *Educational Administration Quarterly, 40*(2), 222–229.

Grumet, M. (1995). The curriculum: What are the basics and are we teaching them? In J. L.

Kincheloe & S. R. Steinberg (Eds.), *Thirteen questions* (2nd ed., pp. 15–21). New York: Peter Lang.

Hacker, S., & Willard, M. (2002). *The trust imperative: Performance improvement through productive relationships.* Milwaukee, WI: American Society for Quality.

Hipp, K., & Huffman, J. (2010). *Demystifying professional learning communities: School leadership at its best.* Lanham, MD: Rowman & Littlefield.

Huffman, J., & Hipp, K. (2003). *Reculturing schools as professional learning communities.* Lanham, MD: Scarecrow Press.

Jones, L., Webb, P., & Newmann, M. (2008). Claiming the contentious: Literacy teachers as leaders of social justice principles and practices. *Issues in Teacher Education 17*(1), 7–15.

Kincheloe, J., & Steinberg, S. (1995). The more questions we ask, the more questions we ask. In L. K. Kincheoloe & S. R. Steinberg (Eds.). *Thirteen questions* (2nd ed., pp. 1–11). New York: Peter Lang.

McKenzie, K., Christman, D., Hernandez, F., Fierro, E., Capper, C., Dantley, M., et al. (2008). From the field: A proposal for educating leaders for social justice. *Educational Administration Quarterly, 44*(1), 111–138.

Murphy, J. (1991). The "Maytag man" of school reform. *The School Administrator, 48*(2), 32–33.

Noddings, N. (1986). *Caring: A feminine approach to ethics and moral education.* Berkeley: University of California Press.

Preskill, S., & Brookfield, S. (2009). *Learning as a way of leading: Lessons from the struggle for social justice.* San Francisco: Jossey-Bass.

Ravitch, D. (2000). *Left bank: A century of failed school reforms.* New York: Simon & Schuster.

Shields, C. (2004). Dialogic leadership for social justice: Overcoming pathologies of silence. *Educational Administration Quarterly, 40*(1), 109–132.

Shields, C., Mazawi, A., & Bishop, R. (2002, December). *Overcoming deficit thinking: De-pathologizing the lived experiences of children.* Symposium presented at the annual conference of the New Zealand Association for Research in Education, Parmerston North.

Siskin, L. S. (2003). Outside the core: Accountability in tested and untested subjects. In M. Carnoy, R. Elmore, & L. S. Siskin (Eds.), *The new accountability: High schools and high-stakes testing* (pp. 87–98). New York: Routledge Falmer.

Skrla, L., & Scheurich, J. J. (Eds.). (2004). *Educational equity and accountability.* London: Routledge Falmer.

Theoharis, G. (2007). Social justice educational leaders and resistance: Toward a theory of social justice leadership. *Educational Administration Quarterly, 43*(3), 221–258.

Tschannon-Moran, M. (2009). Fostering teacher professionalism in schools: The role of leadership orientation and trust. *Educational Administration Quarterly, 45*(2), 217–247.

Tyack, D., & Cuban, L. (1995). *Tinkering towards utopia: A century of public school reform.* Cambridge, MA: Harvard University Press.

Valenzuela, A. (Ed.). (2004). *Leaving children behind: How "Texas-style" accountability fails Latino youth.* New York: State University of New York Press.

Wellman, B., & Lipton, L. (2004). *Data driven dialogue: A facilitator's guide to collaborative inquiry.* Sherman, CT: Mira Via, LLC.

Wheatley, M. (2002). *Turning to one another: Simple conversations to restore hope to the future.* San Francisco: Berrett-Koehler.

CHAPTER 4

PHILOSOPHICAL REFLECTIONS ON MORAL TRANSFORMATIVE LEADERSHIP

JoAnn F. Klinker and David P. Thompson

Leadership for social justice embodies fairness, freedom, respect for persons, truth, and felicity, which are basic principles in all theories of ethics (Barrow, 2006). Grounded in the metaphysical, a philosophical term that concerns itself with the study of or opinion about reality (Craig, 2002, p. 87), these five values are "unverifiable by the techniques of science and cannot be justified by merely logical argument" (Hodgkinson, 1991, p. 99). Moreover, they, like other finer traits of character, are not formed through compulsion but rather are lived through the mind and the heart (Kirkpatrick, 1952).

Discourse, insights, and theories about morality, ethics, and the philosophy of being, *how we want to live*, have merited discussion for over 2,000 years in part because such values were not so easily defined. As an example, professional codes of ethics for educators, those standards of conduct for how educators should conduct themselves in the workplace, usually com-

Educational Leaders Encouraging the Intellectual and Professional Capacity of Others:
A Social Justice Agenda, pages 61–78.
Copyright © 2012 by Information Age Publishing

61

bine elements of deontology, utilitarianism, and virtue ethics. Those are conflicting moral philosophies and at first glance they seem to repel one another, especially when jammed into close proximity within a code of ethics document. Nor has defining leadership for social justice been straightforward as there are many concepts and disagreements as to what social justice is (Theoharis, 2009). But most, we think, would agree that leadership for social justice is value driven and has elements of deontology and virtue theory centered on core values of fairness, respect for persons, and truth. It is our contention as well as Dantley and Tillman's (2006) that leadership for social justice is the expression of a deeply felt belief expressed in thought and action to meet a pressing need. We know that as moral transformative leadership.

Our definition of ethics involves the fact that it is something that we *do*. Moral transformative leadership, a component of leadership for social justice (Dantley & Tillman, 2006), also incorporates that action component of doing, as well as judgment and moral courage. Doing ethics is not something that stands over us or apart and away from us because it concerns the judgments we *make* (Dewey & Tufts, 1908). For example, constructing a code of ethics is the most visible means through which an organization as a whole practices moral leadership. For educational organizations, that action of adopting and enforcing codes of ethics defines what is morally permissible within the social contract of the educational work environment. While a code of ethics fulfills many purposes, among them an increased ethical sensitivity and judgment, doing ethics takes moral courage to live up to ethical standards and to help others live up to them as well. To that end, examining moral transformational leadership for social justice and violations of a professional code of ethics may give us some insight as to why those five values we mentioned earlier are so important for leaders and professionals who advocate social justice practice and promote the practice of those values in a place called school.

MORAL TRANSFORMATIVE LEADERSHIP

Dantley and Tillman (2006) define social justice through the three components of leadership for social justice, moral transformative leadership, and social justice praxis. Our concern in this chapter is with the second component of that definition, moral transformative leadership, and the ethics behind it. Moral transformative leadership is a critical lens that examines the "use and abuse of power in institutional settings" (p. 19) as well as deconstruction of practices that bring about inequities. Inherent in that leadership is the conception that schools are or can be democratic sites that bring about societal reconstruction. Moral transformative leadership then is action based on values about ideals that demand expression through change of the status quo (Dantley & Tillman, 2006). In other words, doing ethics.

In leadership for social justice, examining relationships within the organization and the power distribution among stakeholders (Leithwood & Duke, 1999) is critical as is recognition of Burns' (1978) concept of power (i.e., that it exists in motives or purposes as well as resources). Leadership for social justice derives its power through purpose in changing marginalized lives, which necessitates engagement in value conflicts, which Hodgkinson (1996) noted are at the heart of leadership: "If there are no value conflicts, then there is no need for leadership" (p. 11).

Doing ethics and leading for social justice are not easy because decisions that challenge the status quo never make everyone happy. The point is a powerful one when discussing moral transformative leadership in the chaotic environment of unsettled cultures and student conditions known as school (Larson & Ovando, 2001) because of the tension that already exists. Chaotic environments often lend themselves to heuristic decision making, but that type of decision making solves the surface eruptions of conflict, not the underlying cause or situation that brought about that problem, in other words, the conflicting values at the heart of the situation.

Increasingly, we are coming to realize that decision making is the most important action in which a leader can engage (Agor, 1992; Cuban, 2001). The act deliberately selects an action from a series of options (Demartino, Kumaran, Seymor, & Dolan, 2006). As Berthoz (2006) pointed out, "a theory of decision making cannot assume that subjects evolve in an indifferent world. . . . The world contains living creatures—prey and predators, partners and competitors—that can cause either happiness or misery" (p. 23). In writing about moral leaders and their emphasis on democratic principles such as freedom and equality, Capper (1993) indicated that critical theorists ground decisions in morals and values and move through those decisions to empower and transform followers. As Socrates so aptly illustrated, however, following one's ethic is not always a pleasurable experience, and decisions for social justice, in particular because of their roots in empowerment and transformation, are not easy nor are they always an enjoyable experience (Theoharis, 2009). To empower others and to transform followers indicates changes in the use of power. What is taken away and given to others is not always appreciated by those now bereft of that power or who now have to share it. Moreover, in the midst of this change, leadership still has the responsibility to bring cultural stability and purpose to the school environment. That conflict between role expectations and professional and personal ethics places moral transformative leaders squarely into the uncomfortable arena of moral dilemmas and reactions.

That values can inform decision making is still a contested point in educational leadership because rational choice theory has dominated educational leadership research, practice, and theory. The basic assumption underlying this science is that humans are rational beings. Yet we know humans are consistently irrational beings (Berthoz, 2006). If you have ever gone out shopping for a new car and come home with a vehicle that was nothing like the one you rationally decided upon, you have experienced decision making that was not rational. A decision like that happens all the time because of what is known as framing.

Decision Making

Principals and superintendents are taught from early on in their professional careers that sound decision making relies on logical, rational calculation and that emotion has no place in administrative decision making. But contrary to what school administrators have been taught, emotions and reason are "intimately intertwined and interconnected processes, psychologically and neurologically" (McDermott, 2004, p. 693). Moral transformative leadership for social justice as we have defined it here is a critical lens that does not ignore circumstances and contexts. Instead, it examines them, judges them from a value stance, and moves for change in those circumstances and contexts. Greene and Haidt (2002) have found through brain-imaging studies that "there is no specifically moral part of the brain" (p. 522). Human beliefs about what is and is not moral are neither complete nor consistent, an indication that morality is not completely logical (Bucciarelli, Khemlani, & Johnson-Laird, 2008). If it were, all moral issues would be decided without hedging or uncertainty about whether an issue is moral or not. "When you think about moral issues, you rely on the same independent mechanisms that underlie emotions and cognitions in deontic domains" (p. 137). Emotion is part of the moral evaluation, and emotion cannot be separated from reason in either moral dilemmas or moral reactions (Monin, Pizarro, & Beer, 2007).

To illustrate, consider the following values conflict. An educational leader despises people who live in poverty because he believes (a philosophical stance) that hard work and effort are the only necessary ingredients to rise up out of poverty. However, he rationalizes his decision to treat parents of students in poverty with graciousness because he *fears* that if he does not, the board of education will fire him. To divorce an individual's morality and humanity from reason in theories about decision making is to ignore the circumstances and contexts in which the school administrator acts.

Moral Situations

In their investigation of the reason–affect debate, Monin et al. (2007) differentiated between two different types of moral situations: moral dilemmas and moral reactions. School administrators encounter both and leadership for social justice encompasses both. Despite "the emphasis moral dilemmas place on explicit reasoning and analytical consideration, they also come with their share of emotional content" (p. 102) including anticipatory guilt, least discomfort, and avoidance of averse emotion. Moral reactions, once thought to be centrally located in emotion, are now found to be shaped by prior reasoning. The authors surmised that humans who adopt a moral stance "appear to recruit disgust effectively to serve their moral beliefs" (p. 104), which they arrived at through reasoning. This is dangerous territory for a movement like leadership for social justice. Identifying it with morality is one thing. Identifying it with emotion is quite another.

As English and Papa (2010) noted, a field, especially an applied field like educational leadership, grows from its theories and not from its practices. Articles written by educational leadership scholars about social justice leadership and theory pack a lot of scholarly passion, intended to ignite change in the practitioner world. Scholars who write from a moral imperative perspective are aware of that emotional punch. They use it to engage disgust for the current situation and to change culture, for culture places the boundary around what is disgusting. Disgust and other emotions like it "enable certain experiences and foreclose others . . . they supply powerful motives for action" (Kahan, 1998, p. 3). But this in and of itself is not merely an academic exercise; it takes moral courage and leadership. Dabbling in disgust, or for that matter emotion itself, can be dangerous for social justice scholars. In a discipline like educational leadership, which values rational thinking, to admit that passion drove one's scholarly work would be to contaminate that research. Such discussion "risks personalizing intellectual work, painting it as a less than serious endeavor—even as biased and unscientific—and thus as irrelevant, unimportant, or frivolous" (Neumann, 2006, p. 381).

In contrast, we found no such conflict regarding the use of emotion to support decision making in enforcement of the Texas Educators' Code of Ethics. In fact, in judicial decisions on educational ethics violations in the state of Texas, disgust and other emotions are used to emphasize that the power educators have over students should not be abused. That they find evidence of such abuse, even in something as innocuous as the manner in which a teacher received a gift, illustrates that courts routinely make decisions based on precedent about what is acceptable and not acceptable in our society, what behavior we find disgusting and what behavior our society deems acceptable. The complex interplay of emotion and reason can be seen in the rationale for decisions from administrative law judges, hearing examiners, or the commissioners themselves. As the commissioner noted in *Fenter v. Quinlan Independent School District* (2002), the code of ethics was designed to set ethical standards and to punish those educators who violate those standards. The following decision by a hearing examiner in *Houston*

Independent School District v. Ruiz-Garcia (1999) illustrated two things: the court's refusal to accept an abuse of power and the hearing examiner's disgust at the misuse of that power. Note the emotional words through which the hearing examiner defined the environment the teacher created:

> A damaging educational atmosphere where students have been subjected to corporal punishment against school policy, had money taken and not returned, been humiliated, embarrassed, yelled at and saddened, asked to tie the teacher's shoes, and forced to write multiple sentences as discipline. All of these actions resulted in a significant drop in students' grades and their ability to learn in school. Ms. Ruiz-Garcia's insensitivity toward the students regarding (1) the picture of the students with their former teacher which Ms. Ruiz-Garcia threw away; (2) telling students she had thrown a cake b[r]ought by a student for a party into the trash; and (3) refusing to allow students to take the class party left-over food and drink home with them, further destroyed any atmosphere to nurture the full potential of her students. (Klinker, Thompson, & Blacker, 2011, p. 118)

Implications for Leadership

In the case cited above, all of the behavior took place in a 6-week time period that ended a 23-year career. Clearly the balance of power shifted in that 6 weeks from behavior that emphasized professional ethics to behavior that allowed personal morality to dominate within that brief period of time. Ethics and morality are sometimes used interchangeably, but ethics as it is used in codes of ethics has to do with the social roles in which humans find themselves while personal morality is how a person sees him- or herself as a human being. Sometimes professional ethics and personal morality conflict, and it is in that discussion of value conflicts between the professional and the personal that further motivation for moral transformative leadership might be found.

CODES OF ETHICS

Codes of ethics for educators exist to reassure the public that these certificated professionals can be trusted, are competent, and in the autonomy-for-accountability institutional bargain will behave in an ethical, trustworthy manner. The very existence of the codes is an attempt by a perpetually anxious public to maintain professional accountability as a safety mechanism to check the power inherent in professional autonomy (Klinker, et al., 2011).

Ethical codes are common in educational organizations, and ethics is deemed of sufficient importance to stand alone as the fifth of six Interstate School Leaders Licensure Consortium (ISLLC) standards: "A school administrator is an educational leader who promotes the success of all students by acting with integrity, fairness, and in an ethical manner" (1996, 2008). A close perusal of the 1996 ISLLC dispositions revealed conflicting philosophies of utilitarianism, deontology, and virtue ethics. For example, the ideal of the common good conflicts with individual rights and the character of an administrator challenges both theories. Almost every state in the United States has a code of ethics for educators, and those who do not have a general expectation written in law that educators conduct themselves in an ethical manner.

Underlying Philosophies

To explain the underlying moral philosophies of deontology, utilitarianism, and virtue ethics, we have relied on the work of David Blacker (Klinker et al., 2011). Throughout we have pulled some examples from the Texas Educators' Code of Ethics to illustrate how the philosophical conversation tracks into practice.

Deontology. Most of us have deep-seated principles that, if abandoned, would cause a major identity crisis. For our society, the right of a free and public education has become a fundamental principle. Deontology is the branch of philosophy that takes concepts of rights and principles most seriously. For Immanuel Kant, the philosopher most associated with this moral philosophy, *intentions* are what matter most in assessing the moral worth of actions (Kant, 1785/2009). Another underlying concept is that of *ought versus can*. In other words, it is unfair to hold someone morally responsible for something over which they have no control. In law we can more clearly see the effects of intent in the gravity of the charge. Manslaughter is a lesser crime because the intent to commit murder and the premeditation to do it was not present.

Human dignity is central to Kant's categorical imperative and educators' ethics codes are rife with concerns about human dignity. Concepts of means and ends are inherent in this concept for the unwillingness to see others as fully human or to desensitize oneself to another's humanity is morally corrupt. Rawls's (1971) theory of justice builds on this concept. The touchstone of Rawls's justice theory as it relates to ethical decision making and action, particularly with regard to the distribution of finite resources, is that the actor must place him- or herself in a position of equality with those who will benefit from the distribution of resources by operating behind a "veil of ignorance [i.e., disallowing him- or herself], information concerning our own particular circumstances when making distributive decisions" (p. 29). This concept is readily applicable to education, for example, when it comes to the distribution of resources to students with disabilities, in that the person or body distributing such resources generally does not know the identities of the students to whom resources are being distributed. Operating behind this *veil of ignorance,* the resource distributor would have the incentive of distributing resources in as fair manner as possible.

In our review of the Texas Educators' Code of Ethics, Standard 3.4, which prohibits educators from excluding, denying advantages, or granting opportunities to students "on the basis of race, color, sex, disability, national origin, religion, or family status," best exemplifies Rawls's justice theory. Indeed, this ethical standard places the veil of ignorance between the educator and the student so that the distribution of educational resources is done in an equitable manner. This ethical standard was violated by a high school ROTC instructor who allegedly *outed* several female cadets who complained of inappropriate sexual language undertaken by the instructor and who obtained assistance in securing the signatures of 70 students who signed a petition against two of the complaining students. The district terminated the instructor, in part for violating this ethical standard, and the Texas Commissioner of Education upheld the termination (*Perez v. Laredo Independent School District,* 1996).

Ultimately, the Kantian and Rawlsian perspectives can be boiled into a *rights-based* approach to ethical conduct, which operates under the premise that students, without regard to their circumstances, have a right to an education. This ethical philosophy is embodied into the compulsory education statutes of all 50 states, and has been supported by other state and federal statutes and court cases requiring the states to provide an adequate level of education without regard to the circumstances or attributes of students (see, e.g., *Brown v. Board of Education,* 1954 [race]; *Plyler v. Doe,* 1982 [citizenship], *Public Law 94-142* [disability]). The rights-based approach is not without its challenges, however, particularly when viewed from the natural consequence of an increase of litigation to enforce these rights as well as the issue of competing rights (e.g., the right of students to be free from "hate" speech versus the right of students under the First Amendment to express their views in the school environment).

Utilitarianism. Instead of focusing on rights and intentions, consequentialism goes to consequences or results of actions. With this philosophy, we ask questions and make decisions based on reasons and rationality for doing—in other words, if I take this action, what good will it do? For educators, consequentialism has three advantages. The first is what philosophers of education have called the *success sense of teaching,* meaning that the very idea of teaching someone something cannot be separate and apart from its consequences. The second is that there is no agonizing over which choice promotes the lesser of two evils if one simply does what will result in the most good. And the third advantage in this approach relies on reasoning, on rational justification. Developed by John Stuart Mill and Jeremy Bentham, utilitarianism is the most famous version of consequentialism. The underlying moral action is commonly known as securing the greatest good for the greatest number. Discipline policies tend to incorporate this moral reasoning. In addition, Standard 3.1 of the Texas Educators' Code of Ethics, which generally prohibits educators from revealing confidential information about students, does permit such disclosure for "lawful professional purposes" or if "required by law."

Virtue theories. The two prior theories have relied on rationalism, which is analyzing a situation, making calculations about it, and then employing a rational choice to solve moral dilemmas and take moral action. Virtue theory holds that it is character that promotes good qualities and decision making, not someone who is exceptionally clever at calculating the odds (utilitarianism) or being rigidly logical about basic principles (deontology). Aristotle is the most famous proponent of virtue ethics. To flourish as a human being, to be a person of good quality seems to be the closest one can come to Aristotle's concept of *arête*. Central to this theory is the confusion as to specifics that are not uncommon in ideals that are essential to a society. Phronesis goes to the Golden Mean, that middle state between excess and defect where one can live in moderation to achieve arête.

Traits and context of community play important roles in virtue theory. For example, the role of leader preexists before an individual steps into that role. Those assumptions about what a leader ought to do determine how stakeholders judge his or her actions. And communities and their traditions almost always outlast the individual. A problem from the point of leadership for social justice is that the reliance on community traditions can curtail criticism of those objectionable practices. For example, Aristotle championed slavery, as did many democratic leaders whose ideas formed the United States. The Texas Code of Ethics relies in its enforceable standards on the underlying philosophies of deontology and utilitarianism, and less so on virtue theories. That could be because often virtue dispositions appeal to a common community convention of character that usually is localized. For example, in a pluralistic society, stubbornness as defined by one community may be viewed as integrity in another. However, one could also argue that the ultimate goal of the ethics code is to place virtuous educators into the profession, and this is arguably exemplified by the Statement of Purpose of the Texas Educators' Code of Ethics. We have highlighted those terms in the Statement of Purpose that to us identify a virtue ethics philosophy:

> The Texas educator shall comply with standard practices and ethical conduct toward students, professional colleagues, school officials, parents, and members of the community and shall safeguard academic freedom. The Texas educator, in *maintaining the dignity of the profession*, shall respect and obey the law, *demonstrate personal integrity*, and *exemplify honesty*. The Texas educator, in *exemplifying ethical relations* with colleagues, shall extend just and equitable treatment to all members of the profession. The Texas educator, in *accepting*

a position of public trust, shall measure success by the progress of each student toward realization of his or her potential as an effective citizen. The Texas educator, in fulfilling responsibilities in the community, shall cooperate with parents and others to improve the public schools of the community. This chapter shall apply to educators and candidates for certification. (19 T.A.C. § 247.2 (a), emphasis added)

CONTROVERSY OVER CODES OF ETHICS

The Center for the Study of Ethics in Professions at the Illinois Institute of Technology (IIT) has compiled a collection of ethical codes from a plethora of professional and trade organizations, including educational organizations, business, government, churches, clubs, associations, conferences, universities, foundations, museums, and so forth. Each of these codes is context specific as a guideline to define behavior specific to possible ethical conflicts within that context. But as the website acknowledges, these codes of ethics incorporate competing philosophies and are themselves at the center of the controversy between professional autonomy and public accountability. On one hand is the belief that moral behavior should be intrinsic to the individual, a personal code of conduct developed through reflection and thought about moral autonomy (Ladd, 1991; Luegenbiehl, 1983). From that viewpoint, codes of ethics are useless and harmful to moral growth. Moreover, following a code of ethics erodes moral autonomy and risks confusion with law, thus negating autonomy and choice. On the other hand, others have adopted the viewpoint that a code of ethics serves as an ethical framework, offers protection through defining boundaries of acceptable behavior and thorough discussion, and generates a collective recognition of an environment centered on moral responsibilities (Davis, 1991; Harris, Pritchard, & Rabins, 1995). Moreover, the process of developing and discussing the code can be a bonding experience, an educational tool, and reassurance that the profession is responsible and professional about its moral obligations. In other words, codes of ethics can be seen as reassurance that professional autonomy will not overcome public accountability.

The controversy also exists because of the limitations of discourse to define what cannot be clearly articulated. As Boyd (1992) pointed out, a relationship exists "between the importance of a social issue and confusion in public discourse about that issue. And unfortunately, the relationship is direct: the more important the issue, the more confusion in how people talk to each other about it" (p. 141). Despite the controversy, the proliferation of codes of ethics persists, an indication that ethics is an integral part of defining a professional. This realization is especially important in schools because they are institutions of both moral and academic learning.

Law and Ethics

In democracies, ethics rule us through the rule of law, one of eight dimensions fundamental to all democracies (Diamond & Morlino, 2004). We hasten to add that there are clear differences between law and ethics and that the two should not be confused. But as history indicates they are usually entwined. Socrates' refusal to flee when accused, found guilty by law, and sentenced to die was not a moral reaction but rather moral adherence to a way of life that had made him who he was and he was "not dissatisfied with how it [Athens] did it. So he is bound by its wishes and it is ridiculous to suppose that he might have the right of retaliation against it" (Craig, 2002, p. 27). Compare Socrates' reaction to that of the Chinese who had suffered under the Legalists, rigid quantifiers of the law who ruled from 221 b.c. to 206 b.c. They rebelled against legalism, "the belief that people are fundamentally antisocial and must be bent to laws that place the security of the state above their personal desires" (Wilson, 1999, p. 33) and as a result missed the entry point into "abstraction and the break-apart analytic research attained by European science in the seventeenth century" (p. 33). As Wilson (1999) indicates, their belief in the harmonious whole and subsequent rejection of general law, not their intellect, research skills, or context, took them down a different path than that of the Western world with its belief in fundamental law, otherwise known as science.

For a more recent example of the interplay of ethics and law, in late 2007 the Texas Education Agency *repealed* the specific enforcement rules regarding the Texas Educators' Code of Ethics (instead folding enforcement of the code of ethics into the more general provisions regarding educator discipline), but more often than not allegations of code of ethics violations are often included in local complaints that come through the Texas Education Agency, both in adverse employment actions (i.e., termination, nonrenewal, or suspension of contracts) and in actions taken against educators' certificates (i.e., suspension and revocation). The point to this is that the ideal, the belief that ethical conduct is important for Texas educators to practice, persists despite the repeal of the specific enforcement rules and will continue to persist regardless of what reforms might ensue. The value of ethics is so strong that even when it is no longer inculcated into law, people act as if it is.

We hasten to add, as we have elsewhere, that there are differences between law and ethics of which leaders should be mindful. At the simplest level, the law answers the question of "what can I (or can I not) do," while ethics answers the question of "what should I (or should I not) do." Simultaneously, we subscribe to the sentiments of Bull and McCarthy (1995, p. 614), who view the "boundary-setting" approach to law and ethics at best minimalist and at worst "intellectually and professionally inappropriate," instead arguing that, while educational leaders are not free to ignore legal and ethical principles/mandates, a more robust perspective views "law and ethics as relevant to all their decisions and actions, providing insights and patterns of thought that will strengthen the quality of their deliberations and the effectiveness of their performance."

For example, while the Fourth Amendment of the U.S. Constitution does not *per se* prohibit educators from subjecting students to strip searches (see *Safford Unified School District v. Redding* [2009] for the most recent U.S. Supreme Court decision on the issue of strip searches of public school students), ethical considerations (particularly deontological and perhaps even utilitarian) might give the educator good reason to not conduct such an intrusive search. Similarly, while the U.S. Supreme Court has held that the practice of peer grading does not violate students' rights under the Family Educational Rights and Privacy Act (FERPA) (*Owasso Independent School District No. I-011 v. Falvo*, 2002), a deontological perspective would likely question whether the practice is *ethical* as balanced against what many believe are the rights of students to be secure in the grades that they receive. Taken together, these examples underscore basic differences in legal and ethical conduct, and thus lead us to conclude that ethics in schools is a workable integration of morality, law, and specific educational concerns.

To illustrate the concept of ethics in school as a workable integration, we found it odd that, until the Texas Code was revised in late 2010, it did not require educators to be of good moral character. That seemed odd because it is obvious that Texans expect educators to be of such character. However, with the late 2010 revision to the code came that exact requirement, found in Standard 1.10, i.e., "The educator shall be of good moral character and worthy to instruct or supervise the youth of this state." Good moral character, in turn, is defined as "The virtues of a person as evidenced, at a minimum, by his or her not having committed crimes relating directly to the duties and responsibilities of the education profession...or acts involving moral turpitude" (19 Tex. Admin. Code § 247.1 [b] [9]). Prior to the 2010 revision, the expectation was implicit in the Statement of Purpose and in the enforcement rules. Further, past and current administrative regulations require superintendents and charter school directors to report to the state certification board their knowledge of information that a certificate applicant or holder has committed certain criminal acts, including those that occur outside of school-related activities; or an educators resigns and reasonable evidence supports that the certificate holder be recommended for termination for committing certain misconduct (19 Tex. Admin. Code § 249.14). As we mentioned earlier, ethics in schools seems to be a workable integration of morality, law, and specific educational concerns.

THE STRUGGLE FOR MIND

Social justice advocates would argue that leaders for social justice have no choice but to respond to moral demands. The need is so great and the problems so pressing within our discordant society that we can no longer debate the merit of solutions through the use of logic as if each problem were a moral dilemma or an intellectual exercise. This is a time for moral reaction, that doing of ethics that demands action provoked by values so strong they cannot be denied. But as neuro decision-making studies tell us, choice has always been involved in decision making, be that decision quick or deliberative, because the brain cuts in front of multiple possible solutions to choose one solution over others when a decision is made (Berthoz, 2006). In other words, moral transformative leadership has always been a solution to the issues of social inequities. So now the question becomes why is it not always the optimal selection?

Foster (1989) stipulated that leadership addressed change, transformation, and liberation in the struggle to shape social agendas, what he called the *struggle for mind.* This is not a struggle that can be achieved through cognition and logical analysis, because people "are chained by their histories, their development, and their psyches" (p. 16). That is not to say that people cannot change; what it means is that to bring about change one must understand currents, culture, complexity, time, and ideals. We fully realize that these are words that are acceptable in a culture dominated by rational choice theory and that they allow the myth of value-free leadership to persist. Foster himself understood that the concept of educational leadership was moving toward *doing ethics,* not merely talking about morality even as he suggested that to transform schools, leadership should fall back into the understanding generated by competing moral philosophies that have significantly impacted education. These moral philosophies have through time formed the *keystone* of organizational relationships, especially in schools. Preparing school leaders to understand moral concepts and to talk the talk about morality allows at the very least a development in the understanding of societal expectations. At its best, we agree with Barrow (2006), moral education brings understanding of the nature of morality and provides a framework for practical decisions.

However, as demonstrated, a professional code of ethics by itself does not ensure that leaders will consistently make ethical choices (Dexheimer, 1970; Fenstermaker, 1994). Yet, leaders have power and influence over others. They are in the "business of creating persons" (Strike, Haller, & Soltis, 1988, p. 84), which implies a duty to be proficient in ethical reasoning and to adhere to ethical codes. In our analysis of the Texas Educator's Code of Ethics we also fall back on those age-old concepts while cognizant of the fact that to do so goes to an understanding of societal expectations and not to the question of how moral transformative leadership is practiced. We also know that moral transformative leadership cannot be defined in the acquisition of terms and concepts that illuminate moral theory, or understanding of such theory, any more than resolution of societal ills can be found in accumulation of data. Consider that in our data-driven society, principals and teachers are currently drowning in data, but that collection of data has not yet had the impact we thought it would to change the lives of marginalized groups in schools. What have changed lives are the collective decisions of educators to determine how they want to live (Marshall & Oliva, 2006; Theoharis, 2009).

This indicates that it is from the crucible of conflict between personal needs and wants, professional ethics emphasis, and intractable conflict, problems and issues that can no longer be ignored, for whatever reason, that moral transformative leadership emerges. Decision making evaluates wants through a complex interplay of emotion and reason that results in a choice of a critically evaluated want. Because of that process, the want metamorphizes itself into a value (Kirkpatrick, 1952). Moral transformative leadership is then identified through those values as emphasized in decision making, which results in action.

Equality or Equity

Leadership for social justice gravitates toward equity in that it critically examines the power dynamics and seeks to bring balance to inequities. Krause, Traini, and Mickey (2005) draw this distinction between equality and ethics. They allude to the paradox between equality and equity as contradictory terms. Equality defined in this manner "looks at the individual and the circumstances surrounding him or her" (p. 103) whereas equity focuses on group differences and involves unequal treatment of the group over time, which can provoke feelings of inferiority and even oppression. Wagner and Simpson (2009) define equality as "treating everyone the same" (p. 179), which can result in unfairness if differences are not taken into account. Equity, however, "denotes the spirit and habit of right dealing with others . . . and is defined in terms of principles of fairness and justice" (p. 179). Under these definitions, the roots for equity can be found in ethics as even Aristotle recognized that "when people differ on some relevant characteristic they should be treated differently" (Shapiro & Stefkovich, 2005, p. 105). The juxtaposition of these two definitions of equality and equity illuminates Hodgkinson's (1991) insight that values are rooted in the metaphysical and are not so easily defined or studied.

Our purpose in this chapter is not to define equality or equity, but we do submit that the two are not mutually incompatible. The simple reason is that both have at their core the same five values that are inherent in all philosophical theories: fairness, freedom, respect for persons, truth, and felicity. And as with all philosophical concepts and theories, only the emphasis on values differs as does the road traveled to respond to the issue. For example, our democracy values equality but the influence of equity can be seen in key legal decisions that have advanced social justice, specifically *Brown v. Board of Education* and *Lau v. Nichols* (Dantley & Tillman, 2006). From the Texas Educators' Code of Ethics, we also found an example of how equity secured relief when in *State Board for Educator Certification v. Slovacek* (2006) unusual circumstances, character witnesses, and the will to make a new life for himself saved this educator from having his certificate revoked. As usual the equitable decision making is in the details. Prior to receiving his teaching certificate, the teacher had pled guilty to felony theft against his brother. SBEC sought to revoke the certificate based on this previous criminal history, but when the teacher disagreed with the proposed action at the administrative hearing and presented 14 character witnesses who stated he was fit to teach, SBEC reduced the penalty it sought to suspension of certification for the amount of time the teacher did community service for his felony. The administrative law judge ruled in favor of the educator's request for probation, finding that the witnesses' testimonies carried sufficient weight to find the teacher fit to teach and that the theft occurred in unusual circumstances that would never be repeated. The administrative law judge stayed the suspension and placed the teacher on probation for the remaining time of his community service.

What should not be taken from this juxtaposition of equity and equality is the idea that equality is a bad thing. The tendency may exist to view equity as a response to unfairness in the treatment of marginalized groups because equality could not be realized. Rather, we would submit that while equality has not always been honored in our society, that act does not diminish the laudability of the term or the desire to achieve that goal. To the continuing debate we would contribute the following: both philosophical concepts share an ethical heart of respect for persons, fairness, and freedom. It is only the emphasis one places on values within each concept that differs.

CONCLUSION

Values drive moral transformative leadership, a critical component of leadership for social justice (Dantley & Tillman, 2006). As Kirkpatrick (1952) noted, values are formed through weighing conflicting wants against each other. The want that wins out, the one that has been critically evaluated and found most worthy of choice, ceases to become a mere want and emerges as a value. It has the rightful authority to direct conduct (Dewey & Tufts, 1908). Skills in moral reasoning and knowledge about underlying philosophical keystones can be helpful to moral transformative leaders for social justice, because often, the choice of action is not between a right and a wrong but between two competing right answers (Greenfield, 1993), as the age-old debate between equality and equity emphasizes. It is from this crucible of conflict between personal needs and wants, professional ethics emphasis, and problems as severe as intractable conflict that we think moral transformative leadership for social justice emerges. Such decisions bring with them an inordinate amount of anxiety and emotion, in part because reassurance as to what is right is frequently withheld because of shifting values in our society. In this struggle for mind, discussion of beliefs embodied within codes of ethics offer opportunities for critical conversations about shared values. In schools those conversations are critical because the situations encountered by leadership are morally complex, have high stakes, and resulting decisions about those situations have enormous impact on the organization (Beck, 1996).

REFERENCES

Agor, W. H. (1992). *Intuition in decision making: How to assess, use, and develop your intuitive powers for increased productivity.* El Paso, TX: Global Intuition Network.

Barrow, R. (2006). Moral education's modest agenda. *Ethics and Education, 1*(1), 3–13.

Beck, L. G. (1996). Why ethics? Why now?: Thoughts on the moral challenges facing educational leaders. *The School Administrator, 54*(9), 8–11.

Berthoz, A. (2006). *Emotion and reason: The cognitive science of decision making* (G. Weiss, Trans.). New York: Oxford University Press.

Boyd, D. (1992). The moral part of pluralism as the plural part of moral education. In F. C. Power & D. K. Lapsley (Eds.), *The challenge of pluralism: Education, politics, and values* (pp. 141–167). Notre Dame, IN: University of Notre Dame Press.

Brown v. Board of Education, 347 U.S. 483 (1954).

Bucciarelli, M., Khemlani, S., & Johnson-Laird, P. N. (2008). The psychology of moral reasoning. *Judgment and Decision Making, 3*(2), 121–139.

Bull, B. L., & McCarthy, M. M. (1995). Reflections on the knowledge base in law and ethics for educational leaders. *Educational Administration Quarterly, 31*(4), 613–631.

Burns, J. M. (1978). *Leadership.* New York: Harper & Row.

Capper, C. A. (1993). *Educational administration in a pluralistic society.* Albany: State University of New York Press.

Craig, E. (2002). *Philosophy: A brief insight.* New York: Sterling.

Cuban, L. (2001). *How can I fix it? Finding solutions and managing dilemmas: An educator's road map.* New York: Teachers College Press.

Dantley, M. E., & Tillman, L. C. (2006). Social justice and moral transformative leadership. In C. Marshall & M. Oliva (Eds.), *Leadership for social justice: Making revolutions in education.* Boston: Pearson/Allyn & Bacon.

Davis, M. (1991). Thinking like an engineer: The place of a code of ethics in the practice of a profession. *Philosophy and Public Affairs, 20*(2), 150–167. Retrieved August 4, 2009, from http://ethics.iit.edu/codes/Introduction.html.

DeMartino, B., Kumaran, D., Seymor, B., & Dolan, R. (2006). Frames, biases, and rational decision making in the human brain. *Science, 313*, 684–687.

Dexheimer, R. (1970). Administrative ethics: A study in accommodation. In G. L. Immegart & J. M. Burroughs (Eds.), *Ethics and the school administrator* (pp. 27–42). Danville, IL: Interstate.

Dewey, J., & Tufts, J. H. (1908). *Ethics.* New York: Holt.

Diamond, L., & Morlino, L. (2004). The quality of democracy: An overview. *Journal of Democracy, 15*(4), 20–31.

Education for All Handicapped Children Act, Public Law 94-142, 89 Stat. 773 (1975).

English, F., & Papa, R. (2010). *Restoring human agency to educational administration: Status and strategies.* Lancaster, PA: ProActive.

Fenstermaker, W. (1994). The ethical dimension of superintendent decision making: A study of AASA members finds a lack of awareness of association's code of ethics. *The School Administrator, 54*(9), 16–24.

Fenter v. Quinlan Independent School District, Dkt. No. 055-R10-301, (Comm'r Educ. 2002).

Foster, W. (1989). The administrator as a transformative intellectual. *Peabody Journal of Education, 66*(3), 5–18.

Greene, J. D., & Haidt, J. (2002). How (and where) does moral judgment work? *Trends in Cognitive Sciences, 6*, 517–523.

Greenfield, W. D. (1993). Articulating values and ethics in administrator preparation programs. In C. A. Capper (Ed.), *Administration in a pluralistic society* (pp. 267–287). Albany: State University of New York.

Harris, C. E., Jr., Pritchard, M. S., & Rabins, M. J. (1995). *Engineering ethics: Concepts and cases.* Belmont, CA: Wadsworth. Retrieved August 4, 2009, from http://ethics.iit.edu/codes/Introduction.html.

Hodgkinson, C. (1991). *Educational leadership: The moral art.* Albany: State University of New York Press.

Hodgkinson, C. (1996). *Administrative philosophy: Values and motivations in administrative life.* Oxford, UK: Pergamon.

Houston Independent School District v. Ruiz-Garcia, TEA Dkt. No. 125-LH-599, (TEA Indep. Hearing Examiner, 1999).

Interstate School Leaders Licensure Consortium. (1996, 2008). *Standards for school leaders.* Washington, DC: Council of Chief State School Officers. Retrieved August 4, 2009, from http://www.ccsso.org/pdfs/isllcstd.pdf.

Kahan, D. M. (1998). The anatomy of disgust in criminal law. *Michigan Law Review, 96*(6), 1621–1658.

Kant, I. (2009). *Groundwork for the metaphysics of morals.* New York: Harper. (Original work published 1785)

Kirkpatrick, W. H. (1952). The pursuit of moral and spiritual values. *Teachers College Record, 53*(5), 264–264.

Klinker, J. F., Thompson, D., & Blacker, D. (2011). *Professional responsibility for educators and the Texas Educators' Code of Ethics.* Bulverde, TX: Omni.

Krause, J. K., Traini, D. J., & Mickey, B. H. (2005). Equality versus equity. In J. P. Shapiro & J. A. Stefkovich (Eds.), *Ethical leadership and decision making in educa-*

tion: Applying theoretical perspectives to complex dilemmas (pp. 103–119). Mahwah, NJ: Erlbaum.

Ladd, J. (1991). The quest for a code of professional ethics: An intellectual and moral confusion. In D. Johnson (Ed.), *Ethical issues in engineering* (pp. 130–136). Englewood Cliffs, NJ: Prentice-Hall. Retrieved August 4, 2009, from http://ethics.iit.edu/codes/Introduction.html.

Larson, C. L., & Ovando, C. J. (2001). *The color of bureaucracy: The politics of equity in multicultural school communities.* Belmont, CA: Wadsworth.

Leithwood, K., & Duke, D. L. (1999). A century's quest to understand school leadership. In J. Murphy & K. S. Louis (Eds.), *Handbook of research on educational administration,* (pp. 45–72). San Francisco: Jossey-Bass.

Luegenbiehl, H. C. (1983). Codes of ethics and the moral education of engineers. *Business and Professional Ethics Journal 2,* 41–61. Retrieved August 4, 2009, from http://ethics.iit.edu/codes/Introduction.html.

Marshall, C., & Oliva, M. (Eds.). (2006). *Leadership for social justice: Making revolutions in education.* Boston: Pearson/Allyn & Bacon.

McDermott, R. (2004). The feeling of rationality: The meaning of neuroscientific advances for political science. *Perspectives on Politics, 2,* 691–706.

Monin, B., Pizarro, D. A., & Beer, J. S. (2007). Deciding versus reacting: Conceptions of moral judgment and the reason-affect debate. *Review of General Psychology, 11*(2), 99–111.

Neumann, A. (2006). Professing passion: Emotion in the scholarship of professors at research universities. *American Educational Research Journal, 43*(3), 381–424.

Owasso Independent School District No I-011 v. Falvo, 122 S. Ct. 934 (2002).

Perez v. Laredo Independent School District, Dtk. No. 048-R2-1196 (Comm'r Educ. 1996).

Plyler v. Doe, 457 U.S. 202 (1982).

Rawls, J. (1971). *A theory of justice.* Cambridge, MA: Harvard University Press.

Safford Unified School Dist. v. Redding, 129 S. Ct. 2633 (2009).

Shapiro, J. P., & Stefkovich, J. A. (Eds.). (2005). *Ethical leadership and decision making in education: Applying theoretical perspectives to complex dilemmas* (2nd ed.). Mahwah, NJ: Erlbaum.

State Board for Educator Certification v. Slovacek, SOAH Dkt. No. 701-07-0538.EC (SOAH 2006).

State Board for Educator Certification v. Gomes, SOAH Dkt. No. 701-07-0431.EC (SOAH 2008).

Strike, K. A., Haller, E. J., & Soltis, J. F. (1988). *The ethics of school administration.* New York: Teachers College Press.

Theoharis, G. (2009). *The school leaders our children deserve: Seven keys to equity, social justice, and school reform.* New York: Teachers College Press.

Wagner, P. A., & Simpson, D. J. (2009). *Ethical decision making in school administration: Leadership as moral architecture.* Los Angeles: Sage.

Wilson, E. O. (1999). *Consilience: The unity of knowledge.* New York: Vintage Books.

CHAPTER 5

LEADERSHIP FOR SOCIAL JUSTICE

A Matter of Influencing Policy Development

**Jeanne L. Surface, Peter J. Smith,
Kay A. Keiser, and Karen L. Hayes**

We argue that the first consideration in creating policies for social justice is to strengthen the relationship between schools and communities. Furthermore, in training future leaders we must teach our candidates to take active roles that intervene on oppressive power differences and work to create schools that develop everyone's capacity to think, to critique, and to carry out civil discourse about complex debatable issues. Leaders are stewards of the school and community and are engaged in revitalizing both to serve the needs of all children. The knowledge, skills, and dispositions that surround our work provide a framework for the words that follow. Knowledge: From Abstract to Attitudes

What is it about the connection between schools and communities that creates the cornerstone for this argument? Until recently, we had very little knowledge about the importance of local associations to the health and

Educational Leaders Encouraging the Intellectual and Professional Capacity of Others:
A Social Justice Agenda, pages 79–96.
Copyright © 2012 by Information Age Publishing

well-being of democracy. In *Making Democracy Work*, Robert Putnam (1994) discovered that the economy of southern Italy was weak and depressed and at the same time the economy of northern Italy was thriving and prosperous. The northern and southern region had the same political regimes, cultural heritage, language, and religion. What was different? Northern Italy had grassroots participation in the public square and economic arena. Putnam measured the effectiveness of regional governments in northern Italy. What he found to predict a good and responsive government in Italian regions included local associations, soccer clubs, cooperatives, and even things such as choral societies. Dense networks of civic associations and an active culture of civic engagement characterized some regions, whereas others were characterized by oppressive relationships. He found that regions that have stable cabinets, adopt their budgets on time, spend their appropriations as planned, and pioneer new legislations are, for the most part, the same regions that provide day care centers and family clinics, develop comprehensive urban planning, make loans to farmers, and answer their mail promptly. He concluded that economics does not predict civics, but civics does predict economics, better than economics itself.

Putnam followed up his study of Italy with a study of the American community. *Bowling Alone*, written in 2000, chronicles the collapse and revival of the American community. He indicates that something happened to the social bonds and civic engagement in America over the last third of the 20th century. During the first part of the century, Americans took a more active role in the social and political life of their communities in churches, clubs, unions, and bowling alleys. They served on committees and gave generously to charities. Then, suddenly we began to do all of those things less often. What social bonds we do have are one shot, special purpose, and serve our own self-interest rather than the common good. Unfortunately, we are withdrawing from those networks of reciprocity that once constituted our communities. Though unfortunate, this loss is not something that is a result of modern-day changes.

Unfortunately, the constitutional arguments may be at the root of this unintentional loss of community within our country. Madison believed that the role of government ought to be that of an arbitrator who creates and implements policies that keep citizens apart (Theobald, 2009). Regrettably, the focus of the constitutional convention ended up being more about controlling the voice of the people rather than facilitating it. Without much say in the governance, individuals pursued their own private ends, and the structure of government would balance those pursuits so cleverly that the highest good would emerge without anyone having to will its existence (Kemmis, 1990). In 1776, Adam Smith published the *Wealth of Nations*, in which he argued that an "invisible hand" directed the economy and individuals pursued their own economic ends. Smith's book prized individualism and unfortunately placed the obligation of being a good neighbor and community member far into the background. Because his view was highly influential at the time, our government is based on the rights of the individual, an economy based on accumulation and education that forces students to be machines of the economy.

Over time, the effect of a government that embraced Smith's view clearly set individuals apart and educationally created workers to serve the economy. The long-term results have created an environment that is absent of social justice. Giroux (2004) describes neoliberalism as a concept suggesting that the market should be the organizing principle behind all social, political, and economic decisions. Proponents of neoliberalism are "most concerned with dismantling the segments of the public sector that serve the social and democratic needs of the non-affluent majority of the American populace" (p. 82). Neoliberal institutions are most interested in policies that guarantee the reduction of labor costs, while at the same time limiting expenditures on social programs (Hyslop-Margison & Sears, 2006).

In the development of the neoliberal ideology, education is often reduced to making sure that students possess isolated skills with little regard to the whole person; "education that encourages the meaningful political participation of citizens in public policy decisions, also came under attack" (Hyslop-Margison & Sears, 2006, p. 2). The role of education becomes a means to ensure that business and industry are provided with the necessary human capital. This is apparent in initiatives whose main focus is that of job skills rather than democratic principles. Education policy is being shaped by outspoken criticism of public schools and claims by politicians and others that the public schools are hurting America's chances at maintaining global military and economic power (Spring, 2005). The 1983 document *A Nation at Risk: The Imperative for Education Reform* (National Commission on Excellence in Education, 1983) emphasized that the imperative for education reform must be tied to an education policy that focuses on economic competition, and provided a doomsday forecast of America's global economic power if the school system was not changed. Additionally, increasing educational attainment may do little to change the distribution of income unless the nature of the jobs themselves changes (Barry, 2005). Since 1980, the wage rates paid for lower-skilled workers have been declining, while at the same time the workers in these positions, on average, possess higher education levels.

Public education has not escaped the grips of neoliberalism in the calls for unquestioned faith in competition and accountability, and the demand that teachers and schools be held directly responsible for student success through continual growth of standardized testing (Hyslop-Margison & Sears, 2006). As a result of our obsession with capitalism and developing the economic elite, the United States ranks 18th among industrialized nations in the gap between rich and poor children (Giroux, 2004; Harvey, 2005). Can we close the achievement gap?

> Not if we insist on a mechanistic system that allows federal administrators to judge whether schools are successful or failing simply by examining data reports from annual tests. Not if we redefine the achievement gap as the differences in the rates at which racial minorities and lower-class students approach politically manipulated definitions of proficiency. And not if the purpose of these tests is to assess whether schools are reaching an impossible goal—equalizing achievement between children of different social classes while we fail to reform the economic and social institutions that ensure unequal achievement, on average, for children of different social classes. (Rothstein, 2004, p. 94)

In education, we must consider students as vital participants in society rather than victims who will be manipulated by the economic system. Only in this endeavor will we be able to implement changes that truly reduce inequality and eliminate exclusion (Touraine, 2001). Bull (2008) sees schools as one of the vehicles required to ensure a society that values politically significant personal liberties. We should:

> Conduct public schools in a way that allows children to develop both their own persons—that is, to come to hold personally meaningful conceptions of the good and to acquire the reasonable capacities to pursue them—and as responsible members of their families and communities who respect and support others' politically significant personal liberties and the other political commitments of their society. (p. 25)

Decisions related to social justice must be made within the framework of policies, practices, and political structures existing in schools and districts, and within the context of the public values and policy agendas that impact the education process from the society and community at large. Much of the debate on educational issues focuses on the four competing values of equity, efficiency, choice, and excellence (Sergiovanni, Kelleher, McCarthy, & Fowler, 2009). These values are in a constant state of tension, and the assignment of school effort and resources to one of these values may cause a lack of emphasis on another.

The value of equity is uniquely related to social justice in that it corresponds to the general societal value of fair play and equal opportunity. With No Child Left Behind (2002) legislation and increased local and state accountability efforts, equity may suffer at the hands of excellence. Financial resources and autonomy are intended to motivate schools to strive for excellence. However, it is often the high-achieving schools that receive these rewards, while low-performing schools lose their autonomy, are forced to endure public shame and ridicule, and may eventually be labeled as failing in which they lose much-needed resources. An effort to increase efficiency can cause a decrease in excellence and equity. Attempts to improve efficiency may even backfire. Even though standardized curriculum, testing, and teaching may be an efficient way to approach basic student achievement, they are less effective when considering higher-level student achievement (Elmore, 1995). Does excellence conflict with efficiency? If excellence is measured by standardized tests, perhaps there is no conflict, but excellence related to learning that cannot be measured by standardized tests might cause one to reconsider the purpose of education in general and more specifically what it means to be high performing. Hargreaves and Shirley (2007) looked at a "post-standardization" view of excellence when analyzing schools in Finland, where they found little focus on standardized tests, but high-performing students.

The value of choice in public education may also impact the concept of social justice. The increase of choice may be one measure of the attempts to privatize education, especially in the United States, where there has been consistent growth in the notions of accountability and competition (Hyslop-Margison & Sears, 2006). There is ongoing tension between market choice and democratic choice. While market choice may be more efficient with an overarching factor of self-interest, democratic choice is much more complex, with advocates stressing that some issues are too important to be left to the beliefs in the free market system (Sergiovanni et al., 2009).

Leadership for social justice concentrates on the policies and practices that shape schools and at the same time questions those procedures that perpetuate social inequalities based on race, gender, socioeconomic status, and other factors that define differences. Moral transformative leadership is concerned with the use and misuse of power, and must focus on the identification of leadership practices that perpetuate inequities that exist within the learning community (Marshall & Oliva, 2010).

> Leaders cannot make social justice happen by their passion and will alone. The huge shifts in cultural understandings and societal and school expectations will happen only with the shared values, coalitions, networking, and mutual support that come with the power of engaging groups of people in social movement, which result in the building of social capital and, eventually, political power. (Marshall & Oliva, 2010, p. 14)

Marshall and Oliva (2006) stress that the mission to strive for a more equitable and socially just society begins with educational leadership. Moral, transformative leaders must keep the process of teaching, leading, and research aimed at keeping the social justice movement in the forefront. When school leaders complete their formal preparation programs, they must know how to increase student achievement, how to raise social justice awareness among students and staff, and how to create heterogeneous learning communities for students and staff (McKenzie et al., 2008).

DISPOSITIONS: FROM ATTITUDES TO ADVOCACY

A foundation built on the knowledge of how policy shapes education and how educators shape policy is imperative, but a personal relationship must be made for these concepts to be authentic. Goodman (2001) categorizes support for social justice into self-interest, moral principles, and empathy, all of which are sustained by a connection to self. In addition to knowledge, placing oneself within culture and establishing a role in advancing social justice requires positive diversity dispositions. Dispositions, "the values, commitments, and professional ethics that influence behavior" (National Council for Accreditation of Teacher Education [NCATE], 2002, p. 53), form the basis of what a school leader can bring to the critical and creative tasks of educational administration. These are built over a lifetime, and can be more difficult to teach and assess than knowledge or skills (Edick, Danielson, & Edwards, 2005; Edwards & Edick, 2006). Development of positive dispositions must be vigorously and intentionally addressed by school leadership preparation programs, because administrators who have not developed positive dispositions have trouble being leaders of effective schools (Davis, 1998; Hallinger & Heck, 1996; Heifetz, 2006).

The process of addressing diversity dispositions begins with sociocultural consciousness, or "the awareness that a person's worldview is not universal, but is profoundly influenced by life experiences" (Villegas & Lucas, 2007, p. 31). Educators without this awareness rely too much on their own experience and mental models, and may misinterpret the communication and behaviors of others (Senge, Cambron-McCabe, Lucas, Smith, & Kleiner, 2000). Those who see themselves as monocultural Americans are more likely to perpetuate misconceptions and stereotypes (Dantas, 2007). Yet awareness of positive dispositions—and the savvy to utilize them for social justice—is not only important for administrators to work well with their communities, it is also critical for school leaders as they grapple with the realities of inequalities, conflict, and self-interest sometimes embedded in school, state, and national policy (Bull, 2008).

Sociocultural consciousness may be raised through studying the propositions of culturally relevant teaching: conception of self and others, social relations, and conceptions of knowledge (Ladson-Billings, 1995). These are appropriate concepts as entry points for growth in educational administration graduate students as they view their dispositions from current teaching roles. Understanding the challenges of the demographic divide between an increasingly diverse student population and a much less diverse teaching staff, being inclusive for students and families with exceptional needs, and creating curriculum and assessments that meet both the security of standards and the need for innovation hinges upon the emotional intelligence to be self-aware (Banks et al., 2005). As Parker and Shapiro (1992) state:

> More attention needs to be given to future school and district leaders'…ability to support the education of all children. Opportunities must be provided for leaders to examine and reflect on the meaning of their cultural background, their skin color, and their belief systems as well as the relationship between these attributes and their personal and professional practice. (pp. 387, 388)

For future school leaders, it may be more proactive to move beyond cultural responsiveness to embracing an attitude of cultural proficiency. Those who are culturally proficient "welcome and create opportunities to better understand who they are as individuals, while learning how to interact positively with people who differ from themselves" (Robins, Lindsey, Lindsey, & Terrell, 2006, pp. 4–5). The core values of cultural proficiency are:

1. Culture is a predominant force; you cannot NOT be influenced by culture.
2. People are served in varying degrees by the dominant culture.
3. People have group identities that they want to have acknowledged.
4. Cultures are not homogeneous; there is diversity within groups.
5. The unique needs of every culture must be respected. (Robins et al., 2006)

The number of resources that address teaching social justice in leadership preparation programs is somewhat small (Hafner, 2006), but adoption of a comprehensive framework such as cultural proficiency assists educational administration faculty in infusing social justice across the curriculum in an intentional, developmental manner in order to promote measurable growth.

Success can be found in insights from candidates' comments, in increased depth of reflection, and in a climate of shared vision and commitment, but regular, reliable data needs to supplement the good-feeling feedback. A collection of qualitative data revealed that many of our students are very passionate about social justice. Through the eyes of Jonny, a doctoral candidate, social justice is an issue that needs to be addressed at levels in the educational process, from Pre-K to graduate. "The earliest possible training of humanity with regard to the importance of development of a social conscience that is considerate of all human beings and other living creatures of nature will best prepare our society, locally and globally, for a life in which we can all live among each other in peace." Joel, another doctoral candidate, offered a couple of reflections about social justice: "Do we look at ourselves before we point the finger at others to make a difference?" and "Do we really need more policies or permission to do the right thing?"

Fran, a doctoral candidate, stated that "social justice is a way of living. It cannot be easily defined as that would confine it as more simplistic than its existence. Acting in accordance with social justice means acting with integrity: doing what is right even when no one is looking. It refers to righting the wrongs you know and see through implementation of policies and setting positive examples." Social justice, according to doctoral candidate Janice, "is a moral responsibility of all educators."

Master's candidate Glenn purported that "social justice is about assuming responsibility and accountability for those to advocate for others who cannot advocate for themselves. It's about advocacy and speaking out about inequality that exists in all social aspects of life." He also indicates that "school leaders impact social justice by way of being the voice of the masses they teach, lead, and work for in the community." Jason, a master's candidate, also emphasizes the role that school leaders play in impacting policy that affects social justice, "by developing an environment of awareness and tolerance of differences, school leaders provide positive culture that encourages social justice." Michelle, another master's candidate, offered a warning that "social justice can be impacted negatively if policies are implemented that make all culture conform to the *American way*. This disallows people to practice their traditions and beliefs. Government laws/policies and education policies can impact social justice." Karla, a master's candidate, expresses that "school leaders can impact policy that affects social justice by making sure that they continuously make efforts to speak out against the injustices that occur to the members of their school community. They need to be the voice of those whose voices have been silenced by society." Master's candidate Jay expressed the significant power that school leaders have in impacting policy: "Every decision made by a leader that impacts students, faculty, or the school can be attributed to social justice. When administrators make a discipline decision, they will be looked at and judged by others if their decision is one that is fair. Unfortunately, people need to remember that an equitable treatment does not always come from an equal treatment." We realize that our candidates offer a window where we can look to examine the quality of our programs. We informally assess the attitudes and dispositions during each class session by carefully listening and examining attitudes with class and small group discussions.

We formally assess using focus groups that gather qualitative data from candidates and use valid statistical instruments that measure the development of candidate dispositions and program impact have been developed. Candidates in the University of Nebraska at Omaha educational leadership program are made aware of administrative dispositions by assessing themselves on the Administrator Dispositions Index (ADI). As they progress through their courses, dispositions are directly and indirectly addressed. The ADI is again completed at the midpoint and capstone of the program so that candidates can reflect upon their needs and strengths. The ADI, which was developed by aligning with the Interstate School Leaders Licensure Consortium (ISLLC) Standards, is a 36-item survey that contains a 19-item community-centered subscale and a 17-item student-centered subscale (Schulte & Kowal, 2005).

Annually, faculty has analyzed the ADI and other portfolio results to provide information for program improvement. Yet when trying to understand and explain the beliefs and values of candidates, expressed views could have a tendency to be self-serving. People explain their actions as espoused theories, but their theories-in-use (actual patterns of actions) can only be measured through observation (Argyris & Schön, 1996). Espoused theories, such as those gathered through the ADI and Diversity Dispositions Index (DDI), need to be examined within actual practice (Kane, Sandretto, & Heath, 2002). The EDAD Follow-Up Survey (FUS) was therefore created so that supervisors of practicum candidates could assess candidates' readiness to be school leaders (Smith, 2008). After administering the FUS, it was found that the supervisors ranked candidates as high or higher in professional dispositions (Keiser, 2007; Keiser & Smith, 2009).

As a next step, the DDI was developed and validated to provide a psychometrically sound "self-assessment instrument in graduate teacher education and educational administration programs to help candidates become more aware of and develop the dispositions necessary to be effective educators with students from diverse backgrounds" (Schulte, Edwards, & Edick, 2009, para. 11). It is utilized to measure change during specific courses by administering it during the first and last course meetings.

The educational administrative candidates overwhelmingly espouse positive diversity dispositions on the DDI, with most answering "agree" or "strongly agree." While almost every item shows growth after participating in a course with direct instruction and active learning about culture and community, *educators' beliefs and attitudes about students and teaching/learning* starts at such a high level that there was little room for improvement from pretest to posttest. *Educators' skills in helping students gain knowledge* have slightly significant growth over time. The increase in *educators' connections to the community* is statistically significant. It demonstrates candidate growth in community-based dispositions, but scores consistently lower than the other two factors (Keiser, 2009).

Connecting to the community continues to be the area that candidates show least confidence in possessing throughout the program (Keiser, 2009; Keiser & Smith 2009; Schulte & Kowal, 2005; Smith, 2008). If candidates espouse very positive beliefs and skills in diversity dispositions, then why do they not feel as though they act in a way that connects them to the community?

A disconnect between beliefs and actions—or attitudes and advocacy—can be described as the "knowing–doing gap" (Pfeffer & Sutton, 2000). This gap can occur when individuals or organizations substitute talking for action, fall back on traditions, fear change, focus intensely on short-term measurements, or rely on internal competition. To varying degrees, all of these can be common barriers to active involvement for social justice policy in education. Jeffrey Pfeffer and Robert Sutton (2000) suggest that when uncovering a knowing–doing gap, it was "clear that knowing what to do was not enough. It was clear that being smart was not enough to turn knowledge into practice. It was evident that reading, listening to, thinking, and writing smart things were not enough" (p. ix). The gap that remains was troublesome and discovering how to close the gap was an additional challenge.

Theoretical knowledge is not sufficient to change teachers' sociocultural assumptions (Dantas, 2007). Therefore, it becomes the role of the university instructor to supply opportunities for candidates to actively confront these barriers. Reflection and discussion enhances adult learners' multidimensional consciousness (Grossman, 2009; Scheckley & Bell, 2006; Villegas & Lucas, 2007), and requires them to grapple with the mutuality, solidarity, and diversity of their experience based on their learning. "The ideal end result of transformational learning is that one is empowered by learning to be more socially responsible, self-directed, and less dependent on false assumptions" (Kiely, 2005, p. 7). To move from being believers in social justice policy to advocates who can effect outcomes, candidates must practice demonstrating positive dispositions to be autonomous individuals, progressing in *efficacy* from external to internal locus of control; in *flexibility* from narrow, egocentric views to broader alternative perspectives; in *craftsmanship* from vagueness and imprecision to specificity and elegance; in *consciousness* from lack of awareness to awareness of self and others; and in *interdependence* from isolation and separateness to connection to and concern for the community (Costa & Garmstron, 1994; Lindsey, Martinez, & Lindsey, 2007).

The Elements of Social Justice Education Practice (Adams, Bell, & Griffin, 1997) provide a good framework to address the development of diversity dispositions for advocacy. These elements create an intentional sociocultural environment for active learning. They include:

1. Balance the emotional and cognitive components of the learning process.
2. Acknowledge and support the personal (the individual student's experience) while illuminating the systemic (the interactions among social groups).
3. Attend to social relations within the classroom.

4. Utilize reflection and experience as tools for student-centered learning.
5. Value awareness, personal growth, and change as outcomes of the learning process.

As awareness and personal growth blend together and candidates reframe their actions through a sociocultural lens, speaking and acting courageously for equal opportunities for all replaces a "victim of policy" attitude. "Advocating for social justice is about *our* moral centeredness to do what is in the best educational interest of our students. Advocating for social justice isn't about what *others* do and don't do" (Lindsey, Graham, Westphal, & Jew, 2008, p. 188). Ultimately, by preparing candidates for leadership to be advocates for social justice, positive beliefs can become proactive endeavors for schools today and society tomorrow.

DISPOSITIONS: FROM ADVOCACY TO ACTION

There is an old story of three frogs that were sitting on a log. One decided to jump off. How many remained? Mathematically, the answer is "two," but usually that is not correct—for most situations the actual outcome is, "three." There is a distinct gap between what we decide to do and actually jumping into action. As Adolph Monod said, "Between the great things we cannot do and the small things we will not do, the danger is that we shall do nothing." It takes the building of skill and craftsmanship to jump into action (Costa & Garmston, 1994). This building of capacity is necessary for school leaders to change the system by engaging others in trilevel reforms at the school/community, regional, and state levels (Fullan, 2005).

What do leaders need to do in order to intervene on oppressive power differences? The Department of Educational Administration at the University of Nebraska at Omaha is dedicated to providing the best program that we possibly can. Our mission is to develop effective visionary, intellectual, moral leaders who can cause positive change in education. Educational leaders for social justice typically have a philosophical and dispositional orientation for all students' needs, particularly those groups of students who have been traditionally marginalized. These leaders understand that there is no social justice without providing the opportunities for all students to succeed. This is our moral obligation. Educational justice remains the most significant civil right that has not been provided to all American students and families. It is essential that social justice permeates throughout our programming; all candidates must recognize the fundamental right of all United States citizens to a free and proper education. It is also essential to recognize that our entire society is at risk if a significant group of Americans remains consistently undereducated.

Despite the prolonged struggles over school desegregation, racial segregation, and educational inequality, problems still persist in American public schools. In fact, the segregation of African American and Latino students has actually increased, especially in the nation's urban centers. The percentage of black students attending majority nonwhite schools increased from 66% in 1991 to 73% in 2003–2004. In general, schools in economically depressed, racially segregated communities are almost always unequal schools, characterized by low teacher morale, strained relationships between teachers and administrators, defiant and oppositional behavior from students, an inordinate number of inexperienced teachers, and high turnover in administrative leadership (National Alliance of Black School Educators [NASBE], 2008).

We believe that affecting the policy context is critical to achieving our purpose. This belief is based on the National Staff Development Council's (NSDC) assumption that good policy promotes good practice. We all have witnessed the power of policy in education. The NASBE has declared, "Education is a Civil Right," and insists that this country establish a zero-tolerance policy on illiteracy, dropout, and failure. The basis for this initiative is based on *legal rationale* and the fact that many people in communities across the country consistently identify public education as one of their primary concerns and yet, there are few community-based organizations attempting to mobilize members of the community to work toward improving student achievement at the local level.

The primary focus of NABSE's (2008) *Education is a Civil Right initiative* is to raise awareness and mobilize the public, and especially members of the community, to more actively advocate for strategies that will result in improved academic achievement for all students. The Education is a Civil Right initiative aims to:

- Foster and develop through dialogue, workshops, political and civil action, and other appropriate means, an awareness of the consequences of educational underachievement in every corner of society.
- Initiate activities that will directly address the educational disparities and inequities faced by students and families of color, and bring about intended and measurable improvements in our public school systems.
- Develop the talents, skills, and leadership within our communities that can use its collective expertise and knowledge to continuously monitor, review, and affect needed changes relative to the educational civil rights of the students and families in all parts of our society. To provide strategies and activities for use in school districts serving a significant population of students of color.

The problems that bring about the void of social justice must be addressed. Because of the influence of Adam Smith, our government is based on the rights of the individual, an economy based on accumulation, and an education that creates workers for the economic machine; we must bring together our families in communities to improve the conditions of our country, our communities, and our schools. Our children need to live in cohesive, child-centered communities that are rich in social capital where all community members are cared for and can develop a sense of hope, a sense of purpose, and a sense of future. Communities working together can combat oppressive power differences.

The social fabric of community is formed from an expanding shared sense of belonging. It is shaped by the notion that only when we are connected and care for the well-being of the whole that a civil and democratic society will be created (Block, 2009). In order to change the circumstances before us, educational leaders must be equipped to transform the isolation and self-interest within our communities into connectedness and caring for the whole. The leadership must first have the attitude that they can impact this change and they must be hands-on and deeply engaged in life in the communities in which they serve. As school leaders, we simply cannot afford to view the school as the extent of the community. Certainly, community life exists beyond the walls of a building. While it seems a hopeless task in this age of accountability, staying within the walls of the school simply advances more isolation and makes social justice an impossible goal to reach.

We need to train educational leaders to be community builders. We can begin by bringing together all of the parallel efforts that exist within the world. Churches, law enforcement, businesses, social service organizations, and government are all doing their own good work but they are separated into silos that never really touch each other. This is a tall order under our current circumstances. It is the dividedness that makes it so difficult to create a different future. Intradependence can exist and communities offer the promise of belonging.

Leaders must be prepared to find gifts within the problems. In order to have a more cohesive community we must be willing to trade the problems that exist for the possibilities that are inherent. Our leaders need to be prepared to help build connectedness among and between the organizations that exist. Large established systems are important but not necessary to community transformation. Leadership can energize citizens and a shift in thinking and actions of citizens is more vital than a shift in the thinking and actions of institutions and formal leaders. Most importantly, the small group is a unit of transformation and the transformation is linguistic in nature. The shift in conversation is from one of problems, fear, and retribution to one of possibility, generosity, and restoration.

Leadership must work with the community to create a new community context. Many communities are paralyzed by fear, assigning fault, and the worship of self-interest. In the corporate model, the economy is the center of the story and the media maintains the status quo. We need to help communities shape the media in positive ways and understand its damaging effect on community life. As leaders we must model and help citizens be willing to own up to their own contributions and help them to create an alternative future within the community. The conversation needs to surround the idea that we can either focus on a problem to be solved or a possibility to create. Citizens become powerful when they choose to shift the context within which they act in the world (Block, 2009).

Projection is an act of attributing qualities to others that we deny within ourselves. It is expressed in the way we label others and then build diagnostic categories and whole professions around labeling. Once we move away from projection and labeling, we can begin to hold ourselves accountable for the well-being of the larger community and choose to own and exercise power rather than defer and delegate it to others. If we do not, our projection places accountability for making a better future onto others and allows us to escape accountability. This is the payoff for stereotyping and prejudice and it removes the pressure from us. We project onto the stranger, the wounded, and the enemy, those aspects of our self that are too much to own, in communities where there is poverty, for instance. We focus on their needs and deficiencies, and we think their poverty is central to who they are. We view them as charity or pity and wring our hands at the plight. In order to build our communities, we must drop the labeling and look for the gifts that exist within each person and give them a voice.

A possibility for an alternative future can be created in communities where citizens fully develop the capacity to be a citizen. Unfortunately, the view of citizenship is often limited to the responsibility of voting. The right to vote does not guarantee a civil society (Zakaria, 2007). According to Block (2009), in order to create communities where citizens take back their power, we need to modify our thinking about who is in charge and where power resides. We need to invert our accepted wisdom about what is cause and what is effect. By examining our thinking we develop the capacity to confront our entitlement and dependency. Changing the future then begs the question, "have we chosen the present or has it been handed to us" (Block, 2009, p. 66)?

A powerless community would believe that the past creates the future and that change in individuals causes change in organizations and community, and that people in power create people in a subordinate position. This is all true, but when citizenship moves beyond voting, individuals become aware that they are the creators of their world as well as the products of it. Even more, as long as we see leaders to blame, our communities will be comprised of apathetic, entitled citizens. The pressure on the leadership is a weight that is far too heavy and citizens focus on protecting themselves, which plants the seeds of entitlement. The cost of entitlement is that it is an escape from accountability and soft on commitment. The weakness in the dominant view of accountability is that it thinks that people can be held accountable. While it sells easily, it is a delusion to think that retribution, incentives, legislation, new standards, and tough consequences will cause accountability. Furthermore, this delusion is what creates entitlement and drives us apart. Frighteningly, every autocratic regime rises to power by turning citizens against each other (Block, 2009). "Accountability is the willingness to care for the wellbeing of the whole; commitment is the willingness to make a promise with no expectation of return. The cost of constantly reacting to the choices of others is increased cynicism and helplessness. The ultimate cost of cynicism and helplessness is that we resort to the use of force" (Block, 2009, p. 71).

If a community is to be transformed, the citizenship must shift from a place of fault and fear, oversight and law, systems and corporation, and leadership centered to one of abundance, generosity, gifts, social fabric and chosen accountability, associational life, and the engagement of citizens. Shifts will finally occur when citizens face each other in conversations of ownership and possibility. In order to be successful at this important task, leaders need to change the context within which people gather, name the debate through powerful questions, and listen rather than advocate, defend, or provide answers. Finally, commitment will happen and entitlement and barter will fade (Block, 2009).

Changing communities means understanding our flawed view of change. We cannot count on the aggregation of individual changes to move a community. We must provide a structure of belonging that produces the foundation for the entire system to move. As leaders we must realize that we do not drive change, we must create the structures and experiences that bring citizens together to identify and solve their own issues. Changing communities is about gathering, letting the right questions evolve, and going slow with fewer numbers of people.

Finally, creating a future is different than defining a future. Traditional modes of problem solving will not work with human systems. The image of the future can only be developed with engagement and involvement of citizens. Truly, an alternative future can be built when citizens invest and are willing to pay the economic and emotional price that creating something really requires. This is an organic and relational process, and creates a sense of belonging. If we are to create policies for social justice we must strengthen our communities and the relationship between our schools and communities. Oppressive power differences simply will not be resolved by any other means.

REFERENCES

Adams, M., Bell, J. A., & Griffin, P. (1997). *Teaching for diversity and social justice*. New York: Routledge.

Argyris, C., & Schön, D. A. (1996). *Organizational learning II: Theory, method, and practice*. Reading, MA: Addison-Wesley.

Banks, J., Cochran-Smith, M., Moll, L., Richert, A., Zeichner, K., LePage, P., et al. (2005). Teaching diverse learners. In L. Darling-Hammond & J. Bransford (Eds.), *Preparing teachers for a changing world: What teachers should learn and be able to do* (pp. 232–275). San Francisco: Jossey-Bass.

Barry, B. (2005). *Why societal justice matters*. Malden, MA: Polity Press.

Block, P. (2009). *Community: The structure of belonging*. San Francisco: Barrett-Koehler.

Bull, B. L. (2008). *Social justice in education: An introduction*. New York: Palgrave Macmillan.

Costa, A. L., & Garmston, R. J. (1994). *Cognitive coaching: A foundation for Renaissance Schools*. Norwood, MA: Christopher-Gordon.

Dantas, M. L. (2007). Building teacher competency to work with diverse learners in the context of international education. *Teacher Education Quarterly, 34*(1), 75–91.

Davis, S. H. (1998). Why do principals get fired? *Principal, 78*(2), 34–39.

Edick, N., Danielson, L., & Edwards, S. (2005). Dispositions: Defining, aligning, and assessing. *Academic Leadership, 4*(4).

Edwards, S., & Edick, N., (2006). Dispositions matter: Findings for at-risk teacher candidates. *The Teacher Educator, 42*(1), 1–13.

Elmore, R. (1995). Structural reform and educational practice. *Educational Researcher, 24*(9), 23–26.

Fullan, M. (2005) *Leadership and sustainability: Systems thinkers in action*. Thousand Oaks, CA: Corwin Press.

Giroux, H. A. (2004). *The terror of neoliberalism: Authoritarianism and the eclipse of democracy*. Boulder, CO: Paradigm.

Goodman, D. J. (2001). *Promoting diversity and social justice: Educating people from privileged groups*. Thousand Oaks, CA: Sage.

Grossman, R. (2009). Structures for facilitating student reflection. *College Teaching, 57*(1), 15–22.

Hafner, M. M. (2006). Teaching strategies for developing leaders of social justice. In C. Marshall & M. Oliva (Eds.), *Leadership for social justice: Making revolutions in education* (pp. 167–193). Boston: Pearson.

Hallinger, P., & Heck. R. H. (1996). Reassessing the principal's role in school effectiveness: A review of empirical research, 1980–1995. *Educational Administration Quarterly, 32*(1), 5–44.

Hargreaves, A., & Shirley, D. (2007, December 17). The coming age of post-standardization. *Education Week*. Retrieved November 6, 2009, from http://www.edweek.org/ew/articles/2007/12/21/17hargreaves_web.h27.html

Harvey, D. (2005). *A brief history of neoliberalism*. New York: Oxford University Press.

Heifetz, R. A. (2006). Educational leadership: Beyond a focus on instruction. *Phi Delta Kappan, 87*(7), 512–513.

Hyslop-Margison, E. J., & Sears, A. M. (2006). *Neo-liberalism, globalization and human capital learning: Reclaiming education for democratic citizenship.* Dordrecht, The Netherlands: Springer.

Kane, R., Sandretto, S., & Heath, C. (2002). Telling half the story: A critical review of research on the teaching beliefs and practices of university academics. *Review of Educational Research, 72*(2), 177–228.

Keiser, K. A. (2007). *Between theory and practice: Student teachers' espoused and observed dispositions.* Proceedings from the 6th Annual Symposium on Educator Dispositions.

Keiser, K. A. (2009). Educational administration candidates' diversity dispositions: The effect of cultural proficiency and service learning. *Educational Leadership and Administration: Teaching and Program Development, 21*(1).

Keiser, K. A., & Smith, P. J. (2009). Walking the talk: Educational administration candidates' espoused and observed professional dispositions. *International Journal of Educational Leadership Preparation, 4*(3).

Kemmis, D. (1990). *Community and the Politics of Place.* Norman: University of Oklahoma Press.

Kiely, R. (2005). A transformative learning model for service learning: A longitudinal case study. *Michigan Journal of Community Service Learning, 12*(1), 5–22.

Ladson-Billings, G. (1995). But that's just good teaching! The case for culturally relevant pedagogy. *Theory into Practice, 34*(3), 159–165.

Lindsey, R. B., Graham, S. M., Westphal, R. C., & Jew, C. L. (2008). *Culturally proficient inquiry: A lens for identifying and examining educational gaps.* Thousand Oaks, CA: Corwin Press.

Marshall, C., & Oliva, M. (2006). *Leadership for social justice: Making revolutions in education.* Boston: Pearson Education.

Marshall, C., & Oliva, M. (2010). *Leadership for social justice: Making revolutions in education.* (2nd ed.). Boston: Pearson Education.

McKenzie, K. B., Christman, D. E., Hernandez, F., Fierro, E., Capper C. A., Dantly, M., et al. (2008). From the field: A proposal for education leaders for social justice. *Educational Administration Quarterly, 44*(1), 111–138.

National Alliance of Black School Educators. (2008). *Education is a civil rights toolkit.* Washington, DC: Author. Retrieved October 26, 2009, from http://www.nabse.org.

National Commission on Excellence in Education. (1983). *A nation at risk: The imperative for educational reform: A report to the Nation and the Secretary of Education, United States Department of Education.* Washington, DC: Author.

National Council for Accreditation of Teacher Education. (2002). *Professional standards the accreditation of schools, colleges, and departments of education.* Washington, DC: Author.

National Staff Development Council. (2008). *Education Advocacy Toolkit.* Oxford, OH: Retrieved October 26, 2009, from http://www.nsdc.org.

No Child Left Behind. H.R. 1 U.S.C. § 107-110 (2001).

Parker, L., & Shapiro, J. P. (1992). Where is the discussion of diversity in educational administration programs? Graduate student's voices addressing an omission in their preparation. *Journal of School Leadership, 2*(1), 7–33.

Pfeffer, J., & Sutton, R. J. (2000). *The knowing-doing gap.* Boston: Harvard Business Press.

Putnam, R. D. (2000). *Bowling Alone: The collapse and revival of American community.* New York: Simon & Schuster.

Robins, K. N., Lindsey, R. B., Lindsey, D. B., & Terrell, R. D. (2006). *Culturally proficient instruction: A guide for people who teach.* (2nd ed.). Thousand Oaks, CA: Corwin Press.

Rothstein, R. (2004). *Class and schools: Using social, economic, and educational reform to close the black–white achievement gap.* New York: Teachers College Press.

Senge, P., Cambron-McCabe, N., Lucas, T., Smith, B., & Kleiner, A. (2000). *Schools that learn: A fifth discipline fieldbook for educators, parents, and everyone who cares about education.* New York: Doubleday.

Sergiovanni, T. J., Kelleher, P., McCarthy, M. M., & Fowler, F. C. (2009). *Educational governance and administration* (6th ed.). Boston: Pearson Education.

Scheckley, B. G., & Bell, S. (2006). Experience, consciousness, and learning: Implications for instruction. *New Directions for Adult and Continuing Education, 110,* 43–52.

Schulte, L., Edwards, S., & Edick, N. (2009). The development and validation of the Diversity Dispositions Index. *AASA Journal of Scholarship and Practice.*

Schulte, L. E., & Kowal, P. (2005). The validation of the Administrator Dispositions Index. *Educational Leadership and Administration: Teaching and Program Development, 17,* 75–87.

Smith, P. J. (2008). *Nebraska Department of Education Mini-Folio Advanced Level: Principal K–6 and 7–12.* Report to the University of Nebraska at Omaha College of Education Assessment Committee.

Spring, J. (2005). *Conflict of interest: The politics of American education* (5th ed.). Boston: McGraw-Hill.

Theobald, P. G. (2009). *Education now: How rethinking America's past can change its future.* Boulder, CO: Paradigm.

Touraine, A. (2001). *Beyond neoliberalism.* Malden, MA: Blackwell.

Villegas, A. M., & Lucas, T. (2007). The culturally responsive teacher. *Educational Leadership, 64*(6), 28–33.

Zakaria, F. (2007). *The future of freedom: Illiberal democracy at home and abroad.* New York: W. W. Norton.

PART II

**BUILDING SOCIAL JUSTICE:
INTELLECTUAL AND PROFESSIONAL CAPITAL**

CHAPTER 6

TEACHER INDUCTION

A Process for Advancing Social Justice

Maria B. Roberts and Anita Pankake

INTRODUCTION

The Bill of Rights in the U.S. Constitution guarantees all U.S. citizens fair and equal opportunities to succeed in addition to protecting certain inalienable rights. The No Child Left Behind Act (NCLB) of 2001 is federal legislation developed to set standards for the performance of U.S. schools in an effort to ensure that all students are being provided high-quality learning opportunities. Lawmakers developed this legislation to improve and reform the educational system to benefit all students in response to a perceived unevenness in teaching and learning, evidenced by the low performance of minority students (Noguera, 2004). Specific groups targeted to be addressed by the legislation were African Americans, Hispanics, those who are economically disadvantaged, students in special education services, and English language learners. The mandate requires 100% of the students in all public schools to be proficient in math and reading by the 2013–2014

Educational Leaders Encouraging the Intellectual and Professional Capacity of Others:
A Social Justice Agenda, pages 99–116.
Copyright © 2012 by Information Age Publishing

school year. Without question, the achievement of this aspect of the legislation will constitute a major increase in equity for children and benefit the general welfare of the nation.

In order to ensure that accountability measures are met, and because research indicates that instruction from an effective teacher can overcome various factors imposed on students due to poverty, educational disadvantage, and limited English proficiency (Marzano, 2003), the NCLB legislation incorporated requirements for teacher quality. According to the law, all teachers assigned to campuses receiving federal funds are required to meet "highly qualified" guidelines. All states must submit plans delineating the steps they will take to ensure that high-minority, low-performing schools are staffed with highly qualified, effective teachers. Funding to meet the highly qualified teacher mandate is allocated through various federal grants, including Title II Part A grant of the Elementary and Secondary Education Act (ESEA), the Improving Teacher Quality State grants, and the Higher Education Opportunity Act of 2000. The purpose of these grants is to ensure that all teachers are qualified and effective and, in turn, increase the academic achievement of all students.

Through the U.S. Office of Education, state and local educational agencies receive funds and, in exchange, are held accountable to the public for improvements in academic achievement. ESEA, Title II, Part A provides state and local education agencies with the flexibility to use these funds creatively to address challenges to teacher quality, whether they concern teacher preparation and qualifications of new teachers, recruitment and hiring, induction, professional development, teacher retention, or the need for more capable principals and assistant principals to serve as effective school leaders (U.S. Department of Education, 2006). The funding opportunities encourage teacher induction and mentoring programs for new teachers. For example, a component of teacher-quality grants requires that states incorporate research and evaluation of the programs implemented in order to determine the impact or effect of the programs on teacher retention and student performance. The Higher Education Opportunity Act of 2000 includes provisions such as loan forgiveness of up to $10,000 for students who pursue vital public service jobs, of which educator is one, and grants for partnerships between higher education institutions and local education agencies to improve teacher training and development programs and recruitment of teachers for high-demand areas such as science and technology.

According to Leithwood, Seashore-Lewis, Anderson, and Wahlstom (2004), school leadership and teacher quality are the two most important factors in student achievement. In support of this, a study by Armour-Thomas, Clay, Domanico, Bruno, and Allen (1989) reports that differences in teacher capability can account for as much as 90 percent of the variation in student learning in schools with similar student characteristics (as cited in the National Commission on Teaching & America's Future, 1996). Such data emphasize the importance of providing sustained and purposeful professional development for quality teachers already on the job and recruiting, hiring, and supporting long term those teachers just beginning their careers. Consequently, one of the most important job responsibilities of principals involves recruiting, hiring, retaining, and developing effective classroom teachers. Through teacher quality processes, school leaders can use their positions to promote the concept of social justice in meeting the goals of the NCLB legislation, assuring that every child has an effective teacher. Success in preparing, hiring, and retaining effective teachers and leaders is now a local, state, and national focus and may be among the most powerful means of impacting the injustices that the schools are intended to address, but instead often perpetuate.

The purpose of this chapter is to examine the process of teacher induction as a means for addressing social justice issues related to the lack of support provided to new teachers. The chapter begins with a description of the current situation of teacher turnover, especially as it evidences itself in low-performing schools. Next, information regarding the research on induction processes is presented. The section includes components that make up a quality induction program, and research on the impact quality induction programs have had on teacher turnover. A third section contains the voices of new and veteran teachers from the field regarding the realities of coming new to the profession, job, or workplace. These voices echo the need for quality induction and suggest components educational leaders could consider in generating campus quality induction programs. Finally, the chapter closes with recommended actions that principals, teacher leaders, and personnel administrators can employ in creating a social justice agenda that increases the likelihood that teachers will not only remain in the profession, but continue to develop their instructional effectiveness with all students.

A REVOLVING DOOR: THE CURRENT SITUATION OF TEACHER RETENTION

Although record numbers of teachers are being produced throughout the United States through both traditional and alternative certification programs (Glazerman et al., 2008), too many educators leave within a few years of entering the profession. Smith and Ingersoll (2004) showed that approximately 50% of new teachers leave education altogether before the end of 5 years, and a turnover rate of 29% exists for new teachers after their first year of teaching. Literature on special education teachers (Coleman, 2000) shows a staggering 40% abandon teaching within 5 years. New minority teachers, important role models for minority students, similarly are more likely to leave teaching after their first year on the job. The state of Washington reported annual losses of about 25 percent of its new teachers within their first 5 years in the classroom (Knapp et al., 2005, as cited in Center for Strengthening the Teaching Profession, 2008). Though not as dire as the 50% attrition rate found in some parts of the country, this attrition still represents a significant loss to the K–12 system. This constant turnover results in some schools being prevented from making any coherent multi-year improvement planning because the key players keep changing. The problem, then, may not be so much recruitment of teachers, but rather the development and retention of quality teachers in every classroom (Horn, Sterling, & Subhan, 2002; Smith & Ingersoll, 2004; Webb & Norton, 2009).

The dollar costs to schools and districts to recruit, interview, hire, and train teacher replacement can be major, particularly where turnover is high. One conservative estimate places the cost at a minimum of $12,000 per replacement (Center for Teaching Quality, 2006, as cited in Webb & Norton, 2009). Shockley, Guglielmino, and Watlington (2006) noted that the costs of replacing teachers are not always apparent, particularly since they cannot be identified as a single line in a school district's budget. They identified these costs as being "embedded in expenditures in many areas including teacher recruitment, separation processing, training, and orientation/training requirements for new teachers" (p. 3). In their study of two school districts in Florida, they found turnover rates and replacement costs to vary significantly. For the smaller of the two districts, the turnover rate was 16.4% with a replacement cost per teacher of $4,631; the larger district had a turnover rate of only 7.25%, but an average replacement cost per teacher of $12,652. In another study, this one prepared for the Texas State Board of Educator Certification by the Texas Center for Educational Research (2000), the estimated costs to lose and then replace a teacher in Texas ranged from $48,000 to $50,000. Shockley et al. criticized the Texas study for using "industry cost models" to calculate expenses. The authors of the Texas report gave cost estimates using five different models and provided information regarding cost differences by geographic regions of the state. Perhaps most importantly, the report estimated that with the state teacher turnover rate in 2000 of 15.5%, Texas loses between $329 million and $2.1 billion per year on replacing individuals leaving the teaching profession. Whether the actual dollar costs for teacher turnover is closer to those found in the Shockley et al. study or the report to the State Board for Teacher Education Certification (Texas Center for Educational Research, 2000), the following statement from the Texas report gets to the heart of the issue:

> Teacher turnover results in a high cost to the state and local school districts. Funds used to pay for turnover-related expenses could be used to benefit Texas students and teachers in other ways. Policymakers and district administrators must evaluate how teachers, especially those just entering the pro-

fession, are supported. Implementing strategies to retain qualified teachers must become a priority. By using professional support, time, training, and financial resources, Texas school districts are likely to increase the number of teachers who remain in the Texas teaching force. (p. 17)

A step in correcting a problem is its identification, so it is important to note the reasons teachers are leaving the profession and the obstacles being faced by new teachers. Current literature indicates that new teachers face problems in classroom management, meeting the needs of a diverse student population, solving parental problems, student motivation, and assessing student work (Stansbury & Zimmerman, 2002). Irinaga-Bistolas, Schalock, Marvin, and Beck (2007) summarize various studies, recognizing the following factors: "low salaries; cultural isolation; professional isolation; diverse case load; lack of resources to serve students with low incidence disabilities; lack of pre-service training; significant travel requirements; lack of access to professional development; and limited career opportunities" (p. 13). Horn et al. (2002) cite the reasons proposed by the National Commission on Teaching and America's Future (1996). Those reasons are assignments out of certified area, assignment of extra duties, lack of administration's support, assignment to the neediest students, and professional isolation. Curran and Goldrick (2002) add that "lack of administrative support, poor working conditions, inadequate preparation, low pay, little respect, and limited advancement opportunities" cause new teachers to leave their profession (p. 1). Smith and Ingersoll (2004) added school-level poverty to the list of factors leading to teacher attrition. They found that school-level poverty was proportionally correlated to new teachers leaving education.

Another perspective on the reasons individuals leave teaching emphasizes the particularly challenging situations faced by minority faculty. Brock and Grady (2001) acknowledge that all of the general reasons for teachers leaving the profession apply to minority teachers. However, minority teachers may also face additional challenges because of their minority status. The challenges can include feeling separated from their ethnic group and culture, feeling unwelcome in some school communities, facing biased and bigoted behavior from colleagues and community members, being expected to solve school problems related to instructional issues with minority children, and being given some of the most difficult assignments within the school.

In order to address teacher attrition, it is important to provide them quality induction programs. In addition to retaining teachers in the school and profession (Smith & Ingersoll, 2004), a high-quality induction program moves new teachers beyond survival to increasingly positive impacts on student learning, integrates them into the professional communities in their schools and districts, and encourages them to remain invested in the profession and schools (Center for Strengthening the Teaching Profession, 2008; New Teacher Center, 2007).

INDUCTION PROGRAM COMPONENTS

To ensure a quality education for all students without regard to where they live and to increase the retention of new teachers, the federal government encourages the use of research-proven New Teacher Induction Programs. Induction activities are designed to assist the educator through a smooth and effective transition to becoming an effective leader or teacher on campus. By keeping an effective teacher in every classroom, a district is able to ensure quality instruction and optimal learning conditions for all students, especially the ethnic and low socioeconomic status minority students targeted through NCLB. Social justice and legal requirements are both met through such an arrangement. However, just as the system is set up to provide equal opportunity for success for students, the system must also be fair in providing educators with the skill sets to engage those students in critical inquiry. Induction programs can do that.

Induction is a process. Its purpose is to offer a series of experiences that assist the new or novice educator in learning about the various operations of the school (Brown, 2002). However, an effective induction program must include research-based components that have been proven effective in teacher retention, in teacher skill development, and in increased student achievement. Currently, induction programs vary from one school district to another. Only those districts that receive teacher-quality enhancement grants must adhere to specific state guidelines based on federal reporting requirements. Some states, such as Kentucky, require that all new teachers participate in a prescribed induction program and provide funding for the mandate. It is interesting to note that Kentucky's overall attrition rate is 20% (Clements & Jones, 2003). Smith and Ingersoll (2004) write that 80% of new teachers participate in some form of induction activities, from a one-day pre-service workshop at the district, to a two-year process that incorporates orientation activities, mentoring, and staff development for the new teacher, the mentor, and administrators. High-intensity programs combine various proven activities to ensure success in retaining educators new to the field, in improving the delivery of instruction, and in increasing student performance.

The New Teacher Center of the University of California, Santa Cruz (2007) identifies six components that an effective induction program must have. They are: (1) a multiyear program, spanning at least the first 2 years of teaching; (2) sanctioned time for mentor–new teacher interaction; (3) rigorous mentor selection criteria; (4) initial training and ongoing professional development and support for mentors; (5) pairing of new teachers and mentors in similar subject areas and grade levels; and (6) documentation and evidence of new teacher growth. Sterling, Horn, and Wong (2001) identified nine common components in the literature on effective programs: (1) orientation; (2) mentoring; (3) adjustment of working conditions; (4) release time; (5) professional development; (6) opportunities for collegial collaboration; (7) teacher assessment; (8) program evaluation; and (9) follow-up into the second year (as cited in Horn et al., 2002). A third list comes from the induction program instituted for new teachers in the state of Washington; the Washington program was made up of five components: (1) hiring, (2) orientation, (3) mentoring, (4) professional development, and (5) assessment for teacher growth (Center for Strengthening the Teaching Profession, 2008).

Identifying the various components that may be incorporated to create an effective program is crucial. Smith and Ingersoll (2004) note the importance of new teacher participation in more than two activities. Their study shows that although participation in a program with just two components (i.e., mentoring and campus support) produced a turnover rate of 39%, programs that added a collegial collaborative requirement and an orientation, in addition to mentoring and campus support, resulted in a 27% turnover rate. Finally, by adding a third component consisting of teacher networking, reducing teacher workload, and providing an instructional aid produced the lowest turnover rate, of 18%. After analyzing the literature and numerous induction programs, it seems that the following components should be considered in order to support new teachers: (1) a multiyear induction program, spanning at least the first two years of teaching, (2) sanctioned time for mentor–new teacher interaction, (3) rigorous mentor selection criteria, (4) initial training and ongoing professional development and support for mentors, (5) pairing of new teachers and mentors in similar subject areas and grade levels, (6) documentation and evidence of new teacher growth, (7) orientation, (8) adjustment of working conditions, (9) opportunities for collegial collaboration, and (10) program evaluation. A brief description of each of the 10 program components follows; extensive information on each of the components is available in the literature and should be sought by those interested in knowing more about any one or all of the elements of effective induction programs for teachers.

1. *A multiyear induction program, spanning at least the first 2 years of teaching.* A multiyear induction program is ideal because the new teacher is so engaged in simply learning the system, the culture, the expectations, and the staff of the campus that little energy is left to integrate into truly productive and focused teaching skill development the first year. As a result, student achievement is not significantly impacted after the first year of participation in an induction program, as evidenced in the findings of an evaluation study of the Texas Beginning Teacher Induction and Mentoring Program (ICF International, 2009).

2. *Sanctioned time for mentor–new teacher interaction.* Time must be provided for the new teacher to observe the mentor, for the mentor to observe the new teacher, for the provision of feedback, for the

mentor to model in the new teacher's classroom, for lesson planning, for review of student work, and for discussion of problems that may impede effective teaching. If a new teacher is expected to participate in these activities after working hours, the added stress and hours may increase the risk of leaving.

3. *Rigorous mentor selection criteria.* Providing quality mentors to new teachers is instrumental in "making or breaking" the neophyte educator. The assigned mentor should be an experienced and effective teacher who has experience and success with diverse student groups. In addition, the mentor must be a willing participant in the program, not someone who has been "assigned" the role, because the new teacher will now be in the role of the student, and just as a regular student needs to feel a sense of trust and connectedness in order to be successful as a learner, so does the new educator. Openness to new ideas should also be a quality of mentors in order to encourage the new teacher to implement the most recent best practices learned in the university setting (Clements & Jones, 2003).

4. *Initial training and ongoing professional development and support for mentors.* Mentors should receive initial training on their roles as mentors and coaches and on the skills necessary to communicate effectively. The mentor must recognize and accept the responsibility of guiding the novice teacher through the intricacies and the multitude of tasks to be completed on a daily basis and through those activities that may occur less frequently, such as report card preparation and parent night expectations. The staff development for mentors should include preparation for conducting the observations of the new teacher, for providing feedback, and for developing an improvement plan for future teacher development.

5. *Pairing of new teachers and mentors in similar subject areas and grade levels.* The assigned mentor should be an experienced and effective teacher from the same field and same campus as the novice teacher. Lesson-planning, assessment of student work, meeting for discussions, observations, and frequent feedback will be easier when the content is similar and when the teachers are situated close to each other. Having a mentor from the same field increases the retention rate of teachers by 30% (Smith & Ingersoll, 2004).

6. *Documentation and evidence of new teacher growth.* Documentation of teacher growth can be accomplished through observations, written feedback, and write-ups of follow-up visits to look for improvement. Meeting agendas and copies of the administrator's observations and evaluations will add documentation for evaluation of the mentoring process also (Algozzine, Gretes, Queen, & Cowan-Hathcock, 2007; Brown, 2002). Formal evaluations or observations by administrators was rated among the top five positive induction

program activities by beginning teachers (Algozzine et al., 2007); the feedback about content and process that can be provided to beginning teachers by principals and mentors through observations and conferencing can provide an excellent source of professional development (Wayne, Youngs, & Fleischman, 2005).

7. *Orientation.* Orientation activities usually occur before the school year begins and before other teachers come back for their campus staff development. Orientation is usually conducted through the district office and may include training on best practice, school policy, district curriculum, district programs, and district procedures. New teachers may be taken on a tour of the community, the school district, and local businesses to help them adjust to their new environment. Mentors may be introduced to their mentees during orientation exercises.

8. *Adjustment of working conditions.* New teachers may be given less extracurricular assignments, fewer students, and fewer high-needs students than experienced teachers. However, they may receive more materials and staff development based on the teachers' needs. Secondary teachers may be given fewer preparations, to facilitate a focus on effective lesson planning and quality instructional delivery. Unfortunately, assignment adjustments are among the most often recommended strategies for assisting beginning teachers, but are rarely implemented (Algozzine et al., 2007; Ingersoll & Smith, 2004).

9. *Opportunities for collegial collaboration.* Collegial collaboration equates to the entire grade level or department planning lessons and common assessments together, reflecting on the teaching, evaluating student products, participating in action research, and adjusting future instruction to increase student success in every classroom in the grade level and within the school. This type of induction activity produced a 43% decrease in the risk of leaving and the risk of changing campus by 25%.

10. *Program evaluation.* The induction process must be evaluated to incorporate suggestions and to revise components that are not providing the desired outcomes. The state may also require an evaluation component if the district is using state grant funds for the induction and mentoring of new teachers. The state agency may then use the information provided to evaluate the program at the state level for the desired outcomes of teacher retention, teacher development, and increased student achievement.

Although not exhaustive, the aforementioned components seem to benefit new teachers, with effective induction programs preparing them for the job ahead. In the next section, we report on data collected from new and veteran teachers related to some of the components above.

VOICES FROM THE FIELD

The voices from the field correspond to elementary, middle, and high school teachers; some are new teachers and others are veterans. The participants were teachers in Texas, Louisiana, and Oklahoma with a variety of enrollment sizes and ethnic, cultural, and racial configurations. In an individual, open-ended questionnaire, the participants provided their insights about the importance of creating support systems for new teachers. Their voices provide examples of the importance of the components evidenced by the research.

The need for addressing working conditions at the school is evidenced in these comments by a veteran high school teacher regarding teacher turnover at the school:

> What's been happening with the school is that it's kind of inconsistent here. And you can't blame that on anybody because this is a poor parish. And if you come to work here, you can forget about making a whole lot of money because we are one of the lower paid parishes. And the real good certified teachers, they don't want to come here. But I don't think you teach for money anyway. I think it's a calling. But you're not going to be rich even if you go to another parish—not if you teach. But we can't keep good teachers here. We had some teachers here that were mainstays but what happened is that all the changes that happened last year, those teachers left and went to other parishes. So last year there was an inconsistency with teachers and this year we have a whole new influx of teachers. It's just hard to keep real good teachers here and I don't think we're going to keep them here until we can get up to the national average on salaries or at least with the other parishes.

The words of this teacher attest to the challenges to long-term planning and development that high teacher turnover rates generate in schools. Another new teacher referenced her relationship with a mentor after a classroom observation. Her words seem to echo the claims that documentation and evidence of new teacher growth are an important and positive component of quality induction:

> Well, I think she was better able to relate to me, give me more feedback. And it was nice. I was nervous at first when she came in, but when it was over with, after she talked with me I was a lot closer to her as far as her telling me what I could change. She told me what was good and it did, it helped me improve what I was doing.

In addition to observing working conditions and documented growth processes, a new teacher found that being able to observe others was an important source of support for and improvement of her knowledge and skills:

I observed a second-grade teacher. And I believe that helped me because I was able to see what was needed for background, what first graders needed to know before they went to second grade. And, of course, I'm new, relatively new. This is my second year to teach first grade. And I'm still struggling. I've had lots of help and I still, I know what mainly to teach. But it was interesting to see the first [second?] grade function and see what they needed.

Many of the individuals interviewed mentioned the importance of collaborative environments, especially developing relationships with their peers. In some instances, new teachers provided opportunities for long-time colleagues to engage in team and relationship-building that they might not have, otherwise. Collaboration, care, trust, and support were frequent themes in the comments from these teachers.

Like I said, I think that really brought us closer together. We were a close-knit group before that, but that kind of was the icing on the cake. . . . And it also helped us. We had several new teachers and that kind of helped us bond with those new people, too . . . we have a new vocal teacher coming on board as of today, and I'm planning on just stopping by and seeing how things are going for her, just to check things out. There's a real non-threatening environment that I think accompanies that and it's really neat.

Another teacher added:

We meet as a grade level—our grade has two new teachers—so we need to go ahead and meet again and review the classroom management plans so that they are all the same.

We do that every week when we're planning. Especially as a new teacher has come in, then we just get all her ideas and throw them in with all of ours. So it just gets bigger and better. But through the years I have worked with several teachers and every time a new teacher comes in—those first years are especially good if they've been somewhere, other places where they have lots of ideas. We just discus the things we want to do and we throw all our ideas out on the table. So it's really good.

While the majority of teacher comments related to assistance and the importance of collaborative environments, less than positive experiences in relation to orientation were voiced as well:

The first year that I taught high school, two people talked to me the entire year.

Well, in my own experience and I've only worked in three buildings in my career, but there seems to be a prevailing attitude that I have a teaching certificate, therefore I ought to know how the school works. And that's not always the case. . . . No one bothered to tell me. It is, well, in education I feel like it becomes the teacher's responsibility to seek out school culture and knowledge on how things work. And sometimes you're asked to know things that you don't even know exist. I know in my first school I was asked to submit a report for a school improvement plan and I didn't even know we had a school improvement plan. Well, this is due every September. This is my first year here. But those sorts of issues need to be revisited just for the sake of people who maybe have been here forever and have forgotten or are new to the school. Well, just because you have 20 years' experience in teaching does not mean you know how this school culture works.

Mentoring relationships were, indeed, the most important component of quality induction programs. The aforementioned experience of lack of mentorship echoes the importance of having someone identified as the "go to" person, especially for beginning professionals. Other teachers seemed to be more "fortunate" in receiving mentoring from veteran teachers:

He was my on-site person. So he was able to give me lots of feedback when we would meet. And he would sit and observe my classes and my teaching skills and stuff. And he was giving me feedback on a principal's perspective, because he had done the PDAS appraisals and all of that stuff. So I really took what he told me. I took it to heart because he gave me a lot of good, it was good criticism, and some bad criticism. And he always tried to help me be the best teacher I could be. So he was my, I guess, my on-site mentor observer and then through the district, I was given another mentor. My other mentor ended up being my department head. Once again, I was very lucky to have her because she was very open to me coming and asking questions, to me asking for help, or me running ideas off of her. But also, my department as a whole, all of the teachers in my department, as far as BCIS, I believe there were eight or nine teachers. Everybody kind of played that mentor role for me because if I ever had questions, or if I ever needed help, or if I ever thought, "Hey, do you think that's a good idea?," they were always willing to listen to me, give me their advice. I thought that was really good because I had a great first year because I had all that support.

Other teachers explained how they would go about creating mentoring configurations:

And we try at the beginning of the year to put someone with a new person. "If you need any help,"… So as far as knowing what to do, he didn't need my help. But I still wanted to give encouraging words, smiles, try to make people feel welcome.

Yes, I'm a leader with the first grade because the other teacher is new and I'm helping her out with material and just everything. I'm helping her with the reading, math, social studies, and science curriculums. Kindergarten has two strong teachers, but probably Ms. Colleague is the stronger leader there.

And we would pair new teachers with those that had been there, and we would try and do collaborations and we cooperated on different subjects. Even though I taught math, we tried to incorporate math, language arts, social studies, and all compiled together in one because basically we were all doing the same thing . . .

One veteran teacher talked about the benefits of peer relationships:

> . . . for instance, in the sixth-grade hall the certified teachers got together with the new teachers and gave them some insight. Some things that they could try with their classes to make things better.

Examples of mentoring activities were among the comments these teachers shared regarding their induction programs. Both new teachers and veteran teachers also talked about their schools' orientation. Their responses align with research describing "information giving" formats:

> Usually they come in and are given an overview of the school, of the students, and a handbook. We're still using the same handbook for years. You go down through the handbook and find out if you have any questions or comments or concerns—or maybe something you want to add to it.

> Well, initially there are a couple of meetings held at the central office, which is the school board office. Then we go through training here at the school. We're introduced to some tapes and we watch a couple of those and we go through practical drills of how things will be done when school starts. Then of course you have questions, but overall I do think they make an attempt to get us prepared.

The following words of a third-year teacher emphasize the importance of the affective as well as the intellectual and skill components of induction programs.

> This is my third year and this is the first year I've felt like I have friends. I think it's been a couple of people that have helped and it's been our senior counselor, our secretary that have been the main ones. Just by being friendly. Allowing me to have lunch with them, asking me to sit with at lunch or whatever the case, instead of my feeling like I'm interfering or interrupting somebody else's property.

This same individual goes on to describe a situation in which she found the courage to give voice to feelings that many have in their heads and hearts but are reluctant to share.

> We talked about ... having teacher mentor people come in. Because at one of our meetings last year, I told them what an outsider I felt like and that they were talking about helping new kids come in and having other students help them, and I said well what about teachers? I don't know what pink slips are; I don't know what blue slips are; I don't know what gold ones are. I don't know any of that. And I came in and get all these sheets and I'm like okay, so what.

Though the teacher making the comment that follows is not, at this point, a beginning teacher, she remembers clearly what it was like to be new. Her words also remind us that induction is an important process for veteran teachers who move into new positions and/or different schools.

. . . when you are new in the district, it takes you a few years just to figure out what's going on. And you can hardly see beyond your nose. The people I was around were always extremely helpful and supportive and good teammates. I think much of the staff was kind of a closed community. There were a few of us coming into the staff, just a few every year.

The new and veteran teachers' voices included several of the components we considered from the literature. Interestingly, the teachers helped us understand components that are directly related to teachers. While all of the components are directly related to roles of both beginning and veteran teachers, school administrators have significant influence on whether or not and how much any or all of these components are available in the school.

ROLE OF THE SCHOOL ADMINISTRATOR ON NEW TEACHER INDUCTION

Leadership is essential to the success and effectiveness of teacher induction processes. The context in which new teachers work and the support provided by leadership have been identified as significant factors in teachers deciding to stay in a particular building. According to Brock and Grady (2001), "clearly, beginning teachers view the principal as the most important person in the induction process" (p. 41). They go on to say that leaders who effectively support induction processes are educated about the unique needs of new teachers. They have realistic expectations for new teachers' growth and recognize that beginning teachers are generally at early stages of teacher performance (i.e., emerging or basic level of skill).

With competing expectations from the district, school, and classroom, new teachers can find it challenging to sort out the priorities for their work. Effective leaders serve new teachers well by recognizing the importance of the mentoring relationship, protecting the time set aside for mentoring, and helping new teachers reserve time for their own growth, learning, and reflection. This requires creating structures, schedules, and procedures with new teacher needs in mind, all of which are under the purview of the school leaders, both formal and informal.

Some districts have developed contract language that allows mentors to be invited by new teachers to conferences with the principal. The role of the mentor in this situation is to be a second set of ears and to help the new teacher process the information received in the conference.

Sustainable and adequate program funding allows for program continuity and development and refinement of services provided through the mentoring program. Districts that continue to fund mentoring capitalize on initial training investments—in teachers and mentors—and build an integrated culture that values the learning and contributions of all. Many new teachers purposely request placement in low-performing or high-poverty schools in order to receive forgiveness for their student loans. However, these schools typically present conditions quite unfavorable to the retention of new teachers. New teachers must receive more intensive support in order to survive the various stressful conditions of such needy schools. Because these conditions impact their decision to stay in the profession, it behooves the campus administrator to find ways to minimize the impact of the factors that can impact the new teachers negatively. Brown (2002) suggests that a "building-level induction" be provided to new teachers in low-performing schools.

Building-level induction is meant to ease the transition into a second level of risk factors that come from working at a low-performing school. To help new teachers develop a connection between the school and the students, activities such as a bus tour of the attendance area may be provided. Brown (2002) explains that "teachers' appreciation of culture, aspirations, and barriers that confront children are critical for creating appropriate learning environments" (p. 424). School-specific handbooks may be distributed to the new teachers to provide proactive guidance and to trigger questioning. A campus team can be assigned to answer questions related to curriculum, discipline, or any other items that may surface as the teacher engages in her first year in the profession. The administrator must be actively involved in the instructional support of the novice teachers. This support can be in the form of frequent observations and feedback or scheduled collaborative time between the mentor and mentee and the mentees' support team. An important component to campus-level induction is the development of a matrix for the new teacher. Brown writes that:

> Matrix indicators include but are not limited to: strengths, weaknesses, patterns of growth, focus on teaching and learning, classroom practices, transitions, learning in context, classroom management and discipline, selection and use of resources, alignment of curriculum to student needs, assessments, and resources, and effective use of data driven decisions. (pp. 423–424)

The matrix should be used to guide the support team in developing a plan for the development of the teacher, which may include one-on-one meetings, modeling of lessons, collegial collaboration, and frequent monitoring. The purpose is to provide a seamless and less stressful learning continuum for the new teacher, which will result in better teaching performance, increased student achievement, and a decreased risk of leaving the profession.

ACTIONS FOR IMPLEMENTING QUALITY INDUCTION PROGRAMS

In this section of the chapter, an attempt to translate the information presented into recommended actions is the challenge. Perhaps the most important action recommendation is to recognize that individual needs should be the basis for any assistance provided. Program components and recommended actions for implementing quality programs may or may not align with the needs of the beginning professional in the school. While topics such as classroom management, student motivation, working with students' individual differences, working with parents, and assessment are on the general interest list for beginning professionals, not everyone will need assistance with all of these (Brock & Grady, 2001; Seyfarth, 2005).

Helping new teachers find community is a priority. Community for the new professional can be both inside and outside the school itself. Helping new teachers with community can come through the orientation phase of the induction process by familiarizing individuals with the neighborhoods and businesses in which the school is situated. Another way to assist new teachers in finding community is by providing a mentor. The mentor–mentee match is an important one in all cases, but especially so for minority faculty. Seyfarth (2005) admonishes that teachers who are in a minority in a school may face unique problems and need a mentor who is well informed about and able to freely discuss minority issues.

Both the voices from the field and the literature reviewed advocated providing social interactions with teachers and administrators as ways to assist new teachers in learning about their workplace and develop connection with those who may eventually become sources of assistance. Some of these interactions can be formally planned and scheduled and others can be less formal and held in subunits within the organization. Additionally, participating in school events, athletic, and extracurricular activities can offer new teachers opportunities to meet their co-workers, students, and even the parents and community members. Zepeda and Ponticell (1997) warn of the potential danger of the in and out of school activities is that the new teachers can be overbooked and overwhelmed with opportunities, making them a burden rather than a support. Mentors and administrators can provide support in their area to the beginning teachers; they can monitor themselves in terms of the assignments and demands they impose on new teachers, as well as helping the new teacher to learn to monitor themselves to prevent "overinvolvement."

CONCLUSION

Federal legislation can set the standards for social justice in the area of receiving a quality education. An entire life of existence at a poverty level can be determined by the level of education a child acquires. Yet, the quality of that variable is not an item that the child has control of. The teacher in the classroom and the school leaders are the determinants of that factor. Every child deserves a quality instructor in order to engage in high levels of conversation and become critical thinkers. The child deserves quality instruction to realize that our society values his existence and wants his optimal and genuine participation in the future distribution of goods and services, and a voice in his own governance.

Consciously easing the transition of a new teacher into the first year as a professional educator is a humane action to implement. Administrators can engage in "transformative leadership that supports social justice and works to create democratic and equitable schools" (Gaetane, 2008, p. 340). They can help achieve this goal by using new teacher attrition data to change those factors that impede the retention of quality teachers in the classroom. Improving the circumstances and the professional development of the teachers of all students, especially those who need it the most—our minorities and our high-poverty students—is the first step in ensuring the goal of social justice for students.

REFERENCES

Algozzine, B., Gretes, J., Queen, A. J., & Cowan-Hathcock, M. (2007). Beginning teachers' perceptions of their induction program experiences. *The Clearing House, 80*(3), 137–143.

Brock, B.L., & Grady, M.L. (2001). *From first-year to first-rate: Principals guiding beginning teachers* (2nd ed.). Thousand Oaks, CA: Corwin Press, Inc.

Brown, K. L. (2002). Acclimating induction teachers to low-performing schools: Administrator's role. *Education, 123*(2), 422–426.

Center for Strengthening the Teaching Profession. (2008). *Effective support for new teachers in Washington State: Standards for beginning teacher induction.* Tacoma, WA: Author.

Clements, S. K., & Jones, D. B. (2003). *Teacher educators and KTIP: Promises, problems, and possibilities.* A White paper prepared for the Kentucky Education Professional Standards Board. Commonwealth Policy Associates.

Coleman, M. R. (2000). *Conditions of teaching children with exceptional learning needs: Thebright futures report* [Technical report]. Alexandria, VA: CEC Commission .

Curran, B., & Goldrick, L. (2002). *Mentoring and supporting new teachers.* Issue Brief. Education Policy Studies Division, National Governors Association Center for Best Practices.

Gaetane, J. M. (2008). Leadership for social justice: An agenda for 21st century schools. *Educational Forum, 72,* 340–354.

Glazerman, S., Dolfin, S., Bleeker, M., Johnson, A., Isenberg, E., Lugo-Gil, J., et al. (2008). *Impacts of comprehensive teacher induction: Results from the first year of a randomized controlled study* (NCEE 2009-4034). Washington, DC: National Center for Education Evaluation and Regional Assistance, Institute of Education Science, U.S. Department of Education.

Horn, P. J., Sterling, H. A., & Subhan, S. (2002). *Accountability through 'best practice' induction models.* Paper presented at the annual meeting of the American Association of Colleges for Teacher Education, New York City.

ICF International. (2009). *Evaluation of the beginning teacher induction and mentoring (BTM) program: Executive summary.* Fairfax, VA: Author.

Ingersoll, R.M., & Smith, T. M. (2004). Do teacher induction and mentoring matter? *NASSP Bulletin, 88*(638) 28–40.

Irinaga-Bistolas, C., Schalock, M., Marvin, R., & Beck, L. (2007). Bridges to success: A developmental induction model for rural early career special educators. *Rural Special Education Quarterly, 26(1)*, 13–22.

Leithwood, K., Seashore-Lewis, K., Anderson, S., & Wahlstrom, K. (2004). *How leadership influences student learning*. Minneapolis, MN: Center for Applied Research and Education Improvement and Toronto, Ontario: Ontario Institute for Studies in Education.

Marzano, R. J. (2003). *What works in schools: Translating research into action*. Alexandra, VA: Association for Supervision and Curriculum Development.

National Commission on Teaching & America's Future. (1996, September). *What matters most: Teaching and America's future*. Retrieved from *www.nctaf.org/documents/WhatMattersMost.pdf*.

New Teacher Center at the University of California, Santa Cruz. (2007). *New teacher support pays off: A return on investment for educators and kids* [Policy Brief]. Santa Cruz, CA: Author.

Noguera, P. A. (2004). *Reforming high schools: The greatest educational challenge*. Retrieved 5/10/2007 from http://www.inmotionmagazine.com/

Seyfarth, J. T. (2005). *Human resources management for effective schools* (4th ed.). Boston, MA: Pearson.

Shockley, R., Guglielmino, P., & Watlington, E. (2006, January). *The costs of teacher attrition*. Paper presented at the International Congress for School Effectiveness and Improvement, Fort Lauderdale, FL. Retrieved July 22, 2010, from *http://www.coe.fau.edu/conferences/papers/Shockley%20Guglielmino%20and%20 Watlington.pdf*.

Smith, T. M., & Ingersoll, R. M. (2004). What are the effects of induction and mentoring on beginning teacher turnover? *American Educational Research Journal, 41(3)*, 681–714.

Stansbury, K., & Zimmerman, J. (2002). Smart induction programs become lifelines for the beginning teacher. *Journal of Staff Development, 23(4)*, 10–17.

Texas Center for Educational Research. (2000). *The cost of teacher turnover*. Prepared for the Texas State Board for Educator Certification. Retrieved at: www.tcer.org/research/documents/teacher_turnover_full.doc

U.S. Department of Education, Office of Elementary and Secondary Education, Academic Improvement and Teacher Quality Programs. (2006, October 5). *Improving Teacher Quality State Grants, ESEA Title II, Part A, Non-Regulatory Guidance, Revised*. Washington, DC: Author.

Wayne, A. J., Youngs, P., & Fleischman, S. (2005). *Improving teacher induction. Educational Leadership, 62(8)*. Retrieved 6/28/10 from file://Users/anita-pankake/Desktop/Literature/Induction/ImprovingTeacherInduction. html#db=a9h&AN=16975227

Webb, D., & Norton, S., (2008). *Human resources administration: Personnel issues and needs in education* (5th ed.). Boston, MA: Pearson.

Wong, H. K., Britton, T., & Ganser, T. (2005). What the world can teach us about new teacher induction. *Phi Delta Kappan, 86(5)*, 379–384.

Zepeda, S. J., & Ponticell, J. A. (1997). First-year teachers at risk: A study of induction at three high schools. *High School Journal, 81(1)*.

CHAPTER 7

BARRIERS AND MARGINALIZATION IN FEMALE TEACHER LEADERSHIP

Shirley J. Mills and Janine M. Schall

Female leadership is cracking the "glass ceiling" of public school leadership, and indeed, has broken the ceiling of principal leadership. According to the U.S. Census Bureau (2009), 54% of principals and assistant principals in public schools are females. Yet despite the increasing numbers of female leaders, challenges to successful female leadership remain. In this chapter we discuss barriers and aspects of marginalization related to female teacher leaders through a review of the professional literature and examples of contemporary female teachers who have established themselves as leaders.

As accountability and standardized testing has increased, teacher leadership has been touted as one way to improve test scores (Knight, 2007; Mangin & Stoelinga, 2008; Marshall & Ward, 2004; Randi & Zeichner, 2004; Smylie, 2008). While teachers have been blamed for problems in schools, they are also being looked to for solutions (Smylie, Miretzky, & Konkol, 2004). Leadership models are emerging that call for principals to empower

Educational Leaders Encouraging the Intellectual and Professional Capacity of Others:
A Social Justice Agenda, pages 117–138.
Copyright © 2012 by Information Age Publishing
All rights of reproduction in any form reserved.

teachers to become leaders within the system (Mayo, 2002; Moller & Pankake, 2006), so that teachers can influence policy rather than be impacted by it. Danielson (2007) defined several ways teacher leaders can reach out to others with policies and programs, teaching and learning, and communication and community relations. However, administrative leaders in education are implementing reforms in their schools without questioning the "meaning, implications, and quandaries of equity and social justice" (Marshall & Ward, 2004, p. 531). The bottom line for most administrators is meeting the acceptable cut scores established by their states rather than with issues of social justice. Educational policy encourages student achievement but does so in ways that maintain the status quo and rarely affect the "way it's always been done" attitude pervasive in most school systems (Marshall & Ward, 2004).

MARGINALIZATION AND TEACHER LEADERSHIP

Marginalization is defined in this chapter as being "relegated to an unimportant or powerless position" within a public school system (www.merriam-webster. com/dictionary/marginalize). In fact, research conducted by the American Association of University Women (AAUW) found that just one year after graduating, women earn less than males and ten years later, earn as much as 69% less (Day & Hill, 2008). Female degrees are still associated with fields that traditionally have lower wages, such as education. Women are also sometimes seen as less committed to their jobs because they are perceived to have greater responsibilities in the home, which decreases their prospects of being promoted (Addi-Raccah & Ayalon, 2002). Marginalization can begin as soon as a female with children chooses to work outside of the home. While fathers are actively engaged in the raising of the family, it is still primarily a mother's job (Sweetser & O'Connor, 2008). Female teacher leaders are often stereotypically described as holding one job of teaching when in fact they are often holding many jobs. They may be mother, wife, and teacher, but only one will be categorized as work (Weiner, 2002). Frankel (2007) described this phenomenon by noting that "if you can run a household, you can be strategic" (p. 29), and did not see this feminine description as a hindrance but instead a powerful tool, and indeed makes "leadership a woman's art" (p. 20).

Teacher Leadership

Teacher leadership is a broadly defined term that includes both formal and informal leaders. York-Barr and Duke (2004) discussed the confusing definition of teacher leadership, but concluded that "it reflects teacher agency through establishing relationships, breaking down barriers, and marshalling resources throughout the organization in order to improve students' educational experiences and outcomes" (p. 260). Teacher leadership is related to responsibility for the learning of colleagues (Lambert, 2002; Smylie, Conley, & Marks, 2002). Lambert (2002) stated that "everyone has the right, responsibility, and ability to be a leader; how we define leadership influences how people will participate; and educators yearn to be more fully who they are—purposeful, professional human beings" (p. 37). Teacher leadership should lead to improved practice (Donaldson, 2007). Based on the current understandings of teacher leadership, Crowther, Ferguson, and Hann (2009) developed a framework describing how teacher leaders influence their school communities. The framework includes six elements: (1) school reform should be based on moral underpinnings that work toward a better world, (2) teacher leaders should facilitate communities of learning, (3) teacher leaders should strive for pedagogical excellence, (4) teacher leaders must confront barriers in the school culture and structure, (5) teacher leaders understand how to translate their ideas into effective action, and finally, (6) that teacher leaders nurture a culture of success. Teacher leadership, however, requires a new form of principal leadership.

Moller and Pankake (2006) suggest that intentional leadership built upon relationships is required to take teachers to higher levels. This requires principals to trust that teachers will lead and will be accountable for their decisions. Trust and risk taking are common attributes of teachers developing into leaders (Taylor, 2008; York-Barr, Sommers, Ghere, & Montie, 2001). Leadership is about "learning together and constructing meaning and knowledge collectively and collaboratively" (Harris, 2003, p. 314). The collective action this form of leadership requires has many names. It has been described as shared leadership, distributed leadership, and leadership teams, but all are based on relationships built on strong commitments to improving student learning. Lieberman and Friedrich (2007) noted that this collective action allowed teacher leaders to continue teaching part time while lending their efforts toward the changes needed to improve student achievement. Gronn (2000) described distributed leadership where the line of distinction between leaders and teachers becomes blurred and indistinct and that every person can be a leader. New demands of the accountability system require leadership to be spread over a large number of people (Moller & Pankake, 2006; Picciano, 2006; Sergiovanni, 2001). Teacher leadership is the "sleeping giant" waiting to be awakened to formal and informal leadership roles that assist the schools in moving forward in this complex world of education (Katzenmeyer & Moller, 2001, p. 2).

Formal Teacher Leaders

Moller and Pankake (2006) describe formal teacher leadership roles as those selected through a process by the school administration, central office, or other professional organizations. Teachers with a formal role generally have a job title or description that is somewhat ambiguous. Such positions are often funded by a grant, and are sometimes labeled as literacy coach, lead teacher, staff developer, technology specialist, mentor, department chair, or any other curriculum or instructional leader designated to assist other teachers in developing instructional strategies that increase student achievement (Danielson, 2007; Harrison & Lembeck, 1996; Knight, 2007; Moller & Pankake, 2006; Silins & Mulford, 2002). These formal roles sometimes are defined as power positions but in fact separate these teachers from the rest of the faculty (Katzenmeyer & Moller, 2001). Teachers feel they are members of the teaching staff but are in fact viewed by their fellow teachers as members of the leadership team and therefore, not to be trusted (Knight, 2007). These teachers face isolation because they are no longer "just teachers" yet are not part of the "leadership team" of the school.

Informal Leadership

Leadership often assumes informal roles such as mentoring, volunteering, supporting, promoting the mission of the school, and promoting community relations (Danielson, 2007; Harrison & Lembeck, 1996; Silins & Mulford, 2002). These can be influential positions with a variety of blurred and nebulous roles. Informal teacher leaders often focus on a set of functions or tasks and when these are finished, the leadership position is dissolved (Katzenmeyer & Moller, 2001). These tasks and functions often revolve around issues of student achievement, giving teachers a voice in shaping programs and helping meet goals that support the mission of the school (Gabriel, 2005). Teacher leaders who step into these informal leadership roles are strongly devoted to the issues being addressed and are willing to spend the time, energy, and resources to solve the problems. As education moves toward new leadership models, all teachers should be teacher leaders as they extend their work from their own classrooms to the rest of the school community (Barth, 2001; Gonzales, 2004).

Whether the teacher is functioning in a formal or informal leadership position, the decisions of who becomes a leader, how leaders are chosen, and how successful the leaders are becomes a crucial issue for teachers. Student outcomes are more likely to improve when leadership is distributed throughout the school and teachers are empowered to make the necessary instructional decisions needed to improve their learning (Halverson & Thomas, 2008; Picciano, 2006; Silins & Mulford; 2002; Stone & Cuper, 2006).

MARGINALIZATION AS IT RELATES
TO TEACHER LEADERSHIP

To me a leader is someone who can lead the way to something or try to open doors for people to try to make things happen, finding ways, finding options, finding choices. Bringing people in, trying to make things easier, better, and just trying to change things.　　　　　　　　　　　　　　　　　*—Marisa*

Teacher leaders play an important role as the "school's conscience" and challengers of the status quo in order to improve the learning of all students (Ackerman & Mackenzie, 2006). Issues of marginalization ripple below the surface of daily schooling routines and how these issues interact with the roles of formal and informal teacher leadership create concerns for teachers and leaders alike (Whitehead, 2001). Teachers face many barriers when they are trying to move beyond the boundaries of their classrooms to decision-making roles in order to influence the instruction (Addi-Raccah & Ayalon, 2002; Coleman, 2007; Murray & Simmons, 1994). Only certain teachers are allowed to move into leadership positions and once there, they are only allowed to act in certain ways, which tend to reinforce the status quo, including teachers teaching in isolation and being compliant (Moreau, Osgood, & Halsall, 2007). Marginalized teachers may not even realize they are marginalized because the system appears to support them with resources, time, and with eloquent speeches regarding their importance to student achievement (Coleman, 2007).

Issues of marginalization are about legitimacy and equity—everyone should get what they need; everyone should have the opportunities they need to be effective teachers and teacher leaders. In this context, teacher leadership questions arise. Who really is a leader? Who has the right to be a leader? In the next section, we identify factors that contribute to the marginalization of female teacher leaders.

BARRIERS TO FEMALE TEACHER LEADERSHIP

Most of the principals now are females. They are really harder to work under... the ones I've had are harder because they feel they have to prove themselves in a man's world.　　　　　　　　　　　　　　　　　　　　　　*—Pam*

While teacher leadership is a topic of research interest, barriers that marginalize 75% of the teaching population continue to exist. These barriers include stereotypes about women, the hierarchical system of schooling, school environment, lack of mentoring and support, and the lack of legitimacy of teacher leaders.

Stereotypical Beliefs about Women

Leadership positions, particularly administrative positions, are still thought to be the domain of men even though females are entering the principalship position in large numbers. Women must fight against the idea that leadership is a male domain and sometimes find less acceptance than their male counterparts (Murray & Simmons, 1994). Often they perceive that using their skills of collaboration might be seen as weak leadership. Women are perceived as more caring and nurturing than men and given responsibilities that emphasize these roles. What counts as "good" leadership skills are often skills associated with traditional male traits, resulting in women feeling either unwelcome as leaders or that they must give up parts of their identities as women (Stelter, 2002). For example, men who demonstrate initiative are perceived as leaders, while women who demonstrate initiative are perceived as aggressive or pushy (Moreau et al., 2007). Women are inhibited from seeking positions of power for many reasons, including messages that girls receive in early childhood that equate femininity with dependence, the tendency to label powerful women with pejorative names, and a lack of strong women role models (Frankel, 2007).

Hierarchical Culture

Female teachers function in a system that traditionally has viewed leadership as a hierarchy (Lambert, 2003; Murray & Simmons, 1994). The hierarchical school system where leadership responsibilities are clearly defined and the clear separation of roles and responsibilities within that structure present a major barrier to the idea of teachers as leaders (Harris, 2003). Teacher collaboration and professional dialogue is usually confined to their own schools and controlled by those above them in the hierarchical system (Berry, Norton, & Byrd, 2007). While educational leaders advocate for distributive forms of leadership in which leadership responsibilities are shared, schools continue to be dominated by hierarchical structures that emphasize control and power and discourage teacher leadership (Addi-Raccah & Ayalon, 2002; Moller & Katzenmeyer, 1996; Troen & Boles, 1994). Many schools are structured so that the principal is the main decision maker and teachers have little voice. Shared leadership is an important vehicle for including teachers in the decision-making process (Katzenmeyer & Moller, 2001). The principal, however, retains a powerful role in fostering teacher leadership; without principal support or encouragement, it is difficult for teacher leadership to flourish (Barth, 2001; Childs-Bowen, Moller, & Scrivner, 2000; Crowther, Ferguson, Kaagan, & Hann, 2002; Drago-Severson, 2007; Mangin, 2005). It is the concept of teacher leadership that connects teachers and principals as they seek to improve student achievement (Scherer, 2007).

How to get teachers and principals involved in transition to new leadership roles for teachers is not an easy task in the hierarchical organization of the school. It is clear that the culture of American schools has to change to view teachers as members of the leadership team. With the *No Child Left Behind Act* (2001), mandating that all children be educated to the individual student's full potential; principals will be unable to lead as they have always led. Teachers will have to be a viable partner in the leadership of the school.

The School Culture

Because the traditional hierarchal organization of schools is all that most teachers and principals have known, even when schools attempt to distribute power, current school culture can resist the change. Harris (2003) stated that school culture includes "the prevailing values, norms, philosophy, rules, and climate of the organisation" (p. 314). The current culture is not structured in a way that supports healthy change in teacher leadership (Johnson & Donaldson, 2008; Katzenmeyer & Moller, 2001; Ryan, 2006). It does not foster the image of teachers as leaders beyond their classrooms and may actually discourage it (Coyle, 1997). Teachers have traditionally been socialized to work alone and to lead within the classroom but not within the school. Breaking away from these norms can create tensions (Lieberman & Miller, 1999; Little, 1988; Moller & Katenmeyer, 1996). Teacher leader efforts to share expertise often encounter challenges within the culture of the school (Johnson & Donaldson, 2007; Manno & Firestone, 2008). The only way change will be lasting and marginalization will be reduced is to change the culture of the school (Reeves, 2009; Ryan, 2006).

Elmore (2002) stated that the culture of schools is not working in today's accountability system because our systems focus on a narrow view and educators do not really know why and how the connections operate within the school culture. The culture of schooling promotes isolation of teachers (Drago-Severson & Pinto, 2006; Gonzales, 2004). This type of "egg crate" culture reinforces classroom boundaries and discourages collaboration (Boles & Troen, 1996; Johnson & Donaldson, 2008). In a broader context, teacher isolation is also enforced with policy decision making. Berry et al. (2007) noted that most teachers' experience with policy actions that directly affect their classrooms learn about those policies indirectly; they rarely participate in policy formulation. This often leaves teachers feeling victimized by a system that gives them little or no attention. This attitude impairs their ability to function fully and effectively as teacher leaders.

Bartlett (2001) noted that because the dual roles of teaching and leading were so demanding, teachers choose not to do both. When teachers take on formal leadership roles they are often given more responsibilities than expected so that the leadership position becomes a burden (Gabriel, 2005). The burden is increased when teacher leaders do not have access to a network of support. If teacher leadership is to be effective, it must be embedded within school culture, not marginalized.

Lack of Mentoring and Support

Teachers who wish to take on a leadership role do not always feel supported in their new roles. The transition from teacher to teacher leader is fraught with challenges (LeBlanc & Shelton, 1997; Mangin, 2005; Ovando, 1996; Smylie & Brownlee-Conyers, 1992; Trachtman, 1991). Teachers assuming leadership roles often have to learn how to lead on the job (Ackerman & Mackenzie, 2006; Lieberman & Miller, 2004). Teachers who make their teaching practices available to other teachers or who publicly challenge the status quo risk working against the egalitarian culture that exists in schools today (Ackerman & Mackenzie, 2006; Lieberman & Friedrich, 2007). When there is no process or job description for choosing teacher leaders and designating their roles, their fellow teachers and colleagues may define the appointments as favoritism, again working against the egalitarian society built within the school systems (Johnson & Donaldson, 2008). This concept of teachers discouraging other teachers from moving into leadership positions can be described as the "crab bucket culture" where crabs who try to climb out of a bucket are pulled back down by the other crabs (York-Barr & Duke, 2004). This passive-aggressive behavior that teachers exhibit towards one another often inhibits teachers from aspiring to move towards leadership, and increases feelings of marginalization in teacher leaders.

On the other hand, teachers who do support one another in classroom settings are able to impact student achievement and teacher leadership. Donaldson (2007) suggested teachers needed to build and maintain a sense of purpose by listening to their colleagues and having discussions about learning. Teachers need to feel safe and work within an atmosphere of trust so that they might focus on conversations around student achievement (Lipton & Wellman, 2007; Smylie, Mayorowetz, Murphy, & Louis, 2007). In fact, teachers working together to discuss instructional issues create a powerful version of teacher leadership that requires support within the school culture, structure, and administration (Murphy, 2005; Reason & Reason, 2007).

Lack of Legitimacy

Teacher leaders face challenges to the legitimacy of their knowledge and leadership positions. Because teacher leader roles are often ambiguous, with poorly defined job descriptions or roles, and because teacher leaders are often removed from the classroom, they can face a lack of trust from their colleagues (Murphy, 2005; Smylie & Brownlee-Conyers, 1992). A larger barrier, however, is the lack of belief in their own knowledge. Johnson and Donaldson (2008) concluded that teachers were dedicated to their students but did not share their learning with other teachers, instead keeping their successes to themselves. This attitude kept the instructional capacity of the school static. Ingersoll (2007) described teachers doing what they wanted behind the closed doors of their classrooms, resulting in a lack of trust and/or risk taking by teachers to move into other roles. Teachers are responsible for improved student achievement, but have little voice over how to solve the issues associated with this desired result. School administration and school culture must signal the legitimacy of teacher ideas in order for teacher leadership to flourish (Danielson, 2005). Teachers whose work in leadership was not legitimized felt professional conflict and disappointment (Bartlett, 2001).

VOICES OF ASPIRING AND EXISTING TEACHER LEADERS

To me a leader is someone who's willing to take risks and is willing to look ahead; who's willing to make changes necessary in order to benefit students.
—Emilia

In order to understand the perspectives of practicing teachers and teacher leaders, we interviewed six females who work in South Texas schools in a variety of formal and informal leadership positions. All participants are Latina. The semi-structured interviews took place in a location of their choosing and each lasted between 30 and 45 minutes. Participants discussed their views on teacher leadership, the barriers that they perceived limiting teachers from leadership roles, and their own path to leadership.

Pam

Pam is a bilingual kindergarten teacher with 18 years of experience. She has worked in a variety of teacher leadership positions, mostly related to the field of reading. In her last position, the male principal replaced her with a woman Pam perceived as less capable but more connected politically to school leaders. Pam said, "So who is he going to keep in that position? A lot of times it's politics … it's not necessarily who is most capable."

Pam equated teaching experience with leadership legitimacy, believing that good leaders must have strong teaching experience. She states, "How can they lead if they haven't been in the trenches?...They haven't been in there long enough to know . . . Just because you have a title doesn't mean people are going to follow you."

When asked about her experiences with teachers who go on to be leaders, Pam paused, then said, "They get a big head . . . and they just want to be in charge and they just want to be bossing everybody. That is their idea of being a leader. Not necessarily an educational, teaching instructional leader." She also discussed that the female principals that she worked with are more difficult to work with than male principals are because "they feel they have to prove themselves in a man's world."

When Pam was a school leader, she found that some of her greatest challenges were dealing with other teachers who were resistant to change. She dealt with this issue by trying to gain the respect of the other teachers through her expertise. Pam noted that "if they are going to jump on the train, they will. And if they won't, well, hopefully they will pick up something."

Pam saw several barriers to teacher leadership. She believed that Mexican American culture could be a barrier, saying, "I don't know if you've heard this saying. The Mexicans that are climbing over the bridge, climbing over a fence, instead of helping them by pushing them over, they pull them down." She also saw some gender biases because of the belief that males can better handle discipline issues. Pam believed that while some teacher leaders are supported, "...a lot of the time they just kind of put it on them and tell them 'figure it out.'" She felt that many teachers refuse leadership positions because "they sometimes just don't want to mess with politics. . . "

While Pam was no longer in a formal teacher leadership role, she saw herself as an informal teacher leader and was pleased with this position, saying, "What I do others will say, 'how did you get them to do this? The kids are doing so good. How did you do that?'....I've been a leader where I was literacy coach, but that was with having a title, but not having the power to do anything, so that I was kind of stuck in the middle. This way I feel that I am [a leader] by what I do and what my kids do." She also rejected the idea of ever moving into a purely administrative role because that would put her out of reach of the children. "I tend to connect well with the kids whether it's the little ones, the other ones, even my summer school kids, I feel like they connect with me."

Aricela

Aricela became a teacher later in life. She was not encouraged to obtain higher education. She was a classroom teacher for six years, primarily working with English language learners. She is currently an elementary facilitator, a role that is equivalent to an assistant principal, but also takes on curricular and testing issues. After eight unsuccessful interviews, Aricela had given up hope for a facilitator's job. "It was late July and I was pregnant at the time and I decided that I was tired, I didn't want to interview anymore." However, her principal knew another principal with an open facilitator position and insisted that Aricela interview.

She stated that good leaders lead by example, "You have to walk the talk. You can't just talk the talk because they see it, they'll see right through you." Good leaders have to believe in the students and make student learning the priority. Aricela had trouble seeing herself as someone in charge at her school, stating that her role was to facilitate so that her teachers could do their jobs.

Aricela did not see many barriers toward teacher leadership except that at the district level there was so much competition that it was difficult to get selected. However, throughout her interview she discussed barriers to leadership, though she rarely labeled them as such. For example, the idea of relationships came up repeatedly. While Aricela assured us that in her district it was no longer possible for relatives to hire or supervise each other, it was clear that having a positive relationship, whether with someone in charge or with a friend or relative, was almost essential to obtaining formal leadership positions and to getting things done. Aricela mentioned that most of the formal leaders at the elementary and middle school level in her district are female, but that the high school is predominantly male. She thought it may be because at that level the administrators deal so much with discipline—though she saw no reason a woman could not handle discipline issues—or that it was due to so many of the assistant principals at the high school level also being coaches.

Aricela felt that the teachers at her old school might not have respected her in a formal leadership role since they had primarily known her as a classroom teacher. She was relieved to move to a new school for the facilitator's position. She thought the mentoring and support for teacher leaders was dependent upon the administrators at a particular school. Aricela mentioned that she received no support when she first moved into leadership positions, so it was very important to her that she mentor the teachers on her campus who were working on principal certification or who were in other leadership roles.

Marisa

Marisa had been teaching for ten years, first at the elementary level and now in middle school. She described a leader as "somebody who can lead the way to something or try to open doors for people. To make something happen….someone who can take things and just pull through and change things." She described the best qualities of a good leader as someone who "understands and is willing to listen." Marisa claimed that many leaders "sometimes just tend to fill themselves with paperwork" but a good leader is actually "out there and seeing what is needed and doing something about it." Teacher leadership, according to Marisa, needs many of the same skills that teachers need in their classroom, but with a different focus.

Marisa intends to stay in the field of education for the rest of her working years, but move into formal administrative roles as either a principal or an administrator in a central office. She saw herself as a leader, although she did not have a formal leadership position. She called herself "very outspoken" and said, "If I don't like something I tend to see how it could be made better...when I came back into school I wanted to do something, you know."

Marisa did not see barriers to becoming a teacher leader, other than the need to have the education and the willpower to take on the job. However, she mentioned that "who you know" plays a role in who is chosen for leadership positions. While teachers can apply for leadership positions, they are chosen based on experience, qualifications, and the relationship they have with the administration. Marisa believed that teacher leaders grow professionally more than classroom teachers do because they are seeing more than just their own classroom.

One reason Marisa had not pursued formal teacher leadership positions until now, she said, "I feel I still need to work at some areas because when I take that [leadership] position I want to be familiar with it.... I don't want to ask for too much help because I don't know how much help will be there." While Marisa described some positive models of teacher leadership support, she also stated, "they say in our Hispanic culture it's like, once they see someone go up you try to pull them down . . ." Marisa knew that her district had some training for leaders, but felt that for the most part, the amount of support that teacher leaders get was dependent upon the principal at their school.

Evita

Evita delayed college for several years. At 60 years old, Evita had been teaching for four years, all at an alternative high school. She originally wanted to work within the education system at a prison, but her alternative certification did not meet their requirements. She ended up working at an alternative school within the public school system and became lead teacher. At the time of the interview, she was enrolled in a principal certification program, but was not sure that she would pursue a principal position due to her age.

Evita saw leadership as "more than going in and telling people what you need to do. You need to be able to get those people to find their own solutions." She thought that teachers who wanted to become leaders must first be truthful with themselves and reflect upon whether they truly have the necessary skills for leadership.... "How can you develop or even know that you have these skills when you're so restricted in the classroom?"

She suggested that teachers need to serve in roles in which they have an interest, and once there, be given the tools and knowledge so that they can be good leaders. She appreciated the way that her principal recognized leadership qualities in her and gave her the lead teacher position. She noted that there often seemed to be a lack of support among the teacher leader's former colleagues, saying, "For some reason [there] seems to be the feeling that now she thinks she's better than we are and why should we help her.... My thinking is ... let's just be proud that one of us is there and let's work to climb up."

Evita thought that while both male and female teachers might feel this way, they expressed it differently as "women are catty in the sense that they make these remarks. Men . . . there is more of a closed-door atmosphere." She also mentioned that people at higher levels of the hierarchy may feel threatened by effective teacher leaders. "That's one of the reasons for keeping other people below you, keeping them suppressed, because if you do, then you have nothing to worry about. They're not going to threaten you." She continued, "some of the current leadership thinking needs to change. They need to feel that if I have five people that are capable of taking my job, that reflects on me because I am doing a heck of job training."

Angie

Angie had been teaching for eight years as a foreign language teacher and was the chair of her department at a large four-year high school. Angie aspired to be an assistant principal at a high school as an immediate goal but ultimately wanted to be the director of curriculum for foreign languages in a large high school and meet the needs of students who have English as a Second Language (ESL). She defined herself as a "teacher leader" because she mentored adult students who attended the local university as well as the teachers in her department of foreign languages. "I suppose that fulfills the requirement for teacher leader, right?" Angie did not see her formal leadership role as a role of power. "It's my job, my duty, to deliver information to the best of my abilities and also mediate and facilitate things for my department and as a result for our students."

When questioned about barriers to teacher leadership, Angie shared that she had not encountered many barriers because of the strong mentoring she received from her female principals. "That has been a plus to me as she [the principal] has served as a mentor to some degree." Angie was surrounded by female leadership in her school: "Out of six assistant principals, four are female, so that's a plus!" Angie noted that her principal was supportive of her endeavor to move into leadership.

While she believed there were no barriers to teacher leadership, she noted that "in the long run and I don't see them as obstacles, but rather challenges that need to be overcome and it could be a number of things." When asked to elaborate, she noted, "Teachers may not want you to move ahead, there could be jealousy, there could be the fact that they're not pursuing advancement in their career and they may not want others to do that." When probed as to whether that is typical of female or male behavior, she said, "Mostly female and that's interesting because sometimes it's your own gender that tries to keep you down and not allow you to move up."

When questioned about her fellow female teachers who had assumed leadership roles, she said, "They are positive models. One of our teachers is pursuing a certification for the principal program, and she's been very influential and I see her as a role model." She talked about teachers who enter the teaching field and were not suited to the job. "Are you in it for the passion of teaching and influencing others or are you in it because you think it's going to be an easy job, which it's not."

Angie believed that leadership opportunities were available to her all of the time and "it's up to you to either take them or leave them." She felt that because her principal was such a strong role model, she had opportunities that might not be offered to other females. "She is a very strong leader . . . she's wonderful."

Emilia

Emilia taught foreign languages for thirteen years. She served in teacher leadership positions ranging from mentor teachers to the Site-Based Decision Making committee, but recently moved into a new role as testing strategist for her school. She believed that a good leader was "someone who's willing to take risks and is willing to look ahead. Who's willing to make changes necessary in order to benefit the students?" Later, she explained "a leader has to be someone who does not delegate so much as to not act as a participant...if you keep delegating, delegating, and delegating you are not aware of all the problems." She thought that a leader required different skills than a classroom teacher, saying "As an administrator, you touch so many different aspects. You have to know so many different things."

According to Emilia, leadership was a responsibility that a teacher could not be afraid of and must do because it is a choice. At her school, leadership positions rotated as much as possible, though she noted that the same people volunteered repeatedly. Emilia recognized that not everyone would be willing to take on a teacher leadership role. She called families a barrier to teacher leadership, especially "women with young children."

Emilia believed that colleagues were generally supportive of teachers once they moved into a teacher leadership position, but noted that she had "five good teachers who supported me as a French teacher but then chomped me as a testing administrator..." However, she also stated that some people who move into teacher leadership positions did change. For some of them "it goes to their head."

Emilia moved into leadership positions because an administrator urged her to apply. She believed that "being nurtured by someone above you and someone who sees that potential in you" was important. She saw most of the mentoring and support of new teacher leaders done on an individual level, though her district did have programs in place for this purpose. She concluded, "Sometimes people tell me being a leader . . . can be a very lonely position and the higher up you go the lonelier you are. But I believe that if you nurture those around you and you treat them with respect that it's not such a lonely job because you would have the support of your community."

BREAKING LONG-STANDING TRADITIONS AND MOVING FORWARD

Teachers are already leaders. I mean, we are leading a generation of students. A leader is not necessarily someone in front directing, giving orders. A leader is someone who motivates, that creates that sense of wanting to better yourself constantly.... So teachers, the good teachers, have it in them to be leaders.

—*Angie*

Three broad themes emerged from the participant interviews: the ambiguous definition of teacher leadership, qualities of teacher leaders, and the role of mentoring and/or support in teacher leadership effectiveness and the powerlessness associated with leadership.

The Ambiguous Roles of Teacher Leadership

The literature defined teacher leadership as related to change, relationship, and service (Danielson, 2007; Manno & Firestone, 2008; Moller & Pankake, 2006). The real leaders of schools are found in the ranks of teachers. Defining the concept of teacher leader was different for each of the participants. Participants held a variety of both formal and informal leadership positions, but within their varied experiences, there was little agreement about what a teacher leader is or should be. Pam discussed the difficulty of being a teacher leader who was supposed to promote change, but had no power over the teachers that she worked with within the system. She drew a distinction between her role as a teacher leader and that of an administrator.

Shared leadership roles between administrators and teachers was supported strongly by researchers (Mangin & Stoelinga, 2008; Manno & Firestone, 2008; Moller & Pankake, 2006) but the participants did not seem to believe that administrators shared decision making with teachers. Indeed, they believed that they had very limited power as defined by their roles. The hierarchical structure that emphasized control and power discouraged teacher leadership and hampered their ability to lead (Addi-Raccah & Ayalon, 2002; Moller & Katzenmeyer, 1996; Troen & Boles, 1994).

Researchers noted that student achievement is often directly related to teacher leadership (Picciano, 2006; Silins & Mulford, 2002). Our participants supported teacher leadership as service related to improving the lives of their students. These teachers were in the field of education to help students. They believed that they were able to affect student achievement and make a difference in their lives, especially when they held instructional leadership positions.

Addi-Raccah and Ayalon (2002) noted that women are seen as less committed because of their dedication to their family. Our research concurred, as participants noted that some teachers (particularly females) with young children avoided leadership positions due to responsibilities at home even though they possessed the qualities of leadership.

All of the participants noted the importance of having relationships in order to be chosen for a leadership position. Often, it was not what you knew but whom you knew. School systems traditionally were viewed as a hierarchical system with personalities affecting the choices principals make when choosing teacher leaders (Lambert, 2003; Murray & Simmons, 1994). While the literature did not tackle that issue directly, it clearly was an issue for our participants. Finally, several participants felt that some leadership positions were filled based on gender, with men viewed as better disciplinarians and more equipped to handle a school and its problems.

Experience was an important attribute of a teacher leader. Most colleges and universities require a minimum of three years of teaching experience before candidates can apply to a leadership degree program, while districts closely monitor new teachers with mandated observations for three years, supporting experience as an important attribute of teachers and leaders. Interestingly, many participants noted examples of teacher leaders who had almost no teaching experience. For example, Evita became a lead teacher after only one year of teaching experience. We do not know if that was an anomaly of the group chosen, or a real trend exists. A larger sample of participants studied would help explore this phenomenon.

Teacher Leader Qualities

The participants noted qualities of both effective and ineffective teacher leaders. They said that effective teacher leaders were "well informed," "educated," "organized," "trustworthy," "student centered," and "led by example." They all had experience with good teacher leaders and believed they, themselves, were good leaders. On the other hand, they were familiar with poor leaders as well. One aspect of poor leadership was the influence of relationships within the school and community. All participants discussed examples of teacher leaders chosen based on who they knew rather than their knowledge and skills.

Although all participants were female and had numerous experiences with female school leaders, there were several examples of gender stereotypical leadership styles. Although all six participants described good leaders as possessing what can be thought of as feminine leadership traits, this did not always occur in reality. Pam described her experiences with female administrators as "cold-hearted competition." This led researchers to believe that at least some female leaders are still striving to lead in a perceived masculine manner.

Several participants discussed how good teacher leaders work toward school change and talked about their own hopes for disrupting the status quo. At the same time, several participants noted that this could be viewed as abrasive and that anyone who worked against the norm would find it difficult to get or keep a teacher leadership position. Many of the teacher leadership roles were also shallow and served to enforce the status quo, not promote change, as Moreau et al. (2007) suggested in their research.

Mentoring and/or Support in Effective Teacher Leadership

Both the professional literature and our participants supported the use of mentoring for teacher leaders; however, participants found that often it did not occur. Several of our participants felt they were left to sink or swim in their new positions and many felt that whether or not a teacher leader received mentoring had more to do with individual administrators rather than institutionalized processes found in the culture of the school. Some of our participants had strong mentoring and strong support whereas others felt isolated and alone. They recognized that teacher leadership depended on some of the same skills as teaching, but noted that these skills needed to be used differently.

Marginalization of teacher leaders occurred in both formal and informal positions consistently. It was clear that teachers in formal leadership roles are often sabotaged and resisted in both subtle and overt ways. While the professional literature promotes the end of egalitarian systems, they are still alive and well. Teachers resisted having someone pulled out of their ranks and put in a position above them, as can be seen through the comments made by Pam, Marisa, and Angie that when a teacher sought a leadership position, other teachers tried to discourage and/or undermine their leadership.

The lack of legitimacy within the teacher rank held true when many teachers rejected the instructional help offered by the formal teacher leader, which generated disappointment. For example, when Pam was given the title of literacy coach, she felt powerless and "in the middle" because teachers were free to accept or reject her suggestions based on their relationship and respect for her. Teacher leaders sometimes ended up no longer accepted as teachers but lacking the power and prestige of leaders, leaving them isolated. At least for these teachers, the "crab bucket" is alive and well.

RECOMMENDATIONS FOR TEACHER LEADERS

The literature and our teacher leaders agree that women possess the skills to lead effectively. Female principal leadership was unheard of just 35 years ago. The courageous women who said they could lead with integrity and honor and did it with style cracked the glass ceiling. Female teacher leaders are numerous but few are effectively challenging the status quo. Now women need to focus on challenging the barriers that marginalize their efforts as teacher leaders. Women have to become tired of the culture of schools that currently exist and work to change it. It is when female teachers look at the culture of their schools and say, "I can do it better" that the culture of schools will change.

Johnson and Donaldson (2008) stated, "The success or failure of teacher leaders will depend on their relationship with their colleagues" (p. 13). Much of what teachers and teacher leaders are doing now reinforces the crab bucket culture. Female teachers must take responsibility to lead with integrity and model what they want and experience in great leaders. Teacher collegiality and morale are important issues, as all of our participants noted.

Another issue that is here to stay is school reform. Teacher leader efforts can improve student achievement and create real school reform. Teachers who see themselves as leaders within their classrooms will discover the potential to influence student learning through their own actions. Teacher leaders who are confident about their leadership abilities will take on the responsibility for learning for all students (Katzenmeyer & Moller, 2001). The new models of leadership value the skills of communication, collaboration, vision, life-long learning, and consensus. Education in the United States needs real change in the culture of their schools to empower the "sleeping giant" that Moller and Pankake (2006) refer to in their research.

REFERENCES

Ackerman, R., & Mackenzie, S. V. (2006). Uncovering teacher leadership. *Educational Leadership, 63*(8), 66–73.

Addi-Raccah, A., & Ayalon, H. (2002). Gender inequality in leadership positions of teachers. *British Journal of Sociology of Education, 23*(2), 157–177.

Barth, R. (2001). *The teacher leader.* Providence, RI: The Rhode Island Foundation.

Bartlett, L. (2001). *Expanded teaching roles: Leadership or just overwork?* Paper presented at the biannual meeting of the International Study Association on Teachers and Teaching, Faro, Portugal.

Berry, B., Norton, J., & Byrd, A. (2007). Lessons from networking. *Educational Leadership, 65*(1), 48–53.

Boles, K., & Troen, V. (1996). Teacher leaders and power: Achieving school reform from the classroom. In G. Moller & M. Katzenmeyer (Eds.), *Every teacher as a leader: Realizing the potential of teacher leadership* (pp. 41–62). San Francisco: Jossey-Bass.

Childs-Bowen, D., Moller, G., & Scrivner, J. (2000). Principals: Leaders of learners. NASSP. *Bulletin, 84*, 27–34.

Coleman, M. (2007). Gender and educational leadership in England: A comparison of secondary headteachers' views over time. *School Leadership and Management, 27*(4), 383–399.

Coyle, M. (1997). Teacher leadership vs. school management: Flatten the hierarchy. *Clearinghouse, 70*, 236–239.

Crowther, F., Ferguson, M., & Hann, L. (2009). *Developing teacher leaders: How teacher leadership enhances school success* (2nd ed.). Thousand Oaks, CA: Corwin Press.

Crowther, F., Ferguson, M., Kaagan, S. S., & Hann, L. (2002). *Developing teacher leaders: How teacher leadership enhances school success.* Thousand Oaks, CA: Sage.

Danielson, C. (2005). Strengthening the school's backbone. *Journal of Staff Development, 26*(2), 34–37.

Danielson, C. (2007). The many faces of leadership. *Educational Leadership, 65*(1), 14–19.

Day, J. G., & Hill, C. (2008). *Behind the pay gap.* AAUW Educational Foundation. Retrieved from *http://www.aauw.org/research/upload/ExecSummary_PayGap.pdf.*

Donaldson, G. A. Jr. (2007). What do teachers bring to leadership? *Educational Leadership, 65*(1), 26–29.

Drago-Severson, E. (2007). Helping teachers learn: Principals as professional development leaders. *Teachers College Record, 109*(1), 70–125.

Drago-Severson, E., & Pinto, K. C. (2006). School leadership for reducing teacher isolation: Drawing from the well of human resources. *International Journal of Leadership in Education, 9*(2), 129–155.

Elmore, R. F. (2002). Hard questions about practice. *Educational Leadership, 59*(8), 22–25.

Frankel, L. P. (2007). *See Jane lead.* New York: Warner Business Books.

Gabriel, J. G. (2005). *How to thrive as a teacher leader.* Alexandria, VA: Association for Supervision and Curriculum Development.

Gonzales, L. D. (2004). *Sustaining teacher leadership: Beyond the boundaries of an enabling school culture.* Lanham, MA: University Press of America.

Gronn, P. (2000). Distributed properties: A new architecture for leadership, *Educational Management and Administration, 28*(3), 317–338.

Halverson, R., & Thomas, C. N. (2008). Drawing conclusions about instructional teacher leadership. In M. M. Mangin & S. R. Stoelinga (Eds.), *Effective teacher leadership: Using research to inform and reform.* New York: Teachers College Press.

Harris, A. (2003). Teacher leadership as distributed leadership: Heresy, fantasy or possibility? *School Leadership and Management, 23*(3), 313–324.

Harrison, J. W., & Lembeck, E. (1996). Emergent teacher leaders. In G. Moller & M. Katzenmeyer (Eds.). *Every teacher is a leader: Realizing the potential of teacher leadership* (pp. 101–116). San Francisco: Jossey-Bass.

Ingersoll, R. M. (2007). Short on power, long on responsibility. *Educational Leadership, 65*(1), 20–25.

Johnson, S. M., & Donaldson, M. L. (2008). Overcoming the obstacles to leadership. *Educational Leadership, 65*(1), 8–13.

Katzenmeyer, M., & Moller, G. (2001) *Awakening the sleeping giant: Helping teachers develop as leaders* (2nd ed.). Thousand Oaks, CA: Corwin Press.

Knight, J. (2007). *Instructional coaching: A partnership approach to improving instruction.* Thousand Oaks, CA: Corwin Press.

Lambert, L. (2002). A framework for shared leadership. *Educational Leadership, 59*(8), 37–40.

Lambert, L. (2003). *Leadership capacity for lasting school improvement.* Alexandria, VA: Association of Supervision and Curriculum Development.

LeBlanc, P. R., & Shelton, M. M. (1997). Teacher leadership: The needs of teachers. *Action in Teacher Education, 19*(3), 32–48.

Lieberman, A., & Friedrich, L. (2007). Teacher, writer, leaders. *Educational Leadership, 65*(1), 42–47.

Lieberman, A., & Miller, L. (1999). *Teachers—transforming their world and their work.* New York: Teachers College Press.

Lieberman, A., & Miller, L. (2004). *Teacher leadership.* San Francisco: Jossey-Bass.

Lipton, L., & Wellman, B. (2007). How to talk so teachers listen. *Educational Leadership, 65*(1), 30–34.

Little, J. W. (1988). Assessing the prospects for teacher leadership. In A. Lieberman (Ed.), *Building a professional culture in schools* (pp. 78–105). New York: Teachers College Press.

Mangin, M. M. (2005). Distributed leadership and the culture of schools: teacher leaders' strategies for gaining access to classrooms. *Journal of School Leadership, 15*(4), 456–484.

Mangin, M. M., & Stoelinga, S. R. (2008). Teacher leadership: What it is and why it matters. In M. M. Mangin & S. R. Stoelinga (Eds.), *Effective teacher leadership: Using research to inform and reform* (pp. 1–9). New York: Teachers College Press.

Manno, C. M., & Firestone, W. A. (2008). Content is the subject: How teacher leaders with different subject knowledge interact with teachers. In M. M. Mangin & S. R. Stoelinga (Eds.), *Effective teacher leadership: Using research to inform and Reform* (pp. 36–54). New York: Teachers College Press.

Marshall, C., & Ward, M. (2004). "Yes, but...": Education leaders discuss social justice. *Journal of School Leadership, 14*, 530–563.

Mayo, K. E. (2002). Teacher leadership: The master teacher model. *MiE, 16*(3), 29–33.

Moller, G., & Katzenmeyer, M. (1996). The promise of teacher leadership. In G. Moller & M. Katzenmeyer (Eds.). *Every teacher as a leader: Realizing the potential of teacher leadership* (pp. 1–18). San Francisco: Jossey-Bass.

Moller, G., & Pankake, A. (2006). *Lead with me.* Larchmont, NY: Eye on Education, Inc.

Moreau, M., Osgood, J. Y., & Halsall, A. (2007). Making sense of the glass ceiling in schools: An exploration of women teachers' discourses. *Gender and Education, 19*(2), 237–253.

Murphy, J. (2005). *Connecting teacher leadership and school improvement.* Thousand Oaks, CA: Corwin Press.

Murray, G., & Simmons, E. S. (1994). Women administrators: Leading the way in site-based management. *Equity & Excellence in Education, 27*(2), 71–77.

No Child Left Behind. (2001). Retrieved from: http://www2.ed.gov/nclb/overview/intro/execsumm.html

Ovando, M. N. (1996). Teacher leadership: Opportunities and challenges. *Planning and Changing, 2,* 30–44.

Picciano, A. G. (2006) *Data-driven decision making for effective school leadership.* Upper Saddle River, NJ: Pearson.

Randi, J., & Zeichner, K. (2004). New visions of teacher professional development. In M. Smylie & D. Miretszky (Eds.) *Developing the teacher workforce* (pp. 180–227). Chicago: University of Chicago Press.

Reason, C., & Reason, L. (2007). Asking the right questions. *Educational Leadership, 65*(1), 36–40.

Reeves, D. B. (2009). *Leading change in your school: How to conquer myths, building commitment, and get results.* Alexandria, VA: Association for Supervision and Curriculum Development.

Ryan, J. (2006). Inclusive leadership and social justice for schools. *Leadership and Policy in Schools, 5,* 3–17.

Scherer, M. (2007). Playing to strengths. *Educational Leadership, 65,* 7.

Silins, H., & Mulford, B. (2002). Leadership and school results. In K. A. Leithwood & Hallinger (Eds.), *Second international handbook of educational leadership and administration.* Dordrecht: Kluwer Academic.

Sergiovanni, T. (2001). *Leadership: What's in it for schools?* London: RoutledgeFalmer.

Smylie, M. A. (2008). Effective teacher leadership: Using research to inform and reform. In M. M. Mangin & S. R. Stoelinga (Eds.), *Effective teacher leadership: Using research to inform and reform.* New York: Teachers College Press.

Smylie, M. A., & Brownlee-Conyers, J. (1992). Teacher leaders and their principals: Exploring the development of new working relationships. *Educational Administration Quarterly, 28,* 50–184.

Smylie, M. A., Conley, S., & Marks, H. M. (2002). Exploring new approaches to teacher leadership for school improvement. In J. Murphy (Ed.), *The educational leadership challenge: Redefining leadership for the 21st century: 101st Yearbook of the National Society for the Study of Education, Part 1* (pp. 162–188). Chicago: University of Chicago Press.

Smylie, M. A., Mayrowetz, D., Murphy, J., & Louis, K. S. (2007). *Trust and the development of distributed leadership, 17*(3), 469–503.

Smylie, M. A., Miretzky, D., & Konkol, P. (2004). Rethinking teacher workforce development: A strategic human resource management perspective. In M. A. Smylie & D. Miretzky (Eds.), *Developing the teacher workforce* (pp. 34–69). Chicago: University of Chicago Press.

Stelter, N. Z. (2002). Gender differences in leadership: Current social issues and future organizational implications. *Journal of Leadership Studies, 8*(4), 88–99.

Stone, R., & Cuper, P. (2006). *Best practices for teacher leadership: What award-winning teachers do for their professional learning communities.* Thousand Oaks, CA: Corwin Press.

Sweetser, R. Z., & O'Connor, B. L. (2008). *Breaking through the barriers.* American Association of University Women. Retrieved from http://www.aauw.org/research/statedata/upload/table_data.pdf

Taylor, J. E. (2008). "Instructional coaching: The state of the art." Effective teacher leadership: Using research to inform and reform. In M. M. Mangin & S. R.

Stoelinga (Eds.), *Effective teacher leadership: Using research to inform and reform.* New York: Teachers College Press.

Trachtman, R. (1991). Voices of empowerment: Teachers talk about leadership. In S. C. Conley & B. S. Cooper (Eds.), *The school as a work environment: Implications for school reform* (pp. 222–235). Boston: Allyn & Bacon.

Troen, V., & Boles, K. (1994). Two teachers examine the power of teacher leadership. In D. R. Walling (Ed.), *Teachers as leaders: Perspectives on the professional development of teachers* (pp. 275–286). Bloomington, IN: Phi Delta Kappa.

U. S. Census Bureau. (2009). Statistical Abstract of the United States: 2009. Washington, DC. Retrieved from www.census.gov.

Weiner, L. (2002). Nitpicking: An exploration of the marginalization of gender equity in urban school research and reform. *Urban Review, 34*(4), 363–380.

Whitehead, S. (2001). Woman as manager: A seductive ontology. *Gender, Work, and Organization, 8*(1), 84–107.

York-Barr, J., & Duke, K. (2004). What do we know about teacher leadership? *Review of Educational Research, 74*(3), 255–316.

York-Barr, J., Sommers, W. A., Ghere, G. S., & Montie, J. (2001). *Reflective practice to improve schools: An action guide for educators.* Thousand Oaks, CA: Corwin Press.

CHAPTER 8

PROFESSIONAL DEVELOPMENT TO STRENGTHEN DEPARTMENT CHAIR INSTRUCTIONAL LEADERSHIP CAPACITY

Advancing Social Justice in Urban High Schools

Hans W. Klar and Paul V. Bredeson

The trend toward standardization and accountability for student learning outcomes in the United States, particularly since the enactment of the No Child Left Behind Act, has forced schools to examine the performance of student groups in much greater detail than previously practiced. The disaggregation of academic results has, in many cases, revealed glaring inequalities in achievement and success across student groups. These disparities are most apparent when comparisons are made between students based on differences in race, ethnicity, socio-economic status, levels of English

Educational Leaders Encouraging the Intellectual and Professional Capacity of Others:
A Social Justice Agenda, pages 139–162.
Copyright © 2012 by Information Age Publishing
All rights of reproduction in any form reserved.

language competence, and other special needs. Within urban high schools, these achievement gaps raise critical social justice questions, which challenge traditional structures, instructional practices, and beliefs in meeting the needs of all students.

In some schools, principals, through their instructional leadership practices, have taken the lead in addressing these challenges. Notwithstanding the heroic efforts of these formal leaders, the transformation of cultures, structures, and classroom practices requires an instructional leadership framework that embraces the energies and expertise of the many key stakeholders associated with each school. Principals can realize this transformation in part by supporting the professional development of department chairpersons as instructional leaders. In fulfilling such a role, chairpersons would investigate and pose solutions for "issues that generate and reproduce inequalities" (Dantley & Tillman, 2010, p. 19) whilst creating coherent, purposeful, and sustainable learning environments for all students and staff. A framework reflective of the instructional leadership tasks required to fulfill these roles would suggest that chairpersons learn to effectively:

- Facilitate the development of a shared vision at school and department levels;
- Use data to identify goals and assess instructional effectiveness;
- Support student and adult learning;
- Monitor progress in the alignment of curriculum, instruction, and assessment; and
- Promote continuous improvement in teaching and learning at the school and department levels. (Bredeson, Kelley, & Klar, 2009)

In this chapter, we describe how on-going, job-embedded professional development, provided through a university/school district state department of education partnership, can enhance instructional leadership practices that advance social justice in urban high schools to address inequitable student outcomes. The theory of action employed in the approach is that developing high school department chairs' instructional leadership capacities will support the development of school-wide and department-specific communities of instructional practice, which in turn provide the focus and expertise to examine and revise structures, practices, and beliefs that may be contributing to or perpetuating discrepancies in academic achievement.

CONTEXT

The Wentworth Falls School District (all names used in this chapter are pseudonyms), located in a Midwestern state in the United States, provides the backdrop for this examination of professional development intended to redress inequitable student achievement. The Wentworth Falls School

District (WFSD) is located in a city of approximately 220,000 residents. It has traditionally been viewed as a successful school district, due in part to its large number of national merit scholars, innovative teaching practices, and progressive approaches to educating students with special needs. Yet, the district, like many districts in the United States, has in recent years seen a steady increase in the enrollment of minority, low-income, and otherwise disadvantaged students. Also, like many other districts in the United States, WFSD's growing population of traditionally underprivileged students is not enjoying the same level of success as their White and economically advantaged peers. A demographic breakdown of the students in WFSD and the three high schools featured in this study: Pennant Hills, Hollis, and Winchester is provided in Table 8.1

Despite attempts from many concerned educators within WFSD, large inequities in academic success exist between white students and nonwhite students, as well as between students who are economically disadvantaged and those who are not. The disparities are most apparent when the measures of academic achievement, such as state assessment results, high school completion, and entrance to post-secondary programs, are disaggregated by demographic characteristics. This disparity is illustrated in Tables 8.2, 8.3, and 8.4. Table 8.2 shows WFSD's 2008 tenth-grade state reading and math test results by student group. As can be seen in the table, significantly larger percentages of white students, and students who were economically

TABLE 8.1. 2008-09 WFSD and High School Student Demographics

Student group	All WFSD students	Pennant Hills	Hollis	Winchester
Total enrollment	24, 496	1693	1645	1928
% Female	48.9	49.1	48.8	50.1
% Male	51.1	50.9	51.2	49.9
% American Indian/Alaskan Native	0.8	0.5	0.8	0.7
% Asian/Pacific Islander	10.7	11.3	6.4	12
% Black (not of Hispanic Origin)	22.6	25.9	25.5	21
% Hispanic	14.5	10.7	10.6	10
% White (not of Hispanic Origin)	50.5	51.6	56.7	56.3
% Eligible for Free/Reduced-Price Lunch	44.1	48.6	44.4	66.9
% Limited English Proficient	17.2	15.7	12	10.2
% with Disabilities	*	20	22.5	21.4

Source: State Department of Education website

TABLE 8.2. Percentage of WFSD Students Scoring Proficient* or Advanced on 2008 State Grade 10 Reading and Math Tests

Student group	Reading	Math
American Indian/Alaskan Native	N/A	N/A
Asian/Pacific Islander	68%	71%
Black (not of Hispanic origin)	46%	30%
Hispanic	51%	41%
White (not of Hispanic origin)	81%	80%
Eligible for free/reduced-price lunch	48%	37%
Not eligible for free/reduced-price lunch	83%	81%

Source: State Department of Education website
*State test results are expressed in a range of proficiencies: Minimal Performance, Basic, Proficient, and Advanced.

advantaged, achieved results that were Proficient or Advanced than did students who were not white, or were economically disadvantaged.

A breakdown of the number and percentage of students graduating with a regular high school diploma from each of the three high schools in the 2007–08 school year is provided in Table 8.3. As can be seen in the table, there are significant differences in the graduation rates between White and Asian/Pacific Islander students and Black and Hispanic students. Significant differences can also be seen in the graduation rates of students with and without disabilities.

Table 8.4 further highlights the disparities by examining the percentage of students planning to attend 4-year colleges or universities in each of the schools by student group. As can be seen in the table, significantly higher proportions of white and Asian/Pacific Islander students indicated that they were planning to attend a 4-year college or university than did black and Hispanic students.

Though not included in this chapter, other measures of academic achievement and engagement—such as participation in school activities, enrollment in advanced courses, attendance, and disciplinary actions—further highlight the differences in students' educational experiences in WFSD's comprehensive high schools.

With the knowledge that disparities such as those highlighted in Tables 8.2–8.4 existed in its high schools, WFSD applied for, and, in 2008, received two grants that provided financial resources, additional staff, and external expertise to address the inequities. One grant was from the U.S. Department of Education. The chief aim of this grant was to improve relationships, engagement, and learning for all students through the implementa-

TABLE 8.3. Students Graduating with Regular Diplomas in 2007–08

Student group	Pennant Hills no. of students in grade 12	Pennant Hills % of students graduating	Hollis no. of students in grade 12	Hollis % of students graduating	Winchester no. of students in grade 12	Winchester % of students graduating
Total	483	74.9	430	87.9	504	87.4
Female	228	75.7	230	89.7	230	87.5
Male	255	74.2	200	85.8	274	87.3
American Indian/Alaskan Native	5	75	3	100	2	100
Asian/Pacific Islander	60	77.9	24	92.3	67	90.4
Black (not of Hispanic origin)	113	59.7	68	75.7	65	63.6
Hispanic	36	54.2	51	83.7	38	75.4
White (not of Hispanic origin)	269	84.6	284	91.1	332	95.6
Students with disabilities	121	53.4	97	82.6	99	71.3
Students without disabilities	362	81.6	333	89.1	405	91.1

Source: State Department of Education website

TABLE 8.4.   Percentage of Students Planning to Attend 4-Year College/University by Student Group

Student group	Pennant Hills	Hollis	Winchester
Total Graduates	415	398	498
% of Total Planning to Attend	43.9	48	59.6
% Female	44.1	54.8	57.8
% Male	43.7	40.4	61.4
% American Indian/Alaskan Native	N/A	50	50
% Asian/Pacific Islander	30.2	41.7	69.7
% Black (not of Hispanic origin)	21.6	37.5	22.2
% Hispanic	25.0	31.7	37.2
% White (not of Hispanic origin)	56.1	53.1	67.9

Source: State Department of Education website

tion of small learning communities in its high schools. Commensurate with the ideals of small learning communities, WFSD developed three specific goals for each of its high schools related to the grant. The goals were to increase the graduation rate; improve relationships between students, and between students and adults; and increase post-secondary opportunities for all students.

The Wallace Foundation provided the second grant. This grant was intended to support the development of an aligned system of leadership for learning through a partnership between the state department of education, three universities, and 16 high schools from five districts across the state. The districts selected for the grant represented nearly 90% of the state's African American student population. Each of the districts had large achievement gaps between white and nonwhite students. Given the resources and focus provided by the small learning communities grant, the grant from the Wallace Foundation afforded the WFSD high schools the potential to develop the instructional leadership capacity to realize the goals of the small learning communities grant, thereby enhancing the educational experiences of all high school students in the district.

The following sections of the chapter describe the professional development provided to department chairs in three of WFSD's four comprehensive high schools. In the first section, the theoretical and empirical underpinnings for strengthening department chair instructional leadership capacity to advance social justice and academic outcomes for all students is provided. Next, the Characteristics of Successful Professional Development (Bredeson, 2003, p. 111) are used as a conceptual organizer to describe the professional development provided to the department chairs. In the final section of the chapter, the process of addressing the department chairs' concerns regarding the changes to their professional practice is discussed.

RATIONALE

There are myriad explanations for the poor academic performance of particular groups of students relative to their peers in comprehensive, urban high schools. Explanations for these disparities often focus on attributes of the learners themselves, such as race, ethnicity, language, socio-economic status, ability, and sexual orientation (Dantley & Tillman, 2010; Nieto, 2005). Yet, such a view does not account for a school's potential to impede the academic success of some student groups by contributing to or perpetuating the inequities that may exist within the school system itself. Furthermore, such a perspective does not encourage members of the community to take responsibility for examining and redressing the multitude of factors that may be influencing such disparities. Nieto (2005) highlighted the complex, yet requisite, steps of such an undertaking this way:

> School achievement, always difficult to explain, must be approached by taking into account multiple, competing, and dynamic conditions: the school's tendency to replicate society and its inequities; cultural and language incompatibilities; the unfair and bureaucratic structures of schools; the nature of the relationships among students, teachers, and the communities they serve; and the political relationship of particular groups to society and the schools. (p. 52)

Rather than justify differences in school success by the perceived deficits of their students, then, we concur with Larson and Murtadha (2002) who suggested that achievement gaps found in schools are reflective of an injustich that, though unintentional, is "neither natural nor inevitable" (p. 135). Rather, these achievement gaps should be viewed as issues of social justice, which principals have the wherewithal to amend (Brooks, Jean-Marie, Normorne, & Hodgins, 2007; Riehl, 2000). While the role of the principal in setting direction, developing people, and redesigning the organization is widely recognized (Leithwood, Louis, Anderson, & Wahlstrom, 2004), as Brooks et al. (2007) noted, the role of the principal is particularly important in advancing social justice in the school setting:

> Although many educators throughout school systems can find inspiration in the call to ameliorate hegemony and work toward ethical and equitable educational practice, school leaders are uniquely positioned to facilitate meaningful and substantive change at the building level. (p. 379)

As illustrated in this chapter, one approach to closing this gap in achievement is principals and other instructional leaders working to redress the inequities found within the schools through the development of an inclusive school culture and high-quality instructional practices (Elmore, 2002; Kose, 2007; Leithwood & Riehl, 2003; Theoharis, 2009). This approach is consistent with Leithwood and Riehl's (2003) notion that "school leaders can promote equity and justice for all students by establishing school climates where patterns of discrimination are challenged and negated" (p. 8). This view is also consistent with the work of Kose (2007) and with Theoharis (2009) who argued that it is incumbent upon all leaders of social justice, to maintain a focus on issues of "race, class, gender, disability, sexual orientation, and other historically marginalizing factors" (p. 11). From this perspective, leadership for social justice involves "interrogating the policies and procedures that shape schools and at the same time perpetuate social inequalities and marginalization due to race, class, gender, and other markers of difference" (Dantley & Tillman, 2010, p. 31). Such a view, we suggest, would involve maintaining a focus on advancing inclusion, access, and opportunity for all students while working to develop high-quality classroom instruction throughout the school, frequently acknowledged as a critical factor in academic achievement (Capper, Frattura, & Keyes, 2000; Cohen & Ball 1999; Corcoran & Goertz, 1995; Elmore, 2002; Leithwood et al., 2004; Louis & Marks, 1998; Newmann & Wehlage, 1995; Spillane & Louis, 2002).

Principals are often thought of as the sole instructional leader in schools (Barnett & Aagaard, 2007). Yet, the task of enhancing a school's instructional capacity to improve student achievement is increasingly being viewed as simply too complex and overwhelming a job for a single leader. This inability to provide effective instructional leadership is due in large part to distractions associated with non-instructional issues (Barnett & Aagaard, 2007; Chrispeels, Burke, Johnson, & Daly, 2008; Copland & Boatright, 2006; Fink & Resnick, 2001; Fullan, 2002; Lambert, 2002; Portin, 2000; Resnick & Glennan, 2002; Supovitz & Poglinco, 2001). In complex urban high schools, these distractions tend to be even more disruptive, resulting in even less instructional leadership being provided by principals (Portin, 2000; Resnick & Glennan, 2002).

The extensive, though relatively recent, body of research on teacher leadership (Barth, 2007; Crowther, 2009; Harris, 2003b; Lambert, 2003; York-Barr & Duke, 2004) provides compelling incentives for principals to look within their organizations for assistance. Harris (2003a) suggested that if schools are to cope with the current and future challenges, they must generate the "leadership capacity of the many rather than the few" (p. 5). This approach, she argued, is a "fundamental reconceptualization of leadership as a form of social capital which, if distributed or shared, has the greatest potential to contribute to sustained school development and improvement" (p. 5).

While a great deal of research has focused on principal instructional leadership, and the instructional leadership of teacher leaders such as instructional coaches (Mangin & Stoelinga, 2008), much less attention has been given to the affordances of such leadership being exhibited by academic department chairs. Weiler (2001) referred to the department chair as "the most underutilized position" (p. 1), and suggested that chairs are potentially the most influential people in well-organized high schools. In his research on effective department chairs, Nelson (2004) determined that chairs are the "unsung heroes" of school improvement who are at the frontline of complex change in high schools. Nelson also found that, in comprehensive high schools, effective department-level leadership is critical to improvement and to the implementation of reforms. Wetterson (1992), in conducting multiple case studies of department chairs, found that their position provided chairs the opportunity to influence curriculum and instruction within their own departments as well as promoting ideas for school improvement across the wider school context. Wetterson also found that teachers are more likely to perceive their department chairs, rather than their principals, as the schools' instructional leaders. Given the important role departments play in influencing the work of teachers within them (Harris, 2001; Hill, 1995; Little, 1995; Nelson, 2004; Siskin & Little, 1995), department chairs clearly have an important role to play in converting the aspirations embedded in the school's mission, vision, and values into the reality of daily classroom practice and school improvement efforts.

As the initiative described in this study required a change in a middle-level leadership role already fraught with ambiguity (Zapeda & Kruskamp, 2007) and strain (Bredeson, 1993), it is important to consider the impact of such a change on the department chairs themselves. Hord, Rutherford, Huling-Austin, and Hall (1987) noted that having "specific and individualistic concerns" about the impact of change is a universal feature of change processes (p. 30). Hord and her colleagues also suggested that "the single most important factor in any change process is the people who will be most affected by the change" (p. 29). Hord et al.'s well-researched model for examining concerns related to changes in practice, the Concerns Based Adoption Model (CBAM), provides a useful organizer for discussing the concerns expressed by the department chairs and the manner in which the principals and research team responded to them. The CBAM's three dimensions of self, task, and impact are classified into seven stages of concern as illustrated in Table 8.5. Hord et al. suggested that, though individuals may have concerns associated with each stage of the model, their concerns generally progress from stage to stage as the implementation progresses.

High school department chairs are also typically members of leadership teams. While the compositions and responsibilities of leadership teams may

TABLE 8.5. Dimensions of Self, Task, and Impact

Dimensions	Stages of concern
Self	Awareness, informational, personal
Task	Management
Impact	Consequence, collaboration, refocusing

Source: Adapted from Hord et al. (1987, p. 31)

differ between schools, it is clear they have the potential to play a key role in the manifestation of successful school improvement efforts (Marzano, Waters, & McNulty, 2005). As noted by Chrispeels et al. (2008), "There is a growing recognition that principals cannot lead alone and that school leadership teams are essential to the improvement process" (p. 730).

Members of these teams also benefit from their participation within them. West-Burnham (2004) suggested that teams are the most powerful way to develop leadership capacity, describing them as "nurseries where participants are provided with numerous opportunities to learn and develop leadership skills in a safe and supportive environment" (p. 5). West-Burnham further described teams as "both a powerful vehicle for effective leadership and one of the most effective and fertile contexts for learning" (p. 5). Wenger's (1998) community of practice perspective also provides a useful lens for viewing leadership teams as venues for mutual growth and learning around a shared set of leadership practices.

As illustrated in this review of the literature, there is a sound basis on which this approach to advancing social justice in these three urban, comprehensive high schools has been proposed. This approach suggests that professional development designed to increase leadership capabilities to advance social justice "recognizes the essential nature of building a quality and empowered staff that takes responsibility for the learning of every child and, in particular, the children who struggle the most" (Theorharis, 2009, p. 60). In its effort to provide better educational opportunities for its students who struggle the most, WFSD embraced this approach to school reform in the summer of 2008.

PROFESSIONAL DEVELOPMENT ACTIVITIES

In this section of the chapter, we report on the first year of professional development initiatives carried out in three of WFSD's high schools. The specific purpose of our leader development project was to strengthen the instructional leadership capacity in each school by engaging teams of educators, including the building principal, department chairpersons, and other unit specialists. These school-based teams focused their collective instructional leadership efforts to significantly lift student achievement, especially for students who had traditionally struggled. Addressing glaring gaps in participation and achievement among Whites, African-Americans, Hispanics, English language learners, and students with disabilities in these high schools clearly situated the work of these instructional teams in leadership for social justice. We use Bredeson's (2003) framework- highlighting characteristics of effective professional development- to describe the context, content, design, delivery, and outcomes of professional learning experiences during this initial year of collaboration between our university training team and three high school instructional leadership teams.

Professional Development Context

There were at least three levels of context that affected our professional development project —the political context, district context, and school/ community support context. To begin, the political environment, especially the focus on student learning outcomes required under mandates of the No Child Left Behind Act, has forced educators to examine more closely data revealing substantial inequalities in learning outcomes for particular groups of students. Differences in student achievement have long existed in urban high schools. What has changed in terms of the political context is accountability for those differences. Once explained by factors primarily outside of the school—poverty, community problems, and family indifference—new demands for educational professionals to be accountable for helping all students be successful in school has turned attention to within-school factors—structures, policies, curriculum, and instructional practices—that explain differences in outcomes. Thus, there is a sense of urgency and responsibility for teachers and principals to better understand how changes in instructional capacity and professional practice can address deeply rooted inequalities in student learning outcomes in these urban high schools.

The demographic composition of the school district context reflected changes occurring in most urban districts across the United States. There was an increasingly diverse student population including greater percentages of poor students, students of color, transient populations, and English language learners. As the data displayed earlier in the chapter reveal, there were huge achievement gaps among White students and non-White students and economically disadvantaged students. Finding ways to eliminate achievement gaps among various groups of students is linked explicitly to district goals, and local school vision statements and school improvement plans. Published annual reports from state testing have created both a sense of responsibility and urgency in addressing gaps in student achievement. Over the past decade the high schools in the district have been working together, with varying degrees of success, to confront persistent gaps in student achievement. Within this local environment, the introduction of our instructional leadership development project was viewed as a natural extension of reform and collaboration initiatives in the district to address inequities in student learning and developmental outcomes in schools.

The third level of context was existing support for professional development in these three high schools. In addition to the Wallace Foundation's funding to support professional development, the district received a muli-year small learning community grant providing over a million dollars per year to buy resources, time, and materials to support the development of instructional leadership teams. The two grants provided money to pay for the most expensive element of our professional development project, teacher time. In addition to paying for substitute teachers, these resources funded materials and all costs for whole and half-day off-site professional development. The three high schools were located in a city, which included the state department of education and a major research institution; consequently, the high school team participants, state education department specialists, university experts in various fields, and our university leadership team were able to communicate regularly and coordinate professional development activities. Lastly, the community provided multiple venues— community centers as well as teacher union, university, and private facilities, mostly free, for hosting various professional development meetings.

Professional Development Content

As noted earlier in the chapter, the overall goal of our multi-year professional development project was to strengthen and deepen the social and intellectual capital needed to help all students be successful in these urban high schools. From the beginning, our strategy was to work with existing educator teams (principals, department chairpersons, and other specialists) to build individual and collective professional knowledge, skills, and commitments. By distributing the tasks and responsibilities for instructional leadership among key leaders, especially department chairpersons, we hoped to establish strong and enduring instructional leadership capacities that would help each school address critical issues affecting professional practice and student learning outcomes.

One of the first challenges our university team faced was being able to communicate clearly to all participants what we meant by distributed instructional leadership and what their role(s) would be in creating that capacity in their schools. We believe this challenge also illustrated the reciprocity that developed between our team and the high school teams. Our original intention in the project was guided by knowledge of research and practice in successful instructional leadership, but we resisted the idea of a "one size fits all" approach. We did not want to impose our model. We envisioned the development of instructional leadership teams in each school as organic and reflective of each school's unique qualities. We began by describing a process that we borrowed from the National College for Leadership of Schools and Children's Services titled, *Leading from the Middle* (www.ncsl.org.uk/lftm-index). Unfortunately, the PowerPoint slides and framework used in our introduction to the project appeared to create more confusion than understanding. Participants asked, "What do you mean by instructional leadership?" "How does this affect me as a department chair?" "How is this different from our current practices?" "What does effective instructional leadership look like in actual practice?"

Working with one of our high school principals, we returned to the literature, reviewed national standards for school leaders, and examined various leadership frameworks used by leadership preparation programs and state licensure agencies. We developed a working definition of instructional leadership and identified five key practices that helped us specify the content of professional development activities and desired learning outcomes for individuals and teams. We defined instructional leaders as educators who work to create coherent, purposeful, and sustainable learning environments for all students and staff, and identified the following tasks for development:

- Facilitate the development of a shared vision at school and department levels;
- Use data to identify goals and assess instructional/organizational effectiveness;
- Support student and adult learning;
- Monitor progress in the alignment of curriculum, instruction, and assessment; and
- Promote continuous improvement in teaching and learning at the school and department level. (Bredeson et al., 2009).

Once we specified these tasks for development, department chairpersons immediately recognized differences between their traditional roles and responsibilities as chairpersons and the new expectations for them as instructional leaders. Individuals and teams were now at a critical stage for new learning and changes in professional practice—awareness. They understood that their participation on the instructional leadership team had implications for them as teachers in the classroom, as union members, as colleagues in their departments, and as members of the school leadership team. Their anxiety and uncertainty were predictable affective dimensions of role transition (Bredeson, 1993) in a change process in which individuals and teams consider the implications of changes in professional practice (CBAM) identifies three dimensions of concern related to changes in professional practices: self, task, and impact (Hord et al., 1987). Each of these stages continued to be important as we planned professional development to strengthen instructional leadership knowledge, skills, and commitment.

Professional Development Design

Our professional development team included two professors of educational leadership and four doctoral candidates in the department. Guided by our grant proposal, we coordinated our work in the high schools with a state-wide coordinating team. The state coordinating team was composed of state department of education staff, central office school district personnel from the five participating school districts, a professional association representative, and faculty from the three participating universities.

As our university team began to work at each high school, local context and culture tempered any inclination toward rigid structures or pe-ceived ideas about "right" answers for the development of teams to build instructional leadership capacity. To be sure, there were commonalities across the high schools, but differences in school histories, professional staffs, expectations of their communities, and individual principal leadership styles made us comfortable in adopting a "loose/tight" approach. We were loose in terms of strategies, starting points, and professional development activities we carried out in each school. We were tight in focus and purpose—to build instructional leadership capacity in the school that supports all students' learning and success. Also, given the array of other initiatives already occurring in each of these high schools (e.g., sundry committees, grants for various programs, and partnerships with external organizations), our goal was to begin enhancing and deepening instructional leadership capacities in the schools immediately. We decided to work with the existing and familiar formal leadership structures, i.e., school principals, grant coordinators, and department chairpersons, rather than spend time and resources creating new structures.

As we laid out a general plan and calendars for initiating professional development in the three schools, four design features characterized our work. First, all professional development over the two-year period would be an integral part of these educators' professional work days, not an add-on to already busy schedules. Second, we wanted the training to engage a broad base of participants, generally 1–20 professional staff per building, including academic department chairs and other unit specialists, so that the desired outcomes for students permeated all aspects of school life. Third, our activities with each leadership team were designed to model effective group facilitation processes, instructional leadership behaviors, and active participation. It was important that our plan for leadership development was coherent and aligned with district values, priorities, and individual school improvement goals. Vision and goal statements from the district and one of the high schools illustrate this alignment:

- *District Vision:* "We are committed to successful learning, child by child."

- *Highs School Vision:* "The central goal of Pennant Hills' vision is to increase academic performance and opportunities for all students."
- *Highs School Leadership Team Goal:* "Develop and Implement 'Leadership for Learning Teams' models for high schools that define the behaviors the principal and other team members should employ to positively impact student learning."

As Pennant Hills' vision makes clear, the achievement gap between White and no-White and economically disadvantaged students was no longer acceptable and would not be tolerated.

Lastly, in each of the schools we used one-on-one meetings, surveys, group discussions, data analyses, and participant feedback on professional development activities to assess prior knowledge, individual and team readiness, and learning outcomes from which we could both evaluate leadership development activities and plan future sessions.

Professional Development Delivery

Establishing positive working relationships and building trust among our team and the high school leadership teams were foundational to our interactions with individuals and teams over time. Unlike many of the traditional in-service activities these educators had experienced in their careers, (fragmented, one-off topics involving an array of itinerant presenters), the leadership development project, funded for two years, was designed to assure participants of our commitment of time, resources, research, and expertise to build instructional leadership teams that were effective and sustainable once the initial grant period ended. Our working relationships were strengthened in each case through reciprocal exchanges of expertise and professional knowledge. For instance, our university team brought research and expertise about leadership, team building, group facilitation, change processes, data analysis, and instructional leadership practices that enhanced learning and success for all students. School principals, department chairs, and other specialists were grounded in the daily realities of implementing these ideas in their schools. They knew the students and local culture. They had deep content knowledge and they had years of experience to draw on as they considered new ideas and changes in relationships and practices.

Professional development activities over the first year included such activities as presentations and group work in whole-day and half-day workshops, sharing research and considering its implications for practice, group discussions, readings, videos, and planning meetings with principals and grant co-ordinators, debriefing sessions to assess outcomes and next steps, individual and group assessments, work product development (i.e., vision statements, action plans, and curriculum mapping, and written feedback coming from our team as well as all participants. The wide array of professional learning opportunities was anchored in principles of effective professional development. These include:

- considering how professionals learn and acquire new knowledge and skills;
- identifying successful practices in other settings;
- attending to individual needs as well as team skills and capacities; and
- designing activities that are coherent, continuous, sustainable, and job-embedded.

Creating a supportive learning environment was also an important feature of professional development delivery. Important considerations included the learning venus, both inside and outside of school. Initial sessions were located in conference centers and community facilities that demonstrated to all participants that the work of these instructional leadership teams was valued and would, therefore, be well resourced over time. Warm-ups, ice breakers, group building activities, planned breaks, food, and time to share and reflect were complementary features of professional development sessions over the first year.

Professional Development Outcomes

In this section we identify outcomes based on the first year of professional development work with these three high school teams. Each high school instructional leadership team had laid the groundwork for advancing the project. They had set the direction, shared expectations for their work, and established structures and processes for group and schol-wide initiatives that engaged other teachers and staff. As important, they developed norms of trust, interaction, feedback, relationships, critique, and reflection needed for the challenging professional work to address inequities in student learning outcomes in their schools. Each team also complemented their work with appropriate infusions of fun and humor. Next, we describe changes that we documented in individuals and in the development of instructional leadership teams.

To begin, there was heightened awareness of existing student achievement gaps and a collective sense of professional responsibility to address the various factors that contributed to those gaps. This awareness expressed itself as individuals and teams acknowledged the issues involved and grew increasingly comfortable yet frank in their discussions and critiques of various factors contributing to the achievement gap and its deleterious effects on various student groups. One of the most visible outcomes was the deepening level of engagement and commitment to school improvement goals, especially those centered on equitable student learning outcomes.

For example, in two of the schools, core academic departments (English, math, science, and social studies) met weekly with the principals and their cabinets, while the instructional leadership teams, including all department/unit heads, only met twice a month. The non-core department heads wanted to be included in these weekly meetings. As a result, in two schools, weekly meetings were organized to include all department chairs. As individuals and teams became more familiar with the five key areas of instructional leadership, individual confidence in professional knowledge and skills was affirmed, thereby increasing participation in team tasks and comfort with group process facilitation.

As the agendas in these meetings gained focus, the teams requested school and district data from the principal and central office personnel. Teams asked for supplementary information to support their work, and wanted access to research that provided a foundation for developing action plans.

Despite the short duration of the professional development initiative relative to the scope of the initiatives' goals, there were a number of identifiable outcomes in these three high schools related to the work of department chairs. An illustrative, though not exhaustive, compilation of accomplishments realized by the department chairs working in collaboration with other department chairs as well as the teachers in their own departments can be found in Appendix A. This document utilizes the instructional leadership framework described earlier in the chapter (Bredeson et al., 2009) to highlight the work of the department chairs in each of the schools. Some of these outcomes were focused on structures such as developing teams of teachers who teach and provide academic support to ninth -grade students. Other accomplishments were focused on practices such as revising entrance requirements into higher-level courses to allow for a wider variety of students to apply. Additional outcomes included the examination of existing beliefs, such as the inclusion of English language learners and special education students into all general education classrooms. Other tangible outcomes highlighted by the matrix included:

- major syllabus projects to map course content and objectives within and across district high schools;
- development of shared visions and goal statements;
- identification of necessary professional development for teachers, department chairs, and administrators;
- negotiation between the school district and the teachers' union to provide professional collaboration time for all teachers; and
- school improvement plans tied directly to school/grant goals with specified action plans.

Finally, we also witnessed over the first year how each school principal negotiated his (all principals were male) role in the emerging landscape of distributed instructional leadership. In each of the three schools, the principal's individual personality and leadership style were major energizers for the development of instructional leadership teams and setting the direction for their collective work. Two principals, because of their lengthy tenure in their buildings, had already built strong networks of social trust with their staffs. This form of social capital was a critical resource on which these principals could rely as department chairs struggled to understand new roles and expectations for their work, suspended disbelief in the new distributed instructional leadership framework, and followed the lead of their respective principals as the project initiative progressed. As each of the instructional leadership teams matured and gained confidence in their work, principals became more comfortable as group participants in sessions while other team members assumed responsibility for setting agendas and facilitating activities. Team members expected principals to be engaged and involved. In addition, they wanted to be assured that the principal would follow up with initiatives and support them when they worked within their departments to advance school improvement goals.

COMMENTARY

While the ultimate goal of the professional development activities for the leadership for learning initiative was focused on more equitable student outcomes in these high schools, at this early stage in the project (Year 1) we do not have follow-up student outcome data to report. Nonetheless, our documentation of activities and outcomes for participants in the leadership initiative, and for their schools, provides useful insights into early changes and impacts. As noted in the previous section, in the first year of the initiative the instructional cabinets were transformed into leadership teams focused on issues of school improvement, and the realization of more socially just learning outcomes for their students. In the process of transforming traditional department chairpersons into instructional leaders, through this array of professional development activities that highlighted glaring educational inequities among student groups, the department chairs demonstrated a heightened awareness of their schools' achievement gaps as well as their relationships to existing structures, instructional practices, and beliefs. Reflecting the findings of Barnett and Aagaard (2007), Nelson (2004), and Weiler (2001), these educators recognized that the daunting tasks of instructional leadership in urban high schools is too complex and demanding for any single professional. As department chairpersons reexamined their traditional roles and began to assume new leadership tasks, they collectively understood how critical they were as linchpins in school reform that benefited all students and negated inequitable school structures, cultures, and student learning outcomes.

As the leadership teams matured, they became communities of practice, with team members increasingly trusting and supportive of each other. This environment, combined with the heightened awareness of the schools' status quo, resulted in increased attention to the roles they, as department chairs, could play as instructional leaders. Over time, teams and individuals also became more engaged, empowered, and responsible for the learning of adults and students within their schools. Earlier in the chapter we cited Leithwood and Riehl's (2003) notion that "school leaders can promote equity and justice for all students by establishing school climates where patterns of discrimination are challenged and negated" (p. 8). Clearly these instructional leadership teams have begun to recognize patterns of discrimination in their schools, to challenge the existing status quo, and to lead the development of new structures, instructional practices, and beliefs within their departments and across their schools.

While these gains were heartening to principals, district leaders, research team members, and other stakeholders, we would be remiss if we did not describe some of the challenges that emerged as a result of concerns expressed by the department chairs. In fact, responding to these concerns provided much of the focus of the professional development in the first year. Using the CBAM framework cited earlier in the chapter, our documentation of professional development activities and responses to those learning opportunities revealed individual as well as collective concerns about the shifting role of department chairpersons. For example, in this first year, the department chairs' concerns were primarily associated with the self and task dimensions. In the initial stages of the professional development, the chairs were concerned about issues pertaining to themselves. Concerns were at first heightened when they became aware of the achievement gaps during data retreats (awareness). Following this, the chairs wanted to know what the data from their departments looked like and what would be expected of them as instructional leaders (informational). Once the chairs were satisfied that they understood what was being asked of them, their thoughts, and the focus of the professional development, turned to the skills they might need for leading instructional reform within their departments (personal). Though such concerns varied in concert with the teams' existing capacities, leadership team meetings primarily focused on developing skills related to facilitating effective meetings, team building, data analysis, school improvement planning, and the principles of effective instruction. Generally speaking, at the end of the first year, the three high school leadership teams were situated in the task domain, as indicated by the fact that they were primarily focused on issues related to the transition (management), namely the lack of common time for the teachers within their departments to meet. Looking ahead to the second year of the professional development initiative, we anticipate that the department chairs' concerns related to self and task will wane, in lieu of a focus on issues related to the implementation of their strategies to support the development of a socially just teaching and learning environment. In addition, as these instructional leadership teams continue to mature, the development of supportive school structures and cultures are likely to move each school toward a model of distributed instructional leadership. Similar to the stages of concern experienced by these department chairpersons as they moved through these early instructional leadership training experiences, we anticipate that as chairpersons work with teachers in their respective departments, teachers will also have concerns related to possible changes. Providing the time, resources, support, and learning opportunities for these teachers will be essential as they work to create more socially just and equitable learning environments for all students through the critical examination of schoolwide structures, practices, and beliefs while enhancing their instructional capacity to benefit all students.

APPENDIX: OUTCOMES OF DEPARTMENT CHAIR PROFESSIONAL DEVELOPMENT INITIATIVE

Table A.1

Department chair instructional leadership tasks	Hollis High School	Pennant Hills High School	Winchester High School
Facilitate the development of a shared vision at school and department levels	Developed school action plan Led department members in formation of departmental action plan to support school action plan	Developed school vision and goals Led department members in formation of departmental action plan to support school action plan	Developed three-phase schoolwide process focused on curriculum and instruction, professional development, and interventions and supports
Use data to identify goals and assess instructional/ organizational effectiveness	In departmental meetings, examined data (related to credit attainment, grades and proficiency on state tests, disaggregated by student groups, and individual reading-level assessments) to identify issues for further investigation	In departmental meetings, examined data (related to credit attainment, grades and proficiency on state tests, disaggregated by student groups, and individual reading-level assessments) to identify issues for further investigation	In departmental meetings, examined data (related to credit attainment, grades and proficiency on state tests, disaggregated by student groups, and individual reading-level assessments) to identify issues for further investigation

Department chair instructional leadership tasks	Hollis High School	Pennant Hills High School	Winchester High School
	Presented overview of student performance in department to entire staff using "data walls"		Shared audit of ELL, special education, and African American student participation in each course with department members
Support student and adult learning	Developed model for inclusion of special education and ELL students in general education courses.	Developed model for inclusion of special education and ELL students in general education courses.	Developed model for inclusion of Special Ed and ELL students in general education courses.
	Implemented positive behavior support system to increase student engagement while reducing expulsions and office referrals	Implemented positive behavior support system to increase student engagement while reducing expulsions and office referrals	Implemented positive behavior support system to increase student engagement while reducing expulsions and office referrals
	Provided department members with resources related to assessment, literacy, and using data to improve instruction	Provided department members with resources related to assessment, literacy, and using data to improve instruction	Provided department members with resources related to assessment, literacy, and using data to improve instruction
Monitor progress in the alignment of curriculum, instruction, and assessment	Worked with teachers in department to identify essential questions and enduring understandings for each course	Worked with teachers in department to identify essential questions and enduring understandings for each course	Worked with teachers in department to identify essential questions and enduring understandings for each course
			Facilitated development of course descriptions for school website
			Developed descriptions of how students progress through each department

Department chair instructional leadership tasks	Hollis High School	Pennant Hills High School	Winchester High School
			Adopted textbooks with appropriate grade-level reading levels
Promote continuous improvement in teaching and learning at the school and department level	Utilized departmental meetings and extended employment time to maintain focus on implementing action plan	Utilized departmental meetings and extended employment time to maintain focus on implementing action plan	Utilized departmental meetings and extended employment time to maintain focus on implementing action plan
	Used district-mandated PD sessions to support use of literacy across the curriculum	Provided departmental updates to staff newsletter	Developed a system to foster communication with staff, students, and families

REFERENCES

Barnett, D., & Aagaard, L. (2007). Developing leadership capacity within the teaching ranks: One district's approach. *International Electronic Journal for Leadership in Learning, 11*(9), Retrieved from www.ucalgary.ca/~iejll/volume11/barnett_aagaard.htm

Barth, R. (2007). The teacher leader. In R. Ackerman & S. Mackenzie (Eds.), *Uncovering teacher leaders* (pp. 9–36). Thousand Oaks, CA: Corwin Press.

Bredeson, P. V. (1993). Letting go of out-lived professional identities: A study of role transition and role strain in restructured schools. *Educational Administration Quarterly, 29*(1), 34–68.

Bredeson, P. V. (2003). *Designs for learning: A new architecture for professional development in schools.* Thousand Oaks, CA: Corwin Press.

Bredeson, P. V., Kelley, C. J., & Klar, H. W. (2009). [Instructional leadership framework] Unpublished raw data.

Brooks, J. S., Jean-Marie, G., Normore, A. H., & Hodgins, D. W. (2007). Distributed leadership for social justice: Exploring how influence and equity are stretched over an urban high school. *Journal of School Leadership, 17*(4), 378–408.

Capper, C. A., Frattura, E., & Keyes, M. W. (2000). *Meeting the needs of students of all abilities: How leaders go beyond inclusion.* Thousand Oaks, CA: Corwin Press.

Chrispeels, J. H., Burke, P. H., Johnson, P., & Daly, A. D. (2008). Aligning mental models and school leadership teams for reform coherence. *Education and Urban Society, 40,* 730–749.

Cohen, D. K., & Ball, D. L. (1999). *Instruction, capacity and improvement.* Philadelphia: University of Pennsylvania, Consortium for Policy Research in Education.

Copland, M. A., & Boatright, E. (2006). *Leadership for transforming high schools.* Seattle: University of Washington, Center for the Study of Teaching and Policy.

Corcoran, T., & Goertz, M. (1995). Instructional capacity and high performance schools. *Educational Researcher, 24*(9), 27–31.

Crowther, F. (2009). *Developing teacher leaders: How teacher leadership enhances school success* (2nd ed.). Thousand Oaks, CA: Corwin Press.

Dantley, M. E., & Tillman, L. C. (2010). Social justice and moral transformative leadership. In C. Marshall & M. Oliva (Eds.), *Leadership for social justice: Making revolutions in education* (pp. 19–34). Boston: Allyn & Bacon.

Elmore, R. F. (2002). *Bridging the gap between standards and achievement: The imperative for professional development in education.* Washington, DC: The Albert Shanker Institute.

Fink, E., & Resnick, L. (2001). Developing principals as instructional leaders. *Phi Delta Kappan, 82*(8), 598–606.

Fullan, M. (2002). The change leader. *Educational Leadership, 59*(8), 16–20.

Harris, A. (2001). Department improvement and school improvement: A missing link? *British Educational Research Journal, 27*(4), 477–486.

Harris, A. (2003a). Introduction. In A. Harris, C. Day, M. Hadfield, D. Hopkins, A. Hargreaves, & C. Chapman, *Effective leadership for school improvement* (pp. 1–6). London: Routledge Falmer.

Harris, A. (2003b). Teacher leadership and school improvement. In A. Harris, C. Day, M. Hadfield, D. Hopkins, A. Hargreaves, & C. Chapman (Eds.), *Effective leadership for school improvement* (pp. 72–83). London: Routledge Falmer.

Hill, D. (1995). The strong department: Building the department as a learning community. In L. Siskin & J. Little (Eds.), *The subjects in question: Departmental organization and the high school* (pp. 123–140). New York: Teachers College Press.

Hord, S. M., Rutherford, W. L., Huling-Austin, L., & Hall, G. E. (1987). *Taking charge of change.* Austin, TX: Southwest Educational Development Laboratory.

Kose, B. W. (2007). Principal leadership for social justice: Uncovering the content of teacher professional development. *Journal of School Leadership, 17*, 276–312.

Lambert, L. (2002). Beyond instructional leadership: A framework for shared leadership. *Educational Leadership, 58*(8), 37–40.

Lambert, L. (2003). *Leadership capacity for lasting school improvement.* Alexandria, VA: Association for Supervision and Curriculum Development.

Larson, C. L., & Murtadha, K. (2002). Leadership for social justice. In J. Murphy (Ed.), *The educational leadership challenge: Redefining leadership for the 21st century* (pp. 134–161). Chicago: University of Chicago Press.

Leithwood, K., Louis, K., Anderson, S., & Wahlstrom, K. (2004). *How leadership influences student learning.* New York: Wallace Foundation.

Leithwood, K. A., & Riehl, C. (2003). *What we know about successful school leadership.* Nottingham, UK: National College of School Leadership.

Little, J. W. (1995). Contested ground: The basis of teacher leadership in two restructuring high schools. *The Elementary School Journal, 96*(1), 47–63.

Louis, K. S., & Marks, H. M. (1998). Does professional community affect the classroom?: Teacher's work and student experiences in restructuring schools. *American Journal of Education, 106*, 532–575.

Mangin, M. M., & Stoelinga, S. R. (Eds.). (2008). *Effective teacher leadership: Using research to inform and reform.* New York: Teachers College Press.

Marzano, R., Waters, T., & McNulty, B. (2005). *School leadership that works: From research to results.* Aurora, CO: Mid-Continent Research for Education and Learning.

Nelson, M. (2004). *The unsung heroes of school improvement: High school chairpersons take the lead.* Unpublished doctoral dissertation, University of Wisconsin–Madison.

Newmann, F., & Wehlage, G. (1995). *Successful school restructuring: A report to the public and educators.* Madison, WI: Center on Organization and Restructuring of Schools.

Nieto, S. (2005). Public education in the twentieth century and beyond: High hopes, broken promises, and an uncertain future. In M. Charner-Laird, M. Donaldson, & S. Hong (Eds.), *Education past and present: Reflections on research, policy, and practice* (pp. 43–64). Cambridge, MA: Harvard University Press.

Portin, B. S. (2000). The changing urban principalship. *Education and Urban Society, 32*, 492–505.

Resnick, L. B., & Glennan, T. K. (2002). *Leadership for learning: A theory of action for urban school districts.* Retrieved from *http://ifl.lrdc.pitt.edu/ifl/media/pdf/TheoryofActionResnickGlenna.pdf*

Riehl, C. J. (2000). The principal's role in creating inclusive schools for diverse students: A review of normative, empirical, and critical literature on the practice of educational administration. *Review of Educational Research, 70*(1), 55–81.

Siskin, L., & Little, J. (1995). The subject department: Continuities and critiques. In L. Siskin & J. Little (Eds.), *The subjects in question: departmental organization and the high school* (pp. 1–22). New York: Teachers College Press.

Spillane, J. P., & Louis, K. S. (2002). School improvement process and practices: Professional learning for building instructional capacity. *Yearbook of the National Society for the Study of Education, 101*(1), 83–104.

Supovitz, J., & Poglinco, S. M. (2001). *Instructional leadership in a standards-based reform.* Philadelphia: University of Pennsylvania, Consortium for Policy Research in Education.

Theoharis, G. (2009). *The school leaders our children deserve: Seven keys to equity, social justice, and school reform.* New York: Teachers College Press.

Weiler, L. (2001). Department heads: The most underutilized leadership position. *NASSP Bulletin, 85*, 73–81.

Wenger, E., (1998). *Communities of practice: Learning, meaning, and identity.* New York: Cambridge University Press.

West-Burnham, J. (2004). *Building leadership capacity- helping leaders learn.* Nottingham: National College of School Leadership. Retrieved from *www.ncsl.org.uk/mediastore/image2/randd-building-lead-capacity.pdf*

Wetterson, J. (1992). *High school department chairs as instructional leaders: Four case studies.* Paper presented at the annual meeting of the American Educational Research Association, San Francisco.

York-Barr, J., & Duke, K. (2004). What do we know about teacher leadership?: Findings from two decades of scholarship. *Review of Educational Research, 74*(3), 255–316.

Zepeda, S. J., & Kruskamp, B. (2007). High school department chairs: Perspectives on instructional supervision. *High School Journal.* Chapel Hill: University of North Carolina Press.

CHAPTER 9

LESSONS FROM A PRINCIPAL PREPARATION PROGRAM

Creating Support through Social Justice Practices

**Elizabeth Murakami-Ramalho,
Encarnacion Garza Jr., and Betty Merchant**

A view of school administrators as important agents of social justice is not a recent phenomenon in the field of educational administration. Bogotch (2002), for example, argued that the inquiry about the moral use of power has, in fact, been an ongoing debate for centuries. Reflecting on Dewey's theories, Bogotch discusses the importance of continuously reviewing and critiquing issues of social justice and educational reforms, especially in the field of educational leadership.

Currently, the impetus for examining social justice practices places more emphasis on policies and practices that consistently perpetuate inequalities among children of color, English language learners and their mainstream peers. Committed to inclusiveness, many scholars and practitioners examine the subtractive and hegemonic structures and programs in schools that prevent a disproportionate number of students of color from succeeding

Educational Leaders Encouraging the Intellectual and Professional Capacity of Others:
A Social Justice Agenda, pages 163–174.
Copyright © 2012 by Information Age Publishing
163

academically (Cummins, 2001; Nieto, 2006; Theoharis, 2007; 2008, Valenzuela, 1999). National and state standards for school administrators also enforce the importance of social justice practices. The educational leadership policy standards of the National Policy Board for Educational Administration (ISLLC, 2008), for example, require that educational leaders "promote social justice and ensure that individual student needs inform all aspects of schooling" (ISLLC, standard 5, p. 5). Consequently, there has been a gradual increase across the nation in the number of principal preparation programs that purposefully prepare emerging principals as social justice agents are incrementally being offered around the nation. In this chapter, we share the reflections of emerging leaders being prepared in a master's program distinguished for its preparation of social justice leaders. Our task as coordinators of this program was to equip these leaders with necessary support before, during, and after they became school administrators in an inner-city urban district in south Texas. Their voices exemplify the personal and professional transformations occurred as they learned about concepts and skills related to social justice.

THE URBAN SCHOOL LEADERS COLLABORATIVE: THE CONTEXT OF THE PROGRAM

South Texas, and the city of San Antonio, is a fast-growing area in the nation. The city is located approximately 2 hours from the Mexican border in a culturally rich community with a population that is 58% Latino. In this visitor-friendly city, English and Spanish are often blended in the language and customs, through the city's festivities, printed and visual media, and general public services. The city has also received a new influx of migrants and refugees from economically depressed states and countries.

The city's growth parallels that of other large urban areas marked by demographic shifts and the exodus of affluent families to the suburbs. For the 2008–2009 academic year, the enrollment in the inner-city San Antonio Independent School District (SAISD) was approximately 54,000 students. When comparing SAISD with the demographics of the state of Texas, the district has close to 90% Hispanics in its ethnic composition (compared to 48% in the state).

The school district has a high percentage of students classified as at-risk (67 percent) as well as a large group with limited English proficiency (17 percent). Of greater concern is that 90% of the students are labeled as economically disadvantaged (Texas Education Agency, 2009). SAISD deserves particular attention because it shows an authentic need for investment in children to ensure societal improvement and sustainability. The need for educational leaders committed to the district, acting as social justice agents, is significant when national evidence suggests that public schools where English language learner test-takers reflect, on average, a substantially greater proportion of students qualifying for free or reduced-price school lunches and are significantly more likely to be designated Title I schools (Fry, 2008).

The Urban School Leaders Collaborative (USLC) was based on a strong partnership between the district and the university. The superintendent voiced his interest in advancing the preparation of strong leaders that would partner in his mission to actively support the community. One of the superintendent's concerns was the critical shortage of qualified candidates for principal positions in the district, particularly given the departure of qualified educators and educational leaders to more affluent areas of the city.

The program has been in existence since 2002, and is currently preparing its fourth cohort of master's students. The professional experience of the USLC emerging leaders has ranged from 3 to 20-plus years. The majority of the members has been female and Hispanic. In Cohort I (graduated in December 2004), 10 of the 14 students were curriculum coordinators when they started the program and four were classroom teachers. At the conclusion of the program, three were promoted to administrative positions at their respective campuses. Evidencing the success modeled by the first cohort, Cohort II enrolled two curriculum coordinators and 12 classroom teachers. Cohort II graduated in December 2006 with five students being promoted to leadership roles even before graduation. Cohort III graduated in December 2008. From the 12 members, two now hold leadership positions in the district.

We attribute the success of the USLC, in part to the following four characteristics of the program:

1. The preparation program is driven by a philosophy of social justice advocacy. The focus of preparation is first on attitudes and secondly, on skills.

2. A mentored closed-cohort model was created, in which only employees of the partnering school district would interact; preparation was customized to meet the needs of the children in this specific school district.

3. Professors moved to the field and co-taught with district personnel. All classes were held on campuses throughout the school district and students and professors created direct knowledge application channels, such as neighborhood meetings, and increased community education.

4. A mentoring network was purposefully maintained after students graduated and assumed leadership positions. This relationship supported the improvement of district schools, and through nurturing leadership talents within their own systems.

In the following section, we share some of the reflections of program participants regarding what they learned about social justice and advocacy in the USLC.

A SOCIAL JUSTICE FRAMEWORK: CHANGING ATTITUDES AND MINDSETS

When I heard that there was a program focused on social justice, my antennae wiggled.

It seemed that the students' beliefs were most conducive to being transformed into enacted agency when they were able to discuss personal reflections related to diversity issues. A district counselor in the program asserted, "As an African American, I grew up living social justice, but that terminology is uncommon outside of conversations with my father. So that really had my interest." Social justice is significant in the preparation of emerging leaders, especially in the examination of schools operating within culturally deficient models (Murakami, Garza, & Merchant, in press). Social justice as a theory relates to building a new social order (Capper et al., 2006; Lugg & Shoho, 2006; Merchant & Shoho, 2006). For school administrators, the focus on social justice relates to advocacy and mentorship: the drive to change culturally deficient paradigms, and mentoring teachers, and other stakeholders, in supporting programs and practices that disrupt hegemonic practices. Such practices are revealed through the development of critical consciousness and culturally relevant practices. Capper, Theoharis, and Sebastian (2006) referred to this process of discovery as the development of critical consciousness, "a deep understanding of power relations and social construction including white privilege, heterosexism, poverty, misogyny, and ethnocentrism." (p. 213). Cohort students were ready to reflect on their own experiences, and the implications of these experiences for practice. Through the development of concepts such as critical consciousness (Freire, 1970, 1985), students realized systemic or taken-for-granted evidence. One of the students reflected, "Even growing up in Arizona, I can, with complete certainty, say that not one of my core teachers in secondary school was of any other race than white. In fact, the only time I had a Hispanic teacher was in Spanish class."

DEVELOPING CRITICAL CONSCIOUSNESS

I know the meaning of suffering, and I do whatever I can to help end it. Students misbehave in classes because they are dealing with issues no child or adult should have to experience. The program helped me to stand up for the people who are unable to speak for themselves—especially children who are unable to verbalize their troubles—that's why I want to be a voice for them.

As professors, it is our responsibility to set the stage for critical thinking about social justice. Students in cohort I, for example, cited how one of the program coordinators facilitated critical reflection about social justice advocacy: "We must know ourselves before we can lead a group of students in a school. The main idea is that social injustice is an uncomfortable area of discussion, but the program coordinator had a way of addressing it in a way that was thought-provoking."

Freire (1970, 1985) defined the development of critical consciousness, or *conscientização*—the potential of people submerged in a "culture of silence"—to actively access and exercise their critical worldview. A two-tiered critical consciousness process is embedded in the program. Emerging leaders reflect about their own experiences as children, and transport the meaning behind their experiences to the experiences of their students in school. These reflective exercises generate "out-of-the box" connections and expand their understanding of social injustices.

An educator who had been educated in an international school during her family's military assignment in Europe realized that she had the opportunity to be raised in a culturally relevant school. "Why do we not provide the same opportunity to all students in the United States?" she asked. "We need to teach our children that diversity is good. We also need to stop subtracting from their identity. We should not require, or make them, assimilate." Another educator, who identified herself as a daughter of migrant workers, shared:

> A counselor believed I could never catch up with my work. He would say, "Honey, we are doing you a favor by placing you in easier classes. . . . We have students who are already failing some of those hard courses you want to take, and they are not even migrant students." This experience soon prompted me to develop cynicism toward the word caring. My migrant life had taught me good lessons on how to fight for what was right. Often, I had dealt with housing, employment, and gender discrimination issues on behalf of my family. Nonetheless, in school, I would persist; and with the help of some of my teachers I would end up getting the courses I requested: physics, computer science, and other college preparation courses.

Low expectations are still present in the schools in which these educators work:

> I remember the last class that I taught as a classroom teacher. I had 16 students, but they were 16 who were considered to be the worst behaved and to have the least going for them. They were the ones "bringing down" the fourth grade's data. My students were a mixture of African American and Mexican

American students. They were so accustomed to people viewing them with low expectations that the despair in the room could be cut with a knife. My first question to them on the first day of school was, "Who wants to have a successful year?" They looked at me with such disdain that I wanted to cry. What made this year the most challenging of my career was that the vice-principal never believed these students could show improvement. She would watch me and the students closely to confirm her expectations for failure.

Remarks about ethnicity and gender were prevalent issues in the cohort members' reflections. In critical consciousness discussions, one of the emerging leaders realized, "Sometimes through painful reflection I understand what it means to be a woman . . . leader . . . Latina leader!"

CULTURALLY RELEVANT PRACTICES

Some people do not realize that education should not look the same as it did 20 years ago. We should keep evolving for the sake of the kids.

The preparation of students through critical consciousness invoked a deeper understanding of restrictive political movements in relation to power structures stemming from perpetuated social constructions. Cohort members particularly identified with the concept of subtractive schooling (Valenzuela, 1999), both in their own school experience and the experiences of their students. One of the cohort members, after realizing the "way that education system is made to address the needs of the masses," became well versed in policies for bilingual, gifted and talented, and special education students. Another student stated:

> I began to get more involved in the politics that surround our education system. It is amazing how many cases were supported one decade and then interpreted in an entirely different fashion the next decade. Each and every person needs to become educated on what is happening in American schools today. Policies are implemented onto the school system from the top down. We live in a country where we vote for our representatives, laws, and have freedom of speech, yet we find ourselves voiceless and simply living our lives in a "just get by" state of mind. Educators and parents as a nation cannot allow children to be raised on the belief that they are not intelligent enough to have high aspirations, especially when these children are evaluated only on the basis of placement decisions that may not be accurate, or based solely on scores and state-mandated tests, or other tracking systems.

Cohort members as emerging leaders identified a disconnect between people's needs and a political process of adopting policies that are most often generic and neglect minority issues. The participants were increasingly aware that minority–majority paradigms were quickly changing, but the policies were not necessarily catching up to the progression of events.

Instructors and emerging leaders acknowledged that Texas continues to be the scene of a contentious debate at the Senate level regarding bilingual education. In this program, the participant are confronted with the notion that mandated policies needed to be thoroughly and critically examined before being put into practice. Some of the difficulties encountered by these educators when growing up were a result of the inequities perpetuated by such mandated policies.

The educators in the USLC recognized that the farther one goes from the border, policies related to language, for example, become more hegemonic, with bilingualism less valued and educators less confident about their cultural and language skills or their ability to help students from multiple languages and cultures. Rather than being viewed as a rich asset, bilingualism often becomes tainted with biases that associate particular languages with ignorance and poverty (Valencia & Solorzano, 1997).

Program participants recognized that many of their students, who were considered academically successful in Mexico, were viewed as academically deficient when they moved to the United States, particularly if they were economically challenged. "I see Spanish-speaking immigrants classified as mentally retarded because they do not speak English," reflected one of the students.

MENTORING SPACES THROUGH SAFE REFLECTIONS

When I got into a new school after the age of 12, I was being singled out. I was told to return across the Rio Grande. I had never even heard of the Rio Grande. So, I asked my father what that meant. I recall that day very well, for it would be the day that I was stereotyped and made to assimilate into the white way of life. I was deprived of my culture because of school. It was bad to speak Spanish. I learned the English language at the expense of losing my own identity. I was being asked to no longer be proud to be a Mexican American.

Even though all of the cohort members worked at SAISD, most of them did not know each other at the beginning of the program. At its inception, the program was designed to prepare students through a mentoring structure, with principals recommending potential candidates for the program. The mentoring model was designed based on evidence suggesting that cohort experiences have advantages (Hansford, Tennent, & Ehrich, 2003) that may extend beyond the graduate program by building professional networks and altering other workplace behaviors (Muth & Barnett, 2001). Mentoring, in this case, was a strong component that allowed students to develop a level of comfort in authentic discussions about their racial identity and their goals as educational leaders. The emerging leaders learned to listen and to interpret what they heard toward field applications.

The program interactions were safe places for students to reflect about their own experiences and to develop a stronger advocacy identity. These opportunities were paramount in equipping the educators with the tools to bridge (Merchant & Shoho, 2006) between "who they were" and how they were viewed by others and to use this information to focus their equity and social justice efforts. Facing discrimination and translating it into social agency, for example, was harder when the educators had to confront their own racial identity. One of the students stated:

> I had already come to the realization that schools were tools for assimilation into the mainstream society. My own experiences working in schools awakened me to the notion that education is packaged as one size fits all, and if it is too little or too big it is the student's fault. As a female trying on a garment of a one size fits all, I can say that it feels awful when the garment does not fit. This same concept applied to education can have devastating effects on students.

Cohort members continue the discussion about their commitment to social justice throughout other formal and informal conversations promoted within the program. The focus on social justice as a mission carried out with respect to overseeing instruction (Delpit, 1995; Valencia, 2002), relating to the community (Valencia & Solorzano, 1997), and identifying political implications (Freire, 1985) as they prepare to disrupt and alter institutional arrangements that prevent students from being respected by focusing on equity, equality, and fairness (Gerwitz, 1998; Goldfarb & Grinberg, 2002; Theoharis, 2007).

MAKING CONNECTIONS AND DEVELOPING ADVOCACY

Many cohort members shared the experience of having to change their names (i.e., from Juan to John) upon the teacher's request in elementary school. They also mentioned their parents' effort not to speak Spanish at home in response to teachers' suggestions. Nonetheless, not only was the notion of subtractive schooling (Valenzuela, 1999) perceived, but the cohort members realized that their schools erased their culture and identity. Their grief and confusion accompanies them throughout their lives and careers, with vivid images of teachers defining where "one belongs" or who and how one is worthy of belonging in society.

Although schools are major social institutions and important centers of community activity, educators serving economically disadvantaged communities learn early in the USLC program that the scholarly literature is rich with accounts about the plight and demise of Hispanic and African American students (Cummins, 1989; 1997; 2001; Garza, Reyes, & Trueba, 2004; Ladson-Billings, 2009; Valencia, 2002; Valenzuela, 1999). To set the stage for critical thinking about educational policies and practices that systemically disadvantage certain groups of children, the introductory question posed by one of the facilitators of the Urban School Leaders Collaborative (Garza et al., 2004) is, "What is social injustice?"

The literature is replete with descriptions of the academic challenges facing students of color. Many studies have been conducted to explore why so many Hispanic students, for example, are failing in school (Valencia, 2001; Valenzuela, 1999). These children continue to be plagued with the highest dropout rate, being misplaced and overrepresented in special education, being overage for their grade level, and being underrepresented in gifted and talented and advanced placement programs (Cummins, 2001; Theoharis, 2009; Valencia, 2002). Their poor achievement has been linked to a variety of sociocultural factors that propel Mexican American students into academic failure. The underlying assumption is that Hispanic children do not have the necessary competencies, values, and personal characteristics to succeed in America's schools. This has been attributed, according to a significant body of research (Delpit, 2006; Garcia & Guerra, 2004; Valencia & Solorzano, 1997), to their families, their neighborhoods, and the students themselves. This research typically has defined the students, their families, and their neighborhoods as "culturally deprived" or "disadvantaged." As a result of these deficit-oriented definitions, public school systems have continued to design programs to remediate or compensate for these students' "deficiencies" (Valencia, 2002). The educators running these programs, using a therapeutic discourse, commonly view the children as *pobrecitos* (poor little children) who need to be saved (Garza et al., 2004).

The USLC members are prepared to disrupt these notions. The cohort members' reflections illuminate how their own schooling experiences were meant to only *place* them into a societal status that was being defined for them (Valencia, 2002; Valenzuela, 1999). That *place* never included the possibility of their becoming educational leaders equipped with sophisticated academic and professional skills—which now included the necessary Spanish language fluency to better serve students and their families. Unfortunately, for some cohort members, this required them to a language and culture that has been taken away by the educational system they had experienced as children.

CONCLUSION

We came to the conclusion that we knew too much to go back ... and that stemmed from the fact that administrators go into the principalship position with idealistic aspirations and then, all of a sudden, something happens. We couldn't define it, but we understood that because there were many of us and we were all working in the same district. There was no way that we could actually stray away from our vision or stray away from what's right for kids without somebody calling us on it later on down the line. During reflections, there was always an opportunity to share what it was we believed in, and we developed strength in doing what is right.

Social justice becomes a significant issue only when schools as public assets fail to deliver the same promise of quality education to every child (Connell, 1993; Miller, 1999: Tyler, 1997). People care about social justice or injustice only when they are motivated to break social rules or improve the lives of others (Theoharis, 2007; Tyler, 1997). Program participants learn the true meaning of social justice advocacy, understanding that they will face resistance in doing so, but remaining steadfast in their commitment to equity and justice.

Cohort-to-cohort mentorship has been an important component of the program including workplace visitations, internship opportunities, formal and informal forums, presentations at national conferences, and informal gatherings. Not only are students' scholarship, reflective abilities, and group learning enhanced but their interpersonal relationships are e improved, as evidenced by their collective sense of social bonding, cohesiveness, and community.

The literature about effective schools indicates that principals play a major role in the academic success or failure of students (Garza et al., 2004; Gonzales, 2002; Marshall & Oliva, 2006). Therefore, given the critical role of the principal, it is crucial that school leaders be prepared to meet the needs of all students, particularly those who are marginalized (Gonzales, Huerta-Macias, & Tinajero, 2002; Lomotey, 1989). The importance of sustaining programs that develop social justice through critical consciousness and culturally relevant practices is of utmost importance in developing effective leaders for a diverse society who are able to create educational environments that are conducive to the learning of all students. We carry a similar duty while coordinating this program: we need to continuously reexamine our pedagogy, and curriculum, in our effort to prepare professionals as social justice advocates.

REFERENCES

Bogotch, I. (2002). Educational leadership and social justice: Practice into theory. *Journal of School Leadership, 12,* 138-156.

Capper, C. A., Theoharis, G., & Sebastian, J. (2006). Toward a framework for preparing leaders for social justice. *Journal of Educational Administration, 44*(3), 209–224.

Connell, R. W. (1993). *Schools and social justice.* Halifax, Canada: Lorimer.

Cummins, J. (2001). Empowering minority students: A framework for intervention. *Harvard Education Review Classic Reprint, 71*(4), 649–676.

Davis, S., Darling-Hammond, L., LaPointe, M., & Meyerson, D. (2005). *School leadership study: Developing successful principals.* Stanford, CA: Stanford Educational Leadership Institute.

Delpit, L. (2006). *Other people's children: Cultural conflict in the classroom, updated edition.* New York: New Press.

Freire, P. (1970). *Pedagogia do oprimido.* New York: Herder & Herder.

Freire, P. (1985). *The politics of education: Culture, power, and education.* South Hadley, MA: Bergin & Garvey.

Fry, R. (2008). The role of school in the English Language Learner achievement gap. Pew Hispanic Center Report. Accessed March 23, 2010, at *http://pewhispanic.org/files/reports/89.pdf*

Garcia, S. B., & Guerra, P. L. (2004). Deconstructing deficit thinking. *Education and Urban Society, 36*(2), 150–168.

Garza, E. Jr., Reyes, P., & Trueba, E. (2004) *Resiliency and success: A case of migrant children in the United States.* Boulder, CO: Paradigm.

Gerwitz, S. (1998). Conceptualizing social justice in education: Mapping the territory. *Journal of Education Policy, 13*(4), 469–484.

Gonzales, M. L. (2002). The pivotal role of the principal. In M. Gonzales, A. Huerta-Macias, & J. Tinajero (Eds.), *Educating Latino students: A guide to successful practice.* Lanham, MD: Scarecrow Press.

Gonzales, M., Huerta-Macias, A., & Tinajero, J. (Eds.). (2002). *Educating Latino students: A guide to successful practice.* Lanham, MD: Scarecrow Press.

Hansford, B., Tennent, L., & Ehrich, L. C. (2003). Educational mentoring: is it worth the effort? *Education, Research, and Perspectives, 30*(1), 42–75.

Interstate School Leaders Licensure Consortium (ISLLC). (2008). *Educational Leadership Policy Standards.* Upper Saddle River, NJ: Pearson.

Ladson-Billings, G. (2009). *The dreamkeepers: Successful teachers of African American children.* San Francisco: Jossey-Bass.

Lomotey, K. (1989). Cultural diversity in the urban school: Implications for principals. *NASSP Bulletin, 73*, 81–85.

Lugg, C. A., & Shoho, A. R. (2006). Dare public school administrators build a new social order? Social justice and the possibly perilous politics of educational leadership. *Journal of Educational Administration, 44*(33), 196–208.

McKenzie, K. B., Christman, D., Capper, C., Dantley M., Gonzales, M. L. Cambron-McCabe, N. et al. (2004, April). *Educating leaders for social justice: What every leader should know and be able to do.* Paper presented at the annual meeting of the American Educational Research Association, Montreal, CA.

Marshall, C., & Oliva, M. (2006). *Leadership for social justice: Making revolutions in education.* Boston: Pearson.

Merchant, B., & Shoho, A. (2006). Bridge people: Civic and educational leaders for social justice. In C. Marshall & M. Oliva (Eds), *Leadership for social justice: Making revolutions in education* (pp. 85–109). Boston: Pearson.

Miller, D. (1999). *Principles of social justice.* Cambridge, MA: Harvard University Press.

Murakami-Ramalho, E., Garza, E., & Merchant, B. (2010). Successful school leadership in socio-economically challenging contexts: School principals creating and sustaining successful school improvement. *International Studies in Educational Administration, 32*(2), 1–24.

Muth, R., & Barnett, B. (2001). Making the case for professional preparation: Using research for program improvement and political support. *Educational Leadership and Administration: Teaching and Program Development, 13*, 109–120.

Nieto, S. (Ed.) (2005). *Why we teach.* New York: Teachers College Press.

Texas Education Agency (2009). 2008–9 Academic Excellence Indicator System, State Report. Retrieved April, 2, 2010, from *http://www.tea.state.tx.us/perfreport/aeis/2007/state.html.*

Theoharis, G. (2007). Social justice educational leaders and resistance: Toward a theory of social justice leadership. *Educational Administration Quarterly, 43*(2), 221–258.

Theoharis, G. (2008). Woven in deeply: Identity and leadership of social justice principals. *Education and Urban Society, 41*(1), 3–25.

Theoharis, G. (2009). *The school leaders our children deserve: Seven keys to equity, social justice, and school reform.* New York: Teachers College Press.

Tyler, T. R. (1997). *Social justice in a diverse society.* Boulder, CO: Westview Press.

Valencia, R. R. (2002). The plight of Chicano students: An overview of schooling conditions and outcomes. In R. R. Valencia (Ed.), *Chicano school failure and success: Past, present, and future* (pp. 3–51). New York: Routledge Falmer.

Valencia, R. R., & Solorzano, D. G. (1997). Contemporary deficit-thinking. In R. R. Valencia (Ed.), *The evolution of deficit-thinking: Educational thought and practice* (pp. 160–210). New York: Routledge.

Valenzuela, A. (1999). *Subtractive schooling: U.S. Mexican youth and the politics of caring.* Albany: State University of New York Press.

CHAPTER 10

VOICES OF VETERAN ADMINISTRATORS

Marilyn L. Grady, Marlie Williams, and Julie Gaddie

The chapter begins with our perspective on social justice issues and is followed by a review of the professional development literature that pertains to veteran administrators. Through the voices of veteran administrators, we report the social justice issues they encounter in their work, their descriptions of the "best" professional development they have experienced, the sources of their professional development, their self-directed professional development, and why they "stick with it."

Our perspective on social justice is informed by the literature, interviews with veteran administrators, and our collective years of experience as teachers and administrators.

We acknowledge Ayers and Quinn's (2009) perspectives on social justice. They state, "teaching for social justice begins with the idea that every human being is entitled to decent standards of freedom and justice, and that any violation must be acknowledged, testified to, and opposed" (p. xv). Additionally, Ayers and Quinn note:

> Social justice is surely about a fairer, more just distribution of social wealth and power, but it is also about recognition, disrupting the social structures of

Educational Leaders Encouraging the Intellectual and Professional Capacity of Others: A Social Justice Agenda, pages 175–195.

nonrecognition or disrespect, and cultural equity. Its goals are equity, democracy, and an awareness of social literacy, agency, and activism. (p. xvii)

We also recognize and share Michie's (2009) experience: "Much of what troubles or ensnares some of my former students is directly connected to larger social ills: poverty, lack of opportunity, discrimination, violence" (p. xxiv).

The voices of administrators are the basis for the chapter. The following interview summary is reflective of the 32 administrator interviews that are reported. The summary provides an example of the conversations we had with the administrators. Administrators' responses to questions about social justice were similar to this response in that their comments were embedded in extensive descriptions of their work in schools. Our perspective on social justice issues for veteran administrators is informed by the interviews.

> I was reflecting on how different that looks at the building you go to because it's so based on what your children come with and what they need. I look at little 5-year-olds walking into my building that have never experienced a zoo, never experienced a trip to the museum, never experienced three square meals a day, and I'm to take that child and make sure they're at grade level by the end of the year?

> I come here and staff are struggling with … things feel different. Something's just not right. They're noticing things. So, talk to me, what do you notice? Well, we have kids that are behind in grade levels so you go back and you look at your population and it's like well, in 4 years' time you go from 3% to 27% poverty.

> The teachers were still teaching as if it were a middle-class neighborhood. But once I showed them this is what we're dealing with across the district we have 42% poverty, it's like let's back up and think about what the children lack when they come to school. And are we making sure we're connecting with where they're at, what their knowledge is, and we're trying to give them that new content; are you matching where they're coming from? You look at a little guy coming in with maybe 3,000 words in kindergarten versus a child who has 10,000 words. You can't present the same way.

> I think it's very important that every building principal has to look at who we have in our building and what is it that they're coming to us with and then how can we take where they're at to make sure we're connecting all of that knowledge. Not to excuse it. They still have to have the same high expectations. … I've had the joy of being at three different buildings as administrator and all three had different, unique situations. I'm thrilled we're going to have our kindergarten ELL kids back in our building. But now I realize that I have kindergarten teachers who have never had non-English-speaking students in their class and so what am I going to do as staff development leader in this

building to prepare for that? And how blessed I was to have been at an ELL site previously.

It's going to be a real learning curve for my whole community. So there's that one little piece that comes in and how much I'm going to have to help all my staff members make sure they understand how we're going to welcome and serve these children. So, when you talk about social justice as an issue, it's never ending and it's that educating our teachers that's different. Another huge one that I worry greatly about because our community is not addressing it is mental illness and how many of our children and parents suffer from mental illness but we don't have the support in place for them.

So, there's those easy fixes that I can provide my staff and that's just simple educating them. Who do we have in our building and how are we going to meet their needs?

How can we provide that support in different ways? So you've got from that academic piece to the behavior needs to a little guy coming in—last Friday "I want to go back to my foster mom. I'm just tired of Mom like with her drugs. And the teacher was trying to give a Math CRT that day. Well, that's not what's important to him right then. But how do we provide that support during the day, listen to this little guy, reassure him I'll get the help he needs at home, but right now his job is to know the adults are going to take care of it, and his job is to go back to the classroom and address that. So making sure that support is in place.

I just think I've seen it all and another situation will come up.

So then knowing where I can go for outside resources like my central office... we're constantly looking at ways to improve. So it's like for every given situation, I have to determine my own learning of how can I get better. And I need to realize that I need to rely on outside folks to help me get some information . . .

so much of my learning has been, pick up the phone and call a peer or a colleague; "Have you ever experienced this?"

It's just so funny how every little situation that comes up how you learn just to get a few more tricks in your bag because I've been in education for 33 years and I'm still learning every day. There's never an ending time. And the number one thing is not to be afraid to ask for help and ideas.

REVIEW OF LITERATURE

Recent Developments Increasing Administrative Professional Development Needs

The increased levels of accountability focused on public schools and their administrators is borne by several studies, reports, and legislation directed at improving student achievement levels for students in all of America's public schools. In A Nation at Risk (National Commission on Excellence in Education, 1983), a recommendation was made regarding the necessity of professional development for school leadership:

> Principals and superintendents must play a crucial leadership role in developing school and community support for the reforms we propose, and school boards must provide them with the professional development and other support required to carry out their leadership role effectively. The Commission stresses the distinction between leadership skills involving persuasion, setting goals and developing community consensus behind them, and managerial and supervisory skills. Although the latter are necessary, we believe that school boards must consciously develop leadership skills at the school and district levels if the reforms we propose are to be achieved.

Although this recommendation was made in 1983, little transformation of administrative professional development programs followed. Houle (2006) cites a study completed by the National Center for Education Statistics regarding the focus of principals' professional development, as found through the results of the Schools and Staffing Survey between 1987/1988 and 1993/1994, in which 86% received evaluation and supervision training and 75% received in-service training regarding management practices (p. 145). The National Staff Development Council (NSDC) in its 2000 report, *Learning to Lead, Leading to Learn*, advocates for professional development for school principals that "is long-term, planned, and job-embedded; focuses on student achievement; supports reflective practice; and provides opportunities to work, discuss, and solve problems with peers" (Houle, 2006, p. 146).

The federal No Child Left Behind legislation of 2001 placed additional accountability measures on schools, culminating in 2014 when, according to the legislation, 100% of school children in the United States are required to rate as proficient on math and reading assessments.

All of these recent changes in educational accountability come in stark contrast to the traditional role of the school administrator. Houle (2006) cites Elmore's assessment of traditional school leadership as a model in which the principal is the "manager of the structures and processes around instruction" (p. 144). With traditional master's degree-level educational administration programs primarily focused on the managerial aspects of maintaining the current school culture, "little time is spent helping aspiring and practicing principals learn about transforming a traditional school to meet current and future needs" (Wong, 2004, p. 142). As such, principals are not adequately skillful in leading the large-scale change initiative necessary for achieving 21st century student achievement targets.

Because of the vastly different face of school leadership, Houle (2006) advocates greater attention be paid to the "professional development needs of principals in light of their new roles" (p. 145). With the current short-age of well-trained administrators, it is critical that the professional development needs of veteran principals be tended to adequately. With many research studies underlining the fact that principals are central to the implementation of effective instructional practices, effective veteran school administrators, then, are inextricably linked to increased learning for all students in a school (Peterson, 2002).

Professional Development Sustains Learning and Drives School Improvement

The new accountability levels assigned to school performance places increased pressure on school leadership to provide instructional guidance that translates into student learning outcomes. Sherman (2000) cites the decentralization of authority seen by school administration over the past few years, in addition to a more site-based management approach to school leadership, that has led to "added responsibilities, new aggravations, [and] more accountability" for school administrators" (p. 2). Sherman (2000) further explains that the "principal's pivotal role in school reform makes solid training an imperative" (p. 2). Sherman also cites Education Week reporter Lynn Olson who states, "the sheer abundance of grants and research projects aimed at overhauling principal training reflects a widespread and growing recognition that without strong leaders at the helm, larger efforts to improve student achievement will likely falter, if not fail entirely" (p. 2).

The new recognition being given to the professional development of practicing administrators emphasizes the shift in understanding occurring in regars to the impact of effective school leaders on student achievement. The National Center on Education and the Economy (NCEE) works in concert with the National Institute for School Leadership (NISL) "to provide professional development opportunities to help practicing principals become stronger instructional leaders in high-performance, standards-based schools" (Hale & Moorman, 2003, p. 16). The NCEE focuses on training that assists veteran administrators in "strategic thinking, shared leadership, gaining staff and student consensus, and implementing standards-based instructional delivery models" (Hale & Moorman, 2003, p. 16).

Further support for the importance of a well-trained school leader to provide a foundation for a school's student achievement outcomes is found in the Mid-continent Research for Education and Learning (McREL) 2003 working paper that provides a meta-analysis of 30 years of research on the relationship between a principal's leadership and the achievement of students, which is outlined in the form of leadership responsibilities (Maryland Instructional Leadership Framework, 2005).

Traditional Professional Development Offerings for School Administrators

As the issues and challenges facing school administrators have changed exponentially, professional development offerings to help veteran administrators deal with these changes have not kept pace. Administrative professional development, according to Peterson (2002), is most commonly found to be structured as "one-shot workshops," with more substantive training needing to be designed as "all-day and multiple sessions over an entire year" (p. 216). While the one-shot workshop may leave the veteran administrator feeling inspired, "principals generally return to their schools unprepared to implement change and inadequately educated on the effective implementation of a new instructional practice" (Evans & Mohr, 1999, p. 530). Peterson concurs, stating that "the longer experience with a cohort group can have a greater impact on learning" (p. 216).

Peterson (2002) contends that current administrative professional development offerings are a veritable "crazy quilt" of offerings, leaving veteran principals to the mercy of their desires and their professional organizations to make decisions regarding their professional learning. With the National Association of Secondary School Principals (NASSP), the Association for Supervision and Curriculum Development (ASCD), the National Staff Development Council (NSDC), and the National Association of Elementary School Principals (NAESP), state administrative and educational organizations, universities, along with newly formed for-profit professional development operations, veteran administrators have a dizzying array of choices (Peterson, 2002).

With traditional administrative professional development focusing only on the acquisition of new skills, many veteran principals seek out this type of activity, assuming that learning a new method of teacher evaluation, data analysis, or change leadership will make them more effective school leaders. While this type of logic may seem overtly simplistic, the typical professional development offerings marketed to veteran school administrators support this assertion, mirroring the traditional one-shot, new practice seminars.

Another shortcoming of traditional administrative professional development offerings is that they tend not to be differentiated to the level of experience an administrator possesses. Peterson (2002) cites a report completed by Kelley and Peterson (2002), which finds that effective professional development programs should be "career staged, with specialized training for aspiring, new and experienced principals" (p. 230). Furthermore, with the instructional leadership capacity demands of school administration, professional development offerings should be tailored to meet these needs, focusing less on the traditional, operational roles of school administration.

*Administrative Professional Development Programs that Support
Veteran Principals*

With the increased demands on school principals to lead their schools to
meet student achievement outcomes, the effective professional development of the modern school principals is critical. Conger and Benjamin
(1999, identify four objectives for the support of leaders: "(a) developing individual leadership effectiveness; (b) enhancing career transition
into leadership positions; (c) instilling the vision, values, and mission of
the organization; and (d) developing skills and knowledge to implement
long-term strategic objectives" (Peterson, 2002, p. 214). With the mounting
external pressures of accountability and the community pressures related
to the increased social and emotional needs of children attending public
schools, more than ever veteran school administrators must be given the
professional support necessary to meet these needs.

The NSDC advocates for professional learning programs for principals
that are "long term, carefully planned, job embedded, and focused on how
to reach student achievement goals" (Peterson, 2002, p. 214). Many states
are attempting to develop professional learning programs for principals
that are designed to fit these requirements. "With no consistent national
leadership standards articulated for school principals, the Interstate School
Leaders Licensure Consortium (ISLLC), developed in 1994, provides one
of the most widely known sets of standards for school leaders" (Peterson,
2002, p. 216). Through the leadership actions defined by ISLLC, and
through the various studies and reports available to state educational agencies, the array of principal professional development opportunities is staggering. Because principals are left to navigate these choices individually, it
is virtually impossible to gain momentum toward progress on accountability
measures. Schools rely on the choices made by their own isolated administrators.

Peterson (2002) proposes administrative professional development include several specific designs that will help veteran school administrators
develop the instructional skills necessary to lead schools in the face of 21st
century accountability. He proposes programming that will "address the
needs of well-trained school leaders who have completed existing programs
but who want to deepen their skills in a specific area" (p. 230). The program designs Peterson believes are most effective include "study groups,
advanced seminars, reading and discussion groups, presentations by current thinkers or expert practitioners, attendance at national academies or
conferences, and opportunities to become coaches, facilitators, or trainers"
(p. 231).

The Annenberg Institute for School Reform is a program designed
for principals from all types of schools" "who are implementing substantial school reform efforts, and who agree to participate in the Institute's

programming for a term of one year" (Evans & Mohr, 1999, p. 531). The Annenberg Principals receive intensive professional development and collegial support based on seven principles:

- Principals' learning is personal and yet takes place most effectively while working in groups.
- Principals foster more powerful faculty and student learning by focusing on their own learning.
- While we honor principals' thinking and voices, we want to push principals to move beyond their assumptions.
- Focused reflection takes time away from "doing the work," and yet it is essential.
- It takes strong leadership in order to have truly democratic learning.
- Rigorous planning is necessary for flexible and responsive implementation.
- New learning depends on protected dissonance (Evans & Mohr, 1999, pp. 531–532).

The point of the Annenberg Institute's approach is focused on the tenet that "the principal's work is essential" and that "principals who reexamine their belief systems and transform their practice facilitate change at their schools" (Evans & Mohr, 1999, p. 532).

The Chicago Principals and Administrators Association (CPAA) works with the Chicago public school system to provide a nontraditional approach to administrative professional development. "With differentiated offerings for aspiring, first-year, and experienced school leaders, administrators receive critical training based on their experiential needs" (Peterson, 2002, p. 225).

> The Chicago Academy for School Leaders (CASL) is the program designed by the CPAA specifically for experienced school leaders. With conceptual underpinnings based on the ISLLC standards for school administrators, CASL is designed to assist veteran school leaders seeking to meet the demands of the accountability and governance reforms of the 1990's. (Peterson, 2002, p. 225)

With all three levels of programming based, additionally, on seven tenets of school leadership established by the Chicago Public Schools, the programs are tailored to a balanced leadership approach. The seven principles of leadership of the Chicago Public Schools include:

- School leadership
- Parent involvement and community partnerships
- Creating student-centered learning climates
- Professional development and human resource management
- Instructional leadership: Improving teaching and learning

- School management and daily operations
- Interpersonal effectiveness (Peterson, 2002, p. 225)

The CASL is a "well-designed professional development program for urban principals," and is funded through the local school district and local foundations (Peterson, 2002, p. 228). The CASL is time-bound, in that veteran administrators participate for a period of 2 years and complete long-term seminars centered on 11 content modules aligned to the seven principles of leadership articulated by the Chicago school district, and culminating in the presentation of a professional portfolio.

The Harvard Principals' Academy is a respected administrative professional development program initiated in 1981. With multiple summer offerings, "school administrators may choose institutes designed to meet their specific topical desires, from race and gender issues in schools to managing change" (Peterson, 2002, p. 221). A notable difference of the Harvard Principals' Academies from other state administrative professional development programs is the fact that the Harvard offerings are based on current trends in educational research, rather than being based upon any articulated state or national leadership standards (Peterson, 2002)

The Social Justice Implications of Administrative Professional Development

Social justice implications place additional expectations on school leaders. Houle (2006) cites:

> changing families and communities and the resulting stress placed on children, issues outside of school competing with the available learning time for students and the use of instructional practices that do not respond to the increasing knowledge necessary for success in the context of our ever-changing society as major contributors to the strain placed on school leaders. (p. 144)

If the traditional effects of poverty are to be overcome in our nation's public schools, it is paramount that school leaders have adequate training in how to lead such change initiatives.

Only through a solid understanding of the principles of systemic school improvement will veteran school administrators faced with the challenges of school leadership be able to reform the educational realities facing children in many of this country's school districts. Change of this magnitude is borne not only out of charismatic leadership, it is also the result of leadership that has been trained, systematically over time, to identify and overcome the key struggles of schoolchildren.

PROFESSIONAL DEVELOPMENT OF VETERAN ADMINISTRATORS

There is significant literature concerning professional development, however, little literature was identified about the professional development of veteran administrators. We chose to interview veteran administrators about their professional development. Although we had access to the work of Marshall and Oliva (2010), we were interested in the responses of practicing administrators to issues of social justice in their work in the schools. The administrators we interviewed were women and men who served as principals, assistant principals, assistant superintendents, superintendents, and instructional facilitators.

The individuals identified themselves as "veteran" administrators. Their years of experience in their current positions were between 4 and 28 years. We interviewed 32 individuals noted for their leadership in schools.

SOCIAL JUSTICE ISSUES

The veteran administrators were asked "what does social justice or social justice issues mean to you?" Examples of their responses follow.

- "The concept of justice begins with a search for an understanding of fair and equal. . . . I face the realities of social justice every day. In public schools, social justice is about the parts of the day that happen when students are not in our facility. Our students live without the predictability that comes with stable income flowing through the walls of their homes. The idea that large populations of children do not know where their next meal is coming from, if they will have to move at the end of the month when rent is due, and amidst all of the stress-related adult behavior that stems from living in poverty, is a scenario that educators have not adequately connected to academic achievement."
- "As principals we are challenged with putting our egos aside and admitting that social justice issues are more than we can solve alone. It is time to take off the superhero capes and get tough with the real issues of poverty, immigration, and employment."
- "I think as a building principal you deal with social justice everyday in all the small and big ways you deal with your students, parents, and staff. How you greet them, how you interact, how you deliver financial assistance, how you deliver discipline—it is in the everyday ways you make the most impact ... and deliver the message . . . Social justice issues ... I think that there always are. In my leadership position, it's difficult for me to understand if that's based on equity issues, or if it's based on tradition, which really could be one and the same.

I haven't gone to any training on that. With the exception of maybe the legal training tapped on a few things."

- "Our main area that we have to be ready to [address] is sexual harassment. So many of our classes are gender specific—like automotive. When we get one or two nontraditional [students in a] female- and/ or male-dominant class, we do have issues with sexual harassment."

- "The entire district has social justice issues. I think as a district as a whole, we make that a priority to address those—maybe not real specific professional development days for that, but I think everyone in their own way either reads publications on some aspect of dealing with social justice."

- "Poverty, single homes, people trying to do more than they can … with poverty you bring along the different kinds of abuse—it's not the physical kind—that whole neglect. That idea that that shell is so hard by the time they get here that even the most caring and loving teacher struggles with, you know—getting to that student."

The administrators were asked, "What professional development have you received related to social justice?" Examples of their responses follow.

- "There has been very little focus on the topic of social justice for principals at the local or state level over the past 10 years. However, recently with the pressures of No Child Left Behind rising, principals are searching for answers for lags in student achievement reflected in sub-group data. The sub-group data is a bleak reminder of the academic progress of poverty students, minority students, mobile students, and second language learners."

- "Locally, the urgency for professional development targeted toward improving the academic achievement for students affected by social justice issues has arrived. Through professional literature, I have been challenged to broaden my thinking when considering solutions for these struggling learners. Gone are the days that methodology inside the classroom walls will adequately move all students forward at the pace established by NCLB. The solutions to social injustice are entwined in housing, family stabilization, healthcare, *and* education. The search for educational solutions to social justice extends far beyond the classroom walls."

- "We had an opportunity for diverse individuals to come in one room and ask the hard questions regarding diversity, breaking out of stereotypes, trying to see perspectives of other individuals."

- "Two examples in my world—we find social justice issues always centered around law. And case studies and legislative decisions when I go to professional development to get a law update, we will typically talk about what are issues in school districts surrounding gender or sexuality, not so much poverty, and how they impact your school and what kinds of policies do you have in place and how are they impacting your students and are they legal or not? There's always a whole lot of discussion it's very evident that for administrators—this is a hot topic because this is where they get in trouble."

THE BEST

The veteran administrators mentioned an array of "best" professional development experiences. Two types of experiences were mentioned most often. Being with colleagues and learning from each other were cited as best experiences. Following are examples of administrators' comments.

- "The fact that we can have fun. We know when to be professional and turn it on and get the work done. But to be able to laugh and have a good time and share stories with family when you become close-knit—that's the kind of professional development that we need on a regular basis to support each other and I think to me sometimes that's the most powerful. It reenergizes you, you get your batteries charged because you've had a wonderful time with your colleagues and then you want to go back to work."
- "Learning together ... times that my job-embedded teams sat down at the table and I felt we really made a dent in something ... we learned a lot and have been able to apply it and then we've seen the success through student achievement."
- "The most effective for me is when we have a chance to get to know each other and let our hair down ... I'm bald, by the way."

Professional learning communities were described as examples of "best" professional development activities. The following comments are examples of the administrators' remarks.

- "A couple of topics that really inspired me were when I first started learning about learning communities ... what good teaching looks like ... I can't imagine being prepared to be an instructional leader without being an instructional coach.... (It was the best) whole year of professional development that I've ever had in my whole life because as an instructional coach you're essentially learning how to teach adults how to learn. Having that year of training as instructional coac, gives you some really foundational things to build upon."
- "Working with my school with my teachers in developing special learning communities has made a change in the climate in our building. We had such a separation of teachers because we have very few teachers (who) actually teach subject matter and they realize- I mean

we all realize working together that we do have common goals and common assessment and common working on reading and math and everything else that we do. It's really changed the climate in my building and got people together that had never gotten together before."

- "The move toward a professional learning community, just going and seeing the school that is dubbed the professional learning community in Chicago and . . . witnessing what they are doing in their school. I don't think there's anything better than to go to another school just to look at it, to talk to their teachers, to see how their kids act—that's very rewarding."

Other "best" professional development activities described by the veteran administrators included: (a) leadership academies; (b) assessment training; (c) safety and security issues workshops; (d) legal topics sessions; and (e) parent issues sessions.

SOURCES OF PROFESSIONAL DEVELOPMENT

The veteran administrators were asked where they "looked" for professional development. Their responses indicated that they looked for professional development that met their subject/topic needs or were preparation for the future. Examples of their responses to this question follow.

- "(I look for professional development) related to the different areas that I supervise, (a) content area that is coming up for curriculum revision, ways to learn more about what is new in mathematics, new in science."
- "Last year we worked with assessment, so we were trained under the Stiggins philosophy on assessment. We'll continue to do that again this year. We try to look ahead."
- "(I focus on) middle school reform as far as best practices across our middle schools. We have four middle schools in the district and we work hand-in-hand on professional development..."
- "We try to look ahead as to what it is that we believe we need as professional development for principals and coaches and coordinators and we try to learn a year or two ahead so that we can come back and be the expert voice as much as possible with our colleagues."
- "I choose something that I know to be useful."
- "I really like to have things that are concrete and specific so that I can learn for a purpose."

School Districts

School districts provided professional development activities and focus for the administrators as well. Examples of the administrators' comments follow.

- "Professional development (is provided) through our own school district for our K-12 principals. (At) administrators' meetings, we have monthly professional development provided about leadership."
- "Through our district improvement plan and our school improvement plan … school district professional development topics (have been) diversity training, assessment, leadership."

Advertisements

Sources of professional development were found through emails, universities, and professional associations.

- Typically I will find out about opportunities through email. I'm part of different organizations and so I'll get emails from them advertising. . . . I'm now linked into Twitter and I'm getting a lot of information about other opportunities for professional development."
- Principal associations, educator organizations, the Association for Supervision and Curriculum Development, the American Educational Research Association, Phi Delta Kappa, the National Staff Development Council, leadership academies, and state organizations were cited as sources of professional development by the administrators.
- "More of the formal professional development, you really were inundated with flyers and mailings and emails from everybody and really word-of-mouth and what people—what has worked for other folks—usually gets around, the things that were effective or things that people found had a lot of value. I guess that collaboration and one-to-one communication are probably the biggest development factors."

Data-driven Professional Development

Data-driven professional development was reported by principals.

- "We sit down with our supervisor and talk about student achievement and where our school's at and where it's going and … looking at the achievement gap. Student achievement mainly—that shapes my professional development."
- "Formative assessment has been huge just because I've seen the payoffs… formative and summative assessment really—what it's about is just good teaching, tracking students."

- "Professional development at the building level really does stem from conversations that I have with my boss—with my supervisor. Based-pon our school data.... I receive guidance in what would be the best direction for my building.... It's my job to prioritize and to decid, which direction we need to go first."

SELF-DIRECTED PROFESSIONAL DEVELOPMENT

The veteran administrators were self-directed in their pursuit of professional growth experiences. They described being responsible for their own learning and their professional development.

Professional Reading

Reading was a common form of professional development. Examples of administrators' comments about reading follow.

- "Part of our individual responsibility in this job is to continuously read—whether we're reading on our own during a summer break or we're working together on a book study. We all probably have a passion within us that we want and I think it's important to kind of maintain that line of learning as well as the group learning."
- "I have a primary responsibility of educating my teachers on specific topics that will meet their needs. I receive that professional development through professional reading (and) consulting with my colleagues."
- "(The professional development I) receive during the course of the year is professional reading or stuff that my colleagues are reading up on and, through dialogue, I decide that sounds like something that I need. More informal professional development is probably based on contact with colleagues."

Keep Learning

The administrators described their need to "keep learning." Their comments are reflected in the following statements.

- "You've gotta keep learning—you've gotta keep doing so you can stay active in the whole process, So yo, don't get stale as an administrator."
- "I have to create my own learning, I need to read. You need to go to conferences. You've gotta be around other colleagues in order to grow."
- "I'm challenged by my peers—that would probably be my driving force. I work with really smart people. I see they dedicate themselves to not just learning, but being a part—a contributing part of the pro-

fessional learning and I have recognized in the last 2 year, that's a really important piece for me—I've always aspired to be a growing educator. I love the people that are passionate about it at this level of learning. So, it's fun to be around them."

- "I chose the current dropout rate—persistence to graduation is one that was my own personal research item. And I researched all the different aspects on dropout rates for graduating."
- "I probably learn more when we write our school improvement plans and if there's an area there where I feel deficient, I will get more professional development on that topic."

Learning While Doing

The administrators described the professional development they received through their work. Their comments suggest a "learning while doing" approach to professional growth.

- "A lot of times in my position, we're doing the professional development. That doesn't mean that we're not learning even from the folks that we work with along the way.... I see it as, as ongoing. You focus on serving others instead of helping yourself."
- "I learn alongside my staff during job-embedded professional development every week."
- "Long-term, systematic professional development is most effective. I think that administrators, as well as our teachers, need time to learn, go implement, and come back to the table just to learn."

Personal Interests

Administrators indicated their personal interests and needs led to professional development experiences. Examples of their comments follow.

- "One of the ways that I try to decide where I would like to grow myself is through working with my direct supervisor. She has us reflect upon areas that we need to grow and has us develop our own professional development plan as an administrator.... Reflect upon my own practice and look for holes or weaknesses in my leadership and then try to find books or resource materials that would work along with those."
- "I've selected two themes that I thought both interested me and that I thought were pretty leading edge ... hot topics. One was professional learning communities, [the other was] educational technology integration. I chose those by personal preference and what I thought the educational community was leaning toward."

Beyond the School District

Administrators engaged in professional growth opportunities that took them beyond the school districts. Individuals enrolled in graduate degree programs, participated in accreditation visits, and taught at the college level. Examples of their comments about these experiences follow.

- "The reason I've gone to school as much as I have is (for) the professional development that I really wanted.. . . A lot of my professional development up and through my dissertation and my doctorate, was just me. I just wanted to learn more about lots of things…"
- "I remember sitting in (his) office, 'Why are you doing this doctorate thing? It's not going to do anything for you. You know professional, promotion or anything.' I'm doing it because I like to learn and I might as well transcript it, you know? I might as well learn….What he was saying is very true and I found it to be true other places as well. In education, we don't value being better at our craft. We don't."
- "Another thing that I've been doing that's been very valuable is participated in North Central accreditation visits. And as you learn to do that, it gives you a real opportunity for growth that's been very valuable."
- "I teach a little bit at the college level, which is a great professional development opportunity. When you teach something, you tend to learn a lot more than your students do."

STICKING WITH IT

Variability

The veteran administrators were asked: How were you able to "stick with" your work as an administrator? Their answers varied. One recurring theme was they enjoyed the variability of the days.

- "I like how when I come to work every day, I don't always know what's going to happen—you may know what your day was going to look like, but then something happens. . . . You just never quite know what your day is going to look like."
- "The fact that it is unpredictable I like."
- "I like the challenge. It fits my personality because it's very fast-paced and random."
- "I like the flexibility of the job versus the teacher that is stuck in the classroom for the day. You're busy all the time in many different areas. You kind of know what your day is going to be like in the morning, but you can get to work and it changes, lots of interactions with

many different types of people—students, parents, staff, supervisors, and patrons. Every day something is new. It's not a mundane job at all."

- "A lot of variety in the job, two days are never the same."

Relationships

A second common response was the importance of the relationships the principals developed through their work. Comments about these relationships follow.

- "I also value the interactions and the relationships that I have with other folks. I'm a learner and so I would think whenever I talk with folks—I'm learning just like they are. It's more about how I can work with somebody else to get something moving in the right direction. I love the interactions with folks too and just being able to make an impact."
- "It's the kids and the people you work with."
- "My administrative colleagues help me to persevere every day because it's no secret that this job has many, many, many challenges and many facets. It's really the relationships with my colleagues that help me and also just the relationships that I have with the kids because they do keep me coming back every single day."
- "I do feel I have something to give to the job and the people that I work with. I'm a real people person. I like to talk to people. I like to get to know people and I can accept their points of view and their differences.... [I] like the exposure [and] being able to work with all the people that are associated with the school."
- "It would be extremely difficult to be an instructional leader in any building if you didn't surround yourself with a group of people that were your sounding board that could encourage you and give you feedback regularly on how things were going.... That relationship that we share is so powerful a motivator for all of us. There's a lot more value, for us as a group of middle school principals to collaborate, share, and work together than it is to be competitive. . . . There's always someone there listening so I think those collegial relationships . . . can give you honest feedback are very important."
- "People that stay in this have a definite service mentality—serve other people."

A Calling

The administrators described their work as a calling. Examples of their comments follow.

- "It's just a calling on my life. I feel like I want to do what I feel my strengths are—it's something that I just enjoy… I'm an old coach too… just knowing the kids and staff—I just never get tired of that. That's what keeps me coming back."
- "My entire family comes from teaching and admin—it's just a calling similar to the ministry. Something that you know that you were born to do, if the days and the weeks are something that kind of pass by in a blur to you because you're so engrossed in your work, then clearly you're matched perfectly with what you're doing and I love what I do. I love the kids and I love what I do with my staff…"
- "I think really it's a calling and I think this is where I'm supposed to be and what I should be doing."

Better for Kids

The administrators described the opportunity to make education better for kids as a motivation to "stick with it." Examples of their comments follow.

- "When I have had it with state paperwork, I go out and hang out in the diesel shop. I just like those kids and they're different and I like 'em. The opportunity to impact teachers and therefore make education better for kids. That's what truly motivated me to go into it. The part that I enjoy the most is the opportunity for staff development with teachers and to be able to give them something that they can take back today and use in their classroom that will make learning better for kids. Or make their day of teaching more successful. That's what drives me. If I can do that, then that's what I'm all about."
- "Probably the students. I love working with students. Students that are in trouble a lot—[I] feel a real sense of accomplishment when I can see them graduate."
- "(You) have to have clear goals of what you want to do for kids. I mean you have to love the children and that's the key to survival and staying in this profession."
- "It's all about the kids and I enjoy working with the kids and I always will. So, I really couldn't foresee myself doing anything else at this point."
- "If they can make a difference in even one student, that at the end of that year, especially their first year, that they really realize that's why you're here. It's not, it's not the pay, it's not the hours—it's to make a difference in the individual students."
- "I love being around students. My father was a principal. I've grown up with this. It's only rewarding intrinsically you know—it's not the money."

CONCLUSION

The interviews provided pages of transcripts that chronicle these veteran administrators' professional development experiences. There is far more information available about these individuals' experiences than could be included in this chapter.

A summary of the professional development experiences of these veteran administrators:

- The veteran administrators' responses to the question of social justice issues indicated they are part of the everyday work of an administrator.
- Being with colleagues and learning from each other is the "best" professional development.
- There are many sources of professional development available to administrators.
- The veteran administrators indicated they were responsible for their professional growth and engaged in an array of self-directed activities.
- The administrators were able to "stick with it" because of the variability of the work, the relationships, making education better for kids, and because they described their work as a calling.

REFERENCES

Ayers, W., & Quinn, T. (2009). Series forward. *Holler if you hear me: The education of a teacher and his students.* New York: Teachers College Press.

Conger, J. A., & Benjamin, B. (1999). *Building leaders.* San Francisco: Jossey-Bass.

Evans, P. M., & Mohr, N. (1999). Professional development for principals: Seven core beliefs. *Phi Delta Kappan, 80,* 530–532.

Hale, E. L., & Moorman, H. N. (2003). *Preparing school principals: A national perspective on policy and program innovations.* Washington, DC: Institute for Educational Leadership.

Houle, J. C. (2006). Professional development for urban principals in underperforming schools. Retrieved February 11, 2009, from *http://eus.sagepub.com.*

Kelley, C., & Peterson, K. D. (2002). The work of principals and their preparation: Addressing critical needs for the twenty-first century. In M. S. Tucker & J. B. Codding (Eds.), *The principal's challenge: Leading and managing schools in an era of accountability* (pp. 247–312). San Francisco: Jossey-Bass.

Marshall, C., & Oliva, M. (2010). *Leadership for social justice: Making revolutions in education* (2nd ed.). Boston: Allyn & Bacon.

Maryland Instructional Leadership Framework. (2005). Division for Leadership Development, Maryland State Department of Education.

Michie, G. (2009). *Holler if you hear me: The education of a teacher and his students* (2nd ed.). New York: Teachers College Press.

National Commission on Excellence in Education. (1983). *A nation at risk: The imperative for educational reform.* Washington, DC: Government Printing Office.

National Staff Development Council. (2000). Learning to lead, leading to learn: Improving school quality through principal professional development. Retrieved January 15, 2010, from *http://www.nsdc.org/leadership.html.*

Peterson, K. (2002). The professional development of principals: Innovations and opportunities. *Educational Administration Quarterly, 38*(2), 213–232.

Sherman, L. (2000). Preparing to lead: Seattle invests in new ways to train principal. [Electronic Version]. Retrieved February/16,/2009, from *http://www.nwrel.org/nwedu/spring00/text-prepare.html.*

Wong, P. (2004). The professional development of school principals: Insights from evaluating a programme in Hong Kong. *School Leadership an& Management, 24*(2), 139–162.

CHAPTER 11

CRITICAL DIFFERENCES IN SUPERINTENDENCY SEEKERS

**Ava J. Muñoz, Shirley J.Mills,
Anita M. Pankake, and Elizabeth Murakami-Ramalho**

This chapter illuminates the vast disparity of gender equity in the superintendency from a critical, feminist perspective. The examination, based on a large study of central office administrators in Texas, analyzes critical differences in the aspirations of men and women toward a superintendency, and the common reasons male and female central office administrators chose to apply or not apply for a superintendency. We begin with an examination of the representation of women in early superintendencies, followed by an examination of the representation of women in the superintendency in Texas. Mentoring is considered a social justice equalizer in promoting more women to the superintendency, and an examination of aspirations, preparation, and opportunities for men and women in pursuing a superintendency in Texas completes this chapter.

Public education in the United States continues to experience a leadership crisis (Grogan & Brunner, 2005; Quinn, 2005). The superintendency too is not immune from experiencing these critical shortages in its office. Currently, superintendents are expected to be "CEO" or "Chancellor" in

Educational Leaders Encouraging the Intellectual and Professional Capacity of Others:
A Social Justice Agenda, pages 197–208.
Copyright © 2012 by Information Age Publishing
197

some big-city districts, which signals that their position is intended to be more powerful (Useem, 2009). Adding to the many unappealing attributes of the job, demographical flux, school and policy reform, and increasing demands of society exacerbate the necessity for what can almost be seen as a savior or superhero to direct a district to educational excellence, fiscal stability, and community approval (Kamler, 2009).

Women are increasing their numbers in leadership preparation programs. However, the number of males in superintendency positions continues to outnumber females (Brunner & Grogan, 2005). In general, women continue to serve in low numbers in the superintendent's position, even though the overall workforce is mainly female. The issue of female underrepresentation in the superintendency is of critical importance to a school community and society as a whole. We question whether the school's goals and objectives, as defined by Kamler (2009), were meant to mainly be fulfilled by males:

> Educational reform, changing demographics, and societal and political pressures heighten the need for school boards to select a district leader who will be able to spearhead, facilitate, and manage educational improvement while mediating among the needs of the students, the goals and financial ability of the community, and the demands of the faculty and staff. (p. 118)

If women continue to be excluded or continue to exclude themselves from pursuing a superintendency, future generations will continue to carry the same stereotypical ideas of who should hold these top leadership positions.

REPRESENTATION OF WOMEN IN EARLY SUPERINTENDENCIES

In The Superintendent of Schools, Cubberly (1915) mentions the importance of the superintendency. He comments the following regarding the importance of the office: "Potentially, at least, the most important officer in the employ of the people of any municipality today is the person who directs the organization and administration of its school system, and who supervises the instruction given therein" (p. 147). Throughout the remaining commentary offered by Cubberly, he refers to the superintendent "solely" as male. As a means of justifying his unwavering usage of male to describe the superintendent, he includes a footnote as to why only the masculine pronoun *he* is utilized. According to Cubberly, the masculine form of *he* is employed "for the simple reason that nearly all of our city superintendents are men. What is said, however, is equally applicable to women" (p. 154).

Even though the description reports on 1915 events, 95 years later, males continue to dominate the position of superintendent. Blount (2000) sheds light on four possible rationales related to the superintendency being initially male dominant:

Superintendencies eventually became the school administrative position holding the greatest appeal to aspiring male educators. First, the superintendents possessed growing power and authority as school boards ceded larger responsibilities to them. Second, school district tax bases increased, providing for higher superintendent salaries, an important development at a time when magazines and books became best-sellers with stories of poor young men who, by luck and pluck, worked their way to millions. Third, thickening administrative layers insulated superintendents from the immediacies of school work, thus allowing them to direct others who in turn carried out their wishes. Finally, school superintendents increasingly served in central offices located away from schools, but close to the center of local business and municipal affairs. This arrangement permitted school superintendents to socialize easily with powerful male members of the community. It also widened the physical distance between superintendents and teachers, most of whom were female. (p. 86)

The first female superintendent may have been appointed to public schools circa 1858. Even though Ella Flagg Young (1845–1918) was reported to be the first major city school system superintendent by 1909, Phebe Sudlow (1831–1922) was appointed to the superintendency in Davenport, Iowa, during the Civil War, as a result of a shortage of men, who were going into battle. Sudlow accepted the position, not without having to fight for women's rights in relation to pay parity for herself, and for other female teachers (Davenport Public Library, 2005). She was known for signing school documents as P. W. Sudlow, so as not to stir attention to her gender. By 1910, a promising 6.2% of superintendencies were occupied by women. By 1930, 20 years later, a small increase brought the number of women superintendents to 10.9%. Between the latter part of the 1930s and the beginning of the 1970s the increase of female superintendents took a downward trend, plummeting to 0.3% (Polka, Litchka, & Davis, 2008). Not until the late 1970s and most of the early 2000s have women, again, begun to increase their numbers in the superintendency to a promising 13.2% (Blount, 2000; Brunner & Grogan, 2005; Dana & Bourisaw, 2006). By 2006, 21.7% of superintendents were females. Polka et al. (2008) compiled a graph (Figure 11.1) from various sources to depict a representation of women in superintendency positions between 1910 and 2006:

The Superintendency in Texas

In Texas, the number of females follows national trends, with 20% of superintendencies held by them in 2009. When women are not leading districts in greater numbers, however, we argue that social justice in the representation of females is lacking, and as a consequence, an uneven balance of leadership styles is impacting students in the educational system. In order to facilitate instrumental change, both in representation and in a diversity

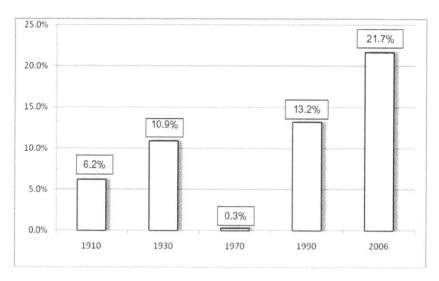

FIGURE 11.1. Percentage of Female School Superintendents between 1910 and 2006
Source: Polka, Litchka, and Davis (2008, p. 295).

of leadership styles, women must be influential, not only in their school communities but by having a voice in the organization of schools, at a local and national level. For example, Johansen (2007) stated that "all managers bring to their jobs different management styles, interpersonal skills, and tools that are a result of their different life experiences" (p. 270). When women are only present in the superintendency in miniscule numbers, their impact is minimal in determining the support for students, participating in school boards, influencing searches for new candidates, or in improving school efforts (Glass & Francheschini, 2007).

Another concern in relation to having minimal voice in school district decisions is that when most of the district superintendents are male, there is a perception from the general public that females in the superintendency are an anomaly, when in actuality this conclusion may be but a consequence of a perpetuation of status quo. In fact, scholars in psychology extensively examined stereotypical norms defined by society of how men and women should behave (Burgess & Borgida, 1999; Glick & Fiske, 1999). Unsurprisingly, a patriarchal society does not perceive, and therefore does not expect women to aspire toward the school superintendency (Blount, 2000; Brunner & Grogan, 2005; Dana & Bourisaw, 2006; Johansen, 2007). Addi-Racah (2006) perceived this inequity when stating, "men are expected to be promoted at school, as this conforms with the dominant male culture and preserves their advantage in society. This pattern of sponsorship may alter as women in school leadership increases" (p. 297).

Interestingly, some scholars are analyzing the superintendency position as one of contemporary renewal. Kamler (2006), for example, asserted that the "graying of the superintendency, a diminished talent pool, and lack of diversity have prompted American educators to develop innovative strategies that encourage, support, and prepare school leaders for the superintendency" (p. 297). This means that an increase in the numbers of retiring superintendents and the lackluster appeal of the superintendency today benefit groups previously denied entry beyond the paper application process for the position (Hayes, 2001). The traditionally male-dominated superintendency may be replacing its "good old boy network" at a faster pace than their mentees can assume their vacant positions.

MENTORING WOMEN TOWARD
THE SUPERINTENDENCY

An important social justice issue to consider, therefore, is the opportunity for current superintendents, presently represented by a majority of males, to provide females with the same opportunities to be groomed for the position. At present, scholars have indicated that mentoring of women, by women, is more frequent than the literature would indicate (Glass, 2000; Grogan, 1996; Dana & Bourisaw, 2006; Muñoz, 2006). The lack of mentoring for women, which may be one of the reasons for some of the barriers for achieving superintendency, is discussed (Grogan, 1996). Grogan (1996) adds that increasing the numbers of women in the superintendency requires cooperation and insight regarding how they arrive at, and function, in the office of superintendent from female role models. Mentoring by women for women has been perceived as rare at the superintendency level due to the lack of female representation in that position. The impact of mentors in supporting and expediting the career success of their mentees at the superintendency level has been proven effective (Dana & Bourisaw, 2006). Glass (2000) added that women also seem to have a less developed mentoring system compared to men.

Researchers observing mentoring systems (Dana & Bourisaw, 2006; Hodgins & Brooks, 2005; Kamler, 2006) concluded that because of society's early definitions of "acceptable" feminine behaviors, women continue to be reluctant to aspire to higher rank positions or ask for mentoring support, whether it be official or unofficial. Consequently, beneficial networking channels are not solidified in order to propel career growth among females in education. Kamler (2006), for example, argued that,

Benefits of this networking configuration as cited by participating aspirants and superintendents may also encourage other superintendents—women and men, white and non-white, alike—to collaborate to ensure that all talented people, regardless of gender and/or color, can access the superintendency. While re-energizing their own spirits to address challenging school issues, mentor superintendents can help to develop a diverse group of aspirants to carry on their life's work and pave the road for inclusive school environments. (p. 314)

Mentoring may be an effective social justice intervention influencing the positive representation of females in the superintendency. Mentoring is important since mentors many times can act as go-getters and go-betweens among superintendent candidates and school boards. In order to create equitable changes for women to participate in the superintendency it is critical that mentors and mentees see values and attitudes beyond *gendered* configurations, and see women as legitimate leaders equipped to lead schools effectively through superintendency positions (Hodgins & Brooks, 2005).

Aspirations, Preparation, and Opportunities for Men and Women in the Superintendency

In a study of aspirations, preparation, and opportunities for males and females for the superintendency, we conducted a survey with 248 responses from assistant, associate, and deputy superintendents, as well as current superintendents in school districts throughout the state of Texas. We examined the career paths of women and men in central office administration and their common reasons for pursuing the superintendency—or the reasons why some were not pursuing the position. The participants contributed with their perceptions related to (1) their aspirations for the position, (2) the connection between aspirations and career advancement, and (3) reasons for pursuing the superintendency. In this section we describe some of the findings of this study.

Aspiration for the Superintendency

When asked if these central office administrators considered pursuing a superintendency position, 11% of women and 25% of men responded affirmatively. When asked to reveal their career aspirations, women made fewer mentions about aggressively pursuing a superintendent's position. Overall, women did not seem as interested in applying for a superintendency position for the position's sake. They seemed content serving in positions up to, but not necessarily into, superintendent positions (assistant, associate, deputy superintendent, etc.). The data also revealed that women were rarely groomed, tapped, or mentored early in their careers about being recommended as good superintendents. As a result, they atypically made the superintendency a career goal.

Male respondents aspired toward a superintendency early on in their careers. One of the reasons reported related to being groomed, tapped, and mentored into the superintendency by mentors early in their careers. In general, males were more articulate in fashioning themselves through language (Gee, 2000), using more "I" statements. They were often referring to their skills, attributes, and achievements in their responses using sentences like "I knew that eventually I would like to be in a position to administer a school district." One of the respondents said:

> I have had extensive life experiences including service as a military officer in addition to experience in business and numerous coaching and teaching situations. While those experiences alone do not qualify me to be a public school/central office administrator, they certainly enable me to bring a larger tool bag to that environment than most of my associates.

In contrast, women often referred to fulfilling the needs of the students and their communities when aspiring to the superintendence with statements such as "Superintendency allows one's influence to reach a broader realm...."

Female respondents considered more choices, reporting to pursue either the superintendency or other central office administration position, while male respondents did not deviate from the pursuit of a superintendency position. Female respondents who aspired a superintendency utilized language that was reactive to the tasks in the position. One of the female candidates said, "I pursued the superintendence because I felt I possessed the skills necessary to fill a superintendent position." Conversely, male candidates were more proactive, responding, "To be a superintendent before I retire has been a goal of mine since very early in my career" and "My career goal has always been to obtain a superintendency." The data informed us that males continue to be socially prepared to aspire for the superintendent's position, followed by women who seem to conform with secondary positions in leading school districts. In the 21st century, women's aspirations to become superintendents are outnumbered by the larger representation and social support given to males.

Connections between Aspirations and Career Advancement

Two hundred and thirty of the 248 survey respondents related their thoughts on why both males and females had pursued their superintendent's certification. From respondents pursuing or that had pursued a certification, an additional question invited participants to share the reasons for pursuing the certification. In general, reasons for obtaining a certification included: (1) career advancement, (2) salary increase, (3) opportunity, and (4) service to students. None of the women referred to salary increases, while 4% of the males mentioned the relation between seeking the superintendency due to salary increase. Females mentioned certification as translating to more opportunities. In relation to serving students, females used relational terms such as "a passion to help" or "a call to make a difference." A majority of males used self-oriented words such as "impacting students and school system" or "impacting students in greater numbers."

Among males, 29% referred to the certification as a means to an end or a "natural path to my career." One of the male respondents reflected:

> I wanted to continue my education. I also wanted to become a leader of a campus and then a district. I was influenced by other administrators who encouraged me. I felt my knowledge of the classroom could be used as a teacher of others. I could make a difference for students in a bigger way. I could touch lives in a more complete way. I was able to mentor adults who could make a mark with other professionals and students.

Thirty-four percent of females reported pursuing a certification to "open up for possibilities." Their responses were presented as explanations, more so than a career-driven decision, confirming Hailman's (2001) observations that there is an expectation that men and women should not only conform with stereotypic expectations but they should avoid behaviors incompatible with these expectations. Females were pursuing degrees in more numbers, but their reasons were often posed as "just-in-case" opportunities, as one participant exemplified:

"I wasn't sure if I was going to ever pursue the superintendency, but it seemed like a good way to gain the certification, just so I would be prepared in the future should that opportunity arise." Another female said: "I had completed all the work necessary for a superintendent's certification while working on my doctorate and wanted to be prepared if the right opening became available."

Male participants seemed to obtain the degree in order to fulfill their aspirations. Females, however, seemed to be less driven in their pursuit of the superintendency, even when equipped with advanced knowledge and certification. The hesitancy of women articulating their aspirations, even when certified, demonstrates that women are still subject to stereotype activation and threat (Hoyt & Blascovich, 2007). Hoyt and Blascovich (2007) argue that women in leadership are vulnerable to the effects of stereotype threats, such as when exposed to stereotypical commercials. Stereotypes threaten the aspirations of women toward leadership, unless they find themselves in a safe environment. Hoyt and Blascovich believe that responses to threat depend on women's assimilation to stereotypes or self-efficacy in reacting against stereotypes.

Females and Mentoring Issues

Surprisingly, many more females as compared to the literature were receiving or providing mentoring opportunities. Based on the data in this study, 66% of males and nearly 72% of females reported having had a mentor or sponsor. On the other hand, 70% of the respondents reported that they themselves were serving or had served as a mentor or sponsor for someone else. In fact, more female respondents in this study reported serving as a mentor than did the male respondents. Additionally, while both male and female respondents in this study indicated that they belonged to a professional learning community or other support group, the largest percent of those belonging to a community of professional learning was reportedly women. Perhaps these data bode a positive change in the mentoring status and activity levels by women for women.

CONCLUSION

When observing the aspirations, preparation, and opportunities of women into superintendency positions, we concluded that positions were not often sought assertively by women in our pool. Overall, women seemed to lack the initiative to apply more specifically for a superintendency. Even though they are preparing for the superintendency through certification, female administrators seem to be waiting for the right opportunity to arise. Conversely, males seemed to continue to be prepared early for the superintendency, and are more purposeful in pursuing the position. These findings are in agreement with previous studies examining the overrepresentation of males in the superintendency (Blount, 2000; Brunner & Grogan, 2005; Dana & Bourisaw, 2006). The positive result from this study is the indication that more mentoring networks are in place to prepare women for the superintendency.

This study showed that women were less driven to pursue the superintendency. However, we also argued that the lack of interest may be a result of a deeper concern that women continue to be exposed to stereotype threats. Nonetheless, "the more social influence women have, the more they are able to introduce change and restructure the gender relations within organizational settings," as Addi-Raccah (2006, p. 313), rightfully recognized. Female leaders of the nation's school systems must have courage, insight, and a clear purpose because they are the ones in the community who are standing up for public education as the cornerstone of our democratic system (Houston, 2007). If, women continue to be excluded or continue to exclude themselves from pursuing a superintendency, future generations of young girls will continue to dismiss the idea of ever holding a superintendency. Moreover, if women are absent from superintendency positions, students and teachers will continue to be exposed to less than representative, unilateral, and gendered forms of leadership, thus perpetuating social justice inequities in the representation of both men and women in significant school leadership positions.

Now, more than ever, the issue of underrepresentation in the superintendency by women is of critical importance to a school community and society as a whole. "Managers no longer 'look' alike in that they no longer share entirely similar backgrounds, and expertise; women bring to an organization personal qualities and life experiences that are different from men" (Johansen, 2007, p. 270). When female school leaders experience a greater amount of "demographic dominance and normative support" (Addi-Raccah, 2006, p. 312), they are more likely to encourage and inform gender-equitable practices in the workplace. They, too, may feel more comfortable using action-oriented terms such as "I have a desire," "I want," and "I always knew I wanted to become a superintendent."

The way men and women operate may be still perceived as at odds. However, women, ultimately, "may choose the strategies that work best for them and/or their organization" (Johansen, 2007, p. 275). Not only have they just begun to talk the talk, they are taking their first steps toward actually walking the walk of the superintendency rather than in minute increments. "First, they are affiliated to the dominant group, and, as noted, their representation in leadership positions is significant. Next, they are found to lead without hesitation, according to their *voice*, which is based on caring and participation" (Addi-Raccah, 2006, p. 300).

Finally, the concept of attainability or realistic career choices often hinders women from pursuing careers that are outside of the status quo. Regarding the lack of women role models in the superintendency, Muñoz (2006) provides one woman's eloquently surmised thoughts regarding the ills of inequity in the superintendency:

> I don't think women have seen themselves in these roles to begin with. How can you aspire if you've not seen yourself in that role? I think women for many years have been content to be behind the scenes. I think women feel ...we feel that we're more connected to the classroom and the students and feel that in having the roles as curriculum directors, as assistant superintendents for curriculum, even human resources where you find a lot of women...that it appeals to our strengths more than the other areas of finance and the management side of large school district[s]. As women become more and more comfortable with those arenas, I believe that and when they are given the opportunity to learn those areas by trial and error or in training...that we will aspire and apply more directly. (p. 134)

It is critical that all those who are involved in preparing future superintendents replicate gender-equitable practices. In anticipation of establishing equitable numbers of female and male superintendents throughout the nation, much work still needs to be done.

REFERENCES

Addi-Raccah, A. (2006). Accessing internal leadership positions at school: Testing the similarity attraction approach regarding gender in three educational systems in Israel. *Educational Administration Quarterly, 42*, 291–323.

Blount, J. (2000). Spinsters, bachelors, and other gender transgressors in school employment, 1850–1990. *Review of Educational Research, 70*(1), 83–101.

Brunner, C. C., & Grogan, M. (2005, November). *Motivation theory and attitudes of aspiration: Why do[not] women central office administrators seek the superintendency?* Paper presented at the annual meeting of the University Council for Educational Administration, Nashville, TN.

Burgess, D., & Borgida, E. (1999). Who women are, who women should be: Descriptive and prescriptive gender stereotyping in sex discrimination. *Psychology, Public Policy, and Law, 5*(3), 665–692.

Cubberley, P. (1915). The superintendent of schools. *The Elementary School Journal, 16*(3), 147–154.

Dana, J. A., & Bourisaw, D. M. (2006). *Women in the superintendency: Discarded leadership.* Lanham. MD: Rowman & Littlefield.

Davenport Public Library. (2005). Phebe W. Sudlow: Iowa's first lady of education. Quad City Memory. Accessed June 19, 2010, from *http://www.qcmemory.org/Default.aspx?PageId=238&nt=207&nt2=229.*

Gee, J. P. (2000). Teenagers in new times: A new literacy studies perspective. *Journal of Adolescent and Adult Literacy, 43*(5), 412–420.

Glass, T. E. (2000). Where are all the women superintendents? *The School Administrator.* Retrieved from *http://aasa.org/publications/saarticledetail.cfm?mnitemnumber=&tnitemnumber=951&i.*

Glass, T., & Francheschini, L. (2007). *The state of the American superintendency: A mid-decade study.* Lanham, MD: Rowman & Littlefield.

Glick, P., & Fiske, S. T. (1999). Sexism and other 'isms': Independence, status, and the ambivalent content of stereotypes. In W. B. Swann, Jr. & J. H. Langlois (Eds.), *Sexism and stereotypes in modern society: The gender science of Janet Taylor Spence* (pp. 193–221).Washington, D.C.: American Psychological Association.

Grogan, M. (1996). *Voices of women aspiring to the superintendency.* Albany: State University of New York Press.

Grogan, M., & Brunner, C. C. (2005). Women leading systems: Latest facts and figures on women and the superintendency. *The School Administrator, 2*(62), 46–50.

Hayes, W. (2001). *So you want to be a superintendent?* Lanham, MD: Scarecrow Press.

Hodgins, D., & Brooks, J. S. (2005). *Paradigm shift or paradigm stasis?: An analysis of research on women in educational leadership from 1980 to 2004.* Paper presented at the annual convention of the University Council for Educational Administration, Nashville, TN.

Houston, P. D. (2007). From custodian to conductor. *The School Administrator, 64*(3), 28–35.

Hoyt, C. L., & Blascovich, J. (2007). Leadership efficacy and women leaders' responses to stereotype action. *Group Processes and Intergroup Relations, 10*(4), 595–616.

Johansen, M. S. (2007). The effect of female strategic managers on organizational performance. *Public Organization Review, 7,* 269–279.

Kamler, E. (2009). Decade of difference (1995-2005): An examination of the superintendent search consultants' process on long island. *Educational Administration Quarterly, 45*(1), 115–144.

Muñoz, A. J. (2006). *"Woman's natural field": The effects of mentoring on women central office administrators.* Doctoral dissertation, University of Texas–Pan American, Edinburg, TX.

Kamler, E. (2006). The aspiring superintendents' study group: Investigating a mentoring network for school leaders. *Mentoring and Tutoring, 14*(3), 297–316.

Polka, W., Litchka, P., & Davis, S. W. (2008). Femperintendents and the professional victim syndrome: Preparing current and aspiring superintendents to cope and succeed. *Journal of Women in Educational Leadership, 6*(4), 293–311.

Quinn, T. (2005). Plan to succeed. *American School Board Journal, 192*(4), 46–49.

Useem, E. (2009). Big city superintendent as powerful CEO: Paul Vallas in Philadelpia. *Peabody Journal of Education, 84*(3), 300–317.

CHAPTER 12

ADVANCING SOCIAL JUSTICE THROUGH SUPPORT PERSONNEL

Fernando Valle and Sylvia Mendez-Morse

The active professional development of personnel in today's schools requires school leaders to share more than accountability stress and instructional savvy; they must breathe life and passion into their mission and vision of producing socially just schools and inspire everyone in and out of the school buildings to join the cause. The effort to establish "socially just schools" continues to be met with inaccurate perceptions of equity and diversity, and limited integration between social justice conceptual frameworks and school practices. It seems that in education, disparities and injustices are becoming an everyday part of America's classrooms (Jacobs, 2006).

The public at large is also hindered by the realities of school personnel burnout; disillusioned and frustrated personnel that believe the harsh realities of inequitable resources and learning outcomes in public education cannot and will not be eradicated. The educational barriers marginalized students face while attending public schools include low expectations, poverty, being an English language learner, having special needs, and ignorance of cultural biases that become associated with deficit characteristics

Educational Leaders Encouraging the Intellectual and Professional Capacity of Others: A Social Justice Agenda, pages 209–228.

of such students and their families. This "business as usual" approach to schooling by adults in the building shifts blame to students and parents, perpetuates stereotypes, and influences policies that do not truly adapt, reform, and advance our school practices. For school leaders seeking to establish equitable schools to persevere and impact school personnel and students, they should frame their work in terms of social justice and equity and enlist all personnel at their campuses. Encouraging participation from all stakeholders in the school building is just as important as acknowledging the equity issues being addressed.

Establishing a socially just and equitable school where all students' needs are met is not an effort that is accomplished by any one person. Undertaking such a task requires collaboration from a host of individuals uniting their passions, visions, and mindsets to achieve the common goal of providing equitable and excellent educational outcomes. It involves the efforts of all personnel—from the custodial staff that maintain the physical conditions of the learning environment to the instructional staff that deliver the lessons in that space. It requires the efforts of the administrative office assistants that provide the front-line communication to students, parents, and community members as well as those of the school leaders that coordinate human, fiscal, and physical resources.

Leading a school that provides an instructional environment conducive to meeting the academic needs of all students continues to be one of the vast challenges facing principals and school leaders. Public schools and their leaders face achievement gaps among White, Latino, and African American children, a growing population of students whose first language is not English, and students with high mobility and poverty rates. In addition, school personnel have an increasing demand to work successfully with special needs children who may also be members of the previously described populations. Moreover, the principals have technological, sexual orientation, racial, religious, health, and financial issues that impact leadership and equity in the building. Each decade brings forth a new generation of students that challenges educators to rethink schooling and provides the catalyst for educators and other school personnel to adapt and improve their roles.

Challenging years of social and organizational norms that created barriers to an equitable education requires having a vision that champions social justice leadership as an effective framework to combat the documented ineffective practices of schools. The idea of taking on enormous responsibility alone may inspire awe, but is typically met with resistance when principals initiate the change processes that confront inequitable practices in schools. Connecting with all staff members, not just teachers, requires a conscious, reflective, and conceptual change of practice for school leaders who strive to transform schools. Engaging all staff members to commit to equity and excellence for all students can no longer be peripheral conversations but rather needs to be a force that confronts and transforms injustices. Embracing support personnel who often feel they are not an active or equal part of the educational community provides leaders the opportunity to erase ideas and practices of marginalization among school staff.

Educational leadership can no longer be viewed as an individual endeavor. Schools are platforms for collaboration where students are not just accountability targets. The role of support personnel is no longer restricted to answering phones, checking out books, and cleaning the school. All staff—professional, certified, and noncertified—are included, empowered, and expected to develop socially just practices with each other and the students they serve. For any school to move toward accepting a social justice identity, it must be endorsed and brought to life by the combined actions of the school leader and the school community. Through this climate of belonging, inclusive conversations about a common vision of what social justice is and can be will occur. As a result, equity will bloom and foster socially just practices between the adults and students who work together.

LEADERSHIP AND SOCIAL JUSTICE

Educational leaders face the constant expectation of advancing and often endorsing countless education policies and practices in their schools. The No Child Left Behind Act of 2001 (NCLB) disturbed fundamental schooling practices across the nation and unveiled discrepancies and disparities among forgotten populations and communities in schools. Although NCLB was met with criticism for its lack of funding, for punishing failing schools, and clearing the path for voucher usage and charter school establishment, it reinvigorated organizations to abandon the "status quo" of marginally acceptable practices with minority and poor students. It pushed school personnel to use "exemplary" practices with all students and provide the firsrate quality education American parents expect.

Some local policies, such as pull-out programs and separate and segregated curricula, have grown out of the grass roots efforts of families, educators, community groups, businesses, and political entities that form the local power structure. District and state policies are often not systematic or orderly; like conversations in social justice leadership, they are messy, ongoing, conflicting, collaborative, and the foundation that changes the daily practices in schools. Theoharis (2009) contends that principals face resistance from within the school site, the district level, and the institutional level; policies and practices can completely alter the direction of a school vision or energize a principal to lead a school toward a social justice vision.

The multicontextuality of leadership in the field, the community context, diverse student populations, facilities, staff, finances, and a host of other variables create a decision-making role for principals that cannot be duplicated. This is where the insights, power of influence, and unique skill sets of the school leader become paramount. It is here that one person can and does make the difference in a school's reputation. Visible leaders, who embrace parents and the community, and are connected with staff and students, understand the air of respect comes from supporting all stakeholders that walk into the building. Principals who have embraced a social justice framework in leading their schools continually scan the educational environment for opportunities to provide lessons of equity and reflective practice toward social justice.

Theoharis (2009) found that resistance to advancing social justice within the local school/community comes through four avenues: 1) the vast scope of the principalship, 2) the momentum of the status quo, 3) the obstructive staff beliefs and behaviors, and 4) the insular/privileged parental attitudes. As principals struggle to make an impact in the education of their most marginalized and oppressed students, the monumental nature of the principalship leaves educational leaders emotionally and physically drained. Principals often find their resiliency to get the job done comes through their students, supportive structures in the organization, relationships at work, and the constant growth due to professional challenges. School leaders can gain strength to battle the constant oppositions of forming socially just schools from supportive relationships in the organization; finding ways of forming and broadening supportive connections with all staff is essential. How educational leaders approach advancing social justice in their schools, not only with students but with support staff, is the focus of this chapter.

SOCIAL JUSTICE

The current collection of social justice rationales argues for improving the background knowledge and contextual accounts of all educators who work with students in our public schools. This charge for critical discourse will help straighten out the creases between practice and policy in our schools. To better understand how the development and inclusion of all personnel in the work of cultivating socially just schools can support educational leaders, it is critical to review various areas of impact that inform the work of a campus leader. These include social justice and leadership, school culture and climate, support personnel, and professional development.

In this first section we present a premise found in the literature on social justice and leadership, how campus leaders promote/cultivate social justice in the schools, and continue defining a socially just school. Next, we extend the definition of a socially just school by describing the school culture and climate in this type of school. We emphasize the importance of relationships and communication and discuss the limited literature found concerning support personnel, particularly nn-instructional and nn-certified support staff. Finally, we present related literature on professional development and advocate for staff training that includes all campus personnel on the social justice aspects of the school. A continued emphasis in this chapter voices the need to develop communication, collaboration, and cultivation skills between general education and specialized education teachers as well as certified personnel and support staff to form a socially just campus, expand staff perspectives, and further develop coherence between campus staff, parents, and community members.

Social Justice Leadership in Schools

Educational leaders rely on the formation of relationships between varied personnel, each with their particular focus and skills, working in collaboration to meet the goals and objectives of the school vision. "Leadership stands at the crossroads, broadening individual aspirations to embrace social change and building a society that responds to human wants, needs, and values" (Burns, 2003, p. 147). These can be delicate issues requiring a principal to arrange situations that promote the articulation of mutual goals and exploration of complimentary processes that lead to productive relationships: a fundamental component and practice to socially just schools.

The school leader is often a "courier," delivering the vision and action plans to implement policies, ensuring instructional leadership, and continuing the rich dialogue social justice work needs from one group to another. Fulfilling the leader's role, the principal becomes a powerful messenger, carrying and delivering both good and bad news of policies, school reforms, and accountability objectives. A principal observes the verbal and nonverbal responses from those receiving the messages, adjusts working timelines, regroups personnel, and ensures equality and integrity is present in the school's finished product.

Those reactions may be tempered when the receiver of the message—a teacher, an administrative assistant, or a counselor—is in a less powerful position than the one delivering it—the school leader. However, in addition to delivering the information, a school leader is also responsible for carrying out the directives of campus and district policies to ensure the highest quality education for all students. As high-stakes testing continues to be part of the educational culture, state and national accountability compels educational leaders to realize that there is no "silver bullet" approach in education and there is no single person or group who can accomplish all that needs to be done.

The responsibility to successfully and effectively educate all of our children to meet the rising benchmarks of accountability is no longer the sole responsibility of the leader or any one individual. The need for the services of support personnel in inclusive classrooms is not a negative reflection on the adequacy of classroom teachers, but instead, reminds us that no single individual, no matter what her or his discipline or experience, has the ability to meet the range of diverse student needs that may be present in a heterogeneous classroom (Stainback & Stainback, 1992).

The need for collaboration, reflective practice, and partnerships has reached new levels and requires new dimensions of educational involvement. The emerging instructional and organizational collaborations result in considering a "new normal" for public education, exploring instructional possibilities and revamping the traditionally isolated roles in education. The "new normal" provokes non-traditional methods of teaching, promotes having the difficult and critical conversations about student realities, leads to the development of unique partnerships, and requires the inclusion of support personnel to contribute in obtaining positive educational outcomes. As schools continue to transform their practices, an untapped talent pool of support staff exists. Often forgotten and frequently found in the peripheral spaces, the non-instructional support staff is an integral part of the school family. Although often neglected, they also contribute to the successful educational development of students, embody the school vision, and act as liaisons between parents, community, and an array of outsider voices.

The Elementary and Secondary Education Act (ESEA), as reauthorized under the No Child Left Behind Act, Sec. 9101, paragraph 36) defines those non-instructional personnel who provide specialized services to students as "school counselors, school social workers, school psychologists, and other qualified professional personnel involved in providing assessment, diagnosis, counseling, educational, therapeutic, and other necessary services..." Furthermore, the definition incorporates *related services* as defined in the Individuals with Disabilities Education Act (IDEA, Sec. 602, paragraph 22). For this chapter we extend our views of those necessary services to the development and advancement of support personnel to include non-certified staff such as administrative assistants, clerks, paraprofessionals, instructional support staff, aides, custodians, bus drivers, and school security officers in our conversation. We see these support personnel as vital to continue the collaboration of the educational community and the development of marginalized staff and student populations.

Supportive Literature

Marshall (2004) recognizes that the knowledge base, research, and professional culture as well as the policies and training programs of the educational administration professoriate and practitioners face chronic but also new challenges for addressing equity and social justice concerns. Schools that have pushed back on the traditional forces that resist change and actively practice social justice in their buildings embrace all levels of participation from personnel and their educational communities and dramatically increase the potential for academic success in their schools. Support personnel are an integral part of the school day, supporting teachers, preventing conflicts, linking community to schools, supporting the development of the whole child, ensuring student safety, and helping school leaders refocus the lens of social justice in our schools.

The past two decades has brought forth a surge in social justice literature and research from practitioners on teaching strategies to support and understand marginalized and oppressed groups in our schools. While a rich literature has grown on the reframing of social justice teaching practices, studies analyzing principals bringing equity and justice to their schools is limited (Theoharis, 2009). As educational leaders contend with an aging workforce, influence the millennial generation, prepare educators to work with children of color (the upcoming statistical majority), and arrange schools to host and lead complex student populations, research on the work principals do to produce more equitable and socially just schools is vital.

Literature, conferences, and resources that address the topics of social justice, leadership, and schools continue to emerge. Among the common themes in these is the need for school leaders to cultivate campuses where students are achieving academically, especially those marginalized because of their race or ethnicity, social economic status, sexual orientation, disabilities, or not having English as their first language. Adding to the current placement of greater and greater demands on the principalship with fewer resources (Kinney, 2003; Langer & Borris-Schacter, 2003; Marshall, 2004). The resistance to advance equity magnifies the stressors of the principalship and provides a strong case to practice socially just leadership strategies in schools.

Another theme in the emerging literature for social just leadership practice is the need for principals to promote such a culture and school climate that ensures teachers actively seek and/or practice instructional methods that meet the educational needs of all their students. Schlechty (2001) stresses, if the principal is to help teachers improve what they do, the principal must continuously be learning to improve what he or she is doing" (p. 145).

A consistent theme in leadership literature is the need to include outreach to the parents, guardians, and community members whose perspectives and concerns are seldom sought and often discouraged. Missing from the literature is discussion on the practices of school leaders that combine efforts and insights of nurses, custodians, librarians, counselors, and support personnel to sustain a campus where all staff members have an equal voice to share cultural, community, and social capital and feel welcomed to participate in delivering an equitable and quality education. Support personnel can easily be a neglected part of the educational community and a resource that is omitted when seeking to form equitable and socially just schools.

When describing the work of social justice principals, Theoharis (2007) argues that social justice supports a process built on respect, care, recognition, and empathy. When school leaders embrace and include personnel, both instructional and non-instructional, into the collective work of all employees at school, the respect and recognition that is part of social justice coherence is extended to these frequently ignored educators. While calling for social justice to be elevated in the school leadership research, Furman and Shields (2005, p. 128) constructed an "interactive model of social justice, democratic community, and learning." Their model explicitly focuses on five areas: moral and ethical leadership, context and community, democracy, pedagogy, and critique.

Bruner (2008) affirms that social justice "is about taking intentional action to create non-discriminatory relationships that transform unequal power structures" (p. 490). Inclusion of support personnel in social justice work can level the traditional top-down hierarchical structures found in schools that frequently contribute to unequal power relationships found between teachers, administrators, and support personnel. This common theme of outreach to marginalized communities both inside and outside of the school building will eliminate the practice of marginalizing support personnel.

Support Personnel and Socially Just Schools

The vast amount of specialized strands in education provides a multitude of opportunities for specialized positions and services. For example, the non-instructional professionally certified personnel such as nurses, counselors, librarians, diagnosticians, social workers, and caseworkers are all important members of a school. In addition, there is also non-certified support staff such as administrative staff, teacher's assistants, custodians, security officers, bus drivers, and food service employees. Support personnel are integral to the school's culture as they contribute meaningful and rich experiences shared by those inhabiting the school. Leadership literature often bulks non-instructional school personnel into "other stakeholder" categories. These stakeholders can be part of isolated subcultures found in schools. When found working in a culture of isolation, support personnel are accepted in their defined roles as long as they do not interfere with daily routines or cultural norms. Theoharis (2009) describes a pervasive attitude in which to many staff members particular children were optional, expendable, and just plain not valued. Such a perspective is often applied to support staff. This attitude is detrimental to inclusive school practices. Extending this fate to support personnel who feel marginalized, demoralized, and unvalued reproduces the idea of oppression and forms the emotional resistance principals face when implementing and advancing social justice work.

As principals face an increased amount of work and agenda overload, and as research continues to provide solutions of carrying this enormous responsibility, the value of support personnel can no longer be overshadowed or neglected. Omitting the active participation of support personnel in the pedagogical, curricular, and emotional well-being of the student is to devalue the essential roles counselors, nurses, librarians, diagnosticians, technology personnel, program coordinators, support and clerical staff, custodians, and security personnel perform in embodying the school vision and educating the whole child. To build a collaborative school, support staff—including bus drivers, cafeteria workers, instructional and library aides, office personnel, and playground supervisors—must frequently meet to receive training and to discuss how they can facilitate and enhance the learning process (Robbins & Alvy, 2003).

A socially just school is a campus where *all* employees and their skills and talents are included and valued in the efforts to support achievement not only of students but the whole school community. The campus leader is the architect, operating in collaboration with all staff members to design the network of structures and foundations that will be built to support the culture of the school. Social justice leaders include the whole school community to be an active component of those school structures and recognize that the contributions of these typically neglected individuals are neither small nor insignificant, but rather are contributory and meaningful. In *The Schools Leaders Our Children Deserve,* Theoharis (2009) sought out principals who were committed and successful in bringing equity and justice to their schools. Their actions served as units of analysis that provided further insight into defining social justice leaders, thus potentially enhancing other school leaders' administrative practice. The principals Theoharis documented were educational leaders who possessed a belief that promoting social justice was a driving force behind what brought him or her to a leadership position. They advocated, led, and kept at the center of their practice/vision issues of race, class, gender, language, disability, sexual orientation, and/or historically marginalized conditions. Moreover, these school leaders had evidence to show that their work had produced more just schools.

Advocating on behalf of societal, emotional, physical, and inequitable issues "conceptualizes and explores a social justice framework for educational leadership, both theoretically and practically" (Marshall & Oliva, 2010). This dimension adds another layer to the principalship that encompasses the complexity of being a just leader, one who would not be a disinterested manager of their environments and contexts, but astute activists, ready with strategies and the sense of responsibility to intervene to make schools equitable (Marshall & Oliva, 2010).

During a school day, a school principal is not the only person doing a walkthrough of the building. Support personnel also have contact with students, out of the classroom, in the hallways, and in the many offices and spaces of a school. Such interactions reveal information about students' life away from the classroom and provide a more comprehensive picture of students' struggles and true lives for teachers and administrators to include in their work with students in and out of the school building. Cafeteria, custodian, bus drivers, security, and administrative support staff are a strong part of the subcultures and informal communication networks established in schools. Compared to a number of administrators and teachers who may not live in the same communities where they teach, school staff may reside in the local community, increasing their knowledge about the complexities of school issues, local politics, power dynamics, and relationships that breed and foster potential conflicts that are under the radar of teachers and administrators.

Principals who do not make time to include or value the efforts of support staff exclude a significant portion of their educational communities. Support personnel, especially non-instructional staff members, are also parents, grandparents, relatives, consumers, and taxpayers in the community with political, business, and civic ties that when left unvalued can be a strong opposition to any principal's efforts. These peripheral support staff members have the pulse of the campus as well as that of the community.

Professional Development

Carol Dweck (2006) defines a growth mindset as the belief that basic qualities can be cultivated. Dweck further points out that although people may differ in their initial talents and aptitudes, interests, or temperaments, everyone can change and grow through application and experience.

A principal who is a social justice leader will utilize Dweck's (2006) perspective of a growth mindset to develop the potential and growth qualities of individuals on their campus, regardless of title, position, or job description. This provides a principal the structures and foundations to extend the conversation of a collective culture of the school and its community and promote and adapt to a growth mindset. Thus a socially just school has a climate that embraces individual roles as important active ones and further develops their talents and skills for the benefit of the individual and the whole school community. Skrla, Scheurich, Garcia, and Nolly (2004) reported that school staffs maintain general lack of understanding about the present levels of inequity and these misconceptions act as a barrier to social justice. These researchers also asserted that the ignorance of present-day inequities was compounded by even well-intentioned staff who treat "differences as deficits, a process that locates the responsibility for school success in the lived experience of children (home life, home culture, socioeconomic status) rather than situating responsibility in the education system.... [They] assign blame for school failure to children and to their families" (p. 114). Professional development that will foster dialogue about how such perspectives and attitudes not only toward marginalized students but also toward support personnel is needed in order to establish socially just schools.

Moreover, principals who have had conversations of school responsibility, equity, and social justice promote a campus where nurses, custodians, support staff, and security guards can serve as mentors, tutors, activists, and role models. Such school leaders further the inclusion of support personnel participating in school-wide trainings, serving on school committees, and being included in professional staff development. This provides a multitude of opportunities to debunk stereotypical staff roles within the culture of the organization. Thus adults are valued for their contributions, utilizing their cultural, social, and intellectual capital, their identities, and various skill sets to contribute to an equitable school culture and climate, and further strengthening their role as a stakeholder in the organization.

Promoting such efforts in leadership preparation and practice are necessary in preparing campus leaders with the knowledge, skill, and desire to examine why and how school policies and practices "devalue the identities of some students while overvaluing others" (Nieto, 2000, p. 183). Hargreaves (2005) contends the moral life of schools runs parallel to the academic life of schools. School personnel need to see themselves in light of the greater good—the broader public purpose of precollegiate education—and continue looking at the ways they connect with and serve the whole community that allows for their existence (Hargreaves, 2005).

Educational leadership, as Hargreaves (2005) continues to describe, was characterized as being practiced by authoritarian, even wounding principals. It was rational, linear, hierarchical, secretive, and controlling (Hargreaves, 2005). It was leadership too often lacking in mission, and almost always bereft of passion that Hargreaves (2005) says describes the paradigm of "power over" rather than "power with," of transactional rather than transformational leadership. Today, the fight for sustainable and transformational practices in educational leadership has created the theoretical and practical support necessary to develop social justice curriculums, and justice-focused strategies for schools and has provided the language and the space for intellectual and experiential experience. The role of today's social justice leader is to create a professional learning community and include all educational stakeholders in this mission of professional learning. Educational leaders need to know that these issues (inequities) run deep for students and staff and that they have obligations to explore, to be nontraditional, to find a way to build capacity for social justice through schooling (Marshall & Oliva, 2010).

Initiating Social Justice Practice in the Field: The Inclusion of Support Personnel

When implementing school-wide reforms and district policies that impact the future academic success of all students, school leaders are faced with ethical, financial, and tough choices. Delivering a unified message to create buy-in among all staff in a school is critical during the change process. The role of the principal moves from instructional leader to social justice advocate and visionary as the realities and complexities of implementing school reform efforts come to life. Fullan (2002) argues that the principal as instructional leader has been a valuable, but too narrow a solution. Instead, the instructional focus must be embedded in a more comprehensive and fundamental set of characteristics, which Fullan (2002) calls "the principal as leader in a culture of change." For educational leaders who champion issues of social justice, it is the conscious inclusion of all staff that encourages professional growth and construction of social justice capacities in our schools.

In Valle's (2008) doctoral dissertation, "Difficult but not Impossible: Initiating Comprehensive High School Reform in a South Texas School District," the superintendent, the central administration, school board, and community aligned their efforts with the high school principals to redesign and reform the district's predominantly Latino high schools. Valle researched the culture of the schools and the messages principals delivered as a unified front to a large educational community. In the midst of initiating various levels of change and facing the pressure to successfully redesign the high schools, the school district personnel formed an alliance with regional partners and a national Comprehensive Reform Model (CRM) that brought in the participation of community members, parents, and all staff together for a full day of staff developments and trainings. The unprecedented involvement of all staff members of both high schools encouraged the cultivation and professional learning of all school personnel. Vital information on high school redesign was presented in both English and Spanish to parents, teachers, counselors, teacher aides, custodians, service staff, and all educational stakeholders present. Veteran personnel commented that in all their years of tenure, the two high schools and their respective campus personnel had never been gathered before in one place to hear a passionate unified message to improve their schooling practices and meet the challenges and needs of all students.

As with many school reform policies, they were met with initial resistance, but educational leaders at all levels led a successful campaign of incorporating the input of all staff, parents, and educational stakeholders. There was a constant examination of leadership proceedings, redesign initiation, and how socially just practices would impact future school business. The superintendent, district leaders, and principals made a conscious effort to focus on initiating change by including all staff during the initial buy-in and trainings, thus validating their voices as they discussed and planned educational improvements for all students.

The reform initiatives in this study created significant changes for school personnel at the campus and district levels. It also provided the school district an opportunity to reconnect with parents, non-instructional staff, and their community as they discussed change, highlighted areas of improvement, and contended with the realities of implementing reform. Consciously including all staff in the conversation of professional learning and change culminated in town hall meetings. The principals and educational leaders embraced the opportunity to utilize their central administration and all staff in their high schools to be active change agents and support the reforms to build equity for the students in their high schools. It took a passionate and socially justice minded superintendent and resilient principals and leadership teams to advance curriculum opportunities for all students, recapture dropouts, create small learning communities, and implement equitable support structures for all student populations.

For superintendents and principals today, implementing reform is no easy task as tenures become overwhelmingly shorter and implementing policies in large public school environments become more complex. The educational leaders in the previous study faced unique cultural challenges and embraced their educational community to support the redesign of their two predominantly Latino high schools. All staff members were challenged to rethink, fulfill, and embrace their new roles during the change process and provide visions of student success by taking advantage of the equitable opportunities.

STRATEGIES TO ADVANCE SOCIAL JUSTICE

Hiring the Right Support Personnel

Support staffs are often the school's invisible army (Schmidt, 2002). Although principals may not get the immediate pat on the back for hiring quality staff, filthy classrooms, a poorly run cafeteria, an absent nurse or counselor, or accidents on school grounds can throw a campus into complete disorder, blaming the school leader for unacceptable practices, mediocre staff members, and unclean rooms. Support personnel perform a list of duties that go largely unnoticed and unapplauded. Hiring quality staff in every aspect of schooling can prevent the spread of dissent and staff resistance. Schmidt (2002) asserts that if educational leaders routinely delegate support-staff interviews to others, it sends a message about hierarchy and status ("She's too busy to interview custodians"). The lessons (Schmidt

(2002) provides in *Gardening in the Minefield: A Survival Guide for Administrators* provides some strategies to make the hiring process successful:

- ***Call in the experts.*** The hiring of support staff may require knowledge and expertise outside the leaders' comfort zone. Having the experts on campus who perform that specific job or duties on the hiring team will help leaders separate good candidates and answers from weak ones.
- ***Call in the central office staff that train and supervise support staff.*** Seeking the advice and questions they would ask or inviting them to be part of the hiring team aligns campus and district philosophies on what kind of candidates they hire. Many departments have interview protocols, questions, and forms they might be able to share to help build a quality workforce.
- ***Central office managers.*** Leaders are eager to share their expertise. Extending your questions to other administrators and central office managers will help build a stronger network of support in your educational community. With combined expertise it is more likely you will hire quality individuals and support staff; if not, you have a team to help undo the mistake.

Creating a Climate of Belonging

To successfully move toward collaboration efforts and create that climate of belonging, school leaders must acknowledge the areas that need improvement with students and staff; take the risk of discussing and collaborating with staff to resolve issues; demonstrate compassion for their educational communities; focus on the work of learning and model it appropriately; and to continue advancing and working on communication efforts with teachers, students, and parents. Theoharis (2009) and the seven principals he worked with in *The School Leaders Our Children Deserve* promoted social justice through their efforts to create a climate of belonging. Collectively, they utilized five strategies in their schools, classrooms, and with their educational communities to establish meaningful connection between the school and its stakeholders. Again we argue that these practices encourage social justice dialogue and proficiency among all staff members. These strategies and talking points provide groundwork for initiating school-wide conversations educational leaders can have with students, the community, and all personnel on:

- Creating a warm and welcoming climate
- Fostering community building in each classroom, among departments, and across the school

- Reaching out intentionally to the community, staff, and marginalized families
- Incorporating social responsibility into the school curriculum, staff meetings
- Using a proactive and process approach to discipline across the school.

Valuing Personnel

When working with the development of all personnel in education, it is fundamental for educational leaders to recognize the importance and value given by all stakeholders: the *Time* spent on educational and noneducational issues, the *Talent* available to develop and value, and the conscious effort to provide time and space for social justice and equitable work that is considered the new normal and *Treasure* in our schools.

Time. As a whole, time is always being negotiated in our schools. Every minute of a student's and staff member's school day is control through schedules, bells, school programs, weekly and monthly plans. As educational leaders we have the opportunity to provide time for our students to embrace teaching moments from a variety of educational stakeholders, like support personnel. Time is the variable that creates and supports peer and mentoring relationships, provides the space to include support personnel in schoolwide discussions, and creates a culture of belonging. The time invested in schoolwide staff impacts the core development of students, distributes the teaching moments throughout the school day and building, and does not isolate learning to the classroom.

Talent. It takes a special adult to work in an educational environment. Reaching parents and students in our public schools takes the savvy of a social worker, the concentrated research efforts of a university professor, the convincing rhetoric of an attorney, and the law enforcement authority of a police officer. In many schools talent pools exist but are not utilized to their full potential. Schools are full of talented staff members who have built various forms of human capital over their careers and have ventured into entrepreneurial experiences, developed second careers and businesses, and have hobbies and interests that educational leaders can harness to educate the whole child. Counselors, librarians, school psychologists, social workers, directors, and support personnel provide an array of talents that are traditionally viewed as one-dimensional in school environments. It is in this pool of noninstructional personnel that principals will find a deep reservoir of expertise and exceptional narratives that supports and fulfills a social justice framework in education.

Treasure. With the conscious involvement and collaboration of all educational personnel, educational leaders can refocus the development on the vast array of educational opportunities for both students and staff. It is conversations surrounding the needed resiliency in the rapidly changing contexts of education and the critical need to erase barriers to equitable educational outcomes that reframes social justice and redesigns job descriptions for personnel. Including school-wide values begins building the educational treasury surrounding the visionary approach to socially just leadership and lifts American public school education to be the important facet of society that our country expects and deserves. Education is one of the true treasures of life. It is an opportunity to build valuable forms of capital and change a child's life beyond measure. It is the reason socially just educational leaders stay up late at night, rethinking the way school business is conducted and why they continue to work tirelessly to improve educational opportunities for all stakeholders.

SUPPORTIVE VIEWS

It takes a conscious partnership between the multiple offices in a school district, central administration, principals, and noninstructional staff to develop consistent equitable support and socially just opportunities for our students. Advancing social justice and increasing the successful performance outcomes for all students has equity implications. In essence, support personnel can contribute to school effectiveness in the following manner.

Facilitate Conditions

School personnel can be part of the distributed and effective leadership practices in schools by assisting principals in the development of a just and capable staff. As collaboration in schools continues to be a necessary strategy for success, educational leaders can create the space necessary for policy implementation, training practices, and inclusion of all staff in staff development opportunities to strengthen the organizational framework necessary to build a community of learners. By incorporating the strengths, various backgrounds, and levels of expertise of staff in the education of our students, school personnel can be an active part of the development of the school culture and effectively support the school to meet student needs and implement the school vision.

Improve School Climate

Support personnel are often privileged to subcultures within schools. They may have community lenses and familial perspectives that teachers and principals miss and, moreover, often to not have the time to focus on. School support personnel can continue to improve school climates by providing alternative lenses to school reality, support various learning outlets for students, inform stakeholders of educational law and policies, and provide additional balance for school leaders who are the first to deal with the harsh realities of public school life.

To work in a public school means encountering both positive and negative aspects of education. School personnel can be a voice in fostering positive teacher attitudes in community relationships, regarding student potential and development and can provide additional avenues for students' personal, academic, and vocational growth. This also means school support personnel can assist educational leaders to sustain and perpetuate order in the day-to-day operations of schools by maintaining a safe and just climate and helping in minimizing the need to discipline. Through continued communication with students and teachers, the typical outsider voice of support personnel can contribute to the organization and support the development of equity and social justice in schools, bringing in additional and needed perspectives to our ever-changing contexts in education.

The participation of support personnel in the development of rewards and incentives for students and staff cultivates collaboration within the school community. It further encourages various district-wide offices to contribute through staff and support personnel in the development of social justice practices. These avenues of cross-collaboration promote communication and clarity between central administration and schools as they face issues of equity and social justice.

Support Personnel: Input is Important

Input from the various brackets of educational stakeholders is important. The input support personnel provide in schools can come from a range of educational spaces, from educational law to strong ties to parents and community, to a nontraditional way of handling school business. Support personnel are often privileged to many conversations, lenses, points of view, and situations that do not reach teachers and principals. For example, diagnosticians, counselors, and school psychologists frequently hear firsthand accounts of parents' perceptions of classroom management, teachers' personalities, teaching strategies, and overall impressions and opinions of the school's efforts in the support for or perceived abandonment of their children. It is receptionists, clerks, and support staff that first receive concerns, complaints, or news. Their constant contact with parents and the community through attendance offices, telephone calls, appointment visits, emails, and conferences assists in creating and maintaining a positive school atmosphere.

This peripheral space is not static but continually shifting between and among the societal views communities have of their educational institutions; it is in this "space" that educational leaders can garner additional support for their schools and continue the encouragement of all personnel. As they protect teachers, communicate with students, and keep a finger on the pulse of the school buildings, support personnel are often the ideal change agents to foster positive parental and community relationships.

Training and professional learning on impacting students should not be limited to teachers and principals. Professional learning is vital to the development of all educators and provides the vital structure to strengthen educational outcomes in our schools. The specialized training school personnel receive and provide schools is a valuable resource for school organizations. School staff personnel have access to a wide school community network and provide valuable resources for teachers and principals.

Like a president surrounded by top advisors, the ongoing professional learning and development of teachers and principals in accountability and specialized areas often depends on the information school personnel provide. Through professional learning, school personnel continue to provide services that address barriers to learning and further assist students to be successful beyond the school walls. These essential services, which focus on prevention and intervention, also promote effective classroom teaching and learning.

Principals and educational leaders who foster ethical environments where all school personnel work collaboratively promote a school culture where social justice dialogue can build the foundations for the equity needed in every school. Maintaining an optimal educational environment and adequate school facilities requires more than routine upkeep. Implementing a social justice framework through support personnel requires a new vision of inclusion, true reflective practice, collaboration, and societal empowerment. What does work for educational leaders is building time within the day to listen to students, teachers, staff, and tackle the school issues that truly matter. This is especially important as principals continue the pursuit of a high-quality education for all students, especially an education that is responsive to the diverse needs and challenges of students today.

Principals who utilize a social justice framework as a strategy to create value for teachers, support personnel, and educational stakeholders will obtain the most out of their students and the people who work in their organizations. Blaming inadequacies, injustices, and low morale on the various macro and micro policies that govern our schools creates incongruent schooling practices. It is essential for educational leaders, who are ultimately the guardians of school policies, to increase the capacity and involvement of support personnel. The conversations and thoughts in these sections provide a framework, direction, and community building opportunities for principals to positively encourage the inclusion of school support personnel in the continued development of a quality education for students.

REFERENCES

Bruner, D. Y. (2008). Aspiring and practicing leaders addressing issues of diversity and social justice. *Race, Ethnicity and Education, 22*(4), 483–500.

Burns, J. (2003). *Transforming leadership: A new pursuit of happiness.* New York: Atlantic Monthly Press.

Dweck, C. S. (2006). *Mindset: The new psychology of success.* New York: Random House.

Elementary and Secondary Education Act of 1965 or ESEA (Pub. L. 89-750). The No Child Left Behind Act of 2001 (Pub. L. No. 107-110) includes the most recent amendments to ESEA. Available at http://www.ed.gov.

Fullan, M. (2002). Principals as leaders in a culture of change. *Educational Leadership, 59*(8), 16–21.

Furman, G., & Shields, C. (2005). How can educational leaders promote and support social justice and democratic community in schools? In W. A. Firestone & C. Riehl (Eds.), *A New Agenda for Research in Educational Leadership* (pp. 119–137). New York: Teachers College Press.

Hargreaves, A. (2005). Sustainable leadership and social justice: A new paradigm. *Independent School, 64*(2), 16–24.

Individuals with Disabilities Education Act. Retrieved from Library of Congress, Bill Text, 108th Congress (2003–2004), H.R. 1350, ENR at *http://thomas.loc.gov/cgi-bin/query/z?c108:h.1350.enr.*

Jacobs, J. (2006). Supervision for social justice: Supporting critical reflection. *Teacher Education Quarterly, 33*(4), 23–39.

Kinney, P. (2003). Leading with less. *Principal, 83*(1), 34-35, 38–39.

Langer, S., & Boris-Schacter, S. (2003). Challenging the image of the American principalship. *Principal, 83*(1), 14–18.

Marshall, C. (2004). Social justice challenges to educational administration: Introduction to a special issue. *Educational Administration Quarterly, 40*(1), 5–15.

Marshall, C., & Oliva, M. (2010). *Leadership for social justice: Making revolutions in education* (2nd ed.). Boston: Pearson

Nieto, S. (2000). Placing equity front and center: Some thoughts on transforming teacher education for a new century. *Journal of Teacher Education, 51*(3), 180–187.

No Child Left Behind Act of 2001 (Pub. L. No. 107-110). Most recent set of amendments to the Elementary and Secondary Education Act of 1965. Available at *http://www.edu.gov.*

Robbins, P., & Alvy, H. (2003). *The principal's companion: Strategies and hints to make the job easier* (2nd ed.). Thousand Oaks, CA: Corwin Press.

Schlechty, P. (2001). *Shaking up the school house: How to support and sustain educational innovation.* San Francisco: Jossey-Bass.

Schmidt, L. J. (2002). *Gardening in the minefield: A survival guide for school administrators.* Portsmouth, NH: Heinemann

Skrla, L., Scheurich, J. J., Garcia, J., & Nolly, G. (2004). Equity audits: A practical leadership tool for developing equitable and excellent schools. *Educational Administration Quarterly, 40*(1), 135–163.

Stainback, S., & Stainback, W. (1992). *Curriculum considerations in inclusive classrooms: Facilitating learning for all students.* Baltimore: Paul H. Brookes.

Theoharis, G. (2007). Social justice educational leaders and resistance: Toward a theory of social justice leadership. *Educational Administration Quarterly, 43,* 221.

Theoharis, G. (2009). *The school leaders our children deserve: Seven keys to equity, social justice and school reform.* New York: Teachers College Press.

Valle, F. (2008). *Difficult but not impossible: Initiating comprehensive high school reform in a south Texas school district.* Unpublished doctoral dissertation, University of Texas–Pan American, Edinburg.

CHAPTER 13

CHARTER SCHOOLS

Meeting the Democratic Mission of Public Education

Ann Allen and Marytza Gawlik

Forty-one states have charter school laws, governing more than 4,000 charter schools across the nation. Established as public schools outside of local control, charter schools attempt to provide educational choice to all students while being more responsive to students and parents than district schools. As an alternative to the traditional school offerings, charter schools introduce several challenges to public school leadership that must be addressed if we are to ensure charter school leadership addresses the social justice goals of public education.

Charter school leaders operate in a political climate in which charter schools compete with district schools for student enrollment. The competition for students presents dilemmas for social justice leaders, who must attend to precepts of equity in educational access. Second, the job of a charter school leader is structurally different than that of a district school leader. Unlike traditional schools, charter schools do not have central office support. Charter school leaders must take on both duties of the traditional principal and traditional superintendent. Third, charter school

Educational Leaders Encouraging the Intellectual and Professional Capacity of Others:
A Social Justice Agenda, pages 229–247.
Copyright © 2012 by Information Age Publishing
All rights of reproduction in any form reserved.

229

leadership preparation is relatively sparse, despite the different challenges charter schools leaders face. To address these challenges, we examine the social justice issues that prompted the rise of charter schools 15 years ago, and the equity and access concerns that have risen within the charter school movement. We consider the challenges charter school leaders face in delivering socially just education in this no-traditional venue. Finally, we consider the potential of professional leadership programs to prepare charter school principals toward a commitment to the social justice goals of public education, including access and equity in educational opportunity for all students.

CHARTER SCHOOLS AND SOCIAL JUSTICE

We use the term "social justice" to mean equity in opportunity and access for all people. In education, social justice is often thought of as a way to ensure all students are treated fairly and have equitable opportunities for learning. One aspect of social justice is the ability of individuals to participate in decisions that affect them. In this way, social justice and notions of democracy go hand-in-hand. Brighouse (2000) and Gutmann (1987) make this connection when they consider that part of a socially just education is education that helps young people learn to think for themselves so that they can effectively participate in democratic society as adults. Charter schools came about as a way to provide greater equity to all students through access to free public schools of choice (Buckley & Schneider, 2007; Chubb & Moe, 1990; Vergari, 2007). Choice is a given for parents who have the resources to either relocate students into public school districts that best fit their expectations or pay to send their children to private schools, but students from poorer families who cannot afford to move or enroll in private schools are "stuck" with the schools to which they are assigned. Charter schools also were designed to be free of political and district control so that charter school educators could be more responsive to the direct needs of students and parents.

Brighouse (2000) examines the equity and access goals of charter schools through his investigation of the liberal aims of school choice policy. Proponents argue that by opening up choice to all students, charter schools aim to create equity in opportunity and increase access of all students to educational opportunities of their choosing. Whether charter schools can fulfill those goals depends on what Brighouse calls "education for social justice." It is not a given, he argues, that either choice or no-choice education systems will promote social justice. What is necessary, instead, is a conscious attention to the following: (a) opportunities for children to develop into autonomous adults through what he calls "autonomy-facilitating education" an, (b) equality of opportunity that allows all students access to education, even if that means more resources are provided to students whose circumstances require more support.

Gutmann's (1987) criteria of non-repression and non-discrimination certainly align with Brighouse's ideas of autonomy and equality of opportunity. Students are not likely to reach autonomous choices if they are repressed by cultures, norms, or rules that keep them from critically examining their world. Likewise, schools cannot provide equality of opportunity if they operate in ways that discriminate against students. We see democratic participation, or the ability of individuals to participate in decisions that affect them, as a means to the individual autonomy Brighouse advocates.

Finally, we want to point out that the goals for public education in America, as discussed by the Center of Education Policy (Kober, 2007) and the Interstate School Leadership Licensure Consortium Standards (Van Meter & Murphy, 1997), reflect similar conceptions of social justice in education. For example, Kober (2007) identifies six common goals of public education in America. They are:

1. To provide universal access to free education.
2. To guarantee equal opportunities for all children.
3. To unify a diverse population.
4. To prepare people for citizenship in a democratic society.
5. To prepare people to become economically self-sufficient.
6. To improve social conditions. (p. 7)

Goals 3 and 5 fit within notions of autonomous-thinking by bringing diverse people together and providing individuals with the skills and talents they need to make autonomous choices, and goals 1, 2, and 6 align with ideas of equity in access. Goal 4 reflects Gutmann's ideas of education for democratic participation, but it also aligns with ideas of autonomous thinking and equality of opportunity as democratic participation requires critical thought and engagement for the purpose of providing equality of opportunities.

These broad goals for public education are also addressed in the standards set forth by the Council of the Chief State School Officers (Van Meter & Murphy, 1997). The five Interstate School Leadership Licensure Consortium (ISLLC) Standards speak to the mission of public education (Figure 13.1). Each of the key standards has a set of goals that further explicates the mission and values of public education as defined by the Council of Chief School Officers. These include goals that reflect the public nature of schooling, the values of equality in access, no-discrimination, no-repression, and the development of free thought. Diversity is a major theme of all six ISLLC Standards, including diversity of students and administrators' engagement with a diverse community (Van Meter & Murphy, 1997).

Standard 1: A school administrator is an educational leader who promotes the success of all students by facilitating the development, articulation, implementation, and stewardship of a vision of learning that is shared and supported by the school community.

Standard 2: A school administrator is an educational leader who promotes the success of all students by advocating, nurturing, and sustaining a school culture and instructional program conducive to student learning and staff professional growth.

Standard 3: A school administrator is an educational leader who promotes the success of all students by ensuring management of the organization, operations, and resources for a safe, efficient, and effective learning environment.

Standard 4: A school administrator is an educational leader who promotes the success of all students by collaborating with families and community members, responding to diverse community interests and needs, and mobilizing community resources.

Standard 5: A school administrator is an educational leader who promotes the success of all students by acting with integrity, fairness, and in an ethical manner.

Standard 6: A school administrator is an educational leader who promotes the success of all students by understanding, responding to, and influencing the larger political, social, economic, legal, and cultural context.

Figure 13.1. ISLLC Standards

It is with these criteria in mind, then, that we examine what we know of charter schools and how we might move forward preparing charter school principals to fulfill the promise of charter schools as avenues of equitable choice and autonomous thought.

Equity in Access

One of the rationales for charter schools was to create greater equity in opportunity for students who could not otherwise "choose" their schools (Abernathy, 2005; Buckley & Schneider, 2007; Chubb & Moe, 1990; Nathan, 1996; Vergari, 2007). By providing all students choice in schooling, charter schools have the potential to increase the equity of educational access. Arguments in early charter school research warned against charter schools "skimming" top students from district schools or "cherry picking" the students who enroll. Buckley and Schneider (2007) found no real evidence for these claims. However, researchers have identified instances in which students who "do not fit" a school's mission or cannot be well served by a school's limited resources are turned away (Allen, 2006; Arsen, Plank, & Sykes, 1999; Bulkley & Fisler, 2002; Fuller, Gawlik, Gonzales, & Park, 2003; Little, Roberts, Ward, Bianchi, & Metheny, 2003).

Although the majority of states' charter school statutes appear adequate in ensuring underrepresented groups have access to charter schools (Ashbrooks, 2001), the question remains whether charter schools abide by their state's statutes. For example, a study of charter schools in California found that 30% of the schools reported that being unable to meet special needs could justify not admitting that student (Bulkley & Fisler, 2002). Arsen, Plank, and Sykes (1999) found that several Michigan charter schools had application procedures, forms, and interviews that could potentially discourage submissions from students who "might disrupt the school community" (p. 75). A study in New York reported similar findings (Little, Roberts, Ward, Bianchi, & Metheny, 2003). Fuller et al. (2003) examined survey data collected from 1,010 charter school principals nationwide during the 1999–2000 school year. The findings disclose that the vast majority of charter schools failed to identify students with disabilities or proved to be uninviting places for them.

Charter schools, like all public schools, must comply with federal laws and regulations concerning special needs students. These laws include Section 504 of the Rehabilitation Act, the American Disabilities Act, and the Individuals with Disabilities Education Act (IDEA). While charter schools generally may be aware of their responsibility to provide special education services, they are not adequately prepared to do so. McKinney (1996) found that charter school administrators had little understanding of special education requirements and procedures. Medler and Nathan (1995) reported that charter school educators in seven states said that they felt unprepared to accept the challenges of students with disabilities. Many charter schools opened their doors without a plan in place for educating these children (Lange, 1997). Some school staff members reported that in starting a new charter school, they focused on special education only after other programs were in place or after the enrollment of children with disabilities. Hence, some charter schools do not develop special education programs until the second or third year of operation (Ahearn, Lange, Rhim, & McLaughlin, 2001). In a case study examining a set of charter schools in Michigan, Allen (2006) describes a charter school board meeting in which the school leadership of a 4-year-old school struggled to come to terms with the school's lack of accessibility for disabled students. "As a result of the board decisions, the student was forced to leave her school and attend one that was handicapped accessible. In this case, the policy of autonomous governance trumped the public goal of equitable access" (p. 111).

The opportunity of charter school policy is that schools can be created in a way that better meets the needs of special needs students. Certainly, some charter schools focus exclusively on students with disabilities, like that of St. Coletta Special Education Public Charter School in Washington, D.C. Yet, as a statement on the school's website notes, there are only a handful of special education charter schools in the nation that "serve students with cognitive disabilities, autism, and secondary disabilities" (Schemo, 2005). For other charter schools, meeting special needs is a challenge that requires resources many schools do not have.

While charter school policy offers the opportunity to develop schools that break down the bureaucratic barriers for all students, or develop schools that meet the special needs of students, the literature on charter schools reflects a different reality: charter schools struggle to meet the needs of special needs students. Rhim, Ahearn, and Lange (2007) examined the issue of charter schools and special education and found several factors that may impede charter schools from meeting special education requirements, including a lack of a specified plan for meeting special education requirements, lack of funding for special education resources, lack of understanding by charter school operators and authorizers as to what is required, and a lack of accountability on the part of authorizers and states for ensuring that charter schools are meeting federal special education requirements. In an earlier report, Rhim and McLaughlin (2001) studied charter schools in 15 states and found those charter schools that partner with school districts for special education resources fare better at meeting the needs of special education students than charter schools that operate completely independent of districts. The researchers also note that one of the biggest struggles charter schools may have in meeting the requirements of special education is the disconnect between the vision of charter schools as autonomous schools and the highly regulated federal requirements for serving special needs students.

Student Achievement

Central to the charter school theory of action is the idea that through various organizational and policy mechanisms, charter schools will lead to increased student achievement. As a measure of quality, student achievement research helps us examine whether charter schools increase options for quality education, providing what Brighouse (2000) calls access to educational options that are at least of equal quality to existing options. The theories that underlie charter schools suggest a market approach to schooling will prompt all schools to improve (i.e., raise student achievement) so they can compete in the marketplace of education (Buckley & Schneider, 2007; Chubb & Moe, 1990). If this is true, then not only do charter schools provide additional options for quality education for students, but they improve the educational options that already exist.

One pressing research question to date, then, is whether charter educators can increase achievement of weaker students, especially given their early success in providing access to low-income families. A synthesis of charter school achievement studies indicates that the charter school impact on achievement is mixed (Miron & Nelson, 2002). Most states that have sponsored formal evaluations of their charter schools document wide variation in school operations and student outcomes (Rhim, Lange, & Ahearn, 2005). Past studies have found that students attending charter schools do not consistently outperform those enrolled in regular public schools, at least on standard achievement measures.

In Michigan, Horn and Miron (1998) assessed test scores, comparing students enrolled in charter and regular public schools. They found that charter students displayed weaker learning gains than students attending conventional schools. Eberts and Hollenbeck (2002) found that charter school students in Michigan scored 2–3% lower than comparable noncharter public schools. No achievement advantage has been detected in average schoolwide scores among charter students in California, compared to regular schools, after taking into account social class, language, and other student characteristics (Brown, 2003).

In Arizona, researchers tracked student-level scores over a 3-year period, and charter students demonstrated slightly higher reading gains across the grade levels on SAT scores, while a mixed to positive impact could be detected in math performance (Solomon, Paark, & Garcia, 2001). Encouraging findings have emerged in Texas, where low-income and "at-risk" students attending charter schools outperformed similar students in regular public schools on the Texas Assessment of Academic Skills (Shapley, Bennr, & Pieper, 2002). Yet for other students, charter attendees did less well than those in regular schools. This research team also found that newly opened charter schools were not as effective in raising achievement as were older ones.

More recent studies also point to achievement gains of students in charter schools (Abdulkadiroglu, Angrist, Synarski, Kane, & Pathak, 2009; Betts & Tang, 2008; Center for Research on Education Outcomes [CREDO], 2010; Hoxby, Murarka, & Kang, 2009). Two of the studies of student achievement in New York City's schools (Hoxby et al., 2009; CREDO, 2010) show achievement gains for students in the city's charter schools. The CREDO (2010) study found that the achievement gains for charter school fourth-grade students are 2 points in reading and 5 points in mathematics. The study also found that 51% of the city's charter schools show academic gains in mathematics, and 30% of the city's charter schools perform better than their traditional school counterparts. Hoxby et al. (2009) found similar effects after studying student achievement of charter school students in K–8 charter schools in New York City. Although the researchers found variability in achievement across schools, their conclusion states, "The vast majority of charter schools for which individual school estimates can be computed with reasonable precision are having a positive effect on students' math and English achievement in the third through eight grades" (p. IV-23). Hoxby et al. cite the following characteristics as possible contributors to the success of New York City charters: a school mission focused on academic achievement, a longer school year, and nontraditional teacher pay.

The success of New York City charter schools cannot be generalized across charter schools nationally. The same group of researchers that examined New York's charter schools (CREDO, 2010) published a study of charter schools in 16 states and found a much different picture, reporting that only 17% of charter schools in the study provided "superior" education, nearly half of the schools performed similarly, and a third of the charter schools in the study performed worse than traditional district schools (CREDO, 2009).

Abdulkadiroglu et al.'s (2009) study of charter school effects in Boston found positive effects of charter school attendance on student achievement for students in middle and high school. In addition to conducting a quasi-experimental lottery analysis on their sample of charter schools and Boston pilot schools, the researchers also conducted an observational analysis of all charter and pilot schools in the city. As a result of the observational analysis, the researchers conclude that the charter schools in their sample are better than other charter schools in yielding large effects. Therefore, they suggest that the positive effects of charter school enrollment on student achievement in their study may be related to the type or model of charter school rather than charter schools overall.

The findings of charter schools with respect to achievement gains remain mixed (Carnoy, Jacobson, Mishel, & Rothstein, 2000; Lake & Hill, 2006; Loveless & Field, 2009). In their review of charter school studies of achievement, Loveless and Field (2009) find that although the quality and methods of the evaluations of charter schools on achievement vary, "none of the studies detects huge effects—either positive or negative" (p. 11). The authors conclude that the important finding in the evaluation of charter schools on achievement to date is not whether the effects are positive or negative, but that the effects are not likely to be large. Given the mixed results of achievement data, what might be said about charter schools as an avenue for equality in opportunity is that the potential for opportunity exists, but more must be done within the schools to ensure that students are getting access to quality education options.

Innovation

Another argument for equity in education might be in the innovation promise of charter schools. If students are not doing well in a district school that does not meet their learning needs, innovative charter schools may provide greater opportunity for students to access education that is a better fit for them. An original intent of the charter school movement was to promote innovation, particularly in the curriculum. Because of the flexibility in charter school policy, charter schools can be designed to meet specific interests. In addition to the market-oriented charter schools that offer choices to students and parents who are looking for options to district schools, charter school policy has been used to develop schools that meet specific needs of neighborhoods and ethnic groups (Lubienski, 2003, 2004). Lubienski (2003) also notes charter schools developed in part as a way to promote innovation in teaching, including child-centered practices such as Reggio Emilia, Montessori, and Waldorf programs. Although these practices are important and the flexibility of the charter school policy may allow for greater ease of experimenting with various curricula, Lubienski argues that use of these programs in charter schools does not constitute innovation unless the programs have been altered through the charter school implementation. In other words, many of these same practices can be found in traditional school districts throughout the last century; they are not unique to charter schools. Yet, as Loveless and Field (2009) note, "These practices are hardly revolutionary, but they do show a willingness to try educational approaches that are not currently dominant in public schools" (p. 109).

Despite the fact that charter school policy allows for innovation in how schools are designed, researchers to date have found little differences in the structure and design of schooling between traditional district schools and charter schools. Henig, Holyoke, Brown, and Lacirena-Paquet (2005) tested their hypothesis that mission-oriented charter schools are more likely to be innovative than market-oriented charter schools. After studying survey results from charter school principals in three states—Arizona, Michigan, and Pennsylvania—and the District of Columbia, the researchers found little difference in innovation among charter schools with different orientations. The authors concluded that the pressures of the market create a convergence among schools that prevents innovation from taking hold.

SOCIAL COHESION AND CHARTER SCHOOLS

Brighouse (2000) argues from a liberal perspective that education must be for the individual child, but that in order to create opportunities that help that child develop autonomous thinking, the child needs to be introduced to ways of thinking beyond what the family proposes. Other scholars make a similar statement arguing for social cohesion, that children from different walks of life come together and learn to be in community with one another (Gutmann, 1987; Levin & Belfield, 2003; Riehl, 2000). Gutmann (1987) maintains that social cohesion is a vital component of democratic education, to teach "responsibilities and rights within a larger and more diverse community" than the community children are exposed to at home (p. 54).

Several recent studies indicate charter schooling may lead to segregation of students by race and socioeconomic status (Institute on Race and Poverty, 2008; Mickelson, Bottia, & Southworth, 2008; Wells, 2009). Studies by Bifulco and Ladd (2006) also point out that charter schools are more segregated than public school districts. The varied missions and orientations of charter schools suggest that while some charter schools may aim to bring a diverse group of students and parents together, the potential for charter schools to segregate students into like-minded communities is a threat to the social justice criteria of both equity in access and autonomous thinking.

Access to Information

A market approach to public education requires that sufficient and objective information is accessible to parents and other stakeholders so informed decisions can be made as to school enrollment or support of school policies. Equality in access depends on parents and students being aware of the choices they have. Research on charter schools and information is limited, but studies that have been done indicate that information about charter schools to parents and other stakeholders is insufficient, creating opportunities for schools to target students, rather than creating opportunities for parents to find choice schools and confusion among taxpayers as to what charter schools are and how they operate (Buckley & Schneider, 2007; Rose & Gallup, 2006).

Abernathy (2005) makes a similar observation about the school choice movement as a whole:

> School choice has the potential to make education in the United States better or the potential to provide another strain on an already strained system. The question is how we go about it. We may be talking about bureaucratic reinvention and democratic reinvigoration, or we may be talking about hastened obsolescence and increasing inequality. Neither outcome is predetermined. (p. 116)

A QUESTION OF LEADERSHIP IN CHARTER AND TRADITIONAL DISTRICT SCHOOLS

Researchers continue to see charter schools as having the potential to provide choice to those students and families who traditionally have not had a choice in education. However, evidence suggests that simply creating new schools is not enough to yield the kind of education that fits the criteria of promoting autonomous thinking and creating equality of access, particularly when the policies that govern charter schools are vague and the autonomy built into charter school policies naturally provide variance that makes enforcement of policies difficult. We believe, however, that attending to the preparation of charter school leadership may help. As the charter school movement grows, some colleges and universities are creating offerings that incorporate the special needs of charter school leaders, while others are developing separate programs specifically and exclusively for public charter school principals.[1] With a new focus of school leadership beginning to unfold, we see a need to think through how leadership programs might address how charter school leaders can fulfill the promise of school choice while maintaining a focus on the core social justice values for public education that apply to all public school leadership positions. The following section looks at the literature on leadership particularly related to the issue of leadership in public schools and specific challenges that charter school leaders face.

LITERATURE ON EDUCATIONAL LEADERSHIP

Traditional school leadership programs approach leadership from a bureaucratic perspective. School principals operate within a system of support, including a central office that typically handles board and public relations, relations with unions, facilities management, human resources, and so on. Studies of educational leadership suggest that in the past principals were able to succeed, at least partially, by simply carrying out the directives of central administration (Perez, Milstein, Wood, & Jacquez, 1999). But management by principals is no longer enough to meet today's educational challenges; instead, principals must assume a greater leadership role. In fact, recent movements in the field have pushed for a greater focus on instructional leadership for school principals and less of a focus on school management (Brookover & Lezotte, 1979; Cotton, 2003; Edmonds, 1979; Goodlad, 1979, 1984; Marzanno, 2003; Sergiovanni, 1992, 1994). The complexity of balancing and integrating dimensions of effective leadership in such a way that practitioners can comprehend and apply them is shown by the long struggle to reconcile two major dimensions: management and instructional leadership. Within the past 25 years or so, principal training programs have changed quite significantly and as evidenced by the ISLLC Standards mentioned earlier, both aspects of school leadership are still represented.

The leader of a school is one of the most important individuals to influence common educational goals yet the pivotal question is, What do we mean by leadership? From a reform perspective, the greatest challenge for the educational administration field may very well be a shift in the mental model of what it means to be a school *leader* instead of a school *administrator* (Cambron-McCabe & McCarthy, 2005; Usdan, 2002). The current conception of leadership supplies an opportunity to reconsider what it means to lead a school where student learning, not the management of daily operations, is at the core of the work (Elmore, 2000). While instructional leadership has been infused into the traditional principal role, leading instruction and managing people is simply not enough. According to Senge (1990), radical action is required to maintain and expand capacity to create results where people are continually learning. The invention of new leadership roles around student learning requires these new challenges not to be met with old approaches and traditional roles (Boris-Schacter & Langer, 2002). Traditional principals have expressed that they are not being trained to deal with classroom realities and in-school politics, work with diverse populations, and prepare for increased testing and accountability (Levine, 2005).

Because charter school leaders are in charge of an independent school with an autonomous board, they not only serve as instructional leaders but also must manage much of the same responsibilities as a district superintendent. Campbell, Gross, and Lake (2008) note that charter school leaders face the same challenges as their district school counterparts, namely setting and maintaining a school's vision, establishing trust between adults and children, managing resources, and balancing pressures that exist both inside and outside the school. However, the job of the charter school principal goes beyond that of a district principal because there is no central office providing support.

Charter school principals are responsible for finding and maintaining school facilities, handling finances, raising money, hiring faculty members, and negotiating relations with boards, parents, and charter school authorizing agencies. They are also responsible for recruiting students, since charter schools operate as schools of choice. In a survey of charter school principals across six states, the National Charter School Research Project at the University of Wyoming, researchers found that facilities issues are one of the top concerns of charter school principals. Charter schools typically must find and fund their own buildings. Other top concerns include personnel and budget issues, particularly recruiting and paying for quality teachers, and finding time for strategic planning (Campbell & Gross, 2008; Campbell et al., 2008; Gross & Martens, 2007).

The core leadership functions for charter school leaders spans seven different functions, namely instructional, cultural, managerial, strategic, human resource, political development, and micropolitical (Portin, Schneider, DeArmond, & Gundlach, 2003). While charter school leaders tend to promote shared leadership around human resources, instruction, and strategy, the principal must be able to "keep a finger on the pulse" (p. 12) of each of the seven core leadership functions. This reconceptualization of roles involves rethinking school leadership development programs and developing new programs that are more relevant for the emerging leadership model of charter schools. However, if charter schools tend to focus more on the private aspects of public education as research suggests they tend to do (Lubienski, 2003; Miron, 2008; Miron & Nelson, 2002), what does a focus on charter school leadership portend for public education? How might we move forward with new approaches to educational leadership without losing the promise of an educated, deliberative, and cohesive citizenry?

CRAFTING POSSIBILITIES FOR CHARTER SCHOOL LEADERSHIP PROGRAMS

As programs emerge for charter school leaders, we suggest program curricula include courses on the core mission of public education, including the role of education to bring diverse individuals together, to create cohesion, and to prepare citizens to be deliberative, engaging, and can work and live in diverse societies. We also recommend that emerging leadership programs look at both management and leadership skills of educational leaders and define how those skills may be balanced in different types of schools. Specifically, we suggest:

- Emerging programs for charter school leaders offer core courses in the foundations of public education, including purposes of public schooling for democratic engagement in diverse communities.
- Leadership programs for both charter and district school leaders offer core courses in working with charter school boards to help board members understand their role in overseeing a public school. These courses should attend to the differences between public and private governance, including the responsibility of board members to provide citizens the opportunity for open access to information and opportunities to engage in discussions with school governors.
- All leadership programs should consider both the management and leadership functions of school leaders and be able to distinguish the right balance for the right context. In the case of charter school leadership programs, the curriculum needs to include management skills similar to superintendents and CEOs, while also providing students with skills in managing the multiple expectations charter school leaders must face.
- Courses in school–community relations should go beyond defining community as the students and parents within a given school, even if the school is a charter school. As a public school, charter schools are a part of the larger public school delivery system, and school leaders must understand how the independent school fits within that larger community. This includes both the responsibility public school leadership has to the local community and the responsibility community members have to the school. School–community perspectives can also offer prospective leaders insight as to how to partner with the community in a way that benefits student development of social justice values.
- Traditional school leadership programs should be expanding their offerings to include courses on the charter school principalship, highlighting both similarities and differences between leadership in traditional schools and leadership in charter schools. While we

acknowledge research on charter school leadership is sparse, we do know from the few studies there are (Campbell & Gross, 2008; Campbell et al., 2008; Gross & Martens, 2007) that charter school principals face unique challenges that stem from operating a public school independent of a district or central office as well as from market pressures. Courses on the principalship for charter schools might, for example, introduce students to the core tenets of social justice leadership in public education and how market pressures and increased job responsibilities challenge those tenets at times. Such a course might ask students to consider how charter school leaders can use the charter school policy to increase attention to social cohesion, better address the needs of special education students, use the flexibility of the policy to create innovation in charter schools that can be diffused to other schools, maintain a focus on open communication, and information that allows stakeholders opportunities to participate in decisions that affect them.

- The core values and standards of public education leadership need to be central to any school leadership program, with an eye on what makes school options "public." Therefore, all programs that prepare public school leaders should offer prospective leaders opportunities to explore the goals of public education, the dilemmas these goals pose such as equity in access and opportunity, and how school leaders might best address these issues.

This perspective also lends itself to a new approach for charter school research. Instead of focusing on charter schools and district schools as separate entities, we might look for the ways in which charter schools and district schools can work together to build a system of public school delivery that is cohesive and connected, while still offering options to parents and students. Possible research questions include:

- How might charter and district schools work together for the benefit of students in the community? What are the opportunities for shared services? What are the opportunities for specialized services? On a deeper level, what is it about these schools that might bring them together around meeting the needs of the local community?
- How much information does the community have about public school options, including district and charter schools? How can information be disseminated to all stakeholders so that stakeholders can make informed judgments about their public schools and the policies and people that govern them?
- What are the shared goals of public education between charter and district school leaders? What are the differences? How do these simi-

larities and differences fit within a broader vision of public education for social justice?

- What would a systems approach to choice look like for public education? How could a systems approach to choice create greater equality in educational opportunity and access?

CURRENT POLICY IMPORTANCE

The freedom charter school policy allows in the development and delivery of public education provides avenues for increasing options for parents and students, but if we are going to use the policy to increase social justice of schooling, we need to pay attention to the social justice aims of public schooling, including equity in access and opportunity, education that provides for independent thought, and nonrepressive, nondiscriminatory practices. As we move forward with both the study and practice of charter schooling, we see the potential of a relationship between charter and district schools that promotes the core principles of social justice.

Charter school leaders face unique and difficult challenges that must be tended to in our school leadership programs. Given the ongoing growth of the charter school movement, ignoring these needs is not an option. While we believe it is necessary to broaden our leadership programs to include the special needs of charter school leaders, we must do so from a systems perspective, maintaining a focus on providing all students with free education that is accessible, nondiscriminatory, nonrepressing, and promotes the development of autonomous thought.

NOTE

1. In our research we found programs specifically focused on developing charter school leaders beginning to emerge, including a program offered by Central Michigan University, and others that are offering strands of programming for the charter school leader, such as Marygrove College in Michigan.

REFERENCES

Abernathy, S. F. (2005). *School choice and the future of American democracy.* Ann ArboI: University of Michigan Press.

Abdulkadiroglu, A., Angrist, J., Synarski, S., Kane, T.J., & Pathak, P. (2009). *Accountability and flexibility in public schools: Evidence from Boston's charters and pilots* National Bureau of Economic Research, Working Paper No. 15549). Retrieved Januar. 13, 2010, fro: *http://www.nber.org/papers/w15549.*

Ahearn, E., Lange, C. M., Rhim, L. M., & McLaughlin, M. J. (2001). *Project SEARCH: A national study of special education in charter schools.* Final report of a research study. Alexandria, VA: National Association of State Directors of Special Education.

Allen, A. (2006). Changing ties: Charters redefine the school-community connection. *Journal of Public School Relations, 27*(1), 84-119.

Arsen, D., Plank, D., & Sykes, G. (1999). *School choice policies in Michigan: The rules matter.* (ERIC Document Reproduction Service No. ED439492.

Ashbrooks, C. Y. (2001). *How equal is access to charter schools?* Paper presented at the annual meeting of the American Educational Research Association, Seattle, WA. (ERIC Document Reproduction Service No. E 45 606)

Betts, J. R., & Tang, Y. E. (2008). *Value-added and experimental studies of the effect of charter schools on student achievement.* Seattle, WA: National Charter School Research Project, Center on Reinventing Public Education, University of Washington Bothell. Retrieved April 17, 2010, from *http://www.crpe.org/cs/crpe/download/csr_files/pub_ncsrp_bettstang_dec08.pdf.*

Bifulco, R., & Ladd, H. F. (2006). School choice, racial segregation, and test-score caps: Evidence from North Carolina charter school program. *Journal of Policy Analysis and Management, 26*(1), 3–56.

Boris-Schacter, S., & Langer, S. (2002). Caught between nostalgia and utopia. *Education Week, 21*(34), 3–37.

Brighouse, H. (2000). *School choice and social justice.* New York: Oxford University Press.

Brookover, W. B., & Lezotte, L. W. (1979). *Changes in school characteristics coincident with changes in student achievement.* East LansiMI: Michigan Stat University, College of Urban Development.

Brown, R. (2003). *Which California schools are improving?: A four-year analysis of performance growth.* Berkeley and Stanford: Policy Analysis for California Education.

Buckley, J., & Schneider, M. (2007). *Charter schools: Hope or hype?* Princeton, NJ: Princeton University Press.

Bulkley, K., & Fisler, J. (2002). *A review of the research on charter schools.* PhiladelphPA: Consortium on Policy Research in Education. Available at *http://www.cpre.org/images/stories/cpre_pdfs/WP-01.pdf.*

Cambron-McCabe, C., & McCarthy, M. (2005). Educating school leaders for social justice. *Educational Policy, 19*(1), 20–222.

Campbell, C., & Gross, B. (2008). *Working without a safety net: How charter school leaders can best survive on the high wire.* Seattle, WA: Center on Reinventing Education.

Campbell, C., Gross, B., & Lake, R. (2008). The high-wire job of charter school leadership. *Education Week, 28*(3): 5–58.

Carnoy, M., Jacobsen, R., Mishel, L., & Rothstein, R. (2000). *The charter school dust-up: Examining the evidence on enrollment and achievement.* New Yoty: Teachers College Press.

Chubb, J. E., & Moe, T. M. (1990). *Politics, markets, and America's schools.* Washington, DC: Brookings Institution.

Center for Research on Education Outcomes (CREDO). (2009). *Multiple choice: Charter school performance in 16 States.* Stanford, CA: Stanford University. Retrieved January 6, 2010, from *http://credo.stanford.edu/reports/MULTIPLE_CHOICE_CREDO.pdf.*

Center for Research on Education Outcomes (CREDO). (2010). *Charter school performance in New York City*. Stanford, CA: Stanford University. Retrieved January 6, 2010, from *http://credo.stanford.edu/reports/NYC%202009%20_CREDO.pdf.*

Cotton, K. (2003). *Principals and student achievement: What the research says.* Northwest Regional Educational Laboratory.

Eberts, R. W., & Holleneack, K. M. (2002). *State notes: Charter school teachers and finance.* Denver, CO: Authors.

Edmonds, R. (1979). Effective schools for the urban poor. *Educational Leadership, 37*(12), 1–24.

Elmore, R. F. (2000). *Building a new structure for school leadership.* Washington, DC: The Albert Shanker Institute.

Fuller, B., Gawlik, M., Gonzales, E. K., & Park, S. (2003). *Charter schools and inequity: National disparities in funding, teacher quality, and student support.* PACE Working Paper Series. Available online at *http://gse.berkeley.edu/research/pace/reports/WP.03_2.pdf.*

Goodlad, J. (1979). *What are schools for?* Bloomington, IN: Phi Delta Kappa International.

Goodlad, J. (1984). *A place called school: Prospects for the future.* McGraw-Hill: New York.

Gross, B., & Martens, K. (2007). *Leadership to date, leadership tomorrow: A review of data on charter school directors.* Seattle, WA: Center on Reinventing Public Education.

Gutmann, A. (1987). *Democratic education.* Princeton, NJ: Princeton University Press.

Henig, J. R., Holyoke, T. T., Brown, H., & Lacireno-Pacquet, N. (2005). The influence of founder type on charter school structures and operations. *American Journal of Education, 111*(4), 48–522.

Horn, J., & Miron, G. (1998). *Evaluation of Michigan public school academy initiative: Performance, accountability, and impact.* Kalamazoo: The Evaluation Center, Western Michigan University.

Hoxby, C., Murarka, S., & Kang, J. (2009). *The New York City charter schools evaluation project: How New York City's charter schools affect achievement.* Retrieved Januay. 13, 2010, frm: *www.nber.org/~schools/charterschoolseval/.*

Institute on Race and Poverty. (2008). *Failed promises: Assessing charter schools in the Twin Cities.* Minneapolis: University of Minnesota Law School.

Kober, N. (2007). *Why we still need public schools: Public education for the common good.* Washington, DC: Center on Educational Policy. Retrieved March 21, 2009, fro :*http://www.cepdc.org/index.cfm?fuseaction=Page.viewPage&pageId=490&parentID=481.*

Lake, R. J., & Hill, P. T. (2006). *Hopes, fears and reality: A balanced look at American charter schools in 2006.* Seattle, WA: National Charter School Research Project Center on Reinventing Public Education.

Lange, C. M. (1997). *Charter schools and special education: A handbook.* Alexandria, VA: National Association of State Directors of Special Education.

Levin, H. M., & Belfield, C. R. (2003). The marketplace in education. *Review of Research in Education, 27*(1), 18–219.

Levine, A. (2005). *Educating school leaders*. Washington, DC: The Educating Schools Project. Retrieved February 15, 2009, from *http://www.edschools.org/pdf/Final313.pdf*.

Little, D., Roberts, G., Ward, D., Bianchi, A. B., & Metheny, M. (2003). *Charter schools: Investment in innovation or funding folly?* LathNY: New York State School Boards Association. (ERIC Document Reproduction Service No. D 42 408)

Loveless, T., & Field, K. (2009). Perspectives on charter schools. In M. Berends, M. G. Springer, D. Ballou, & H. Walberg (Eds.), *Handbook of research on school choice* (pp. 9–114). New York: Routledge.

Lubienski, C. (2003). Instrumentalist perspectives on the"'publi'" in public education: Incentives and purposes. *Educational Policy, 17*(4), 47–502.

Lubienski, C. (2004). Charter school innovation in theory and practice: Autonomy, R & D, and curricular conformity. In K. Bulkley & P. Wohlstetter (Eds.), *Taking account of charter schools: What's happened and what's next?* (pp. 7–92). New York: Teachers' College Press.

Marzanno, R. (2003). *What works in schools: Translating research into action*. Alexandria, VA: Association for Supervision and Curriculum Development

McKinney, J. R. (1996). Charter schools: A new barrier for children with disabilities. *Educational Leadership, 54*(2), 2–25.

Medler, A., & Nathan, J. (1995). *Charter schools: What are they up to?* Denver, CO: Education Commission of the States.

Mickelson, R. A., Bottia, M., & Southworth, S. (2008). *School choice and segregation by race, class, and achievement*. TemAZ: Arizona State University Education Policy Research Unit. Retrieved Januay. 13, 2010, frm: *http://epsl.asu.edu/epru/documents/EPSL-0803-260-EPRU.pdf*.

Miron, G. (2008). The shifting notion of publicness in public education. In B. Cooper, J. Cibulka, & L. Fusarelli (Eds.). *Handbook of education politics and policy* (pp. 338–349). New York: Routledge.

Miron, G., & Nelson, C. (2002). *What's public about charter schools: Lessons learned about choice and accountability*. Thousand Oaks, CA: Corwin Press.

Nathan, J. (1996). *Charter schools: Creating hope and opportunity for American education*. San Francisco: Jossey-Bass.

Perez, A. L., Milstein, M. M., Wood, C. J., & Jacquez, D. (1999). *How to turn a school around: What principals can do*. Thousand Oaks, CA: Corwin Press.

Portin, B., Schneider, P., DeArmond, M., & Gundlach, L. (2003). *Making sense of leading schools*. Seattle, WA: Center of Reinventing Public Education.

Rhim, L. M., Ahearn, E., & Lange, C. (2007). Charter school statutes and special education: Policy answers or policy ambiguity? *The Journal of Special Education, 41*(1), 194–206.

Rhim, L. M., Lange, C. M., & Ahearn, E. (2005). *Congestion at the intersection of federal and state policy implementation: An analysis of special education in the charter school sector*. Paper presented at the annual meeting of the American Education Research Association, Montreal, Canada.

Riehl, C. J. (2000). The principal's role in creating inclusive schools for diverse students: A review of normative, empirical, and critical literature on the practice of educational administration. *Review of Educational Research, 70*(1), 55–81.

Rose, L.C., & Gallup, A. M. (2006). The 38th annual Phi Delta Kappan/Gallup poll of the public's attitudes toward the public schools. *Phi Delta Kappan, 88*(1), 41–56.

Schemo, D. (2005). A dream not denied: A building with a mission. *New York Times.* Retrieved April 17, 2010, from *http://www.nytimes.com/2006/11/05/education/edlife/autist.html.*

Senge, P. (1990). *The fifth discipline.* New York: Currency Doubleday.

Sergiovanni, T. (1992). *Moral leadership: Getting to the heart of school improvement.* San Francisco: Jossey-Bass.

Sergiovanni, T. (1994). *Building community in schools.* San Francisco: Jossey-Bass.

Shaplet, K. Sl, Bennr, A. D., & Pieper, A. M. (2002). *Texas open-enrollment charter schools: Fourth year evaluation.* Austin, TX: Texas Center for Education Research.

Solomon, L., Paark, K., & Garcia, D. (2001). *Does charter school attendance improve test scores?: The Arizona results (Arizona education analysis).* Phoenix, AZ: Center for Market-Based Education, Goldwater Institute.

Usdan, M. D. (2002). Reactions to articles commissioned by the National Commission for the Advancement of Educational Leadership Preparation. *Educational Administration Quarterly. 38*(2), 300–307.

Van Meter, E., & Murphy, J. (1997). *Using ISLLC standards to strengthen preparation programs in school administration.* Washington, DC: Council of Chief State School Officers.

Vergari, S. (2007). The politics of charter schools. *Educational Policy, 21*(1), 15–39.

Wells, A. S. (2009). The social context of charter schools. In M. Berends, M. G. Springer, D. Ballou, & H. Walberg (Eds.), *Handbook of research on school choice* (pp. 155–178). New York: Routledge.

PART III

MENTORING STRATEGIES FOR BUILDING INTELLECTUAL AND PROFESSIONAL CAPACITY

CHAPTER 14

SERVICE LEARNING PROVIDES UNIVERSITY STUDENTS WITH A VEHICLE TO ADDRESS

Inequities in Urban Education

Diane Schiller and Mary Charles

In this chapter, we demonstrate the efficacy of collegiate service learning in the development of intentional and sustained awareness of social justice. The literature review establishes that there is an abundant resource of college student volunteers; the second section of the literature review utilizes studies about time to support a theoretical perspective that underscores the value of the college tutor's work; and the third section of the literature review focuses on the long-term value of civic engagement for the college student. The chapter describes two replicable projects: one in an elementary school and another in a secondary school. The chapter concludes with suggestions and resources that have been used and developed.

Educational Leaders Encouraging the Intellectual and Professional Capacity of Others:
A Social Justice Agenda, pages 251–267.

SERVICE LEARNING LITERATURE REVIEW

Theoretical and Historical Framework

John Dewey's educational philosophy provides the theoretical base for service learning: learning from experience, reflective activity, citizenship, community, and democracy (Cummings, 2000; Giles & Eyler, 1994; Varlotta, 1997; Hildreth, 2004). The civil rights movement, the formation of the Peace Corps, and VISTA invigorated activist education by providing real opportunities to make a difference in the world. The early pioneers of the service-learning movement emerged, combining "service" and "learning." During the 1980s campus service accelerated. Initiatives to promote community service among undergraduate students became a national effort: the National Youth Leadership Council (1982), the Campus Outreach Opportunity League (1984), the National Association of Service and Conservation Corps (1985), Youth Service America (1985), and Campus Compact (1985). Both the Office of National Service and the Points of Light Foundation were created in 1990. These efforts led to the National and Community Service Act of 1990, legislation that authorized grants for schools to support service learning and demonstration grants for national service programs to youth corps, nonprofits, and colleges and universities. The legislation created Serve America with a goal to "distribute grants in support of service-learning in order to simultaneously enrich the education of young people, demonstrate the value of youth as assets to their communities, and stimulate service-learning as a strategy to meet unmet community needs." The new millennium renewed attention to the civic mission of fully engaged universities, a vision of a partnership of scholars, students, and citizens who have the support and resources to transform education and communities (Stanton, Giles, & Cruz, 1999; Stanton & Wagner, 2006). Information from the 2007 Campus Compact survey (available at www.compact.org/about/statistics/) indicates that the most common issues addressed by student service and service-learning work are poverty, reading/writing, housing/homelessness, hunger, the environment, health care, multicultural understanding, and senior services.

Research Support for the Benefits of Service Learning

Service learning positively affects participants as to social development, academic achievement, civic awareness, and career exploration. High-quality programs maximize student outcomes (Billig, 2000). In a longitudinal study of over 22,000 undergraduates in a national sample comparing experience of community service (46%), service learning (30%), and no service (24%), service had a positive effect on academics, values, self-efficacy, leadership, career plans, and plans to participate in community service after graduating from college. More than 80% of the service learning participants felt that their service made a difference and that they were contributing to a better world (Eyler, Giles, Stenson, & Gray, 2001). Participation in service learning during college is associated with increased civic leadership, charitable giving, and political engagement after graduation. These same results were found in a later study funded by the Corporation for National and Community Service, Learn and Serve America subgrant through the National Service-Learning Clearinghouse.

Impact on Communities

One-fourth of all students are at Campus Compact member colleges and universities and approximately one-quarter of all U.S. higher education institutions belong to Campus Compact. In 2007 students contributed more than $7 billion in service.

Value of Tutoring

The pool of college students available as tutors and mentors is expansive. University students as tutors provide an inexpensive way for a school district to increase the number of academic instructional hours for students. In 1994, the National Education Commission on Time and Learning advocated an extended school day and year to ensure that American students had an opportunity to meet world-class standards. There is increased pressure to provide more instructional time to improve K–12 student achievement. Multiple studies have confirmed John Carroll's (1963) mathematical model of school learning: degree of learning = time spent learning/time needed to learn. In testing this simple equation, educational researchers have developed complex ways to understand the use of time in schools (Berliner, 1990; Fischer et al., 1980). Time variables include allocated time or the time available based on the school calendar and the length of the school day. In one metropolitan area, the difference in allocated time between two neighboring districts is 95 minutes per day for middle school students. The variable academic learning time tries to measure the time that students are working at rigorous tasks at an appropriate level of difficulty (Berliner, 1990; Fischer et al., 1980). English language learners (ELL) present a "time" challenge to many school districts. On the 2005 National Assessment of Educational Progress, 96% of ELL eighth graders scored below the basic level (Perie, Grigg, & Donahue, 2005). A third time variable considers student engagement.

According to Walberg's well-tested model of educational productivity, if there is no motivation, there is no learning (Walberg & Uguroglu, 1980). If all of these measures of time are maximized, students can be expected to learn (Aronson, Zimmerman, & Carlos, 2002). Policymakers will be disappointed if they do not consider all aspects of time (Rangel, 2007). Research has consistently shown that extended time has a powerful impact on student learning in schools serving low-performing students (Gandara, 2006; Smith, 2000). For many school districts, the cost of extending academic learning time might seem prohibitive. One cost-effective way to simultaneously provide for more allocated time, academic learning time, and engaged time is the use of college tutors, both in volunteer and paid positions. Escalating tuition costs have increased the number of undergraduate and graduate students eligible for the Federal Work-Study Program (FWS). There are approximately 3,400 participating post-secondary institutions. The federal work-study program provides employment either on campus or in a nonprofit off-campus community agency. Eligible undergraduates and graduates can earn $500–2,500 per academic year as federal work-study students.

SERVICE LEARNING IN ACTION

Compulsory public education is one of the anchors of American democracy. Public schools are mandated to accept all students without regard to their race, religion, social class, family income, special needs, or personal characteristics. While the law demands that all students are accepted equally, it does not guarantee that they are educated equally. The geographic expansiveness and open availability of the U.S. education system too often mitigate the enormous inequities rooted in many of America's schools. Insufficient attention is given to the disparities in teacher quality, the variance of rigor across the curriculum, the inconsistent number of instructional minutes, and the contrasting condition of school facilities that exist across the country. These noted discrepancies and many others contribute to the vast education gap that separates underrepresented students in densely populated urban areas from their peers in more affluent communities. The persistence of the education gap challenges education experts, raises nagging questions of social justice, and short-changes millions of our country's students annually.

While there are no easy answers or quick fixes for narrowing the education gap, there are hopeful practices that offer productive support for students currently trapped in the abyss of education inequity. Colleges and universities across America have underutilized resources in the undergraduate and graduate students who attend their institutions. College/university students have the time, energy, and intellectual curiosity to reach beyond their campuses into the community and grapple with issues of social justice. The untapped idealism of college students puts mind and muscle into the action and implementation of service learning. This unique combination of bright college students and students in underperforming urban schools often yields transformative results for both groups.

Service learning is a powerful response to social justice because of the tremendous benefits it offers both the server and the served. According to Kaye in *A Complete Guide to Service Learning* (2004), students engaged in service learning will:

- Apply academic, social, and personal skills to improve the community;
- Make decisions that have real, not hypothetical results;
- Grow individuals, gain respect for peers, and increase civic participation;
- Experience success no matter what their ability level;
- Gain a deeper understanding of themselves, their community, and society; and
- Develop as leaders who take initiative, solve problems, work as a team, and demonstrate their abilities while and through helping others.

Next, two different community-based student interventions that respond to inequity in the educational opportunities of urban youth are presented. The first example is a required clinical experience related to university coursework and the second intervention is a university-sponsored community-based student job opportunity. While only our first example is officially considered service learning, the other example demonstrates how the theoretical framework of service learning can guide meaningful community-based student employment opportunities.

Clinical Requirement for Elementary Education Majors: Experiencing Service Learning

Students who hope to be admitted to a specific elementary education teacher preparation program enroll as freshmen in Mathematics for Elementary Education I, a course that incorporates a service-learning component. During the first half of the semester, college freshmen experience service learning as they teach math to fourth and fifth graders. All of these clinical activities take place weekly during regular school hours over the course of 7 weeks at a very diverse Chicago public elementary school located near the university campus. The freshmen work with a group of three students in a supervised environment and receive timely feedback on their performance.

In addition to regular classroom instruction, the undergraduates receive training on math pedagogy by reviewing instructional math videos on a free website supported by the university. The website hosts over 800 short movies featuring expert teachers working on specific math concepts. As part of their assignments, the undergraduates are emailed links to specific movies so they can prepare a teaching script for the instructor's review prior to each class. Each week's lesson focuses on a different math concept and consists of approximately three 15-minute segments, including an extended response math problem that children must not only solve but also explain in writing how they arrived at their answer; a second activity that presents the specific math content such as fractions; and a third segment that includes a math game designed to build computation skills and reinforce the concept. The following is a sample of one of these assignments.

Sample Assignment Emailed to Clinical Students

Below is an outline for the lesson you will teach. Please gather the materials you will need for the lesson and create a "script" for each part of the lesson, planning exactly what you will say to your students. The first script is done for you. Please note directions are highlighted in italics. You should come to the school with a two-pocket folder. The lesson plan (script) should be on the left side and the materials you will use should be on the right side. You should have your folder open as you teach.

Part I: Introduction: Algebra Name Tags

Materials needed: name tag model, crayons

Script (**directions in bold**; *questions in italics*)

Good morning, students. I am happy to be here today.

(**Show name tag.**) *What do you see?*

Can you guess my name?

I would like to learn your names and review fractions at the same time.

Please make a name tag using an equation to show the value of your name if vowels are worth ½ and consonants are worth ¼.

Tell me your name and we will check your equation.

Do you think you will remember my name next week?

Part II: Problem Solving

Materials needed: Completed companion website Challenge Sheet to use as model, which can be found on the website below movie.

Script: Create your Problem-Solving script as you watch the two videos linked below (**directions in bold**; *questions in italics*)

• Fraction Design: Solution Part 1
  http://countdown.luc.edu/NCTM_cat/ExtendedResponse/Number_Operations/050217/FractDesignSolutPt1/index.html

• Fraction Design: Solution Part 2
  http://countdown.luc.edu/NCTM_cat/ExtendedResponse/Number_Operations/050217/FractDesignSolutPt2/index.html

Part III: Game: *Fractions Nearest to One (computation practice)*

Materials needed: Completed companion website Challenge Sheet to use as model, which can be found on the website below movie. ALSO deck of cards, number line, Post-Its.

Script: Create your Fractions script as you watch the two videos linked below. (**directions in bold**; *questions in italics*)

- Fraction Card Game: Hand 1
  http://countdown.luc.edu/NCTM_cat/NumberOperation/Fractions/060126/FracCardGameHand1/index.html
- Fraction Card Game: Hand 2
  http://countdown.luc.edu/NCTM_cat/NumberOperation/Fractions/060126/FracCardGameHand2/index.html

The grade-level teachers at the schools guide the math concepts used for the clinical experiences to maximize the impact of the focused instruction delivered by the freshmen. Three different measures of math achievement gains paint a compelling case for improving the math achievement of underserved elementary school students with undergraduate tutoring.

First, we compare achievement on the state math test from 2008 and 2009 by grade level. Second, we compare achievement across similar schools in the state. The third achievement measure compares fourth- and fifth-grade students' achievement on a six-item fraction computation quiz that was administered by teacher education candidates before and after the undergraduate intervention.

The above data indicate that the service learning interventions were successful in all grades except fourth grade. Since the content was exactly the same for fourth and fifth grade, it may be that fraction computation lessons

TABLE 14.1. Comparison of the Percentage of Students Who Meet or Exceed Math Goals on State Test After Service Learning Intervention

Grade	2008	2009	Change	Undergraduate course	Size of group
3	72	90	+18	Philosophy elective	1–2 students
4	75	70	–5	Education requirement	3–5 students
5	78	85	+7	Education requirement	3–5 students
6	80	85	+5	Education requirement	3–5 students
7	64	81	+17	Education requirement3	–5 students
				Philosophy elective	1–2 students
8	83	80	–3	No intervention	

were too difficult for the fourth graders. It may also be the case that fraction computation was not tested for fourth graders on the state math test. We see in Table 14.3 that the fourth-grade students did make some gains on computation with fractions. Double-digit gains were made in third and seventh grades. Since the professional development for the undergraduates was similar and provided by the same math education specialist, we may tentatively conclude that the size of the group had an impact on achievement.

A second way to look at the impact of undergraduate tutoring is to compare achievement at Millenium School with similar schools. Using the state databases "compare schools" feature, we were able to find four other schools in the state which matched Millennium. The factors were type of school (elementary), district (unit), size (400–1,000 students), low income (> 70%) and demographics: 20–40% black; 20–40% Hispanic; 0–20% white, and instructional expenditure per pupil (>5,200). Two features that were not part of the available database comparison were % mobility and % LEP (limited English proficiency). Both of these rates are an important factor in comparing school achievement. In the comparison schools, mobility ranges from 11% to 33%. The mobility rate at Millennium School is 21%, the median of the comparison schools. The range for % LEP in the comparison schools is larger, 2–34%. At 34%, Millennium School has the highest rate. The comparison schools are arranged in Table 14.2 from highest to lowest LEP rate.

Students in grades 3, 6, and 7 outperformed all comparison schools. Grade 5 was only 2% lower than the highest-scoring School C. School C has a mobility rate of 11% and an LEP rate of 6%. Grade 4 with the service learning intervention and grade 8 with no intervention rank in the middle of the comparison schools.

TABLE 14.2. Comparison of the Percentage of Students Who Meet or Exceed Math Goals on 2009 State Test for Similar Schools by Grade Level

Grade	Millennium	Comparison School A	Comparison School B	Comparison School C	Comparison School D
3	**90**	46	55	74	(grades 4–6)
4	70	65	53	79	81
5	85	69	35	87	74
6	**85**	50	55	69	69
7	**81**	71	65	80	(grades 4–6)
8	81	74	49	89	(grades 4–6)

TABLE 14.3. Percentage of Fourth- and Fifth-Grade Student Change in Achievement from Pretest to Posttest on Fraction Computation

Grade	% Students who improved	% Students with no change	% Students who performed poorer	Mean gain	N
4	79	17	4	1.5	48
5	95	5	0	2.7	34

The third measure of achievement is the result of a pre/posttest given by the undergraduates to fourth and fifth graders. Prior to the first fraction lesson, undergraduates gave the students a six-item pretest of computation of fractions. On the last day of instruction, they gave the students the same test to assess progress.

From an analysis of a pre/posttest measure of fraction computation conducted by the undergraduates, in the fourth grade 38 students improved; eight showed no change and two children achieved less on the posttest than they did on the pretest. The mean gain was 1.5 points out of 6. In the fifth grade, 32 students gained; two students showed no change and no student scored lower on the posttest of fraction computation. Mean growth for the fifth graders was 2.7 points out of 6.

The impact of the experience on the undergraduates supports the tenets of service learning advanced by Kaye (2004). In reflections sent to the classroom teachers at the clinical site, the Loyola students detailed how they had become problem solvers and grown in self-awareness with a deeper awareness of the challenges of urban education. The following excerpts are samples from the teacher letters.

> These four students have probably taught me more than I have taught them. Here are some of the important things that I learned through this experience: concepts often need to be explained in more than one way, and often lessons need to be tweaked in order to accommodate the needs of all students. Also, students need to be able to make connections to other areas of math and to the world around them in order to truly master a concept. ... I think the most important thing the students learned was how to better explain their steps when solving a problem.
>
> Student A—University freshman

> Your students really helped me to see how guided questions can help students arrive at even the most difficult answers. I have also learned how much a teacher's enthusiasm affects the students' capacity to learn and I am ever thankful to you and your students for this opportunity.
>
> Student B—University freshman

I have learned so much from them and from the experience of teaching them math. One thing that I learned was how I have to sometimes explain an idea in more than one way….as they grow, I need to grow with them…when they understand how to do something better and it becomes second nature, I have to come up with new ideas to challenge them and make them think. It not only attempts to challenge them, but also challenges me to become a better and smarter teacher.

Student C—University freshman

Everything that I learned in your class is irreplaceable and I will always remember the three students I worked with. Each student had something special to offer to our time together and they were allowed to bring their ideas to the table. Many times I would let them know that they taught me something and they would be surprised, because they said that they were not the teachers. I could only laugh because sometimes I did feel like the student, and we had a give-and-take relationship.

Student D—University freshman

I came to this school hoping the students would learn something from me, but in teaching them, I too ended up learning so much. I learned that sometimes it takes thinking outside of the box to explain things. Each child is different and so each of their learning styles may differ as well. Therefore, I came to realize that the way I plan on teaching a subject may not work for all students, so I need to be ready to think of outside strategies.

Student E—University freshman

Clinical Requirement for Elementary Education Majors: Teaching Service Learning

The prospective teachers enrolled in Mathematics for Elementary Education I, the course that incorporates a service-learning component, complete the clinical experience during the second half of the semester by teaching service learning to middle school students. Like the math component, all of these clinical activities take place weekly during regular school hours over the course of 7 weeks at the same very diverse Chicago public elementary school located near Loyola's lakeside campus.

Drawing on their personal service-learning experiences from the previous weeks of student engagement with fourth and fifth graders, the undergraduates use a curriculum that marries math and theater.

A theater piece entitled "The Power of Two" provides the base for all student work because it has numerous possibilities beyond the binary implications of math. Strong messages of cooperation and the power of working together are woven throughout the curriculum. For these clinical experiences, four undergraduates work together as a team, modeling what they hope the middle school students will do. Each lesson includes a performance piece and a related math activity. Leadership for preparation of the teaching script rotates among the members as do responsibilities for other parts of the lesson including presentation and rehearsal. Each team works with half of the students in the classroom.

During the 2008–2009 school year, each undergraduate freshmen team taught the middle school students about service learning and then coached them in a math/theater activity that they in turn presented to younger students in the school. The focus each week was the performance piece and a related math activity. Each teaching script began with a theater game that was initially done as a generic activity and then done with specific math content incorporated. After learning the necessary math instruction and rehearsing the theater piece, the middle school students performed for the fourth or fifth graders. Following the performance the middle school students then helped the younger students with the related math activity.

A sample of the theater games used as a warm-up along with the math adaptation follows. In the generic version of *Agree/Disagree*, students move to the appropriate side of the room in response to a statement such as my favorite food is pizza; I watch TV for more than 2 hours daily; my favorite subject in school is math; I have a dog; I am a Cubs fan. In the math version, students respond to statements such as: three is a prime number; 27 is a multiple of four; a right angle is 180 degrees; another name for one half is five tenths; the probability of tossing an even number on a dice is one half.

The second math/theater experience connected math to a performance. For example, middle school students acted out the story of how *The Librarian of Basra* saved 33,000 books. After the performance, they helped the younger students calculate the volume of the books saved by the librarian. There were no pre/post assessments of this intervention. Instead, the undergraduates engaged the middle school students in reflective conversation about the experiences they had learning math content, rehearsing a theater piece, and performing for the younger students. The undergraduates shared some of the middle school students' reactions in letters sent to the classroom teachers. Again, the undergraduates' reflections are aligned with Kaye's (2004) observations about the impact of service learning. Excerpts of those letters follow.

> Each of the students that I worked with gave me a different perspective of how I might teach in the future. The kids helped me develop different teaching strategies and learn how to compromise what I had planned for the day. … I believe the seventh graders really benefited from the service learning because they began to understand what type of influence they could have on someone younger. … The thing I love most about teaching or even working with kids is that they teach you more than they will ever know.
>
> Student F—University freshman

This experience taught me just how important it is for a teacher to work on creating a classroom environment that promotes learning. In the beginning of the semester, we talked about service learning with our students and they showed a real desire to help the fifth-grade class we worked with.... I noted several students who were genuinely invested in teaching the fifth graders the concepts we had discussed earlier, even though it was a challenge for them to do so. They were eager to share their knowledge and enlighten their younger peer group, which was fantastic.

Student G—University freshman

It was a valuable learning experience to be in a school environment during the first year of college.

Student H—University freshman

When we described to them what we were going to be doing in order to perform service learning, many of the students stated that they did not like the fourth graders and they did not want to do it.... As the weeks went on, many of the students stated their excitement of going to help the students.... I have seen the progressive change in the students' opinion of service learning throughout the weeks we were at Swift...in our last discussion together when we asked what our students' favorite part of the class was, about six of the eight students stated their favorite part was the service learning and teaching the fourth graders.

Student I—University freshman

Another experience I bring away from your classroom is confidence. I have gained much more confidence in myself as a teacher, and that will carry on with me forever.... Throughout the service-learning classes that we taught, I noticed that students learned several things. Some learned how to cast away their shyness and speak up more to read, some learned how to work better with a big group, some learned basic skills of math, and some students even learned how to read and act out a play.

Student J—University freshman

I have learned a great deal from your students. They have taught me how to become more patient, since many of your students are still learning how to speak English.... I believe that the students' enthusiasm grew over time. They were able to ask us questions about Loyola and the classes we were taking. It was great to know that the students are already taking an interest in college.

Student K—University freshman

Academic Coaching: A Paid Position that Serves Targeted Urban Students

The economic realities of college life necessitate that many college students work while going to school. Academic coaching is a hybrid form of tutoring and mentoring that offers college students an employment opportunity that combines a regular paycheck with the rewarding effects of community service. As academic coaches, the college students travel to one of the city's underperforming high schools on Saturday mornings where they provide homework support and build "near-peer" relationships with at-risk students over the course of 3 hours. Transportation to and from the school site is provided by the university.

The requirements for academic coaching are stringent. Interested students must meet the following qualifications to be considered: full-time sophomore status or higher; cumulative 3.0 GPA; academic and work references; approved background check; submit a quality writing sample; pass algebra competency exam and make a full academic year commitment to training plus 22 Saturday mornings at a school site.

Diversity is integral during the hiring process so academic coaches reflect a blend of gender, ethnicity, and college majors. Once hired, academic coaches receive 7 hours of concentrated project orientation and professional development before the first study session at the school site. Team-building activities are introduced to promote familiarity and build camaraderie among the coaches. A literature review is incorporated to frame the general challenges of urban education and specific site information provides background on the school where they will work. The coaches, who are not necessarily education majors, are introduced to a wide variety of effective tutoring methods in different content areas with special attention devoted to supporting activities. In addition to the academic content covered during training, the coaches are also exposed to common milestones in adolescent development and transition activities targeted at high school freshmen. The academic coaches receive continued professional development throughout the school year. The entire group meets every 6 weeks for a general sharing session and presentations relative to the implementation support they have identified as significant during individual school gatherings. During the large group meetings, Loyola faculty with expertise in urban issues provides coaches with effective strategies to address gang influence, violence, and sociopolitical concerns of the high school freshmen. The supporting grant office hosts regular "resource hours" weekly when coaches can access supplies and use materials in preparation for Saturday study sessions. In total, coaches receive 18 hours of paid training over the course of one academic year.

Academic coaches work in teams of two at the school site and are paired according to their complementary college majors. For example, a female math major would likely be paired with a male history major. Because of their academic prowess, academic coaches are often diagnostic in their assessment of the high school students' content needs and responsively collaborate with the university support staff to identify supportive solutions. The ratio of academic coaches to high school freshmen is 1:4, allowing students to be grouped so a cohesive learning environment that fosters respect and responsibility evolves over the course of the 9-month project. Academic coaches deliver homework help for 3 hours on Saturday mornings in a climate of high expectations. Rather than following any scripted curriculum, academic coaches facilitate homework support and offer productive interventions like algebra basics and vocabulary development, which are tailored to meet students' needs and to challenge their competency. In addition to educational support, the academic coaches also provide "near-peer" guidance addressing issues like time management and goal setting as well as the social skills integral to high school success, such as self-awareness, team building, and decision making.

While the academic support of high school freshmen is the primary focus of academic coaching, a secondary benefit is the transformative experience the project affords the academic coaches. Academic coaches to communities and cultures that reach well beyond the boundaries of their college classrooms and campuses are exposed when working weekly on site in poor urban schools. The coaches experience a growing awareness of their abilities and how these talents can be harnessed to help others. The consistent interaction with students and administrators in urban school settings often yields a deep sense of commitment and initiative. The coaches' immersion in a service environment over a sustained amount of time conceivably lays the foundation for a future life path that is guided by social responsibility. This experience also introduces and reinforces the value of community-based employment.

During the 2008–2009 school year, 40 academic coaches worked with 204 students at High School "A" as part of the grant-funded dropout prevention initiative. The project focused its energies on at-risk freshmen and garnered impressive results. Together the group accomplished 1,246 homework assignments and tallied 4,401 hours of study time outside of school hours. The number of school days missed by students in the project was six while the schoolwide average was 26. TNT students performed better than their freshmen peers academically. Seventy-three percent of the project's students passed English as compared to 68% of their peers and 64% of the project's students passed math class compared to 57% of their peers.

Academic coaching is a model of a successful interactive project. High school freshmen receive consistently encouraging academic and social

TABLE 14.4. Comparison of Percentage of Project and Nonproject Students Passing English and Math—4th Quarter

N = 50	Project students	Nonproject students
English	77%	63%
Math	62%	50%

support that they need to succeed in high school and beyond. College-age academic coaches learn invaluable lessons about themselves and the world around them as they share their time and talents with deserving high school students.

Periodically throughout the school year, academic coaches are asked to think and write reflectively about the impact the work is having on them personally. The excerpts from reflections quoted below give evidence to the transformative power this experience has on college students. These reflections were shared during the project's pilot semester and first year of program implementation.

> University student L, Sophomore, wrote about coaching at High School "A":
> This has opened my eyes, warmed my heart, given me an extra push to follow my dreams.... I have lived in the community surrounding this high school all my life, but only attended a neighborhood school in preschool. From kindergarten to 12th grade I went to selective-enrollment schools in the city. These schools had enthusiastic teachers, a wealth of resources, and high standards. I know that my kids at this high school have had a very different experience in the urban public school system than I had.... I know that I want to work in an urban school to fight the inequality that I see. There is no good reason why these kids should have a different experience than I did in school. We live in the same city and are part of the same system. My kids at this high school have given me the motivation to teach. As a teacher I hope to empower my kids the way my teachers empowered me. I cannot wait to teach!

> University student M, freshman, wrote about coaching at High School "B":
> I think the biggest thing I've learned is just how lucky and fortunate I am.... Thinking about my high school in comparison to this school is shockingly eye opening.... The students who show up to our program on Saturday are trying so hard to obtain something that was so easy for me to obtain: an education. They want to do well in school. I'm grateful to be a tool for these capable students to achieve success.

> University student N, junior, wrote about coaching at High School "C":
> This semester I've learned a great many things. I've learned or, rather, remembered that in high school to be embarrassed in front of a group of peers is a nightmare.... I have learned that showing a student your weaknesses and telling them you struggle with some of the same things helps them to be okay with the fact that they are struggling, yet gives them the perseverance to keep going.... I have learned that some of these kids have experienced way more than I ever did when I was in high school and some more than I will in my lifetime.... This truly has been a wonderful experience.

> University student O, freshman, wrote about coaching at High School "D":
> Throughout my experience at this school, I have learned many things...I have seen firsthand the pressures of violence and gangs. Of course I knew of these things prior to my academic coaching experience, but I have now received

a closer look. Each Saturday our team recounts what we believe the problems to be with our students and their schoolwork: absence, feeling lost and confused, and sometimes pure laziness. It is *never* that we think our students are stupid or incapable. From this experience, I have been reminded of the necessity of individual attention for every student and therefore have come to see great value in my work.

University student P, junior, wrote about coaching at High School "E":
I have learned many things since I have been with my students at this school. First of all, I've learned that I have been given an extremely good life by my parents. I have learned that the students at this school are truly amazing... most of them just need a positive influence in life to help them get through school.... Four of my students came into a Saturday session not knowing how to do anything regarding addition, subtraction, multiplication, or dividing exponents. Within 2 hours, all four of them had been through numerous problems I made up. We went through this information very thoroughly because they had a test that next week. The following Saturday, they came back to me and told me that they had all passed their tests! I was thrilled.

CONCLUSION

The two scenarios presented in this chapter demonstrate how the enthusiastic naiveté of committed college students can be shaped into very productive results. Conscientious college students involved in interventions like these detailed here are in an ideal position to facilitate change in others because they are embroiled in an evolving developmental process of change themselves. As college students, they are experiencing a new sense of autonomy and establishing their own identity away from familiar surroundings, family, and friends. Their coursework and connections with faculty and classmates are challenging them to develop their intellectual capacity while simultaneously learning to manage interpersonal relationships. And myriad life choices associated with collegiate independence are stimulating character development and personal growth.

The untapped idealism of dedicated college students is a perfect antidote to the cycle of despair perpetuated by American's education gap... their hopefulness may contribute to the cure that makes the system fairer.

REFERENCES

Aronson, J., Zimmerman, J., & Carlos, L. (2002). *Making time count.* WestEd Policy Brief. San Francisco.
Berliner, D. (1990). What's all the fuss about instructional time? In M. Ben-Peretz & R. Bromme (Eds.), *The nature of time in schools: Theoretical concepts, practitioner perceptions* (pp. 3–35). New York: Teacher College Press.
Billig, S. (2000). The effects of service learning, *School Administrator, 57*(7), 14–18.

Campus Compact, (2007) *Annual membership survey final report.* Providence, RI:Campus Compact. Available at *http://www.compact.org/about/statistics/.*

Carroll, J. (1963). A model of school learning. *Teachers College Record, 64,* 723–733.

Cummings, K. C. (2000). John Dewey and the rebuilding of urban community: Engaging undergraduates as neighborhood organizers. *Michigan Journal of Community Service Learning, 7,* 97–108.

Eyler, J. S., Giles, D. E., Stenson, C. M., & Gray, C. J. (2001). *At a glance: What we know about the effects of service-learning on college students, faculty, institutions, and their communities, 1993–2000.* Funded by the Corporation for National and Community Service, Learn and Serve America subgrant through the National Service-Learning Clearinghouse. Available at *http://www.compact.org/resources/downloads/aag.pdf.*

Fischer, C. W., Berliner, D., Filby, N., Marlieve, R., Cohen, L., & Dishaw, M. (1980). Teaching behaviors, academic learning time and student achievement: An overview. In C. Dehman & A. Liberman (Eds.), *Time to learn* (pp. 7–22). Washington, DC: National Institute of Education.

Gandara, P., & Rumberger, R. W. (2006). *Resource needs for California English learners.* Stanford: University of California Research Institute.

Giles, D. E., & Eyler, J. (1994a). The impact of a college community service laboratory on students' personal, social, and cognitive outcomes. *Journal of Adolescence, 17*(4), 327–339.

Giles, D., & Eyer, J. (1994b, Fall). The theoretical roots of service-learning in John Dewey: Toward a theory of service-learning. *Michigan Journal of Community Service Learning,* pp. 77–85.

Hildreth, R. W. (2004). *John Dewey as a critical resource for the theory and practice of civic engagement.* Paper presented at the annual meeting of the Midwest Political Science Association, Chicago.

Perie, M., Grigg, W., & Donahue, P. (2005). *The nation's report card. Reading 2005* (NCES 2006-451). U.S. Department of Education, Institute of Education Sciences,

National Center for Education Statistics. Washington, DC: U.S. Government Printing Office.

Rangel, E. (Ed.). (2007). Time to learn. *Research Points: Essential Information for Educational Policy* [Special issue], *5*(2).

Stanton, T., Giles, D., & Cruz, N. (1999). *Service-learning: A movement's pioneers reflect on its origins, practice, and future.* San Francisco: Jossey-Bass.

Stanton, T. K., & Wagner, J. W., (2006). *Educating for democratic citizenship: Renewing the civic mission of graduate and professional education at research universities.* Stanford, CA: California Campus Compact.

Varlotta, L. E. (1997). Confronting consensus: Investigating the philosophies that have informed service learning communities. *Educational Theory, 47*(4), 453–476.

Walberg, H., & Uguroglu, M. (1980). Motivation and educational productivity: Theories, results and implications. In L. J. Fyans, Jr. (Ed), *Achievement motivation: Recent trends in theory and research* (pp. 114–136). New York: Plenum Press.

CHAPTER 15

MENTORING WOMEN AND MINORITY EDUCATIONAL LEADERS

The Need for Research

Gloria Crisp

The underrepresentation of women and minorities in leadership positions is one of many important social justice issues facing the PreK–12 educational system. According to a recent NCES report by Snyder, Dillow, and Hoffman (2009), disparity exists in the number of women and minorities holding school leadership positions. For instance, in 2003–2004, although 75% of teachers were women, only about 48% of women held a position as principal. Additionally, as of 2000, only 11% of principals were African American and 5% classified themselves as Hispanic (Kamler, 2009) and a mere 13% of school superintendents were female (Glass, Bjork, & Brunner, 2000). Moreover, findings by the American Association of School Administrators (AASA) revealed that it often takes African American women longer to obtain a position as superintendent when compared to nonminority women applicants (Brunner & Grogan, 2005).

Educational Leaders Encouraging the Intellectual and Professional Capacity of Others:
A Social Justice Agenda, pages 269–285.
Copyright © 2012 by Information Age Publishing

Although some argue that the underrepresentation of women and minorities in leadership can be attributed to a lack of interest in pursuing administrative positions (Sherman, 2005), there is mounting evidence that suggests that the lack of representation among women and minorities in educational leadership positions is, in part, due to a lack of access to mentoring relationships (Ehrich, 1995). For instance, we have evidence to suggest that mentoring is a primary way that men have been traditionally socialized and prepared for leadership positions (Scanlon, 1997). In addition, mentoring has been shown to effectively combat the residual effects of sexism and racism in the workplace (Bohlander, Snell, & Sherman, 2000).

Mentoring is generally accepted by both researchers and practitioners as an effective form of professional development that offers numerous benefits to both individuals and institutions, including opportunities for networking and personal reward or growth (e.g., Hansford & Ehrich, 2005). As such, mentoring programs/experiences are prevalent, and in some cases mandated by policy, throughout the educational system. In turn, although the literature is not well developed, we have an increasing body of empirical research on mentoring educational leaders. Despite the need to increase the representation of women and men in leadership positions, throughout the PreK–12 educational system, however, until recently very little attention has been given to how gender and race affect mentoring relationships/outcomes. Fortunately, some of the newer programmatic efforts are focused on promoting the development of women and/or minority leaders and recent studies have begun to consider the roles of gender and ethnicity in mentoring relationships.

However, the literature with regard to how race and ethnicity affect mentoring relationships/outcomes has not been critically synthesized and discussed. It is therefore thought that a synthesis of the empirical and theoretical work around mentoring might guide future research and/or the design and implementation of mentoring programs that promote the advancement of diversity in leadership. In turn, the following chapter provides a substantive, focused review of the literature regarding mentoring PreK–12 educational leaders and the link between mentoring and advancing the cause of social justice.

The chapter begins with a brief overview of mentoring programs and characteristics to provide context to the review. Relevant empirical work to date is synthesized and critiqued, with a focus on mentoring studies that contribute to our understanding of gender and ethnic inequities among educational leaders. Next, a review of relevant theoretical perspectives of mentoring from the business, psychology, and education literature is provided. The chapter concludes with a proposed research agenda in an effort to help frame future research around mentoring leaders and how research might advance efforts toward social justice.

MENTORING PROGRAMS/CHARACTERISTICS

As with many educational movements, mentoring efforts have been characterized by (1) rampant growth, (2) high levels of decentralization, and (3) little research to support practice (Johnson & Sullivan, 1995). Mentoring programs/relationships are prevalent throughout the educational system (Hall, 2008) and are considered a critical component of effective pre-service leadership programs across the United States (Daresh, 1995). In addition, professional standards for school leaders have mandated that numerous university-based preparation programs redesign their curriculum to include field-based experiences with mentoring opportunities (Browne-Ferrigno & Muth, 2004). Likewise, over the past decade, 32 states have enacted policies and laws that mandate formal support programs for school administrators who are in the earliest stages of their careers (Daresh, 2004).

The National Principals Mentoring Certification Program is a year-long program designed to train current principals to be master mentors (Hall, 2008). There are also numerous statewide or regional programs that provide mentoring for new principals such as the California School Leadership Academy, First-Time Campus Administrators Academy, and the Albuquerque Public Schools' Extra Support for Principals (Hall, 2008). Furthermore, as discussed by Barnett and O'Mahony (2008), mentoring programs for school leaders are becoming increasingly common in other countries, including the SAGE Mentoring Programme in Australia and the New Zealand First-Time Principals Programme. Additionally, the Diploma in Educational Administration (DEA) program in Singapore is one of the most established formal mentoring programs for aspiring principals (Hean, 2004), and Bush and Coleman (1995) report that formal mentoring programs for principals have existed in England since 1992.

Despite the prevalence of programmatic efforts, there is currently no clear definition of mentoring within the context of educational leaders or leadership students (Ehrich, 1995). Existing definitions of mentoring have been extremely broad or used synonymously with other related activities/processes such as coaching, counseling, or leadership development (Barnett & O'Mahony, 2008; Sherman, 2005). For example, Hubbard and Robinson (1998) broadly define a mentor as any individual who is trusted, is willing to guide, advise, and listen to the aspiring or beginning leader, and who helps them solve problems and create opportunities to advance in his or her career. In other cases, mentoring is defined as a process, as in the work of Browne-Ferrigno and Muth (2006) who define *leadership mentoring* as "the formal and informal social construction of professional performance expectations developed through purposeful interactions between aspiring and practicing principals in the context of authentic practice" (p. 276). Furthermore, a small number of researchers have begun to frame mentoring from a multicultural perspective, including Rodriguez (1995) who defines *multicultural mentoring* as "the mentoring of individuals from diverse cultural backgrounds, from traditionally underrepresented populations, and of many cognitive perspectives" (p. 70).

Although there continues to be disagreement within the literature about what mentoring is and what characteristics it entails, mentoring generally applies to the development of educational leaders through pre-service preparation and the process of professional induction (Daresh & Playko, 1990). Mentoring relationships can be informal or formal, short or long term, planned or spontaneous (Luna & Cullen, 1995; Sherman, 2005). Informal mentoring relationships are not structured, managed, or formally recognized by the school (Chao, Walz, & Gardner, 1992) and tend to naturally develop, involve the mentor and mentee seeking each other out, and are typically focused on long-term goals (Campbell & Campbell, 1997). In contrast, formal mentoring relationships have been shown to be managed and sanctioned by the school (Chao et al., 1992) and are typically included as part of a university- or school-based leadership program.

According to Kram (1983), mentoring relationships naturally progress through a series of four stages. The first stage, initiation, lasts between 6 months and 1 year and is seen as the time a relationship between the mentor and mentee begins. The next stage, which was found by Kram to last between 2 and 5 years, is termed the cultivation stage. This stage is defined as the time in which the range of mentoring functions expands. Separation, the third mentoring stage, is characterized by psychological or structural changes in the organizational context. This period disrupts the cultivation stage whereby the established relationship between mentor and mentee is altered and the mentee gains independence. The fourth and final stage of mentoring, redefinition, is characterized by the relationship evolving into a new, significantly different relationship, or in some cases the stage that the relationship ends.

STUDIES CENTERED ON MENTORING WOMEN AND/OR MINORITY EDUCATIONAL LEADERS

The following section provides an overview of narrative reviews focused on mentoring followed by a synthesis and review of empirical studies specific to the development of PreK–12 women and/or minority educational leaders.

Narrative Reviews Focused on Mentoring Educational Leaders

The mentoring literature contains a number of narrative reviews specific to mentoring educational leaders, including early reviews between 1984 and 1994 by Daresh (1995) who found that the majority of research on mentoring utilized descriptive surveys, quasi-experiments, and action research designs. The most comprehensive and critical review to date has been conducted by Ehrich, Hansford, and Tennent (2004). They reviewed over 300 studies from education, business, and medicine. Of the 159 education studies, the most frequently cited positive mentoring outcomes were encouragement, support, counseling, and friendship. The next most frequently reported benefit was help with classroom teaching, reflecting the large number of studies focused on mentoring teachers. Other commonly reported positive mentoring outcomes included sharing ideas or information and feedback or constructive criticism. Similarly, the most commonly reported mentor benefit was related to collaborating, sharing ideas, or networking, followed by reflection, professional development, and personal reward or growth. It should be noted that nearly half of mentoring studies identified negative or problematic outcomes, such as those associated with a lack of mentor expertise, a poor personality match between the mentor and administrator, or a lack of time the mentor devoted to the relationship.

Hansford and Ehrich (2005) also published a literature review and critique specific to mentoring programs for principals. Their review revealed at least one positive mentoring outcome for the participating principals in 31 of the 40 reviewed studies. Commonly reported types of support leading to positive outcomes included support, empathy, counseling, shared problem solving, opportunities for professional development, and opportunities to reflect and network. Negative outcomes previously identified by Ehrich et al. (2004), such as a lack of time for mentoring, were also identified. Similar findings were noted by Hobson and Sharp (2005) who reviewed mentoring articles specific to head teachers in England, Wales, Ireland, the United States, Canada, and Australia from 1982 to 2002.

Mentoring Women Leaders

Research specific to mentoring women and minority educational leaders is lacking in the literature. There is, however, some evidence to suggest that mentoring experiences are perceived as beneficial to women. This includes qualitative work by Morris (1993) that described women's perceptions of factors that helped or hindered their involvement in educational leadership. Interviews with seven women, four Afro-Trinidadians and three Indo-Trinidadians revealed that women who were successful in administration were likely to have been supported by mentors, especially in male-dominated schools. Similarly, research by Kamler (2009) indicated that support for women superintendents in Long Island was perceived as crucial to their ability to deal with the stressors of the position as well as their growth and development.

The value of mentoring women has also been supported by work by Young and McLeod (2001) who found that women who go into school leadership are different from women who do not in three areas: (1) exposure to role models, (2) exposure to transformative leadership styles, and (3) support received. In addition, there is research that suggests that mentoring might be more important for women than men. For instance, descriptive findings by Hubbard and Robinson (1998) indicated that females utilized mentoring to help them obtain their current position more often than males. Moreover, a literature review by Daresh (1995) suggests that women more often prefer women mentors, although research has not found same-gender relationships to be more effective in producing positive outcomes.

In terms of mentoring outcomes, there is little quantitative research that empirically demonstrates a significant relationship between mentoring women and leadership performance. However, Sherman (2005) interviewed 15 women who were in or aspired to be in a leadership program. Framed using critical theory, findings indicated that women who had not been mentored perceived themselves as less confident in terms of leadership ability and had more difficulty in seeing themselves as participants who belonged in the leadership program. Moreover, the participants indicated that participation in the leadership program may not be helpful unless it is paired with a mentoring relationship with an experienced leader.

Noe (1988) evaluated the impact of a comprehensive program designed to develop educators who aspired to school leadership positions through participation in simulation exercises and support from mentors who held upper-level administrative positions at one of nine districts across the country. Quantitative scales were used to assess several aspects of mentoring, including the quality of interaction and time spent with mentors and the functions of the mentoring relationship. A dummy variable was also used to capture whether the mentoring relationship was homogeneous in terms of gender. Results indicated that heterogeneous mentoring relationships were perceived as more effectively utilizing the mentor. Moreover, females indicated that they perceived receiving significantly more psychological benefits from mentoring when compared to males. Noe hypothesized that women may have been more motivated to use mentors because of a perceived lack of mentoring opportunities for women.

Mentoring Minority Leaders

While there is little empirical work specific to women leaders, there is even less research to date that has focused on mentoring aspiring or existing minority leaders. However, we have some evidence to suggest that district-based leadership (or mentoring) programs support the status quo rather than promote diversity and equity (e.g., Samier, 2000). In contrast, mentoring has been identified as a central theme related to the promotion of underrepresented groups in administrative positions in the United Kingdom (Burton, 1993).

Loder (2005) used a qualitative life course design to examine similarities and differences in how white and African American women school administrators negotiated their work and family conflicts. Findings indicated that participants used different life course strategies based on their race and generational locations. For example, African American administrators were found to rely more on other women to assist with child care and household support. In contrast, white women revealed that they primarily sought support from their spouses. Similarly, Mendez-Morse (2004) interviewed six Mexican American educational leaders in Texas. The mentoring discussion revealed two themes, including (1) mothers as the strongest role model and first mentor, and (2) participants constructing a mentoring experience from the talents of various individuals in a way that facilitated their professional growth and met their specific needs.

CONCEPTUALIZING MENTORING

With the exception of a few studies that have been framed using theory not specific to mentoring (e.g., Ehrich, 1995), the majority of published work on mentoring educational leaders has been atheoretical and focused on problem solving (Daresh, 1995). Although several conceptual pieces have been advanced (i.e., Mertz, 2004; Samier, 2000), no dominant model has emerged, as existing models do not fully explain how mentoring might apply or be experienced by educational leaders and/or are not well supported by empirical evidence (Bush & Coleman, 1995). Moreover, there is little, if any, theoretical work that explains how the mentoring experiences of women and minorities might be different from the experiences of white males. The following section reviews mentoring frameworks from the psychology, business, and education literature in order to frame future mentoring research specific to women and minority educational leaders.

Arguably, Roberts (2000) conducted the most comprehensive mentoring theory to date by using phenomenological reduction to conceptualize mentoring. Mentoring was defined by Roberts as "a formalized process whereby a more knowledgeable and experienced person actuates a supportive role of overseeing and encouraging reflection and learning within a less experienced and knowledgeable person, so as to facilitate that persons' career and personal development" (p. 162). Roberts developed his theory from a review of research articles in a variety of fields published between 1978 and 1999. The review revealed that a comprehensive mentoring experience involves several *essential* attributes, including the existence of an underlying helping, teaching–learning, reflecting, career development, formalized process; a supportive relationship; and a role constructed by or for a mentor. In addition, Roberts identified several *contingent* mentoring attributes including coaching, sponsoring, and role modeling.

Mentoring from a Psychological Perspective

The theoretical work of psychologists Levinson, Carrow, Klein, Levinson, and McKee (1978) has been used by researchers in numerous fields to understand how mentoring is perceived and experienced by individuals (including women and minorities). Levinson et al. proposed that mentors served several functions including teacher, sponsor, host or guide, exemplar to admire and emulate, and a counselor who gives moral support. Serving as a teacher, the mentor enhanced the protégé's intellectual development and skills. In situations where a mentor acted as a sponsor, he or she used their power and influence to facilitate the protégé's advancement or entry into employment. As host or guide, it was the mentor's role to assimilate the protégé into his or her social world. This process involved introducing the protégé to the customs, values, and resources available. Within the third function, serving as an exemplar to admire and emulate, the mentor modeled his or her virtues, achievements, and way of living. Finally, Levinson et al. proposed that a function of mentoring was providing moral support to protégés in times of stress.

In addition to the functions mentioned above, Levinson et al. (1978) proposed that the most important role of the mentor was to support and facilitate the realization of the protégé's dream. According to Levinson et al., it was the mentor's role to define the protégé's emerging self in their place of employment, creating a space for the protégé to work on a life structure that supported their dream. Within this function, it was also the mentor's role to foster the protégé's development by sharing in his dream. However, it should be noted that Levinson et al.'s work was limited to men and there has been little research conducted to validate their theory using more diverse samples including women and minority leaders.

Similarly, psychologists Schockett, Yoshimura, Beyard-Tyler, and Haring (1983) identified a mentoring framework containing eight mentoring functions, four psychosocial and four vocational. The four psychosocial functions included the mentor serving as a role model, encouraging the mentee, counseling and providing emotional support, and acting as a friend. The first psychosocial function, role-modeling, offered the protégé the opportunity to observe his or her mentor dealing with conflict, interacting with others, and balancing professional and personal demands. Encouraging, the next function, was shown through the mentor's confidence in the protégé's ability. Motivating the protégé by providing emotional support was shown to facilitate the growth of his or her self-confidence. The third mentoring function, counseling, involved the mentor allowing the protégé time to discuss his or her anxieties, fears, and uncertainties about professional as well as personal issues. Finally, the process of moving from a superior to a friend allowed the protégés time to see themselves as a peer or friend whose ideas and work were valued.

Schockett et al. (1983) posited four vocational functions of mentoring including educating, consulting, sponsoring and protecting. The education function was broadly defined as providing challenging work assignments, constructive criticism of work, evaluating potential for success, and enhancing intellectual development or technical skills for the protégé. The second vocational function, consulting, introduced the protégé to the politics and informal power dynamics of the organization or institution. More specifically, the consulting function introduced the protégé to the norms, values, and resources of the social environment. Providing "good press" for a protégé through nomination, discussing the protégé's accomplishments with others, and vouching for his or her ability made up the third vocational function, sponsoring. The final function, protection, involved shielding the protégé from potentially damaging situations or negative publicity, and taking the blame for the protégé when appropriate.

Schockett et al.'s (1983) model was tested 2 years later in a study involving 152 participants who were asked to rate on a scale of one to seven the desirability of mentoring activities described in four vignettes (Schockett & Haring-Hidore, 1985). Each vignette was approximately 50 words and incorporated quotes from the mentoring literature. Factor analysis verified the validity and reliability of the two-factor model.

Mentoring from a Business Perspective

Kram's work (1983, 1985, 1988) has provided the most detailed and systematic work on the mentoring process (Noe, 1988). Kram's (1983) original framework was developed from in-depth biographical interviews in the public business sector with 18 managers. Interviews were analyzed using content analysis, revealing two major mentoring functions, career and psychosocial. The career function included aspects that facilitate the enhancement of the protégé's career. In contrast, the psychosocial function promoted a sense of identity, competency, and effectiveness in the protégé.

In 1985, Kram and Isabella used a grounded theory approach to investigate the nature of peer relationships at different career stages (i.e., early, middle, late). Results indicated that peer relationships contained career-enhancing (information sharing, career strategizing, and job-related feedback) and psychosocial (confirmation, emotional support, personal feedback, and feedback) functions. Moreover, their findings revealed peer relationships often served many of the core functions of a mentor, and peer mentors were more available to students.

In 1988, Kram developed a theoretical framework from both her prior work and the limited number of investigations involving mentoring in business. Similar to her previous findings and the model provided by Schockett et al. (1983), Kram (1988) hypothesized that mentoring relationships are comprised of two major functions, career and psychosocial. More specifically, Kram proposed that five components make up the career function of mentoring including sponsorship, exposure and visibility, coaching, protection, and challenging work. Sponsorship was the most frequently observed function and primarily involved nominating the protégé for promotions and allowed for empowerment of the protégé through knowledge and opportunities for advancement. Similarly, exposure and visibility involved giving the protégé opportunities to work with higher-ranking or senior employees. Exposure and visibility also served a socialization function, preparing the protégé for more authority and responsibility through exposure to life at middle or senior management levels.

As the name implies, coaching involved the mentor offering strategies for how to complete work, achieve career goals, and receive recognition and praise. This function involved sharing ideas, providing the protégé with feedback, and providing inside information about key members of the company and the political process. More broadly, coaching offered the protégé the knowledge and understanding of how to function in the organization. Coaching was found to be mutually beneficial for the mentor as it confirmed the value of the mentor's experience, built respect from one's peers, and contributed to the next generation of managers (Kram, 1988). Taking credit and blame in tough or controversial situations and intervening when necessary were the major functions within the protection component of the career function. The final component, challenging work, provided the protégé with opportunities to develop the necessary knowledge and skills to succeed. The mentor in this case served as the teacher, providing technical knowledge and constructive feedback regarding the challenging work assignment.

Role modeling, acceptance and confirmation, counseling, and friendship were the major components that comprised Kram's (1988) psychosocial mentoring function. Role modeling was the most frequently observed psychosocial function. Role modeling offered the protégé with an image of who they might become, providing a model of values, behaviors, and attitudes to emulate. The second component, acceptance and confirmation, involved both the mentor and protégé developing an identity from the positive regard conveyed by the other person. "A relationship provided psychological nurturance through this function" (Kram, 1988, p. 35). Counseling was the third component within the psychosocial function, providing the protégé with a sense of self. Counseling involved enabling the protégé to resolve problems through feedback from the mentor about fears, anxieties, and other issues faced by the protégé. The final component, friendship, was demonstrated when social interaction turned into mutual understanding and liking for the other person. This component allowed the protégé to feel they were a peer of the mentor. Over time, friendship benefited the protégé by allowing him or her to interact more easily with middle or upper management (Kram, 1988). Research validating the existence of Kram's two mentoring functions has been substantiated within the context of industry (Chao et al., 1992; Ragins & Cotton, 1999).

Mentoring from an Academic Perspective

Developed from a review of the literature from business, psychology, and education, Anderson and Shannon (1988) proposed a theory of mentoring, thought to be specific to PreK–12 teachers. The researchers proposed that the process of mentoring teachers included five functions: teaching, sponsoring, encouraging, counseling, and befriending. The first function, teaching, involved basic behaviors guided by adult education principles including informing, modeling, confirming or disconfirming, questioning, and prescribing. Sponsoring, the second function, involved the mentor serving as "guarantor." Moreover, sponsoring included three essential mentor behaviors: (1) supporting teachers by participating in assigned activities, (2) protecting teachers from something in the environment, and (3) promoting teachers within the social and instructional systems of a school program.

The third mentoring function hypothesized by Anderson and Shannon (1988) was encouraging, defined by the mentor affirming, inspiring, and challenging teachers. Similarly, counseling was described as a problem-solving process involving the mentor probing, listening, advising, and clarifying. Finally, befriending, the last mentoring function, was identified by two critical behaviors: relating and accepting. Unfortunately, no attempt was made to test Anderson and Shannon's theoretical model and so it is uncertain whether the model accurately explains the mentoring experiences of teachers and/or educational leaders.

Attempts to conceptualize mentoring within the context of graduate students have also been made by Fiason (1996) and Edwards and Gordon (2006). Fiason examined mentoring roles that were perceived to contribute to the success of mentoring relationships between African American graduate students attending a predominantly white university. Guided by a constructivist paradigm, data revealed that graduate students perceived mentoring as being comprised of several roles including academic, facilitative, professional development, career, and personal support. Edwards and Gordon interviewed faculty, doctoral students, and alumni in an attempt to understand the characteristics of successful mentoring of online graduate students. Similar to Fiason's findings, Edwards and Gordon found that mentors and students both perceived online mentoring relationships to involve academic and social–emotional interactions. Beneficial personal attributes, relationship prerequisites, and communication were also found to have enhanced the mentoring relationships of doctoral students.

Few studies to date have attempted to develop and test a conceptual framework of mentoring for PreK–12 leaders beginning with Noe (1988) who, as previously mentioned, studied the determinants of formal mentoring relationships among educators aspiring toward leadership positions. A 32-item survey, based on Kram (1988) and others' work, was used to assess how aspiring leaders experienced mentoring. In line with Kram's findings, the results of an exploratory factor analysis revealed mentors provided two functions to the aspiring leaders, career and psychosocial.

Similarly, Cullen and Luna (1993) explored the mentoring functions provided by senior women who were higher education administrators. Twenty-four women were interviewed about their experiences with mentors, current mentoring activities, their career progression, and barriers or obstacles to mentoring leaders. Similar to Noe's (1988) quantitative findings, leaders reported receiving both career and psychological support functions from mentors. A prominent theme in the data was the career functions of coaching, sponsorship, and challenging work. Counseling and role modeling were two of the most frequently mentioned psychosocial mentoring activities.

PROPOSED RESEARCH AGENDA

Mentoring efforts designed to enhance the representation of women and minorities in PreK–12 educational leadership positions should be based on methodologically sound research that is grounded in theory. However, research with regard to mentoring women and minority educational leaders is largely underdeveloped and many questions remain to be answered. Moreover, a literature review by Daresh (1995) found that the majority of mentoring studies have been completed by educational leadership students through doctoral dissertations rather than by experienced academic researchers. As such, the following paragraphs detail some specific ways in which researchers, specifically those focused on promoting gender and ethnic diversity among educational leaders, might consider engaging in research around mentoring a diverse group of minority leaders.

Although there are a few evaluations of formalized mentoring programs (e.g., Pocklington & Weindling, 1996), more empirical work is needed that systematically evaluates formal and informal mentoring relationships (Johnson & Sullivan, 1995; Sherman, 2005). As one example, although there is a wealth of literature that documents issues of inequity within educational leadership, little is known about how to implement management structures and approaches (e.g., mentoring programs) that promote equity (Burton, 1993). As such, there is a need for research that investigates how mentoring can enrich diversity within educational leadership.

Descriptive research is also needed that examines how the characteristics of minority groups may be different from "traditional" educational leaders.

For instance, there is minimal knowledge about how Latinas compare to other minority or white female leaders (Mendez-Morse, 2004). Research is also needed that examines how mentoring is perceived and experienced by individuals who have traditionally been underrepresented in leadership positions. For instance, few studies to date have been conducted specific to mentoring women who aspire to advance to top administrative positions (Cullen & Luna, 1993). In addition, empirical findings suggest that researchers should investigate gender differences in motivation for participating in mentoring programs and how mentoring benefits women leaders who seek or hold positions in a traditionally male occupation (Noe, 1988). Moreover, empirical work is needed to understand how women or racial/ethnic minority groups might serve as role models for other women or minorities who desire to become school leaders (Daresh, 1995). Furthermore, longitudinal data are needed to track outcomes of women and minorities who participate in leadership (mentoring) programs (Sherman, 2005).

Although we have a wealth of descriptive work describing the perceived benefits of mentoring, little attention has been paid to studying mentoring outcomes (Barnett & O'Mahony, 2008; Daresh, 1995; Grogran & Crow, 2004). Rather, evaluation efforts have primarily focused on input measures (Johnson & Sullivan, 1995). As such, there is a need for researchers to study the specific impacts (both short and long term) of mentoring educational leaders (Daresh, 1995). For instance, research is needed that provides evidence of the effectiveness of leader mentoring, including assessment of the longitudinal impact of mentoring on the psychological health and performance of school leaders (Hobson & Sharp, 2005). Research is also recommended that examines the relationship between mentoring and various outcomes, including leadership skills/performance, leadership capacity (Grogran & Crow, 2004), and student learning (Barnett & O'Mahony, 2008). In addition, research that examines mentoring outcomes in terms of gender, racial/ethnic group, disability, and so on, warrants attention (Grogran & Crow, 2004).

West and Milan (2001) offer several recommendations to advance the mentoring literature including (1) increasing the use of data triangulation from different stakeholders to reduce the bias of mentors' and mentees' impressions and (2) using quasi-experimental designs that include a control group for comparative purposes (as cited in Barnett & O'Mahony, 2008). Moreover, there is a need to isolate and measure the various individual and organizational factors that influence mentoring outcomes. For instance, future research should measure the impact of leaders' career attitudes and behavior on the success of a mentoring experience (Noe, 1988).

The majority of mentoring research to date has focused on formal or arranged mentoring relationships (Daresh, 1995). As such, research is recommended that explores the impact of naturally occurring relationships among educational leaders and how informal mentoring experiences compare to formalized programs in terms of the learning process (Grogran & Crow, 2004; Noe, 1988). In addition, little attention has been given to the various individuals that might contribute to leaders' mentoring experiences. For instance, drawing from the graduate mentoring literature from other fields, it is recommended that research be conducted that examines the role of university faculty in mentoring students in educational leadership programs. On the other hand, it would also be beneficial to better understand what mentees contribute to the mentoring process (Grogran & Crow, 2004).

In light of the absence of theory guiding the mentoring literature (Daresh, 1995), a final recommendation is for future research to be framed using theory from other disciplines (e.g., psychology, business) including Critical Race and feminist theories. Theoretical work should explore how mentoring might be experienced or perceived differently by different individuals. For instance, it has been noted that there is no discernable body of knowledge or theoretical frameworks that have been applied toward Latino/a leaders (Martinez, 2005). Similarly, despite empirical findings that suggest mentoring might be experienced differently by women and men, theoretical work is lacking that attempts to explain these differences. As such, future research on mentoring that is framed around social justice issues may consider a more inclusive definition of mentoring, such as Rodriguez's (1995) concept of *multicultural mentoring*.

REFERENCES

Anderson, E. M., & Shannon, A. L. (1988). Toward a conceptualization of mentoring. *Journal of Teacher Education, 39*(1), 38–42.

Barnett, B. G., & O'Mahony, G. R. (2008). Mentoring and coaching programs for the professional development of school leaders. In J. Lumby, G. Crow, & P. Pashiardis (Eds.) *International Handbook on the Preparation and Development of School Leaders* (pp. 232–262). San Francisco: Jossey-Bass.

Bohlander, G. W., Snell, S. A., & Sherman, A. (2000). *Managing human resources* (12th ed.). Mason, OH: South-Western College Publishing.

Browne-Ferrigno, T., & Muth, R. (2004). Leadership mentoring in clinical practice: Role socialization, professional development, and capacity building. *Educational Administration Quarterly, 40*(4), 468–494.

Browne-Ferrigno, T., & Muth, R. (2006). Leadership mentoring and situated learning: Catalysts for principalship readiness and lifelong mentoring. *Mentoring and Tutoring, 14*(3), 275–295.

Brunner, C., & Grogan, M. (2005). Women leading systems. *School Administrator, 62*(2), 46–50.

Burton, L. (1993). Management, race and gender: An unlikely alliance? *British Educational Research Journal, 19*(3), 275–290.

Bush, T., & Coleman, M. (1995). Professional development for heads: The role of mentoring. *Journal of Educational Administration, 33*(5), 60–74.

Campbell, T. A., & Campbell, D. E. (1997). Faculty/student mentor programs: Effects on academic performance and retention. *Research in Higher Education, 38*(6), 727–742.

Chao, G. T., Walz, P. M., & Gardner, P. D. (1992). Formal and informal mentorships: A comparison on mentoring functions and contrast with nonmentored counterparts. *Personnel Psychology, 45*(3), 619–636.

Cullen, D. L., & Luna, G. (1993). Women mentoring in academe: Addressing the gender gap in higher education. *Gender and Education, 5*(2), 125–137.

Daresh, J. C. (1995). Research base on mentoring for educational leaders: What do we know? *Journal of Educational Administration, 33*(5), 7–10.

Daresh, J. (2004). Mentoring school leaders: Professional promise or predictable problems? *Educational Administration Quarterly, 40*(4), 495–517.

Daresh, J. C. & Playko, M. A. (1990). Mentoring for effective school administration. *Urban Education, 25*(1), 43–54.

Edwards, J. L., & Gordon, S. M. (2006). *You should—I should: Mentoring responsibilities as perceived by faculty, alumni, and students.* Paper presented at the annual meeting of the American Educational Research Association, San Francisco.

Ehrich, L. C. (1995). Professional mentorship for women educators in government schools. *Journal of Educational Administration, 33*(2), 69–84.

Ehrich, L. C., Hansford, B., & Tennent, L. (2004). Formal mentoring programs in education and other professions: A review of the literature. *Educational Administration Quarterly, 40*(4), 518–540.

Fiason, J. J. (1996). *The next generation: The mentoring of African American graduate students on predominantly white university campuses.* Paper presented at the annual meeting of the American Educational Research Association, New York.

Glass, T., Björk, L., & Brunner, C. (2000). *The study of the American school superintendent.* Arlington, VA: American Association of School Administrators.

Grogran, M., & Crow, G. (2004). Mentoring in the context of educational leadership preparation and development: Old wine in new bottles? *Educational Administration Quarterly, 40*(4), 463–467.

Hall, P. (2008). Building bridges: Strengthening the principal induction process through intentional mentoring. *Phi Delta Kappan,* 449–452.

Hansford, B., & Ehrich, L. C. (2005). The principalship: How significant is mentoring? *Journal of Educational Administration, 44*(1), 36–52.

Hean, L. L. (2004). Educational practice in leadership mentoring: The Singapore experience. *Educational Research for Policy and Practice, 2,* 215–221.

Hobson, A. J., & Sharp, C. (2005). Head to head: A systematic review of the research evidence on mentoring new head teachers. *School Leadership and Management, 25*(1), 25–42.

Hubbard, S. S., & Robinson, J. P. (1998). Mentoring: A catalyst for advancement in administration. *Journal of Career Development, 24*(4), 289–299.

Johnson, A. W., & Sullivan, J. A. (1995). Mentoring program practices and effectiveness. In M. W. Galbraith & N. H. Cohen (Eds.), *Mentoring: New strategies and challenges* (pp. 43–56). San Francisco: Jossey-Bass.

Kamler, E. (2009). Decade of difference (1995–2005): An examination of the super-intendent search consultants' process on Long Island. *Educational Administration Quarterly, 45*(1), 115–144.

Kram, K. E. (1983). Phases of the mentor relationship. *Academy of Management Journal, 26*(4), 608–625.

Kram, K. E. (1985). *Mentoring at work: Developmental relationships on organization life.* Glenview, IL: Scott, Foresman.

Kram, K. E. (1988). *Mentoring at work: Developmental relationships in organizational life.* Lanham, MD: University Press of America.

Kram, K. E., & Isabella, L. A. (1985). Mentoring alternatives: The role of peer relationships in career development. *Academy of Management Journal, 28*(1), 110–132.

Levinson, D. J., Carrow, C. N., Klein, E. B., Levinson, M. H., & McKee, B. (1978). *The seasons of a man's life.* New York: Ballantine.

Loder, T. L. (2005). Women administrators negotiate work-family conflicts in changing times: An intergenerational perspective. *Educational Administration Quarterly, 41*(5), 741–776.

Luna, G., & Cullen, D. L. (1995). Empowering the faculty: Mentoring redirected and renewed. *ASHE-ERIC Higher Education Reports, 3*, 1–87.

Martinez, R. O. (2005). Latino demographic and institutional issues in higher education: Implications for leadership development. In D. J. Leon (Ed.), *Lessons in leadership: Executive leadership programs for advancing diversity in higher education* (pp. 17–55). Amsterdam: Elsevier.

Mendez-Morse, S. (2004). Constructing mentors: Latina educational leaders' role models and mentors. *Educational Administration Quarterly, 40*(4), 561–590.

Mertz, N. T. (2004). What's a mentor anyway? *Educational Administration Quarterly, 40*(4), 541–560.

Morris, J. (1993). Women in educational management: A Trinidad and Tobago perspective. *British Educational Research Journal, 19*(4), 343–356.

Noe, R. A. (1988). An investigation of the determinants of successful assigned mentoring relationships. *Personnel Psychology, 41*, 457–479.

Pocklington, K., & Weindling, D. (1996). Promoting reflection on headship through the mentoring mirror. *Educational Management & Administration, 24*(2), 175–191.

Ragins, B. R., & Cotton, J. L. (1999). Mentor functions and outcomes: A comparison of men and women in formal and informal mentoring relationships. *Journal of Applied Psychology, 84*(4), 529–550.

Roberts, A. (2000). Mentoring revisited: A phenomenological reading of the literature. *Mentoring and Tutoring, 8*(2), 145–170.

Rodriguez, Y. E. (1995). Mentoring to diversity: A multicultural approach. In M. W. Galbraith & N. H. Cohen (Eds.) *Mentoring: New strategies and challenges* (pp. 69–77). San Francisco: Jossey-Bass.

Samier, E. (2000). Public administration mentorship: Conceptual and pragmatic considerations. *Journal of Educational Administration, 38*(1), 83–101.

Scanlon, K. C. (1997). Mentoring women administrators: Breaking through the glass ceiling. *Initiatives 58*, 39–59.

Schockett, M. R., & Haring-Hidore, M. (1985). Factor analytic support for psychosocial and vocational mentoring functions. *Psychological Reports, 57,* 627–630.

Schockett, M. R., Yoshimura, E., Beyard-Tyler, K., & Haring, J. J. (1983, April). *Proposed model of mentoring.* Paper presented at the annual meeting of the American Psychological Association, Anaheim, CA.

Sherman, W. H. (2005). Preserving the status quo or renegotiating leadership: Women's experiences with a district-based aspiring leaders program. *Educational Administration Quarterly, 41*(5), 707–740.

Snyder, T. D., Dillow, S.A., & Hoffman, C. M. (2009). *Digest of Education Statistics 2008* (NCES 2009-020). Washington, DC: National Center for Education Statistics, Institute of Education Sciences, U.S. Department of Education.

Young, M. D., & McLeod, S. (2001). Flukes, opportunities, and planned interventions: Factors affecting women's decisions to become school administrators. *Educational Administration Quarterly, 37*(4), 462–502.

West, L., & Milan, M. (2001). *The reflecting glass: Professional coaching for leadership development.* New York: Palgrave.

CHAPTER 16

BUILDING BRIDGES AND EPISTEMOLOGIES AMONG PRACTITIONERS AND RESEARCHERS IN EDUCATIONAL LEADERSHIP

Ashley Oleszewski and Elizabeth Murakami-Ramalho

The purpose of this chapter is to examine social justice issues related to building collaborative bridges and epistemologies among practitioners and researchers in education. Dr. Murakami, a professor, and Ashley, a doctoral student, began this conversation after Ashley's second year as a full-time student in an educational leadership doctoral program. Both professor and student have spent time as practitioners working in the public school setting and experienced differences between the work of practitioners and researchers. This conversation evolved when Ashley expressed concerns of practitioners like herself not being treated with the same respect as researchers in academia.

Students enter doctoral programs for different purposes: They may be seeking a higher salary, a promotion within PreK–20 education, or a career

Educational Leaders Encouraging the Intellectual and Professional Capacity of Others:
A Social Justice Agenda, pages 287–300.

in academia. Ideally, everyone involved in education, including teachers, administrators, and higher education faculty, would be working toward one common goal: to improve the field of education (Young, 2001). An education doctorate is unique because this degree prepares both scholars and practitioners. "The doctoral degree in educational leadership, for example, provides practitioners with the skills to analyze organizational systems, improve the practitioners' research skills, and become proficient in analyzing and diagnosing broader educational concerns," reflected Dr. Murakami. Because many educational leadership students are full-time teachers or administrators, they rarely enroll in doctoral programs full time. However, even as they begin the program, students seem to sense a tension related to the value given to practitioners versus scholars. Ashley added, "As a student, I am living the constant struggle doctoral students experience when enrolling part time or full time to complete the degree. In many ways, the doctoral program and structure do not seem conducive to part-time students."

These tensions are not new in educational leadership preparation programs. Nonetheless, doctoral students coming into higher education are still exposed to historical divides in relation to the purpose and meaning of practitioners and researchers in education. These tensions are explored in this chapter through current research and personal experiences, followed by possible considerations derived from this dialogical process. Our reflections were informed by cases from individuals experiencing the divide between the practitioner/researcher epistemologies. Here, we reproduce short cases that sparked our discussions.

COMPELLING CASES: DONNA AND ERNIE

Dr. Donna Smith (pseudonym) is a compelling example of the divide between practitioners and researchers. Donna is currently serving as the assistant superintendent for a school district, a position that she has held for 8 years. Her previous work experiences include being an assistant professor for 7 years at two universities and an administrator of another school. These positions followed the completion of her doctorate degree at a large tier-one research university where she also held a research and teaching assistantship. Her knowledge regarding state tests, 21st century learning, engaging curriculum, state standards, technology, and grant funding is impressive, as all of these areas fall under her domain as a assistant superintendent. Because of her previous work in academia and her interest in graduate studies, Smith is also highly knowledgeable about research practices.

Donna is trying to reenter academia for several personal reasons. The hours and responsibilities of public education have limited her independence as an educator. Donna would like to return to the collaborative nature of academia. In consulting with a colleague in academia, the professor asked Donna about the number of publications she has written in the past

5 years while she was away from academia. While a university professor, Donna had published several articles. However, when she moved to her job as a central office administrator, her schedule had provided her with time for researching, but job demands did not include writing and publishing. After listening to Donna, her mentor-professor commented: "If you haven't published anything recently, don't bother applying for a university position." Donna has an expanse of knowledge and experience to share with a classroom of graduate students, especially those entering K–12 education. Why is her experience and knowledge as a practitioner not rendered as valuable in academia?

Professor Ernie Duncan (pseudonym) is another example of this divide. When entering academia, and after a career as an educator in K–12 schools, Ernie sought to be published in *Educational Leadership* because of the journal's large practitioner readership. He knew that any published work in this journal could have a great impact on those working in the schools. However, Ernie soon learned that publication in a non-peer-reviewed journal would not be as valued in his professional portfolio in higher education. He learned that an article published in *Educational Leadership* would not count toward his tenure. On the other hand, many of the peer-reviewed journals in which he was asked to submit his manuscripts were not directly informing K–12 educators.

Professors in education enter academia with ideals to influence schools (Metz & Page, 2002). Similarly, many practitioners wish to use their knowledge and experience to contribute to the education research. However, both researchers and practitioners have been limited in their abilities to contribute to the opposite field. Situations like these send a message to new doctoral students that their experiences as practitioners may not be valued by researchers.

DEBATES REGARDING THE "FISSURE" BETWEEN EDUCATIONAL PRACTITIONERS AND RESEARCHERS

The debate about the preparation of practitioners and researchers in education has been a contested one for decades. Levine (2005) reignited this debate when he indicated that this divide has continued to grow, and could now be described as a "fissure" (p. 15). The rift between practitioners and researchers has existed since the development of educational leadership programs in the 1920s. In the early 20th century, James Earl Russell, Dean of Teachers College, supported a program for experienced practitioners who would enroll part time. The focus of the curriculum was on topics and skills students needed in order to perform their job responsibilities, a practitioner focus (Levine, 2005). Henry Holmes, Dean of Harvard's education school, refuted this model. He created a 2-year program with an academic focus for students without previous experience in education. Russell dismissed this model, saying that students needed experience and practical instruction. Charles Judd, Director of the Department of Education at the University of Chicago, felt that education schools were not rigorous enough and in response developed a program that focused on the science of education research and preparation (Powell, 1976). From these examples, it is evident that during the development of educational leadership degrees in the 1920s, programs were created for practitioners and researchers. University administrators could not agree on the purpose of an education leadership program, the student population, the length of the program, or the design of the curriculum. Levine (2005) summarized this century-long struggle between practitioners and administrators:

> The education school deans agreed to disagree, thus laying the foundation for what has evolved into polar differences regarding the goals and purposes of educational administration programs. No consensus exists on whom programs should enroll, what they should prepare their students to do, what they should teach, whom they should hire to teach, what degrees they should offer, and how educational administration relates to teaching and research. (p. 16)

Levine's report generated a strong oppositional response from across the nation, stemming from policymakers and analysts, scholars, school leaders, and professional organizations. They contested the existence of a divide between practitioners and researchers, showing that drastic reforms had indeed been made in improving preparation programs (Irby & Lunenburg, 2007; Young, Crow, Orr, Ogawa, & Creighton, 2005). However, we assert that in relation to improving the connections between researchers and practitioners, there remains room for improvement—with practitioners contributing with researchers, and researchers contributing with practitioners, in building knowledge.

Practitioners can be well prepared to utilize research in the field, and many of them are working toward improving these skills in doctoral programs. Murakami and her colleagues, in fact, stated, "Practitioners need to understand and use research to set targets, implant strategies, and measure growth" (Militello, Murakami-Ramalho, & Piert, in press). Pilkington (2009) also added that not only can practitioners use their research in schools and classrooms, but the reflective nature of practitioner research can provide new insights that may lead to successful change. Anderson (2002), in fact, recognized that practitioner research "can make contributions beyond the scope of traditional research" (p. 22). The responsibility to contribute to improving education is mutual. Doctoral students who intend to practice in K–12 education will improve the field by developing research skills, and doctoral students who intend to pursue a position in higher education could foster stronger collaborations with practitioners. This divide, however, may not be caused by practitioners and researchers alone. The divide may lie in the different role expectations in their corresponding institutions.

PRACTITIONERS AS DOCTORAL STUDENTS IN EDUCATIONAL LEADERSHIP

Part-time students in educational leadership programs in particular feel the effects of the aforementioned divide. Levine once argued that "students... are so busy at their day jobs that they have little time to devote to their graduate programs" (p. 33); future researchers make up less than 10% of educational administration students. If a professor perceives students who are practitioners as too busy for graduate school, are these students being treated fairly? This issue, we argue, relates to social justice issues regarding individuals' worth as professionals and diminished opportunities for certain students. The literature and the cases posed have demonstrated that university-tenured or tenure-track faculty may be placing more value in research over practice. Ashley describes her experience:

The program offers an EdD in educational leadership, which services both students in K–12 and higher education. The department offers five large research fellowships a year, which provide full-time doctoral students with a salary for 20 hours of work as a research assistant, a stipend, and tuition. The fellowships have enabled a few students like myself to attend school full time who may not have done so otherwise.

With a majority of educational leadership students being practitioners, attending school part time, these students are left feeling inferior; a common sentiment among colleagues, who are practitioners, is that their work is not valued. "From my own personal experiences," attested Ashley, "when my colleague was penalized for missing class because of a work commitment, he responded, 'I signed my contract, which requires me to cover evening duties, before I began this program. I have a responsibility to put food on my family's table. I cannot risk losing my job to attend class. If my grade is penalized, so be it.'" Other students have hoped faculty would understand their work commitments because the program was sold as one for "working professionals."

"Research and practice should work together to advance the field of education," reflected Ashley. She continued:

Unfortunately, in education these two fields seem to act in isolation. This has created competing factions within the field. Specifically, the population in educational leadership doctoral programs consists of students with varying educational and career goals. The program must meet the needs of those pursuing careers in educational administration and higher education, both part time and full time.

As practitioners by day, many of these doctoral students work "in the trenches" with children, parents, teachers, and administrators. Other doctoral students work in higher education administration. While pursuing a degree in educational leadership, doctoral students are encouraged to follow strict research guidelines that seem disconnected from their daily practices. The question remains: Are educational leadership students who serve as practitioners treated the same as those who are pursuing a career in research or higher education?

Doctoral students in educational leadership and their professors seem to belong to different work realities that clash during their programs. Students seem to face the challenges of balancing work and school in a program structure that may not be conducive to their success. In addition, the university structure sometimes limits students from fully using their services (with labs only open 5 days a week during working hours, for example), and many students referred to limited opportunities to build strong relationships with faculty.

FULL TIME VERSUS PART TIME: SOCIAL JUSTICE ISSUES IN THE REPRESENTATION AND ENGAGEMENT OF DOCTORAL STUDENTS

The majority of education doctoral students, and not just educational leadership students, attend school part time (Anderson, 2002; Shulman, Golde, Bueschel, & Garabedian, 2006). In a study of 29 nationally representative universities and departments of education, 73% of the alumni said they worked full time while attending school (Levine, 2005). At this south Texas university, about 82% of the students are part time. Unfortunately, most doctoral students do not receive enough financial support to leave their jobs and attend school full time (Hoyle & Torres, 2008; Metz & Page, 2002).

Part-time students tend to be older than full-time students and must balance responsibilities, such as family and work (Watts, 2008). Because of the challenge of effectively managing work and school, Metz and Page (2002) believed that part-time students cannot fulfill both professional and academic responsibilities without jeopardizing the quality of either duty or both.

In order to meet the needs of these students, some education doctoral programs are conducted in intensive evening classes or weekend formats (Shulman, et al., 2006). However, even within this structure, professors rarely seem to understand a student's nonacademic commitments. Unexcused absences, for example, place students in a quandary, which is not really a "choice" for the majority of the students. If such penalties are held by faculty teaching in educational leadership programs, then part-time students seem to come into the program at a disadvantage. As a result, some professors may be perceived by students as not respecting their professionalism, or not expecting the same quality work from students who are enrolled part time.

In addition to balancing work and school, part-time students encounter challenging program structures, and less than encouraging underlying messages about the value and dedication of practitioners. "It is interesting how the values of typical educational leadership programs are not often purposeful about accommodating the needs of part-time students," attested one student in the program. The same student reflected that because part-time students are frequently balancing multiple responsibilities, and commute for classes, they often feel isolated. In fact, in a study of 26 full and part-time students, Deem and Brehony (2000) found that part-time students have the most difficult time accessing peer and academic cultures, feeling isolated from the research community and penalized for having commitments outside the university (Militello et al., in press).

PART-TIME STUDENT FACULTY INTERACTIONS

Watts (2008) added that part-time doctoral students in education may not receive the same treatment and guidance from faculty as full-time students. Some institutions seem to be more apt to support full-time students who will complete the program faster and enhance the university's research profile (Watts, 2008). Anderson (2002), in turn, acknowledged that there are fewer rewards for faculty who work with practitioners, with faculty often discouraged to work with students who enroll part time, due to higher institution demands for tenure.

Time limitations and scheduling seem to also limit these interactions. Watts (2008) again stated that "where there is such minimal face-to-face contact, getting to know the student, let alone developing a productive and engaged supervisory relationship can be very challenging both for student and supervisor" (p. 370). A part-time student's schedule does not allow enough time to meet with professors during office hours. Such limited interaction with faculty "leads to little socialization into communities of inquiry or practice" (Shulman et al., 2006, p. 26). Studying current and past educational administration doctoral students, Militello et al. (in press) added that building relationships with faculty was dependent on the availability of faculty and being at the right place at the right time, both of which are difficult for part-time students. They stated, "In fact, accessibility to colleagues and faculty members was found to be a privileged experience" (p. 21).

FULL-TIME DOCTORAL STUDENTS

"There is quite a disparity between part-time and full-time students," attested one of the doctoral students in the university, referring to limited opportunities and isolation. On the other hand, full-time students are provided numerous educational advantages. As a full-time student and graduate assistant, Ashley has been provided numerous opportunities to assist with professors' research and contribute to publications. She stated:

> By attending school full time and working closely with various faculty members, I have been able to fully immerse myself in my coursework. As a result, I have gained a deeper understanding and appreciation for various types of research. I have also had the opportunity to assist professors in all stages of their research, including securing grants, seeking approval from the institutional review board, gathering and reviewing literature, collecting data, and publishing. These opportunities have created a rich learning experience and will truly benefit me when I begin conducting my own research. In addition, I have been able to build relationships with various members of the department as I work for them, serve on committees with them, and spend time with faculty throughout my work in the department. Unfortunately, my part-time counterparts have not been provided these same opportunities. In many ways, I have a distinct advantage.

What changes could be made, both structurally and in value systems, so that we more fully recognize the value of the epistemological knowledge practitioners and scholars jointly bring? These social justice issues in relation to doctoral students, and later perpetuation of the disconnect between practitioners and scholars, seem to work counter to building the capacity to prepare professionals invested in improving the field of education and leadership.

CONSIDERATIONS FOR REDUCING THE DISCONNECT

Apart from scientific debates about the improvement of educational leadership programs, licensure, or recruitment, this chapter focused on different value systems practitioners encounter upon entering doctoral programs in educational leadership. State and national efforts to improve the structure, content, or method of delivery in educational leadership have been undertaken (Young et al., 2005; Young, Petersen, & Short, 2002), but more can be done to improve the dispositions of both practitioners and scholars in creating seamless collaborations when contributing to research. Young, et al. (2002), for example, reminded us that the work of practitioners and researchers is fundamentally interdependent. Bridging capacity and engagement among practitioners and researchers, in the PreK–20 and advanced programs in education, however, continues to be a challenge.

Doctoral programs in educational leadership are successful when researchers and practitioners are valued equally in their contributions to improve educational systems. Professors/researchers who are invested, and involved in the work of PreK–20 practitioners, and practitioners that continuously incorporate research, and involve professors, are intentional in bridging the gap between the two fields. The challenge for universities lies in the examination of social justice issues that continue to disrupt these connections. We concur with Young (2001), who accurately indicated the "pressure and urgency to be truly inclusive" (p. 4). It is not acceptable to continue to have doctoral students feeling discouraged or unappreciated for their knowledge as they begin their doctoral program.

Recommendations for building capacity for both practitioners and researchers include reexamining: (1) higher education expectations for researchers and practitioners; (2) the creation of cohorts; (3) mentoring; and (4) part-time program adaptations. Following, we expand on these recommendations.

Higher Education Expectations for Researchers and Practitioners

During our dialogues, we questioned whether or not the expectations for both professors and practitioners have been revisited. For example, practitioners often teach in universities, contributing highly, as adjunct faculty, for the advanced preparation of principals and superintendents. However, they are usually hired as instructors with little or no voice in higher education faculty senates, departmental faculty meetings, or curricular planning. Generally, involvement of adjunct faculty in higher education is limited to teaching hours, and consequently limits opportunities for dialogues with professors and students outside of the classroom. Adjunct faculty is often removed from any research discussions or collaborations with tenure-track faculty. As a result, a practitioner aspiring to reenter academia, as presented in Donna Smith's case, earlier, is impacted by this separation of roles.

In terms of tenure-track faculty, have we really addressed the problem of generating investigations and research with practitioners? Recognizably, the roles and expectations for professors are very different from the work of practitioners. In general, higher education professors are required to dedicate a portion of their time to research. However, the pressure to publish may, in certain cases, be perceived as deterrents in building collaborative bridges and epistemologies among practitioners and researchers in education. Some professors, especially untenured faculty, sacrifice the time that could be used in developing connections with schools, in order to publish. So, even though many professors are prolific in publishing articles, not all professors are closely involved with PreK–20 schools. Those heavily involved in schools, in fact, seldom obtain tenure, often engaging in more active roles in schools, and less involved in writing research (Foley & Valenzuela, 2005).

The push to develop a vast knowledge base in policy, in the examination of national datasets, or writing grants should not replace the engagement of these scholars within the field. University professors are expected to write research, but tenure-granting systems in education departments do not include or generally value direct participation in PreK–12 schools. If, on the one hand, practitioners are expected to have a publication track when seeking a job in higher education, then, on the other hand, researchers could also be required to have more direct involvement in PreK–12 activities. Elmore, in fact, addressed this very concern in a University Council of Educational Administration convention keynote address, raising much controversy (*www.scottmcleod.org/2006UCEAElmore.mp3*). After the uproar, however, little was done to address the creation of clinical teams to investigate educational problems.

In addition, issues such as student attrition, retention, and successful completion among doctoral students are tightly related to faculty guidance and support (Ferrer de Valero, 2001; Golde, 2000). Professors are highly supportive of their doctoral students; however, the relationships between full-time professors and part-time students are indeed limited by constraints in time, even if they meet at equidistant settings. Nonetheless, considering the recent emergence of fully online doctoral programs in educational leadership, it is important to consider whether or not doctoral students feel less disconnected in face-to-face programs offered by traditional universities, when compared to online programs. Several online universities offering doctoral degrees in educational leadership advertise the importance of a supportive and mentoring faculty, sometimes providing 24-hour support for doctoral students (even though it is unclear if support is provided by tenured or tenure-track professors). Structural issues may need to be revisited to address this concern.

Creating Cohorts

There have been debates as to whether students who are practitioners should pursue a different degree than those who intend to conduct research (Levine, 2005). However, programs that combine both groups of students in cohorts seem to provide practitioners and researchers with fruitful opportunities where practitioners and aspiring professors can learn from each other. By enabling students of differing careers and research interests to communicate and develop research identities together, the gap between practitioners and researchers begins to narrow (in the case of Ashley and her colleagues, the cohort is composed by PreK–12 school leadership and higher education administration students).

Perceived advantages of cohort groups have been extensively studied. Among the advantages of cohorts, scholars include easier integration of students with the program sequence and structure; enhanced social and academic support, which encourage success; and increased cohesiveness in matriculating and completing degrees (Barnett, Basom, Yerkes, & Norris, 2000; Everson, 2006; Scribner & Donaldson, 2001). These scholars also caution that not all cohorts necessarily develop positive interactions. Nonetheless, cohort groups may be the ideal environment to encourage research capacity building, with projects in which both professors and students can develop research projects and field-based research. Purposefully building a culture of bridging epistemological perspective among cohort group members may generate lasting interdisciplinary collaborations.

Mentoring

"The greatest benefit that I have experienced as a doctoral student has resulted from the coaching and mentoring provided by faculty members," attested one of the doctoral students in our program. As was previously described, a faculty mentor is seen as a privilege that is much more accessible for full-time students. However, a mentor is perhaps even more crucial for part-time students. By establishing a positive mentor relationship with a faculty member, part-time students are able to advance their knowledge of the research process. In providing for mentored research opportunities for part-time students, both student and professor may want to set research-oriented sessions, in addition to sessions focused on the craft of research for the student's dissertation. Some professors develop current research endeavors with their students in their schools. Sense-making opportunities with experienced scholars, coupled with exposure to informal research communities, offer opportunities for research knowledge and growth (Militello et al., in press). An example of where this sort of mentoring has worked well is the doctoral program at St. Louis University. The institution has a unique mentor program that has built-in structures to facilitate a relationship between students and faculty (Everson, 2006). In this program, students are grouped according to their area of interest and experience. Then, each group is assigned a faculty mentor that shares a similar interest. The faculty advisor teaches a one-credit course to his or her advisees for multiple semesters. The structure creates time for students and faculty to converse despite the student's schedule or enrollment status (part time or full time). Everson (2006) described the success of this program:

> Because of the regularity of interactions between team members and their advisor, a collaborative culture is often created. This collaborative culture models good practice and can influence the associations that students have in their current positions or hope to create in new leadership positions. (p. 7)

With a strong knowledge of both practice and scholarly research through mentor relationships, students who complete this program are more likely to become well rounded and prepared for various research-informed career paths.

Part-Time Program Accommodations

Several formulas have been implemented to accommodate part-time doctoral students. However, instead of changing things to preserve the status quo, the challenge seems to be to determine the significant role of universities as centers of creation, discovery, application, and dissemination of knowledge. Abeles (2006), and other scholars, including Levine (2001), gave us a glimpse of the contemporary challenges of university structures, with doctoral students now having the opportunity to choose between brick or click universities.

Online and combinations of online and on-campus courses are becoming more of a norm, especially for commuting part-time students paying high service fees they are unable to use. Universities are indispensible centers of learning, and provide collaborative spaces for the development of new knowledge. However, these traditional structures need to provide state-of-the-art programs and be more fluid in developing new knowledge if they are to compete in the world of customer service. There is, however, one caveat: While virtual learning spaces may meet the needs of part-time doctoral students, they may not necessarily meet the need to increase the connections between practitioners and researchers. These and numerous other issues seem to be just ahead of us; unfortunately, few of us are able to think outside the box to determine the future of programs transitioning from rigid structures of teaching and learning. Perhaps this is one of the pressing issues that both practitioners and researchers choose to examine together.

CONCLUSION

Building collaborative bridges and epistemologies among practitioners and researchers, we argued, is a pressing task. Breaking historical divides in relation to the purpose and meaning of practitioners and researchers in education is but the beginning of a larger mission to improve education. A change in the language used to determine schools and institutions of higher education (trenches, or ivory tower) is needed to promote the collaboration among practitioners and researchers. Shulman and Hutching (2004) remind us that "authentic and enduring learning works best when the processes of activity, reflection, emotion, and collaboration are supported, legitimated, and nurtured within a community of culture that values such experiences and creates many opportunities for them to occur and to be accomplished with success and pleasure" (p. 25).

Contributions from practitioners and researchers alike are needed in the development of educational research and policy. Similarly, a call for collective advocacy is posed, especially when decisions about education are made unilaterally, or from those outside of education. We, too, like Shulman and

Hutching (2004), carry the hope that a commitment to reenvisioning the doctoral degree may highly contribute to building a new community of visionary educational researchers.

REFERENCES

Abeles, T. P. (2006). Do we know the future of the university? *On the Horizon, 41*(2), 35–42.

Anderson, G. L. (2002). Reflecting on research for doctoral students in education. *Educational Researcher, 31*(7), 22–25.

Barnett, B. G., Basom, M., Yerkes, D., & Norris, C. (2000). Cohorts in educational leadership programs: Benefits, difficulties, and the potential for developing leaders. *Educational Administration Quarterly, 36*, 255–282.

Deem, R., & Brehony, K. J. (2000). Doctoral students' access to research culures-are some more unequal than others? *Studies in Higher Education, 25*(2), 149–165.

Everson, S. T. (2006). The role of partnerships in the professional doctorate in education: A program application in educational leadership. *Educational Considerations, 33*(2), 5–9.

Ferrer de Valero, Y. (2001). Departmental factors affecting time-to-degree and completion rates of doctoral students at one land-grant research institution. *Journal of Higher Education, 72*(3), 341–367.

Foley, D., & Valenzuela, A. (2005). Critical ethnography: The politics of collaboration. In N. K. Denzin & Y. Lincoln (Eds.), *The Sage handbook of qualitative research* (pp. 217–234). Thousand Oaks, CA: Sage.

Golde, C. M. (2000). Should I stay or should I go?: Student descriptions of the doctoral attrition process. *Review of Higher Education, 23*(2), 199–227.

Hoyle, J. R., & Torres, M. S. (2008). Students' reflections on the relevance and quality of highly ranked doctoral programs in educational administration: Beacons of leadership preparation? *Journal of Scholarship and Practice, 5*(2), 5–13.

Irby, B. J., & Lunenburg, F. C. (2007). Doctoral program issues: Accreditation of programs. In C. Mullen, T. Creighton, F. Demoboski, & S. Harris (Eds.), The handbook of doctoral programs in educational administration: Issues and challenges. NCPEA Press: Connexions. Retrieved from http://www.connexions.soe.vt.edu/docbook.html. Levine, A. (2001). The remaking of the American university. *Innovative Higher Education, 25*(4), 253–267.

Levine, A. (2005). *Educating school leaders.* New York: Education Schools Project.

Metz, M. H., & Page, R. N. (2002). The uses of practitioner research and status issues in educational research: Reply to Gary Anderson. *Educational Researcher, 30*(7), 26–27.

Militello, M., Murakami-Ramalho, E., & Piert, J. (in press). A view from within: How doctoral students in educational administration develop research knowledge and identity. *International Journal of Graduate Education.*

Pilkington, R. (2009). Practitioner research in education: the critical perspectives of doctoral students. *Studies in the Education of Adults, 41*(2), 154–174.

Powell, A. G. (1976). University schools of education in the twentieth century. *Peabody Journal of Education, 54*(1), 3–20.

Scribner, J. P., & Donaldson, J. F. (2001). The dynamics of group learning in a cohort: From nonlearning to transformative learning. *Educational Administration Quarterly, 37,* 605–636.

Shulman, L. S., & Hutching, P. (2004). *Teaching as community property: Essays on higher education.* New York: Jossey-Bass.

Shulman, L. S., Golde, C. M., Bueschel, A. C., & Garabedian, K. J. (2006). Reclaiming education's doctorates: A critique and a proposal. *Educational Researcher, 35*(3), 25–32.

Watts, J. H. (2008). Challenges of supervising part-time PhD students: Towards student-centered practice. *Teaching in Higher Education, 13*(3), 369–373.

Young, L. J. (2001). Border crossings and other journeys: Re-envisioning the doctoral preparation of education researchers. *Educational Researcher, 30*(3), 3–5.

Young, M., Crow, G., Orr, T., Ogawa, R., & Creighton, T. (2005). An educative look at educating school leaders. Retrieved on July 28, 2006, from *http://www.ucea.org/pdf/EducLeadersRespMar18.pdf.*

Young, M. D., Petersen, G. J., & Short, P. M. (2002). The complexity of substantive reform: A call for interdependence among key stakeholders. *Educational Administration Quarterly, 38*(2), 137–175.

CHAPTER 17

MENTORING AS A SOCIAL JUSTICE EQUALIZER IN HIGHER EDUCATION FOR WOMEN

Whitney H. Sherman and Margaret Grogan

While mentoring has been studied between mentors and protégées in the K–12 setting, by comparison, less is known about mentoring in higher education. Hall and Sandler (1984) established the presence of a "chilly" patriarchal climate in higher education for women, but few studies have followed that demonstrate how mentoring has been used to promote individuals, particularly women, in the higher education setting to make practice more equitable and inclusive. Therefore, the purpose of this chapter is to challenge commonsense assumptions about mentoring and to revision the practice to one that is an inclusive, social justice equalizer for women in higher education. This work is distinct because it frames social justice and mentoring in action-oriented strategies and is situated in a mentoring relationship that has existed for almost 10 years in the higher education setting between two women: a mentor and protégée.

Educational Leaders Encouraging the Intellectual and Professional Capacity of Others: A Social Justice Agenda, pages 301–319.

CONTEXT FOR WOMEN IN HIGHER EDUCATION

Women represent only 38% of faculty nationwide (American Association of University Professors, 2001). They are most well represented at community colleges and least represented at doctoral institutions. Women are disproportionately represented at lower ranks among full-time faculty and least well represented among full professors. Women make up 46% of assistant professors, 38% of associate professors, and 23% of full professors. The percentage of women with tenure fell from 52% in 1998 to 43% in 2007 (Marcus, 2007). Furthermore, in 2005, only 16.5% of the nations' full-time professors were from minority groups, making minority women faculty even scarcer (Gose, 2008).

Studies of university faculty have shown that women face isolation due to the lack of mentors and face slower rates of promotion and tenure than men (Washburn, 2007). Isolation can occur as fewer opportunities for advancement and rewards along with less visibility (Hermsen, Litt, Hart, & Tucker, in press). According to Valian (1998), biases that deem men as more competent work in combination with institutional structures to marginalize women. In addition, Riger, Stokes, Raja, and Sullivan (1997) reported that the proportion of women in a department is related to perceptions of the environment and that departments with fewer women are seen as more hostile environments.

According to Acker and Feuerverger (1996), women faculty members of education reported an unequal division of labor in comparison to their male colleagues and having to take responsibility for the nurturing and housekeeping side of academic life in addition to taking on these responsibilities at home. Studies have also shown that women faculty report increased service responsibilities, numerous requests from students for mentoring and advising, assignment of larger and introductory classes, and few leadership opportunities (Hermsen et al., in press). The division of labor is discouraging for women (Newton, Giesen, Freeman, Bishop, & Zeitoun, 2003) as they are expected to achieve a sense of balance between home and increasing work responsibilities on their own (Ward & Wolf-Wendel, 2004).

Women faculty are less likely to have children compared to women in professions such as law and medicine (Cooney & Uhlenberg, 1989) and only 31% of current women faculty have children (Perna, 2001). Wolfinger, Mason, and Goulden (2008) found that family and children account for the lower rate at which women obtain tenure-track jobs. Further evidence comes from the "Do Babies Matter?" studies (Mason & Goulden, 2002, 2004; Mason, Goulden, & Wolfinger, 2006) that report women who have children within 5 years of receiving their doctorates are less likely to have tenure.

While women are better represented among the faculty in higher education now than ever before, they progress more slowly through the ranks of assistant, associate, and full professor than their male counterparts and are much less well represented than men in positions of power (Wolf-Wendel &Ward, 2003). Moreover, these authors argue there are fewer women and fewer leadership opportunities for women at more prestigious institutions. It is much more likely that, as institutions respond to economic crises, women and faculty of color make up a large proportion of adjunct and non–tenure track faculty (Schuster & Finkelstein, 2006). Clearly, there is a need for the deliberate mentoring of women to help equalize this imbalance.

Concerns in regard to bias, institutional structures, and masculine cultures have triggered calls to action to address inequitable advantage in the academic setting. "Mentoring women is understood to address unconscious bias, isolation, and gendered organizations" (Hermsen et al., in press) and has surfaced as a key strategy to address the status of women in higher education. However, in their study of a faculty mentoring program, Laursen and Rocque (2009) found that combining mentoring with organizational need and systemic change produced the most effective approach to negating barriers to women's advancement and success.

LACK OF INCLUSIVE MENTORING PRACTICES FOR WOMEN

Career mentoring is most strongly associated with the practices and support individuals receive as they move into leadership positions in K–12 education. It is well established that mentoring, including practices of networking and support, provide benefits to some practicing educational leaders and to some of those seeking leadership positions (Browne-Ferrigno & Muth, 2004; Crow & Matthews, 1998; Daresh, 2003, 2004; Ehrich, Hansford, & Tennent, 2004; Gardiner, Enomoto, & Grogan, 2000; Hubbard & Robinson, 1998; Mertz, 2004; Sherman, 2005). The support, sharing, encouragement, and feedback for protégés as well as increased opportunities for reflection, personal growth, and professional development for individuals serving as mentors has been well documented (Ehrich et al., 2004).

According to Zhao and Reed (2003), "mentoring is a personal relationship that we experience in many areas of our lives" (p. 399). "Mentors, then, are those special people in our lives who, through their deeds and work, help us to move toward fulfilling our potential" (Kochan, 2002, p. 283). In K–12 settings, mentoring has traditionally existed as a top-down, one-on-one relationship. However, more recent accounts of the practice have emerged that describe it as a network of support to help a protégé achieve career success (Sorcinelli & Yun, 2007). More traditionally in the leadership literature, men together or individually groomed their successors. There were many established practices including accompanying a mentor to important meetings, receiving targeted advice on professional development and acquisition of degrees, and receiving opportunities to gain valuable experience. On the other hand, "It is often common practice for women administrators to experience no mentoring throughout their career trajectory" (Gardiner et al., 2000, p. 6). Glass (2000) also asserted that women seem to have a less developed mentoring system compared to men and, thus, women and men do not share similar levels of mentoring support (Wales, 2003).

Yet, in their study of women superintendents, Sherman, Muñoz, and Pankake (2008) found that almost all of the women interviewed spoke about mentors who had played significant roles in their career advancement. However, somewhat contrary to other studies such as Gardiner et al.'s (2000), lacking in the majority of the women's descriptions of mentors and the process of mentoring in this study were *actions* or highly action-oriented behaviors. Current definitions of mentoring indicate that mentoring *is* active rather than passive and deliberate rather than happenstance, including descriptors of the process such as teaching, coaching, advising, promoting, directing, protecting, and guiding (Gardiner et al., 2000; Grogan, 1996; Brunner, 2000; Kochan, 2003; Shakeshaft, 1989). It is troubling that most of the women in the Sherman et als' study were unable to describe the actions of their mentors and fewer were able to describe a process that was anything other than passive. Sherman et al. stated:

> While receiving positive feedback and having someone believe in one's capabilities are important, they do not necessarily constitute the act of mentoring. For instance, mentoring entails support, but support does not necessarily result in mentoring. Women found themselves waiting to be deemed as worthy to pursue leadership positions and, many times, waited to be tapped for roles rather than being proactive and pursuing them independent of nudges from others. (pp. 261–262)

FEMINIST APPROACH TO MENTORING

While reported advantages of mentoring are numerous, feminists who have taken a critical look at mentoring have found that not only is it not as accessible to women as men, but that the practice itself often discourages women from leading in ways with which they are most comfortable, and that it sometimes serves to promote the status quo of an organization through exclusionary practices that are based on male-centered faculty models (Hermsen et al., in press; Mendez-Morse, 2004; Ortiz, 2000; Reskin, 2003; Samier, 2000; Sherman, 2005). Most often, in the career literature, the power to change the system resides with those who do the mentoring.

> [But] because [the opportunity to be mentored] depends on being approved of by those who wield the power, successful protégés grow to think and act like those who mentor them—even if they had differing philosophies initially...

many protégés are being mentored by those who lack a critical perspective or the desire to change the status quo. (Grogan, 2002, p. 126)

A feminist approach to mentoring is based on mutuality between mentor and protégé and is focused on empowerment and rejection of the status quo (Hermsen et al., in press) for the purposes of enhancing self-esteem, addressing inequities, and promoting recruitment and retention of women faculty (Benishek, Bieschlke, Park, & Slattery, 2004). The leadership that can bring about real change in higher education belongs to the faculty, first and foremost to the full professors with tenure. Therefore, access to career mentoring is a crucial prerequisite for those whose moral vision includes the desire for a more inclusive society. The diversity that women bring to the professoriate, having been for so long excluded from positions of power, has the potential to facilitate greater social justice in the academy. This establishes the need for deliberate mentoring of women graduate students into the field and for long-term active support that is tailored toward the tenure and promotion process. And it should not stop there. "Women should be encouraged to seek positions as deans, department and division chairs, changing the rules of the game and becoming advocates as well as mentors of other women" (Glazer-Raymo, 2003, p. 108).

MICRO AND MACRO VIEWS OF MENTORING THROUGH AUTOETHNOGRAPHY

In problem-posing education, people perceive critically the way they exist in the world in which they find themselves and, thus, come to see the world not as a static reality, but as a reality in process (Freire, 1993). According to Ellis and Bochner (2000), autoethnography is a genre of writing that makes the experiences of the researchers "a topic of investigation in its own right" (p. 733) and that "displays multiple layers of consciousness, connecting the personal to the cultural" (p. 739). It places the self within a social context, for the purposes of this chapter, mentoring in the higher education setting, and allows the self or selves to serve as the vantage point (Cole & Knowles, 2001). Autoethnographers "ask their readers to feel the truth of their stories and to become coparticipants, engaging the storyline morally, emotionally, aesthetically, and intellectually" (p. 745).

We, as the authors, recognize the power in dialogue and the sharing of stories to explore issues of social justice in mentoring. There is a need to locate women who have engaged in mentoring relationships and to make their experiences and strategies visible if mentoring is to be a social justice equalizer. We considered questions such as "What does it mean to mentor or to be mentored?" and "What does it mean to be a woman mentored by another woman or a woman who is mentoring another woman?"

Due to the highly individualized and personal nature of mentoring relationships, we believe this form of writing can contribute to discussions on mentoring, particularly mentoring for social justice. It seemed counterintuitive to us, as researchers and teachers of educational leadership and social justice in education who have engaged in a mentoring relationship for almost 10 years, to fail to include our experiences in the body of work that we have contributed to on mentoring in educational leadership. By combining our previous individual work on mentoring with our personal experience in a mentoring relationship, we formed a more authentic, inclusive, and collective understanding of mentoring issues and strategies. Furthermore, there is an absence of academic work that addresses mentoring in action from such an approach.

The following brings pieces of our individual experiences, memories, and thoughts centered around our mentoring relationship together in a dialogical and autoethnographic fashion to allow readers a window into our relationship. We use micro and macro views of mentoring to depict our relationship (Kochan & Trimble, 2000). The micro view consists of our narrative of our mentoring relationship, how it developed, and our reflections. The macro view is depicted through the strategies we offer for mentoring that might serve as social justice equalizers. These strategies can be used strategically by other women, mentors, and protégées who wish to promote equity and social justice in higher education.

OUR MICRO VIEW OF MENTORING

Margaret Grogan is a professor and dean of educational studies who has been a faculty member in higher education for 16 years and who has extensive experience as a teacher and administrator in K–12 education. Whitney Sherman is an associate professor in educational leadership who has been a faculty member in higher education for 8 years and who has some experience as a teacher and administrator in K–12 education. Margaret and Whitney have been engaged in a mentoring relationship for approximately a decade that began when Whitney was a graduate student and Margaret an assistant professor at the same university. We outline the micro view of our mentoring relationship below in two phases: building the foundation and passing along the torch.

Building the Foundation

Whitney:

After one semester in my doctoral program, I knew that I wanted to engage in research for my dissertation that focused on women in leadership. Knowing that Margaret studied women in leadership, the professor who was serving as my advisor at the time suggested that I talk to Margaret about serving as my chair. I had several conversations with Margaret about my interests and she agreed to guide me through the dissertation process. While this seems like a fairly common occurrence between professors and doctoral students, for me, it was a pivotal act in what has become my career largely due to the fact that, at the time, dissertations on women in leadership tended to be frowned upon. So, Margaret's concession to serve as my chair was never only about being my chair. It also required creative thought in which courses would serve me best (i.e., a feminist theory course that was not only offered outside of the department, but outside of the school of education, and was only offered at the undergraduate level); buffering when it became clear that I needed to take the required dissertation seminar out of sequence (because not all instructors value the study of women) so that I could study a topic of my choice; and honest discussions about opportunities for fellowships and awards that might not come to fruition for me due to a distaste for research on women.

Margaret:

When Whitney joined our PhD program I had been an assistant professor for a few years, though I was much older than she was. I was just learning how the system worked in academe. I remember being delighted that Whitney wanted to study women in leadership at the K–12 level just as I had. I think mentoring emerges very easily when someone seems eager to follow a path similar to the one a mentor has followed. I found myself doing the same for Whitney as my academic mentor and dissertation chair, Mary Gardiner, had done.

Whitney:

Once I had become acclimated to the academic environment of a full-time doctoral student and had served as a teaching assistant for a year while also teaching part time in an elementary school, I knew that by being pulled in so many directions, I was missing out on key experiences. I made the decision to quit teaching altogether and focus only on my doctoral program. I approached Margaret and asked her if she would be willing to have me serve as her graduate assistant. I had an honest discussion with her and told her that I was looking for the kind of opportunity that would allow me to actually apprentice with a professor in a way that cannot be taught in a classroom environment. I wanted to conduct authentic research and learn how to analyze it, write about it, and present it at conferences.

Margaret:

I felt extraordinarily lucky. To acquire a graduate assistant, interested in the same research agenda as me, as focused and energetic as Whitney was, seemed a bonus. At the time, I already knew that many professors work with graduate assistants who are not studying the same area. Once I understood that Whitney was considering going into higher education, I became energized. At that point, as I was nearing tenure, I loved my job, and I wanted to help someone else get this kind of professional fulfillment.

Whitney:

Margaret agreed to take me on as a graduate assistant and, as a result of this one act and all that it entailed, I gained experience traveling to and conducting interviews while making connections with the district leaders with whom I talked (and to always be prepared with two audio recorders in case one malfunctioned). I learned how to analyze interview data, write a literature review, and construct a coherent Results section of a manuscript. Margaret gave me my first opportunity to publish in a way that was fairly safe and less stressful for a graduate student by allowing me to serve as her co-author on a book chapter based on our research. She then maximized this opportunity for me by allowing me to switch roles and serve as first author on a peer-reviewed journal publication based on our research. Each time, she had me focus on writing different portions of the manuscript. So, while for the first publication I focused on writing the literature review, for the second, I focused on the interpretation of the data. Margaret's mentorship did not stop with teaching me how to be a researcher. She also created opportunities for me to take on both leadership (i.e., I directed a UCEA ethics conference as her graduate assistant) and teaching (i.e., under Margaret's guidance, I taught my first graduate-level course while still a doctoral student) roles. Again, while agreeing to allow a student to work with you as a graduate assistant might not seem like an act out of the ordinary, when a professor takes mentorship seriously and views her protégée's success as a reflection of herself, it indeed becomes a pivotal act. For me, this opportunity was key because it allowed me to have presentations, publications, and teaching experience on my curriculum vitae when seeking a professorship. Margaret was able to contextualize for me the gaining of confidence through experiences she allowed me to have in a more "safe" way grounded in her perception of me as a competent researcher, writer, and teacher (see Grogan, 2002).

Margaret:

It was definitely a two-way street. As an overloaded assistant professor (and a wife and mother of a school-age daughter), I was very grateful to have a graduate assistant as competent as Whitney. She provided me with the kind of assistance that allowed me to do research, to publish, and to serve the university. In framing this relationship as a mentoring one, and highlighting the advantages of it for the protégé, we mustn't neglect the mentor's self-serving aspect of it. I don't remember any more how much I simply involved Whitney in my activities because she was my graduate assistant and how much I actively sought opportunities for her. I am flattered by the account Whitney gives above, but I am not sure to what extent I did it for my own benefit.

Whitney:

One of the least talked about aspects of mentoring is the ability to connect with a protégée outside of the work environment and on a more basic human level. While I was in my second semester of doctoral work, my mother was diagnosed with breast cancer, had a mastectomy, and underwent a year of intense chemotherapy. Amidst all of the busy, day-to-day activities of her academic and personal life, Margaret quietly, compassionately, and authentically remembered to ask about my mother's progress and how I was managing the stress of home and student life.

Margaret:

I remember that period as very stressful for Whitney and I really admired her ability to handle it as well as she did. I saw an amazing strength that I think has carried her through a lot these past years.

Whitney:

Networking is a multifaceted act and, thus, must be taught and modeled in many ways and in multiple environments. As a graduate student and, more importantly, a graduate assistant for Margaret, I was able to travel to conferences and co-present the research I helped her with. Margaret gave me visibility at conferences by introducing me to faculty at institutions who had faculty vacancies; giving me "on the spot" training through both planned and unplanned presentations (i.e., I can remember almost having a heart attack at a taped session at an AERA conference where Margaret was on a panel and she called out to me in the audience to come up to the microphone and talk about my research on women); and helping me feel included during social events when all I really wanted to do was take up my position as a "flower on the wall," partially due to feelings that I was a fish out of water and partially due to a disdain I had developed for networking because of its privileging nature. As she says in one of her articles, "Few can manage without the support of an individual or individuals who will speak on their behalf, sponsor or promote them when it counts. Mentoring leads to networking, which is an activity limited to certain individuals in certain situations" (Grogan, 2002, p. 125). For me, Margaret has always seemed to have a keen sense of when and how to promote and network me.

Margaret:

During this period of our relationship, I found myself thinking more and more of Whitney as a colleague. Somewhere along the line, because of her own skills and abilities, she shifted into a novice researcher/writer and instructor. I can't pinpoint when and how that happens, but when it does, mentoring in the form of including the protégé in professional and social events becomes very easy. We always had an easy kind of relationship and it seemed just an extension of the colleagues we had become that she participated in more of my activities—especially since she was researching the same areas I was. I knew from my study of mentoring that the most important support I could give her was to make sure she was out in front of people demonstrating how good she was.

Whitney:

Lisa Delpit talks about the importance of making sure that everyone has basic skills in the most explicit of ways. When I think about all of the things Margaret did for me as a mentor in the early years, this seems to be the most simple, yet critical combination of acts that contributed to my success in not only gaining my first professorship, but in actually knowing what to do once I secured the position—the building of my basic skills as a researcher, a writer, and a teacher. According to Grogan (2002), this can be characterized as "access to the unwritten rules" that can only be made explicit in the mentoring relationship. I know from experience that not all graduate students are as fortunate as I and that many of them end up in their first positions without a clue of what to do—how to build a research agenda, how to establish a network of support, how to write for publication successfully. I have had several frank discussions with junior professors who have to come me about their lack of knowledge about the university environment and have been confronted in a "Why didn't you tell me this?" type of manner and have responded in a "I thought you knew that!" way. After this happened several times, I learned that it was my responsibility to start "paying it forward" by extending what Margaret taught to me to other students and junior professors in the field. While it has always been my mission to extend the knowledge I have gained to others, it was shocking to learn how lacking some of my colleagues' skills were—the ability was there, but some of the most innovative and brilliant minds had simply never been taught how to do some of the most fundamental tasks of the professorship.

Passing along the Torch

Whitney:

As a young woman doctoral student in educational leadership who lacked the typical twenty-plus years in K–12 administration, needless to say, I have taken some serious and hurtful ridicule and disrespect from those in the field who have chosen to be closed-minded over the years. As a graduate student, I was conflicted over whether or not I belonged in the higher education setting and wavered back and forth about whether I was worthy of applying for an academic position because of my own insecurities that were fed by comments from others. But Margaret never let me disrespect myself or the unique gifts I could bring to the university and went over and beyond the call of duty as a mentor and advisor to build my confidence and to help me acquire the thick skin she knew I would need to survive the first few years at the university. She helped me identify and understand my strengths and, more importantly, helped me to be able to convey this to others by holding numerous discussions with me about how to prepare for university interviews and teaching me how to match my strengths with the content of position announcements to make myself more marketable. She was explicit in teaching me the steps of the interview process, practiced mock responses to interview questions with me, and acted as a cheerleader, confidant, and networker who wrote countless letters of reference for me and who made phone calls and face-to-face contacts in some cases with department faculty who had posted vacant positions in their departments. Margaret also shared knowledge with me about how and what to negotiate as a new professor. As a result, I secured a position with the first university with which I interviewed.

Margaret:

I really enjoyed this part. By this time, I knew that Whitney would move into higher education and would be successful. My role was to help smooth the way by drawing on my own experiences and on others' experiences that I had had the opportunity by then to understand. The phrase "passing it forward" comes to mind here. Others had helped me along the way and I was delighted to use that knowledge that comes with passing the test of tenure to bring another very talented woman up with me. I really saw myself acting out much of what I was researching. I kept thinking the more I could meet such women as Whitney, the more I could help change the face of academe.

Whitney:

Though Margaret had prepared me well for the academic environment, I still had numerous questions and the need for continued mentorship after securing my first position. Margaret served as a sounding board, read manuscripts, and made suggestions for revisions as well as appropriate journals to send my work. In one particular instance, she helped me negotiate a review process with a specific journal that I found confusing. Margaret always found time (and still does) to meet with me at conferences, talk with me on the phone, and, especially during that first year, reminded me over and over again that I belonged in higher education despite comments to the contrary from some and helped me visualize the progression that was taking place in my career. She continued to help me network with others at conferences to widen my net of support and recommended me for committee and taskforce work that, otherwise, as a new professor, I would not have had the opportunities to participate in. Five months into my first professorship, I had a family emergency that led to my living in a state of crisis for several years. Ultimately, I made the decision to leave the field after completing only my first full year at the university. While I will likely never forget some of the biting comments I received from a few colleagues, like "You'll ruin your career if you leave after only one year," "You'll never get tenure if you leave," and "You'll be black-balled if you leave after only one year," I will forever be grateful for the support Margaret provided to me during that time. She never questioned my decision to leave and remained in contact with me during the 2 years I dropped off of the university map.

Margaret:

Well, by then, I was not going to let Whitney slip away. She had demonstrated her capacity to conduct research, to publish, and to teach well. For the reasons mentioned above, Whitney was going to help me pave the way for many more women researchers in educational leadership. I was highly motivated to do what I could to keep the flame alive.

Whitney:

During the 2 years that I left the field, Margaret maintained regular contact with me and helped me find opportunities that I could manage alongside my family emergency situation such as adjuncting for a local university where I had moved to be with my family and making revisions to a manuscript that I had submitted for review before leaving the academic environment full time. The isolation I experienced from the academic setting those years brought back old insecurities about whether I belonged in the field and, again, Margaret helped me visualize and make concrete the strengths that I could offer a university environment. As the time neared that I was ready to reenter the field, Margaret, once again, undertook the role of networker, reference-writer, and cheerleader as I applied for my second position and helped me renegotiate the academic world that seemed a bit frightening after being gone for what seemed like a long time. By this time, she had positioned/established herself in such a way that the mere mention that Margaret was my mentor, advisor, and dissertation chair was enough to help me gain interviews. Once I gained my second position and reentered the field, I had been gone so long that I wanted to jump into the "academic process" as quickly as possible and not experience the delay that first-year professors often experience as they establish their research agendas (i.e., I did didn't want to turn my tenure clock back and start all over again). I needed to begin multiple research projects quickly and one of the things that helped me to do this was being able to conduct follow-up studies on the research Margaret and I had worked on together when I was her graduate assistant several years before. That work was like the gift that kept on giving and allowed me to conceive of new projects to begin immediately that took me quickly through my next 2 years at the university. Margaret's mentorship took on a new shape during these years as she gave me advice on "next steps" for my career and helped me negotiate new opportunities. She recommended me to become a Jackson Scholar mentor; recommended me for two additional taskforces that led to research, writing, publishing, presenting, and networking opportunities; and continued to not only track but facilitate my career. She encouraged and supported me once again as the opportunity arose for me to change university settings for the third time to bring my home and work lives into greater balance (I spent 2 years commuting an hour and a half each way when I reentered the field). Ten years after meeting Margaret as a graduate student, working with her as a graduate assistant, and asking her to serve as my dissertation chair, I have been able to negotiate and weather both work and home challenges through a young career that has spanned three university settings and myriad setbacks. On July 1, 2009, I was awarded tenure and promotion (and was able to remain on the tenure clock under which I first entered the field). I know, unequivocally, that I would not have been able to do this without the purposeful, action-oriented mentorship Margaret has provided to me over the years.

Margaret:

I am struck by how enjoyable this process was and continues to be. I think the realization that we are now pretty well networked into a wide set of colleagues makes me feel good. I made a pledge to myself after my first study of women aspiring to the superintendency that I would do everything in my power to facilitate women's access to leadership in whatever form it took. Now that I have been in higher education for more than 15 years, I am excited about the many more opportunities that unfold each year. As colleagues continuing to engage in this work, Whitney and I are doing the same thing. It seems clear that the more we connect and share experiences with each other and with other women, the more change we'll see.

OUR MACRO VIEW OF MENTORING

After the authors reflected on our mentoring relationship, we utilized our autoethnographic dialogue to develop strategies that we present in this section of the paper for mentoring that might serve as social justice equalizers.

These strategies can be used by other women, mentors, and protégées who wish to promote equity and social justice in higher education.

Strategies to Mentor for Social Justice

Gewirtz (1998) describes social justice in action-oriented terms as the practice of the disruption of marginalization. As we engaged in the autoethnographic process, we gained a sense of specific actions that were helpful to Whitney that, in and of themselves, disrupted traditional university practices and assert that these might also be useful to other women protégés in the field. We outline strategies for career mentoring for women in higher education below that we envisioned while analyzing our dialogue that include the following:

- *Develop strength of self.* Those involved in the fitness culture understand that to be truly fit, one must make the foundation or core of the body strong. Similarly, to be able to successfully negotiate graduate school and the process toward securing a position in higher education, the most important goal for a protégé—one that supersedes all others—is to understand who she is, what she stands for, and how this sense of self can be utilized to her advantage. If you are in a position to mentor someone, actively seek a protégé and help her identify research and teaching interests that speak to her individuality rather than what might be more mainstream and readily acceptable by others in the field. Help your protégé gain self-confidence by buffering her when necessary (i.e., Margaret helped Whitney take courses outside of the department that would be most beneficial and to take her dissertation seminar out of course sequence) and helping her stand on her own when appropriate (i.e., Margaret allowed Whitney to teach a course and to coauthor manuscripts). Help her identify her strengths and formulate a plan of improvement for her weaknesses. Give her opportunities to work with you on research and teaching projects. If you are a protégé, be proactive, work to make connections with faculty, and network with those who have similar goals and who demonstrate that they are willing to spend time with you. Actively seek a mentor(s) (i.e., Whitney asked Margaret if she could work as her graduate assistant because she knew her interests were similar to Margaret's). Be specific about what you need your mentor to help you with. Be specific about what you desire to gain from a mentoring relationship. Strive to be an academic weightlifter —slowly work all of your muscles and work toward additional weight. Seek balance so that all areas are strong.
- *Grow a core of knowledge.* Runners know that it is virtually impossible to get a good stride going if they lack knowledge about what consti-

tutes a good stride, proper breathing, and a competitive pace. Many who are new to running find it helpful to master best practices a few at a time. If you are a mentor, it is important for you to engage in "think alouds" with your protégé. Talk out loud about the academic culture and share knowledge (especially any hidden rules). Margaret explained to Whitney that research on women is often a difficult road to take) explicitly and do not assume that your protégé understands the culture. Help your protégé develop knowledge a little at a time by sharing information, giving instructions, modeling, and then scaffolding as your protégé tries a task on her own (i.e., Margaret co-presented with Whitney and then encouraged her to present on her own). Teach your protégé to conduct research, write, and disseminate this information through publications and presentations (Margaret coauthored with Whitney and allowed her to write different pieces of the manuscript to build experience a little at a time). Do not assume that she gained this knowledge through coursework. In essence, teach your protégé to be an academic runner who can go the distance and jump hurdles when necessary. If you are a protégé, ask questions, soak up knowledge from those who came before you, and respond to feedback positively. Your stride will eventually improve.

- *Live and respond to life.* Unquestionably, life can be difficult enough without negotiating graduate school or a first-time professorship along the way—especially for women, as they are often expected to take on the bulk of family and home responsibilities in addition to work. It is crucial for mentors to show their protégés what successful juggling of home and work looks like. If mentors cannot demonstrate this themselves, it is unlikely that their protégés will be able to either. Mentors might also let their protégés understand that when juggling, at least one ball will drop eventually (this could take the form of a project deadline not met, a child's softball game missed, etc.). However, more importantly, it is helpful for protégés to know that the ball can be picked back up and thrown back into the mix when ready (i.e., Margaret encouraged Whitney to put family first when her mother was diagnosed with cancer and helped Whitney maintain connections and get back into the field during and after her leave of absence from the field). If a protégé has a curveball thrown at her in regard to her home life, the mentor should acknowledge this and demonstrate care (the act of care is neither feminine nor masculine, but, rather, human), but also hold the protégé accountable in fulfilling responsibilities and help her negotiate a new process if necessary. Protégés must be honest with mentors when unexpected circumstances arise and ask for help.

- *Be a fisher of women.* Fishing can be enjoyed in many different ways whether you are seeking a specific type of fish with special bait or whether you are simply throwing a pole in the water ready for anything that comes to the surface. Mentoring can be this way as well. Social justice agendas for women demand that mentors specifically seek women and minorities and promote them due to lack of access to mentoring in the past, except for a select few. Women mentors may seek women protégés who are like themselves for both the protégé's and mentor's benefit (i.e., Who doesn't want to work with someone who has similar interests?). But, they may also seek women and minorities who have strengths and interests different from their own for the sole purpose of promoting someone who otherwise would not receive the benefits of mentoring. Both practices are acceptable and work toward promoting more equitable and socially just environments. The point is to get out there and fish for other women so that networks can be built for those that come after you. If a mentor demonstrates the act of fishing for other women, the protégé will likely also practice paying it forward when she is in the position to do so.

CONCLUSION

The purpose of this chapter was to challenge commonsense notions about what mentoring is and who can be mentored. We reflected on our mentoring relationship and specific actions that were taken that resulted in Gewirtz's (1998) notion of the disruption of marginalization. As we analyzed our individual and collective memories about our mentoring relationship, we came to understand that mentoring is, indeed, an active rather than passive process that requires effort on the part of both the mentor and protégé and one that requires care, honesty, and commitment. Whether the relationship develops naturally or due to specific actions or intent on the part of the mentor or protégé, women benefit from one-on-one relationships with other women practicing in the field of higher education. By allowing readers a window into the mentoring relationship that has taken shape over a decade between us, we hope it shed light on specific actions that Margaret took to facilitate and advance Whitney's career development and advancement so that other women might use these to promote even more women into higher education so that, ultimately, the climate will become less chilly.

REFERENCES

Acker, S., & Feuerverger, G. (1996). Doing good and feeling bad: The work of women university teachers. *Cambridge Journal of Education, 26*(3), 401–422.

American Association of University Professors. (2001). Statement of principles on family responsibilities and academic work. Retrieved March 13, 2009. from *http:// www.aaup.org/AAUP/pubsres/policydocs/contents/workfam-stmt.htm*.

Benishek, L., Bieschlke, K., Park, J., & Slattery, S. (2004). A multicultural feminist model of mentoring. *Journal of Multicultural Counseling and Development, 32,* 428–442.

Browne-Ferrigno, T., & Muth, R. (2004). Leadership mentoring in clinical practice: Role socialization, professional development, and capacity building. *Educational Administration Quarterly, 40*(4), 468–494.

Brunner, C. C. (2000). *Principles of power: Women superintendents and the riddle of the heart.* Albany: State University of New York Press.

Cole, A. L., & Knowles, J. G. (2001). *Lives in context: The art of life history research.* Walnut Creek, CA: Alta Mira.

Cooney, T. M., & Uhlenberg, P. (1989). Family-building patterns of professional women: A comparison of lawyers, physicians, and postsecondary teachers. *Journal of Marriage and the Family, 51,* 749–758.

Crow, G., & Matthews, L. J. (1998). *Finding one's way: How mentoring can lead to dynamic leadership.* Thousand Oaks, CA: Corwin Press.

Daresh, J. (2003). *Teachers mentoring teachers.* Thousand Oaks, CA: Corwin Press.

Daresh, J. (2004). Mentoring school leaders: Professional promise or predictable problems? *Educational Administration Quarterly, 40*(4), 495–517.

Ehrich, L. C., Hansford, B., & Tennent, L. (2004). Formal mentoring programs in education and other professions: A review of the literature. *Educational Administration Quarterly, 40*(4), 518–540.

Ellis, C., & Bochner, A. P. (2000). Autoethnography, personal narrative. Reflexivity: Researcher as subject. In N. Denzin & Y. Lincoln (Eds.), *The Sage handbook of qualitative research* (2nd ed., pp. 733–768). Thousand Oaks, CA: Sage.

Freire, P. (1993). *Pedagogy of the city.* New York: Continuum.

Gardiner, M. E., Enomoto, E., & Grogan, M. (2000). *Coloring outside the lines: Mentoring women into school leadership.* New York: State University of New York Press.

Gerwitz, S. (1998). Conceptualizing social justice in education: Mapping the territory. *Journal of Education Policy, 13,* 469–484.

Glass, T. E. (2000). Where are all the women superintendents? *The School Administrator.* Retrieved from http://aasa.org/publications/saarticledetail.cfm?mnitem number=&tnitemnumber=951&ite.

Glazer-Raymo, J. (2003). Women faculty and part-time employment. In B. Ropers-Huilman (Ed.), *Gendered futures in higher education* (pp. 95–110). Albany: State University of New York Press.

Gose, B. (2008). Whatever happened to all those plans to hire more minority professors? *Chronicle of Higher Education, 55*(5), B1.

Grogan, M. (1996). *Voices of women aspiring to the superintendency.* Albany: State University of New York Press.

Grogan, M. (2002). Influences of the discourse of globalization on mentoring for gender equity and social justice in educational leadership. *Leading and Managing, 8*(2), 123–134.

Hall, R. M., & Sandler, B. (1984). *Out of the classroom: A chilly classroom climate for women.* Washington, DC: Project on the Status and Education of Women, Association of American Colleges.

Hermsen, J. M., Litt, J. S., Hart, J., & Tucker, S. A. (in press). In B. J. Bank (Ed.), *Gender and higher education.* Baltimore: Johns Hopkins University Press.

Hubbard, S. S., & Robinson, J. P. (1998). Mentoring: A catalyst for advancement in administration. *Journal of Career Development, 24*(4), 289–299.

Kochan, F. (Ed.). (2002). *The organizational and human dimensions of successful mentoring programs and relationships.* Greenwich, CT: Information Age.

Laursen, S., & Rocque, B. (2009). Faculty development for institutional change: Lessons from an ADVANCE project. *Change.* Retrieved July 6, 2009, from *http://www.changemag.org/Archives/Backpercent20Issues/March-Aprilpercent202009/full-advance-project.html.*

Marcus, J. (2007). Helping academic families have families and tenure too: Universities discover their self-interest. *Changes, 39*(2), 27–32.

Mason, M. A., & Goulden, M. (2004). Marriage and baby blues: Redefining gender equity in the academy. *Annals of the American Academy of Political and Social Science, 596,* 86–103.

Mason, M. A., Goulden, M., & Wolfinger, N. H. (2006). Babies matter: Pushing the gender equity revolution forward. In S. J. Bracken, J. K. Allen, & D. R. Dean (Eds.), *The balancing act: Gendered perspectives in faculty roles and work lives* (pp. 9–29), Sterling, VA: Stylus.

Mendez-Morse, S. (2004). Constructing mentors: Latina educational leaders' role models and mentors. *Educational Administration Quarterly, 40*(4), 561–590.

Mertz, N. T. (2004). What's a mentor anyway? *Educational Administration Quarterly, 40*(4), 541–560.

Newton, R., Giesen, J., Freeman, J., Bishop, H., & Zeitoun, P. (2003). Assessing the reactions of males and females to attributes of the principalship. *Educational Administration Quarterly, 39*(4), 504–532.

Ortiz, F. I. (2000). Who controls succession in the superintendency?: A minority perspective. *Urban Education, 35*(5), 557–566.

Perna, L. W. (2001). The relationship between family responsibilities and employment status. *Journal of Higher Education, 72*(5), 584–611.

Reskin, B. F. (2003). Including mechanisms in our models of ascriptive inequality. *American Sociological Review, 68,* 1–21.

Riger, S., Stokes, J., Raja, S., & Sullivan, M. (1997). Measuring perceptions of the work environment for female faculty. *Review of Higher Education, 21*(1), 63–78.

Samier, E. (2000). Public administration mentorship: Conceptual and pragmatic considerations. *Journal of Educational Administration, 38,* 83–101.

Schuster, J., & Finkelstein, M. (2006). *The American faculty: The restructuring of academic work and careers.* Baltimore: Johns Hopkins University Press.

Shakeshaft, C. (1989). *Women in educational administration.* Newbury Park, CA: Corwin Press.

Sherman, W. H. (2005). Preserving the status quo or renegotiating leadership: Women's experiences with a district-based aspiring leaders program. *Educational Administration Quarterly, 41*(5), 707–740.

Sherman, W. H., Muñoz, A., & Pankake, A. (2008). The great divide: Women's experiences with mentoring. *Journal of Women in Educational Leadership, 6*(4), 239–259.

Sorcinelli, M., & Yun, J. (2007). From mentor to mentoring networks: Mentoring in the new academy. *Change, 39*(6), 58–61.

Valian, V. (1998). *Why so slow?: The advancement of women.* Cambridge, MA: MIT Press.

Wales, S. (2003). Breaking barriers in business: Coaching women for career advancement in the United Kingdom. In F.K. Kochan & J.T. Pascarelli (Eds.), *Global perspectives on mentoring: Transforming contexts, communities, and cultures* (pp. 165–189). Greenwich, CT: Information Age.

Ward, K., & Wolf-Wendel, L. (2004). Academic motherhood: Managing complex roles in research universities. *Review of Higher Education, 27*(2), 233–257.

Washburn, M. H. (2007). Mentoring women faculty: An instrumental case study of strategic collaboration. *Mentoring and Tutoring, 15*(1), 57–72.

Wolf-Wendel, L., & Ward, K. (2003). Future prospects for women faculty: Negotiating work and family. In B. Ropers-Huilman (Ed.), *Gendered futures in higher education* (pp. 111–134). Albany: State University of New York Press.

Wolfinger, N. H., Mason, M. A., & Goulden, M. (2008). Problems in the pipeline: Gender, marriage, and fertility in the ivory tower. *Journal of Higher Education, 79*(4), 388–405.

Zhao, F., & Reed, C. J. (2003). Love, trust, and concern: Ingredients for successful mentoring relationships. In F. K. Kochan & J. T. Pascarelli (Eds.), *Global perspectives on mentoring: Transforming contexts, communities, and cultures* (pp. 399–415). Greenwich, CT: Information Age.

CHAPTER 18

MENTORING RELATIONSHIPS IN HIGHER EDUCATION

An Important Means of Encouraging the Development of Others

Marie Simonsson and Ava J. Muñoz

"Being a professor is creative, exciting, and energizing work; however, transitioning into that role can be difficult, daunting, and draining," once affirmed McCormick and Barnes (2008, p. 16). Challenges abound when initially entering a career (Cawyer, Simonds, & Davis, 2002). Regardless of which avenue from which the junior faculty member enters into the academic setting, just completing the terminal degree (master's or doctoral), or arriving from practicing in their discipline after earning their terminal degree, she or he has a rather steep learning curve to climb. Initial mentoring when transferring from role of student to faculty is critical to the new faculty members' long-term success (Austin, 2003; Colbeck, O'Meara, & Austin, 2008; Holmes, Land, & Hinton-Hudson, 2007).

According to Strathe and Wilson (2006), "The entry-level faculty member has a narrow view of an academic institution that probably does not extend beyond the department level; where multiple specializations exist

Educational Leaders Encouraging the Intellectual and Professional Capacity of Others:
A Social Justice Agenda, pages 321–334.

within the department, the view may even be more limited to the specialty area. Perspectives of academic administration are equally as narrow—perhaps limited to the department chair, or head, or the section chair, if specializations exist" (p. 7).

The purpose of this chapter is to explore the links between successful mentoring relationships and the theme of this book (i.e., *Leadership for Social Justice: Encouraging the Development of Others*). The chapter begins with an overview of mentoring, including what it is and the forms it takes. Next, comments from mentors and mentees are used to bring voices to the characteristics and practices mentoring. The final section is an attempt to use the information from the literature and the voices from the field to formulate recommendations for practice.

NEW FACULTY IN ACADEMIA

Numerous unfamiliar practices and a limited knowledge base are experienced by new faculty as they make their entry into the field of academia. Research on new faculty reveals that junior faculty are more prone to experiencing vast amounts of stress in their initial quest to achieving professional success in all areas of the professoriate (Sorcinelli, 1994). It takes considerable time to learn about an organization that serves thousands of students: maneuvering teaching, scholarly and service responsibilities, and getting to know the personnel, students, governance of the university, and its surrounding community. The many different components of work (social, cognitive, or affective) make the new faculty member's challenges astronomical.

What may appear to be common knowledge regarding the institution's operational methods is often unknown to new faculty, contributing to being uninformed (Simplicio, 2008). One of the most significant skills to acquire is to be aware of one's faculty responsibilities, and also to determine which responsibilities are timely or have deadlines and need to be dealt with first (Olsen, 1993). Many junior faculty members are predominantly engaged in and prioritize the tasks that may earn them tenure in the future (Rice, Sorcinelli, & Austin, 2000).

In an across-disciplines study of 350 junior faculty members on their perceptions of the tenure process, Rice et al. (2000) found that "expectations for performance were ambiguous, shifting, and inconsistent" (p. 43), including increased expectations especially in research, limited structured feedback or mentoring, concerns about the tenure peer-review process, and the tenure timeline. "The tenure process was described as inflexible and unresponsive to decreased funding, publication backlogs, the learning curve for teaching and preparing courses, the time needed to exploit the advantages of new technologies, and the personal demands made on scholars struggling to balance their lives" (Rice et al., 2000, p. 43). "In fact, being mentored during the pre-tenured years can spell the difference for a new faculty member between getting promoted and tenured and getting the proverbial 'boot'" (McCormick & Barnes, 2008, p. 8). Consequently, it is of the utmost importance that at the onset of their pre-tenure careers, new faculty be provided with a supportive mentor and that they also take responsibility for successfully assuming the role of mentee (McCormick & Barnes, 2008).

MENTORING

Mentoring in higher education is a common topic of discussion, but is not a consistently implemented or regulated practice. Savage, Karp, and Logue (1996) claim that the critical need for faculty mentoring "has longstanding support in higher education research" (p. 23). The benefits of mentoring for the mentee seem obvious and the rewards of the relationship to the mentor are not difficult to envision. However, successful mentoring relationships also impact the organization in important ways. Mentees tend to remain in their university assignments when mentoring has been obtained (Gardiner, Tiggeman, Kerns, & Marshall, 2007) and, through the utilization of mentoring, "a new faculty member may become a vital and productive member of the professoriate" (Cawyer, Simonds, & Davis, 2002, p. 239).

It takes considerable time to learn about an organization and its stakeholders in order to successfully function in and contribute to it at one's full potential. An individual's first appointment in academia may, initially, be a somewhat intimidating, overwhelming, and humbling experience. Researchers have discovered that new faculty members are expected to execute their new responsibilities and respond to the new culture and job descriptions without much allowance for a socialization process (Olsen, 1993; Sorcinelli, 1988).

Defining Mentoring

The very essence of successful mentoring is the encouraging the development of others. A mentor is an individual who collaborates with protégés (or mentees) to guide and provide support for them on research efforts, teaching methods, creative service options, and other opportunities and issues that one or both of them see as necessary for the protégé's success (Bower, 2007; Wasburn, 2007). Generally, mentors are conceptualized as senior individuals providing support to and advocacy for those more junior, typically from within the organization (Settles, Cortina, Stewart, & Malley, 2007). For example, a successful academic who has published can be helpful in guiding a new faculty member regarding such issues as topic selection, research methods, and outlets for publication (Ugrin, Odom, & Pearson, 2008).

Mentoring relationships can be established with or without formal procedural channels (Wasburn, 2007) and generally have two configurations: dyadic (one on one, consisting of a mentor and a mentee) or groups. These relationships can involve a mentor with seniority over another individual or they can be made up of peers (Gardiner et al., 2007). This can be enhanced by paying particular attention to mentor/mentee pairings (Ugrin et al., 2008). They report "responses from junior faculty (mentees) seem to indicate that they feel they get along better with a mentor that has common research interests and can help them achieve their career goals" (p. 348).

Mentors may also increase individuals' sense that they have voice or influence within the workplace. Effective mentors watch over their mentees, making sure that they are not overwhelmed with teaching, research, and service (Bower, 2007). This is often done by coaching the mentee in acceptable ways to decline them from among the flood of opportunities that often come to the less seasoned faculty. The mentor can offer advice about the way in which the mentee voices concerns within the organization and can even be the voice for the mentee by raising concerns on their behalf (Settles et al., 2007).

Mentees benefit most when familiarized with the socialization process of a particular institution. Through their mentors' tutelage, mentees are better equipped to navigate academia when informed of its social mores (Cawyer et al., 2002). Information as simple as what power structures are in place in a department, college, or university are critical and beneficial to assisting new faculty in how to navigate the system (Cawyer et al., 2002). Informal yet informative dialogue assists a mentee in familiarizing herself with the rudimentary operational processes of an organization (Cawyer et al, 2002.).

Not surprisingly, "successful mentoring relationships are often seen as a combination of common goals, individual personalities, and a great deal of luck" (Wasburn, 2007, p. 59). Availability of the mentor to the mentee and offering them activities that reinforce mentorship is more important to establishing a quality mentoring experience than mentor/mentee compatibility. However, not surprisingly, not all mentor–mentee relationships get off to a smooth start. Working out the nuances of both individuals is critical to whether or not effective mentoring will ever take place (Mathias, 2005). Cawyer et al. (2002) advise that it is good practice to look for other social contacts when the assigned mentor turns out to be more of a hindrance than a help.

The Social Justice Dimensions of Mentoring

Social justice in this chapter relates to organizational functioning (i.e., "attempts to describe and explain the role of fairness as a consideration in the workplace" [Greenberg, 1990, p. 400]). As an example, Bova (2000) asserts that "mentors tend to gravitate toward younger versions of themselves" (as cited in Wasburn, 2007). Given the demographics of faculty, this can be an issue of equity in that ". . . women and minorities are mentored less frequently than white males, making it more difficult for them to advance in their careers" (Wasburn, 2007, p. 59). Considering that "faculty of color make up only 12% of the typical graduate department" (APA Research Office, 2005, as cited in Shin, 2008, p. 188), social justice issue dimensions of mentoring may be related to the limited role models and support systems for faculty of color. Consequently, the likelihood of mentees interacting with tenured, minority faculty are few and far between (Holmes & Murray, 1996), which, in turn, minimizes the opportunities for successful mentoring of minorities to occur.

Going back to Bova's assertion that mentors are drawn to younger versions of themselves, it should not come as a surprise that faculty of color and women obtain less mentoring than their white male counterparts or even white female counterparts, where they exist. In fact, according to Baez (2000), "There is little opportunity for faculty of color to meet others like them in their department and, therefore, race-related service may provide the only opportunities of faculty of color to meet others for support" (p. 366).

Holmes et al. (2007) declare that the ideal is for mentors and mentees to be of the same race/ethnicity and gender in order to provide students and newer faculty with role models that empower them to envision just what they can achieve. This scenario is highly improbable because of the low number of minority faculty available to mentor. This, of course, is especially true at predominantly white institutions. Consequently, "the idea that higher education has deceived itself, by seeming to change through touting the value of racial diversity, while actually staying the same by supporting an underlying pattern of discrimination, is not an easy conclusion to accept" (Beaton & Tougas, 2001, p. 235).

Belonging to a social group is important to whether or not the new faculty member forms a long-term connection with his or her colleagues. A social group, as defined by Adams et al. (2000), primarily provides a sense of identity, not just a set of shared attributes (p. 38). In part, a person's sense of history, affinity, and separateness—even the person's mode of reasoning, evaluating, and expressing feelings—come from his or her affinities with one or more groups. If the new faculty member has no group with which his or her affinities align, then their sense of self cannot be nurtured, and therefore sustained. The lack of identity affinity can be a particularly important source of stress. The isolation that can occur for faculty of color can be particularly problematic. These faculty members often must find other outlets for what sociologists call "ethnic participation," while opportunities for "ethnic participation" for white faculty members are pervasive and consequently taken for granted (Baez, 2000). Faculty of color may experience discrimination among colleagues or students. Different experiences for women and faculty of color adds increased importance to the mentoring process. While mentoring is important for new faculty, mentoring faculty of color is a social justice issue as well as a professional obligation.

GIVING VOICE TO FACULTY MENTEES AND MENTORS

In this section of the chapter, comments from five senior and five junior faculty members from different universities are presented. The senior faculty members' comments come from career experiences they have had over the years, whereas the junior faculty members present their experiences during the past 2 years. The content of these voices from the field echo the research and, in some instances, add to it. By presenting reflections from both mentors and mentees, the reader will be exposed to these two different but mutually dependent perspectives.

Voices of Faculty Mentees

The literature reports that relationship can be identified through formal or informal processes; time to interact is an important condition; compatibility is ideal but not always available and the lack of mentors for minority faculty is a reality. Each of these elements was echoed to some extent in the comments from the new faculty we interviewed.

Process for identifying a mentor. The junior faculty members were asked if a mentor was provided during their first year as a tenure-track faculty member. Both formal and informal processes were used. Two of the junior faculty members were assigned a mentor within the college, one within the department, one outside the college, and one was not assigned a mentor. Half of the faculty who were assigned a mentor indicated that the mentor successfully helped them navigate the system.

Time to interact as an important condition. The activities of which the mentees reported taking part varied, as well as the perceived levels of success. One junior faculty member described an initiative called "Writing Fridays" where the mentor and mentee met weekly to discuss college, department, and university requirements and policies for tenure, annual review, creating scholarly works, publishing, and the like. Another junior faculty member stated, "I have been blessed to be mentored by my chair and a mentor from [another] university," and presented mentoring activities such as university-sponsored socials (luncheons, wine and cheese, end-of-the-year reception), and informal mentoring activities (lunch meetings, emails, networking activities).

One junior faculty member stated that the mentor has not had enough time for mentoring due to other responsibilities. Cawyer et al. (2002) advised that it is good practice to look for other social contacts when the as-

signed mentor turns out to be more of a hindrance than a help. The mentee found a self-appointed faculty member in the department who helped
with scholarly writing, presenting, and being more successful in teaching.
The mentee stated that "My year has been really stressful, and I believe I
would not have made it without the guidance of a 'self-appointed' mentor."

Lack of mentors for faculty of color. A Latino junior faculty member
sought out a Latina faculty member in the college, and established a informal mentee–mentor relationship. As the only Latino faculty member in
his department, he further stated, "I gravitated toward the very few Latino
faculty. Not all were able to serve as mentors, but many provided valuable
advice, lent an ear and a hand, and went out of their way to illuminate first-
year academia issues. They 'understood' my needs, my struggles, and were
ready to include me in an 'informal' mentor network."

Voices of Those Who Mentor

In addition to the junior faculty perspective, we included highlights from
senior faculty members serving as mentors, which included department
chairs and senior faculty in education. The literature on mentors' perspective is less available. Much of the content from these senior faculty members
adds to, rather than echoes, the work that has been done.

Mentoring experiences. To gain better insight into the mentors' backgrounds, senior faculty members were asked to describe the extent of their
mentoring experiences. One of the mentors stated:

> I have served in a mentor's role at most every institution where I've been em-
> ployed since 1990—that would be three. Early on it was as a peer, when new
> faculty was hired. Mostly, in our discipline, we hire people "fresh from the
> field" who know nothing about how universities operate. So I've spent a lot
> of time inducting individuals into their new culture and getting them on the
> road to publishing. Others that I have worked with are faculty who may have
> been in place for a while but have either not published or have been isolated
> or isolated themselves regarding collaboration. Asking these people to join
> in a project or make a contribution to developing a project has resulted in
> renewing some veterans along the way.

Another senior faculty member had mentored two new faculty members.
In this instance, both the formal and informal processes were used in identifying a mentor. The senior faculty member reported being assigned one
mentee as an official mentor and collaborating with another as an unofficial mentor. Both relationships proved productive: "My unofficial protégé
and I collaborated on a study and submitted a manuscript for publication.
My official protégé and I collaborated on producing a conference proceeding." Yet another mentor stated, "I currently have one mentee assigned to

me; however, I try to help all new faculty in any way I can." A department chair/mentor added:

> As department chair, I work with all new faculty on assignments and activities related to teaching, research, and service. I try to help them focus in ways that will lead to promotion and tenure, a clear growth in their research agenda and grant getting initiatives, and developing their reputation as a teacher.

The majority of the senior faculty interviewed had, on their own initiative, taken on the mentorship of faculty members who needed assistance rather than being assigned as a mentor to another faculty member. Some of the typical activities that the mentors provided to new faculty included:

1. Providing assistance in understanding university compliance issues (helping them get to know the ropes)
2. Pointing out opportunities for staff development (such as learning more about teaching, tenure, and promotion activities)
3. Helping them navigate the politics of a department
4. Assisting them in research (collaborating with mentors, including them in publications and presentations, or matching the new faculty interests with other scholars)
5. Explaining the process of developing and submitting a proposal and a manuscript; and
6. Discouraging involvement in too many projects during their first couple of years.

In summary, all of the mentors stressed the importance of engaging in scholarly activity such as research. One mentor reflected:

> Almost always, my first admonition is to get busy writing for publication. I spend a lot of time talking with these folks to determine what they may already have done that could be developed into a publication (and usually there is something). I also talk with them a great deal about teaching—constructing a syllabus, setting expectations for student performance, creating a classroom culture, and working with reluctant or challenging students.

Some of the more atypical activities that the mentors were involved with included social events and other time-consuming but somewhat tangential activities. One mentor mentioned that, "most recently, my mentoring has included helping with locating a place to live, finding yard service personnel, locating the department of public safety offices, and other survival issues."

Some of the positive experiences that the mentors indicated were getting to know new colleagues and developing collegiality, seeing the mentee achieve well, seeing the mentee become self-directing, and reciprocating with opportunities for the mentor or adopting a mentee of their own.

Mentoring takes time. The negative experiences were related to the amount of time mentoring takes and takes away from the mentor's job responsibilities. Added to that is the frustration of utilizing all of one's mentoring skills and realizing that the mentee still does not respond or progress well, or realizing that, as one mentor pointed out, "we have a long way to go." One of the mentors stated:

> There have been a few along the way that take whatever they can get and then move away from me as a colleague/mentor. These are some of my greatest hurts. These individuals, instead of giving back to me or to others, become selfish in their activities and opportunities. Though they succeed, they are unlikely to credit anyone but themselves; and some have even become mean and vindictive toward myself and others who mentored them. But mostly, my mentees have done well, share their opportunities as they mature, and stay connected in some form or another so that they can share their joys, frustrations, and achievements.

The mentors also provided additional reflections on the mentoring relationship such as those in the following collage of comments: "Mentoring is a personal, time-intensive, and human activity. Both parties need to get something out of it"; "This can be a great experience for both if there is a good match between the two; if not, it is not a positive experience"; "Mentoring, for me, has been among my greatest joys and some of my saddest experiences"; "I think it is important that mentors be assigned to each new faculty member and begin their mentoring activities at the moment the new person signs the contract or accepts the position."

Perhaps as with other behaviors, having a role model can be a powerful teacher. One of the senior faculty spoke of their own journey from mentee to mentor:

> I have to credit others in higher education for whatever success I have had as a mentor. When I was a full-time student in my doctoral program, I worked for an individual who epitomized the word mentor. I have tried to model my behavior after hers and have added a few of my own. But without question, I have been very fortunate to have had excellent mentors in my own career development, so my mentoring skills were "passed on" to me as a new faculty member and I feel compelled to "pass on" these skills to others as they come to higher education. Mentoring is somewhat like raising children. You do your best and it is up to them to use it positively or not so positively with the next generation. At this stage of my career, I wonder if I spent too much time worried about the success of others and not so much on my own success. This has become a point of reflection recently. I wonder how things might have been different in my own career opportunities if mentoring had not become

such a major component of my higher education persona. Just wondering... but not worrying.

After reading the perspectives presented in the voices of mentees and mentors, readers may develop their own thoughts of best practices. As authors, an attempt was made to use both the literature and the voices from the field to identify actions that could increase the likelihood of both a successful mentoring relationship and the ultimate objective developing productive professionals who remain at the institution and contribute to the profession.

LESSONS FROM MENTEES AND MENTORS

The voices of mentees and mentors provided additional points to be considered, especially in relation to mentoring faculty of color. We noticed, however, that mentors provided recommendations less directed to a specific group of new faculty, choosing instead to focus on mentoring strategies that worked best for them. In encouraging the development of others in education, much is discussed in supportive systems in the PreK–20 continuum, but introducing new faculty into their professions as educators in schools, or in higher education, seems to be often overlooked or delivered through short faculty orientations, faculty writing across the curricula, speaker series, workshops, administrative- and technology-related training, or brown-bag sessions.

It is important to provide insight into faculty mentoring at universities and perhaps distinguish them from faculty orientations. Mentoring systems require investment from the department colleagues and the institution in the same way college students need support to complete their degrees. The lessons learned from the voices of mentees and mentors suggest the following recommendations: (1) department-level support, (2) development of mentoring relationships, and (3) the socialization of faculty of color.

Department-level support. Department chairs play an important role in guiding the new faculty member in the process of becoming acclimated. Matching minority faculty with senior members, and allowing new faculty to work together according to research, teaching, or service interests, can create healthy and productive organizational cultures. Concurrently, valuing collaborative efforts and creating circumstances for the recognition of mentoring roles similarly provides opportunities for the development of a department invested in its growth and productivity.

Development of mentoring relationships. Developing relationships between mentors and mentees take time. Opportunities for the establishment and cultivation of successful mentoring relationships may depend on (1) creating opportunities to get acquainted with research agendas and mutual interests for collaboration; (2) safeguarding common time for the development of objectives and common focus; (3) allowing for co-teaching opportunities; and (4) providing common service tasks at the department and institutional level.

In addition, mentoring relationships may guide mentees in managing time effectively. They may find themselves consumed in service and teaching unless there are guided efforts to orient new faculty to develop research. Characteristic of educators, and education advocates, many new faculty focus on service issues. Although service is an important part of the tenure and promotion process, it is often seen as the least important of the three (research, teaching, and service). Especially minority faculty members being considered for tenure and promotion, should be cautious about "engaging in professional activities that typically receive little or no consideration in the tenure and promotion process" (Shin, 2008, p. 186).

Socialization of faculty of color. Considering that many forms of support systems have been created for students in schools and colleges, especially interventions geared toward the retention of students of color (Rendon, Jalomo, & Nora, 2000), it is ironic to find an absence of support systems for the very educators preparing these students. The lack of support systems for the promotion and retention of faculty of color still speaks to a deeper concern about perpetuating exclusionary educational systems—based on an individual's race. Such disparity exists when the faculty in a university does not reflect the diversity of the population it serves (Engerman & Waller, 2000; Stanley, 2006). Faculty of color finds fewer mentoring opportunities, especially in fields such as educational leadership, historically represented by white males. This chapter therefore adds to the examination of social justice issues related to the retention of faculty of color as a reminder that recruitment does not necessary result in retention if institutions of higher education do not address the preparation and mentorship of new faculty.

At universities where specific programs to support junior faculty development are nonexistent, informal mentoring may develop. This type of mentorship usually evolves through collegial interaction between and among faculty members, and may lead into future collaboration in scholarship. The award for a mentor is to see new faculty established as productive, contributing colleagues. Higher education faculty members who enjoy mentoring open their lives and careers for the benefit of their colleagues, the improvement of programs, and the improvement of the field. According to Baldwin and Chang (2006), "at many institutions, ambitious orientation programs, mentoring systems, and grant opportunities targeted specifically at new professors help to ease their transition into the academic profession" (p. 28).

It is our hope that guidelines for best practices provided by the participants will be placed in a context of social justice practices that respect individual gender, cultural capital and preferences, personality, knowledge, time in the position, and personal lifestyles. A newly hired faculty member of assistant or associate professor rank aspiring to become tenured may have quite different needs for development than a full professor that has a long tenure at one or multiple institutions.

CONCLUSION

This chapter explored issues of social justice and ways to support new faculty in academia. Mentoring relationships in higher education are important not only for the students, but equally important for faculty preparing them. The voices of mentees and mentors in our study highlighted contemporary issues still to be fulfilled in order to exemplify ways to encourage the development of others.

Mentees reported that they benefitted from interacting, with some degree of regularity, with their mentors. Mentors overwhelmingly agreed that mentoring was a worthwhile experience and agreed that mentoring arrangements provide for a healthy organizational culture, enhanced productivity, and a positive transition for faculty new to academia. Structured mentoring activities were mentioned by several of the mentees, but for the most part, mentoring played a significant role for mentees successful in their learning curve into becoming faculty in higher education. For some, mentoring involved personal, out-of-work connections, while other mentorship arrangements occurred strictly at the workplace.

Ethnicity was a significant topic of discussion for one mentee, who chose to be mentored by an individual from his own culture. The participant's voice, in fact, represents contemporary faculty compositions, and one can infer that due to the limited availability of mentors of similar ethnic backgrounds in institutions, some may have failed to mention cultural similarity as a critical attribute of being successfully mentored. In the words of one of the mentees, "It would be futile to ask for a mentor who is ethnically similar to you, when you are the only 'diverse' person in the department."

The ethnic makeup of the department, college, and university contributes to whether or not a mentee will encounter a mentor of similar ethnicity. Recalling the disproportionately low numbers of faculty of color throughout the nation, and fields still dominated by males, social injustices in the way minority faculty is introduced and evaluated may still require further examination. It is critical, for the professional survival of minority faculty, that institutional safeguards are established to maintain and augment the participation of this diverse group of scholars. Purposeful mentoring arrangements and department, college, and university efforts that sustain a healthy organizational culture—and that recognize mentors for their positive efforts—may be the initial step for the well-being of new and experienced faculty.

REFERENCES

Adams, M., Blumenfeld, W. J., Castañeda, R., Hackman, H. W., Peters, M. L., & Zúñiga, X. (2000). *Reading for diversity and social justice: An anthology on racism, anti-Semitism, sexism, heterosexism, ableism, and classism.* New York: Routledge.

Austin, A. E. (Winter, 2003). Creating a bridge to the future: Preparing new faculty to face changing expectations in a shifting context. *Review of Higher Education, 26*(2), 119–144.

Baez, B. (2000). Race-related service and faculty of color: Conceptualizing critical agency in academe. *Higher Education, 39,* 363–391.

Baldwin, R. G., & Chang, D. A. (2007). Collaborating to learn, learning to collaborate. *Peer Review, 9*(4), 26–30.

Beaton, A. M., & Tougas, F. (2001).Reactions to affirmative action: Group membership and social justice. *Social Justice Research, March, 14*(1), 61–78.

Bower, G. G. (2007). Factors influencing the willingness to mentor 1st-year faculty in physical education departments. *Mentoring and Tutoring: Partnership in Learning, 15*(1), 73–85.

Cawyer, C. S., Simonds, C., & Davis, S. (2002). Mentoring to facilitate socialization: The case of the new faculty member. *Qualitative Studies in Education, 15*(2), 225–242.

Colbeck, C., O'Meara, K., & Austin, A. E. (Eds.). (2008). *Educating integrated professionals: Theory and Practice on Preparation for the Professoriate* (New Directions for Teaching and Learning No. 113). San Francisco: Jossey-Bass.

Engerman, K., & Waller, R. (2000). *Recruitment and retention of faculty of color in higher education.* Paper presented at the fifth annual conference of Building Diversity in the University and the Community, University of Nebraska, Lincoln.

Gardiner, M., Tiggeman, M., Kerns, H., & Marshall, K. (2007). Show me the money! An empirical analysis of mentoring outcomes for women in academia. *Higher Education Research & Development, 26*(4), 425–442.

Greenberg, J. (1990). Organizational justice: Yesterday, today, and tomorrow. *Journal of Management, 16,* 399-432.

Holmes, J. G. & Murray, S. (1996). Interpersonal conflict in close relationships. In E. T. Higgins & A. W. Kruglanski (Eds.), *Social psychology: Handbook of basic mechanisms and processes.* New York: Guilford Press.

Holmes, S. L., Land, L. D., & Hinton-Hudson, V. D. (2007). Race still matters: Considerations for mentoring black women in academe. *Negro Educational Review, 58*(1/2), 105–129.

McCormick, C. B., & Barnes, B. J. (2008). Getting started in academia: A guide for educational psychologists. *Educational Psychology Review, 20*(1), 5–18.

Olsen, D. (1993). Work satisfaction and stress in the first and third year of academic appointment. *Journal of Higher Education, 64,* 453–471.

Organ, D. W. (1988). *Organizational citizen behavior: The good soldier syndrome.* Lexington, MA: Lexington Books.

Rendon, L. I., Jalomo, R. E., & Nora, A. (2000). Theoretical considerations in the study of minority student retention in higher education. In J. M. Braxton (Ed.), *Reworking the student departure puzzle* (pp. 127–146). Nashville, TN: Vanderbuilt University Press.

Rice, R. E., Sorcinelli, M. D., & Austin, A. E. (2000). *Heeding new voices*. Washington, DC: New Pathways Working Paper Series.

Savage, H. E., Karp, R. S., & Logue. R. (1996). Faculty mentorship at colleges and universities. *College Teaching, 52*(1), 21–24.

Shin, R. Q. (2008). Advocating for social justice in academia through recruitment, retention, admissions, and professional survival *Journal of Multicultural Counseling and Development, 36*, 180–191.

Simplicio, J. S. C. (2008). Shared governance: An analysis of power on the modern university campus from the perspective of an administrator. *Education, 126*(4), 763–768.

Settles, I. H., Cortina, L. M., Stewart, A. J., & Malley, J. (2007). Voice matters: Buffering the impact of a negative climate for women in science. *Psychology of Women Quarterly, 31*, 270–281.

Sorcinelli, M. D. (1988). Satisfaction and concerns of university teachers. *To Improve the Academy, 7*, 121–131.

Sorcinelli, M. D. (1994). Effective approaches to new faculty development. *Journal of Counseling and Development, 72*, 474–479.

Stanley, C. A. (2006). Coloring the academic landscape: Faculty of color breaking the silence in predominantly white colleges and universities. *American Educational Research Journal, 43*(4), 701–736.

Strathe, M. I., & Wilson, V. W. (2006, Summer). Academic leadership: The pathway to and from. *New Direction for Higher Education*, pp. 5–13.

Ugrin, J. C., Odom, M. D., & Pearson, J. M. (2008). Exploring the importance of mentoring for new scholars: A social exchange perspective. *Journal of Information Systems Education, 19*(3), 343–350.

Wasburn, M. H. (2007). Mentoring women faculty: An instrumental case study of strategic collaboration. *Mentoring and Tutoring: Partnership in Learning, 15*(1), 57–72.

CHAPTER EPILOGUE

"I'M STILL HERE, GOD"

Fenwick W. English

This is a book about social justice. Most readers who traverse this text will be familiar with social injustice. They may have been even victims of social injustice: been discriminated or marginalized or even silenced because of their race, national origin, religion, or gender. This book has included many authors of many persuasions and perspectives. The book is inclusive. Schools and society are not. Schools in most of the world represent only the "haves" in their populations and social structure. The "have nots" are marginalized or silenced. There is no channel for them to protest and many have been silenced long before they experience the overt discrimination that will punctuate their awareness that they have been excluded on some or all of the criteria outlined in this text.

I salute the editors, Elizabeth Murakami-Ramalho and Anita Pankake, for their courage in constructing this text. And equal plaudits go to the authors and coauthors that contributed to it. It is not easy to talk about one's isolation and/or exclusion in this world. It is even more difficult to take action to change it.

The world as we know it is a social construction. There is nothing "natural" about it. That is what is most infuriating about being marginalized or silenced in it, but also what gives one hope to change it.

Educational Leaders Encouraging the Intellectual and Professional Capacity of Others: A Social Justice Agenda, pages 335–336.

In the final analysis I remember the film *Papillion.* At the end Steve Mc-Queen leaps from the cliffs into the sea. As he emerges from the brine and foam and clings to his homemade life raft, he looks up at the sky and says, "I'm still here, God."

All of the scholars and authors in this text can also say, "I'm still here, God." We live to make schools and the societies in which they exist better and more equal, equitable, and fairer places than they are today. We must persist. If we are silenced millions of schoolchildren around the world will have no hope. There is no alternative. We cannot live without hope, nor can they.

Someday when we are all gone, the living legacies of our fight will be the beneficiaries of a better life. What better tribute to our labors can there be?

MEET THE AUTHORS IN THIS VOLUME

EDITORS

Elizabeth Murakami-Ramalho is an Associate Professor and director of the Doctoral Program in Educational Leadership and Policy Studies at University of Texas-San Antonio where she prepares school administrators through master's and doctoral courses in school leadership, human relations, school change, and principal certification. She is a South American native who received her MA in Curriculum and Teaching, and her Ph.D. in Educational Administration with specialization in International Development from Michigan State University. Dr. Murakami coordinates the doctoral program and co-coordinates the Urban School Leaders Collaborative, preparing principals in urban areas, and is one of the researchers in the International Successful School Principals Project, as well as a member in the National Latino Leadership Project. Her research focus includes leadership for Latin@ populations, and urban and international issues in

Educational Leaders Encouraging the Intellectual and Professional Capacity of Others:
A Social Justice Agenda, pages 337–346.

educational leadership. Her research includes leadership dynamics, hybrid identities/communities, social justice, race, and gender.

Anita Pankake is a professor in the Department of Educational Leadership at The University of Texas—Pan American, Edinburg, TX. Her Bachelor's and Master's degrees are from Indiana State University and her doctorate is from Loyola University Chicago. Prior to joining higher education, she worked as an elementary teacher, team leader, assistant principal and principal in public schools in Indiana and Illinois. In higher education she has been a faculty member, department chair and interim associate dean for research and graduate studies, and doctoral program director. Her research and teaching interests include organizational change, leadership, women's issues, teacher leadership and professional learning communities. Among her honors are the Texas Council of Women School Executives' *Margaret Montgomery Leadership Award*, The *Outstanding Contribution to Staff Development Award* from the Texas Staff Development Association, the awards as the *Outstanding Mentor Award* and for *Research Excellence Award* from the UTPA College of Education. She has seven books, numerous book chapters and over 60 refereed and non-refereed publications to her credit.

CONTRIBUTORS

Jesus (Chuey) Abrego, Jr. is an Assistant Professor of Educational Leadership at the University of Texas at Brownsville. Prior to his work in higher education he served as a science teacher, administrator for the Texas Education Agency in the departments of Statewide Staff Development Program with the Office of Curriculum, Assessment, and Professional Development; Middle School Education and Migrant Education. In addition, he served as an assistant principal at an inner-city urban high school, and middle school principal in Texas. He presents regularly at national and state conferences—including AERA (American Educational Research Association) and SERA (Southwest Educational Research Association).

Ann Allen is an associate professor in the School of Educational Policy and Leadership at The Ohio State University. Her work centers on democratic representation in school governance, how that representation is affected by policies, and the politics that influence policy. Her research examines governance policies and politics as they relate to charter schools, school-community relations, and school boards. Dr. Allen holds a Ph.D. in Educational Policy from Michigan State University.

Paul V. Bredeson is a Professor in the Department of Educational Leadership and Policy Analysis at the University of Wisconsin-Madison where he teaches courses in Professional Development and Organizational Learning,

Instructional Leadership and School Improvement, and Research Methods. Prior to his appointment on the faculty in 1991, Professor Bredeson was a Professor at Pennsylvania State University and also served as the Executive Director of the Pennsylvania School Study Council from 1985-1991. Professor Bredeson also served three years as a Professor of Educational Leadership at Ohio University. Dr. Bredeson is also an International Faculty Associate at Umea University.

Mary Charles holds a B.A. in English, Clarke College, Dubuque, Iowa; M.A. in Curriculum and Instruction, Loyola University Chicago; Certificate in Philanthropy, Loyola University Chicago. She is an Apple Distinguished Educator and has taught at the elementary, high school and college levels. Ms. Charles has been actively involved in professional development, dropout prevention and post-secondary access work at the secondary level in Chicago for the last 17 years. During that time she has created and directed outreach programming that has allowed more than 300 high achieving undergraduates to deliver more than 60,000 hours of academic coaching to underrepresented students in chronically underperforming urban high schools, She is an invited presenter at national education conferences and provides consulting services in the area of mentoring. Publications include text book chapters, journal articles, electronic media, and education periodicals.

Gloria Crisp is an Assistant Professor in the Educational Leadership and Policy Studies Department at The University of Texas at San Antonio (UTSA). The focus of Dr. Crisp's scholarship includes understanding how mentoring is perceived and experienced by students, the factors that influence the success of community college and/or Hispanic students, and the impact of institutional and state policy on student transfer and persistence.

Fenwick W. English currently teaches at the graduate level in the Educational Leadership Area at UNC College of Education. He has served in administrative capacities in higher education as department chair, dean and vice chancellor of academic affairs. English has held leadership positions throughout the country and has served in an executive capacity at the national level with the American Association of School Administrators in Arlington, Virginia, and with KPMG Peat Marwick, a private accounting and consulting firm in Washington, D.C. English has lived or worked in all 50 states and two U.S. territories during his career. He has headed task forces sponsored by the National Secondary School Principals, and by the Association for Supervision and Curriculum Development. He is now serving on the Executive Board of the National Council of Professors of Educational Administration.

Encarnación Garza, Jr. is the son of Mexican born parents who originally came into the United States in the late 1940s. He is a former migrant farmworker and worked in the fields until he graduated from college. Professionally, he has extensive experience working with students with backgrounds very similar to his own. He has been a teacher, counselor, director of an alternative education center, elementary school principal, educational specialist, field service agent and a school superintendent. Currently Encarnación is an assistant professor at the University of Texas at San Antonio in the Department of Educational Administration and Policy Studies. His major focus is the preparation of future school leaders that will primarily serve minority children. His book, *Resiliency and Success: Migrant Children in the U. S.* (2004, Paradigm Publishers) was co-authored with Professors Pedro Reyes and Enrique Trueba.

Marytza A. Gawlik is a faculty member of Florida State University. She holds a Ph.D. in Policy, Organization, Measurement and Evaluation from the University of California at Berkeley. Dr. Gawlik draws from both organizational sociology and political economics to investigate and assess the contributions made by policy and school reform initiatives. Her scholarship and research focuses on charter schools, accountability, professional autonomy and teacher quality. Dr. Gawlik employs both qualitative and quantitative methodologies in her research to address enduring policy reforms that impact both school leaders and teachers.

Marilyn L. Grady is professor of educational administration at the University of Nebraska-Lincoln (UNL). She is the author or coauthor of 23 books. Her research areas include leadership, the principalship, and superintendent-board relations. She has more than 175 publications to her credit. She is the editor of the *Journal of Women in Educational Leadership*. She is the recipient of the Stanley Brzezinski Research Award, NCPEA's Living Legend Award, the Donald R. and Mary Lee Swanson Award for Teaching Excellence, UNL's Distinguished Teaching Award, and UNL's Award for Outstanding Contributions to the Status of Women.

Margaret Grogan is a Professor of Educational Leadership and Policy, and Dean of the School of Educational Studies at Claremont Graduate University, California. Originally from Australia, she received a Bachelor of Arts degree in Ancient History and Japanese Language from the University of Queensland. She taught high school in Australia, and was a teacher and an administrator at an international school in Japan. After graduating from Washington State University with a PhD in Educational Administration, she taught in Principal and Superintendent Preparation Programs at the University of Virginia and at the University of Missouri-Columbia. She served a term as President of the University Council for Educational Administration in 2003-04. Her current research focuses on women in leadership, the moral and ethical dimensions of leadership, and leadership for social justice.

Karen Hayes is an associate professor in the Department of Educational Administration and Supervision in the College of Education at the University of Nebraska at Omaha, where her focus is on developing leaders for Urban Schools. Dr. Hayes' research interests include Professional Development, Cultural Proficiency, Leadership Development and Social Justice. Dr. Hayes previously worked for the Omaha Public School district as Director of Staff Development, Elementary Principal, Administrative Assistant to the Superintendent, Administrator for Educational Service Unit # 19, Assistant Principal and teacher.

Stephanie Hirsh is the executive director of Learning Forward (formerly the National Staff Development Council [NSDC]). Prior to her appointment as executive director in 2007, Hirsh served the association as deputy executive director for 18 years. She began her educational career as a junior high teacher and also served as a school district administrator in the Richardson (Texas) Independent School District. In 1996 she was elected to the Richardson school board and served for three terms. Hirsh has published numerous books and articles on educational leadership, professional development, and school improvement. She speaks to a variety of audiences and advises federal and state policymakers on issues related to professional development, leadership, and teaching.Hirsh received her B.S. in Social Studies Education from The University of Texas, her M.Ed. in Education Administration from The University of North Texas, and her Ph.D. in Curriculum and Instruction from The University of North Texas.

Shirley Hord is Scholar Laureate with Learning Forward (previously, National Staff Development Council), following her retirement as the first Scholar Emerita at the Southwest Educational Development Laboratory in Austin, Texas. Prior to this work, she served on faculty in the College of Education, Science Education Center, University of Texas, Austin; she engaged in research on school change and improvement for ten years in the federally funded R&D Center for Teacher Education, University of Texas at Austin. She authors articles, chapters, and books on school-based professional development, leadership, school change and improvement, and professional learning communities. In addition to working with educators at all levels across the US, Canada, and Mexico, she makes presentations and consults in Asia, Europe, Australia, and Africa.

Jane Huffman is a Professor of Educational Administration, teaches master's and doctoral courses at the University of North Texas. Her areas of interest include organizational change management, leadership, parent involvement, and professional learning communities. In 2009 she was a Visiting Scholar at National Taiwan Normal University and she received the University of North Texas Outstanding Doctoral Mentoring Award. Huffman holds bachelors, masters, and doctoral degrees in Administration, Curriculum, and Supervision from the University of Oklahoma. She worked in the Norman, Oklahoma, public schools for 10 years as a teacher, school administrator, and staff development administrator.

Kay A. Keiser is an Associate Professor in the Department of Educational Administration and Supervision at the University of Nebraska at Omaha. A former instructor and administrator in the Omaha Public Schools, she teaches School Community Relations, Interpersonal Relations for School Leaders, and Achieving School Excellence. Leadership motivation and dispositions, school climate, and individualization of instruction are her research interests.

Hans W. Klar is an Assistant Professor of Educational Leadership at Clemson University. His current research interests include the development of instructional leadership capacity as a means for sustainable school improvement. Dr. Klar previously held teaching and administrative positions at the University of Technology, Sydney, in Australia and at the Sydney Institute of Language and Commerce, in Shanghai, China. Dr. Klar's most recent publication is "Fostering department chair instructional leadership capacity: Laying the groundwork for distributed instructional leadership" in the *International Journal of Leadership in Education.*

JoAnn F. Klinker is a university professor and former high school principal with almost 20 years experience in K-12 education. As an associate professor at Texas Tech University, Dr. Klinker works with masters and doctoral students in the Educational Leadership program. She also teaches graduate courses in instructional supervision, community relations, the internship, democracy and schools, ethics, and postmodernism. A frequent presenter at various conferences, Dr. Klinker has also worked with the Wallace Foundation and Community Foundation of Texas to construct and implement a pilot preparation program for urban principals in collaboration with Lubbock Independent School District. She is the director of the Institute for Leadership and School Improvement within the College of Education at Texas Tech.

Sylvia Mendez-Morse is an Associate Professor in the Educational Leadership Program at Texas Tech University. She teaches graduate courses in the Masters/Principal Certification and the Doctoral programs. Dr. Mendez provides instruction via face-to-face, web assisted, and instructional television in the courses Organizational Communication in Education, School and Community, Equity Issues in Educational Leadership, Gender Issues in Educational Leadership, Leadership for Social Justice as well as others. Her previous research work focused on effective leadership for at risk student populations, Latinas in the superintendency, and Latina school leaders. Sylvia's current research efforts continue to investigate Latina educational leaders: their resistance, resilience, and ability to thrive. In addition she studies the influence of racial/ethnic identity in aspiring principals' potential for social justice leadership. She is a member of the National Latina/o Leadership Project. Dr. Mendez has been published in *Educational Administration Quarterly, Urban Education, Journal of Cases in Educational Leadership,* and *Educational Policy Analysis Archives.*

Betty M. Merchant is a Professor and dean of the College of Education and Human Development at the University of Texas at San Antonio. Before going to Texas, she taught at the University of Illinois Urbana-Champaign and in public schools, preschool through high school, and in tribally controlled Native American schools in the southwest. Her research interests focus on educational policy, equity, student diversity, and school leadership.

Shirley J. Mills received her Ph.D. in Educational Leadership and Higher Education from the University of Nebraska Lincoln in 2005. In 2007 she became an Assistant Professor at the University of Texas Pan American where she teaches in the Master and Doctoral graduate programs for the Department of Educational Leadership. Shirley's research interests are in K-12 leadership in public schools, teacher leadership, and technology.

Ava J. Muñoz is an Assistant Professor in Educational Leadership and Policy Studies at University of Texas at Arlington where she prepares school administrators through master's and principal certification courses (Principalship, Foundations of Educational Administration, Internship and Diversity in the Educational Setting). She, also, teaches a doctoral course in Organizational Theory. She is a native Texan (Rio Grande Valley) who received both her M.Ed. and Ed.D. in Educational Leadership from the The University of Texas-Pan American. Dr. Muñoz is the master's in educational leadership with principal certification program director. Her research focus includes gender equity in educational leadership (superintendency), social justice, mentoring, and student college access and retention.

Ashley M. Oleszewski is a doctoral student in Educational Leadership and Policy Studies at the University of Texas at San Antonio. Her research interests include issues related to the assistant principalship and transitioning from the assistant to the principalship. Ms. Oleszewski earned her M.S. in educational administration from Gwynedd Mercy College and her B.S. in psychology from Allegheny College.

Maria B. Roberts is an assistant professor in the Department of Educational Leadership at The University of Texas—Pan American, Edinburg, TX. She holds a B.S. in Chemistry from Pan American University, an M.Ed. in Educational Administration from The University of Texas at Brownsville and a doctorate from The University of Texas—Austin. Prior to entering higher education, she served in PK-12 public schools as a teacher, instructional facilitator, assistant principal, principal and curriculum director. Her teaching and research interests include instructional leadership, the principalship, socio-cultural issues particularly as the related to minority and bilingual populations. She has numerous presentations at state and national associations and conference including the American Educational Research Association, National Association of Bilingual Educators, American Association of Hispanics in Higher Education, Women in Educational Leadership, and the Texas Association of School Administrators.

Janine M. Schall received her Ph.D. in Language, Reading and Culture from the University of Arizona in 2004. She is currently an Associate Professor in the Department of Curriculum and Instruction at the University of Texas-Pan American. She teaches reading courses at the graduate and undergraduate level and coordinates the Reading Specialist M.Ed. program. Janine's research interests include the cultural identities of teachers, multicultural children's literature, and children's literature and response.

Diane Profita Schiller is Professor of Education at Loyola University Chicago. She earned her Bachelor of Arts degree at the University of Illinois, Chicago; her Master of Arts degree at the University of Illinois, Urbana, and her doctorate at University of Illinois, Chicago. For ten years she worked as a middle schoolteacher in a small, urban school where service learning was an expected part of the curriculum. As a professor, Dr. Schiller has included service learning in all of her undergraduate education classes. In 2008 she won 2nd place in the Jimmy and Roslyn Carter School Community Partnership award based on the work of her students in the local public school. For the past three years, she has developed and supervised a work/study program called MathTEAMS. Thirty undergraduates work with a team of six underserved students at neighboring elementary schools to improve math achievement and develop critical thinking. For 20 years, Dr. Schiller has led a team of on air educators to create and produce a weekly, hour-long call-in cable access television show that offers students and hour of high quality math instruction on TV. Edited clips from the TV show are available at MathFLIX.luc.edu.

Whitney H. Sherman is an Associate Professor in the Department of Educational Leadership at Virginia Commonwealth University in Richmond, Virginia, USA. Her research interests include: leadership preparation and mentoring; women's issues in leadership; social justice in leadership; and ethical leadership. Dr. Sherman's work has been featured in journals including: Educational Administration Quarterly; the Journal of School Leadership; the Journal of Educational Administration; Educational Policy; and the International Journal for Qualitative Studies in Education.

Marie V. Simonsson is an associate professor and director of the Educational Leadership Doctoral Program at The University of Texas—Pan American (UTPA). She holds both a bachelor's degree and master's degree in physical education from Drake University in Iowa. She completed her doctorate in Educational Leadership, Education Administration & Supervision from the University of Houston, TX. Dr. Simonsson has taught graduate and undergraduate classes at UTPA in the departments of curriculum and instruction, health and kinesiology, educational psychology and educational leadership. Prior to her work in the U.S. she served as a teacher and athletic consultant in her home country of Sweden. Her teaching specialties are research, statistics, program evaluation and assessment. She has numerous articles and presentation focused on student assessment, programs for gifted and talented students, and culturally and linguistically diverse learners.

Peter Smith, an Assistant Professor of Educational Administration and Supervision, received his doctorate at the University of Nebraska at Omaha. He teaches School Finance, Governance and Politics, and Intermediate and Advanced Statistics. His research interests include educational leadership standards and dispositions, social justice, and the use of portfolios with leadership candidates. He spent 30 years serving as a teacher and administrator for the Omaha Public Schools.

Jeanne Surface is an Assistant Professor of Educational Administration and Supervision at the University of Nebraska at Omaha. She teaches School Law, School Business Management and Leadership and Administration of schools. Her research interests include Social Justice, Rural Education and School Law. Jeanne, the former Superintendent of Park County School District #16, Wyoming and received her doctorate at the University of Wyoming.

David P. Thompson is Professor and Chair of the Department of Educational Leadership and Policy Studies at The University of Texas at San Antonio. He received his B.S. (Physical Education), M.S. (Educational Administration), and Ph.D. (Educational Administration) from Texas A&M University. For his doctoral dissertation, titled "Job Satisfaction: A Synthesis of Research in the Educational Administration Quarterly," David received outstanding dissertation awards from both Division A (Administration) of the American Educational Research Association and the National Council of Professors of Educational Administration. David has over 20 years of experience in public education at both the PK-12 and higher education level, having served as a mathematics teacher and golf coach in the Lamar Consolidated Independent School District, a high school assistant principal in Spring Independent School District, and a faculty member and department chair at both UTSA and Texas A&M University-Commerce. In 2008, David was named an Outstanding Alumnus of the College of Education and Human Development at Texas A&M University.

Fernando Valle is a native of South Texas and serves as an Assistant Professor in the Educational Leadership Program at Texas Tech University. He received his bachelors of Science degree in education from The University of Texas—San Antonio and both Masters degrees in Guidance and Counseling and School Administration from The University of Texas at Pan American. In 2008, Valle received a Doctorate in Educational Leadership from The University of Texas—Pan American. After twelve years of service in South Texas public schools, he transitioned to higher education. Valle currently teaches graduate and doctoral level courses in process of school change, school and community, equity issues in education, the principal internship, and research in educational leadership education.

INDEX

Educational Leaders Encouraging the Intellectual and Professional Capacity of Others: A Social Justice Agenda, pages 347–350.
Copyright © 2012 by Information Age Publishing
347

CPSIA information can be obtained
at www.ICGtesting.com
Printed in the USA
LVHW03s1233111018

593191LV00001B/1/P

9 781617 356230